A Christian Critique of American Culture

The Julian Hartt Library

Series Editor
Jonathan R. Wilson

****

Toward a Theology of Evangelism
Being Known and Being Revealed
The Lost Image of Man
Theology and the Church in the University
A Christian Critique of American Culture
The Restless Quest
Theological Method and Imagination
What We Make of the World: Memoirs of Julian Hartt

A Christian Critique of American Culture

An Essay in Practical Theology

Julian N. Hartt

Series Foreword by Jonathan R. Wilson
Volume Foreword by David H. Kelsey

Wipf and Stock Publishers
Eugene, Oregon

Wipf & Stock Publishers
199 West 8th Ave, Suite 3
Eugene, OR 97401

A Christian Critique of American Culture
By Hartt, Julian N.

ISBN: 1-59752-233-3
Previously Published by Harper & Row Publishers, 1967

Library of Congress Catalogue Card Number: 67-14932

To my wife, Neva

Contents

Series Foreword

Why is Wipf and Stock reprinting the works of Julian Hartt? Certainly his faculty appointments and administrative responsibilities at Yale (1943-1972) and Virginia (1972-1981), after an initial term at Berea, indicate something of his participation in a formative period for American theological education. That observation, however, does not identify the impact of his work or the reasons for reprinting his books. His work deserves reprinting and renewed attention for at least four reasons.

One reason for reprinting Hartt's work is the depth of theological reflection represented in it. The books are not easy to enter. They are densely packed and cannot be read quickly. My first encounter with his work occurred in the basement of the library at the University of British Columbia. I was browsing in the religion section and was drawn to a book by its aesthetic appeal. Its size and proportions as well as its dusty blue color drew me in. I could not read the title on its spine, so I took it off the shelf: *A Christian Critique of American Culture*. Intrigued, I borrowed it from the library and renewed the loan several times while I managed to read about one-third of the book. I finally returned the book to the library and did not read it again until many years later.

So, let's be clear. Hartt's work makes significant demands on readers. His own erudition and his ability to bring it together in concentrated form means that his work cannot be skimmed for the "high points." Every book is packed with high points. Each paragraph makes an important contribution to the argument or exposition. Hartt's books, then, are not quick and easy reads. But such characteristics also mean that reading carefully through one of Hartt's books teaches more than sprinting through numerous other works. In an age that values short paragraphs, shallow thinking, and predigested ideas (that is, pablum), Hartt's books are strong meat not thin gruel.

Our age needs the kind of work that makes us slow down, chew on a sentence, a paragraph, an argument, until it has nourished our lives. That's what Hartt's work provides for us.

A second reason for making Hartt's work more readily available is not just its character but also its content. Hartt's work is not only densely packed, it is also sharply penetrating. One of Hartt's friends told me about once hearing him preach in a British Methodist church on Good Friday. "I felt like I had been laid bare, stripped of every pretense, lacerated by the truth, so that I could be healed by the gospel."

In Hartt's work, readers will find a severe truth-telling grounded in the conviction that only the truth revealed in Christ will set us free. So Hartt's penetrating insight and prophetic truth strips away our platitudes and the thin lies that we wrap around ourselves to protect us from the admission that our emptiness and anxiety go to our very core. Even though—perhaps precisely because—Hartt exposes these lies in their particular cultural expressions, his severity continues to administer healing grace to us today. Our particular cultural expressions of the lies and illusions that we create for ourselves may differ, but our propensity to live by lies and illusions remains a part of every human condition.

We must go one step further to understand why the content of Hartt's work is so penetrating. Its power lies not only in his clear-eyed perception of the lies we live by; even more, the power of his work lies in his apprehension of the gospel of Jesus Christ. My use of the word *apprehension* here is very important. Hartt has been apprehended by the gospel, and in the outworking of that gospel in his life, he has also apprehended it. This notion of apprehension is crucial to Hartt's thinking. Though he had this understanding of apprehension early in his intellectual development, it is highly developed in the work of Austin Farrer, who contributed significantly to Hartt's thinking. Today, a similar notion may be found in Reinhard Hütter's notion (in *Suffering Divine Things*) of being "rapt" by God.

For Hartt, to be apprehended by the gospel is to be so captured by God's grace in Jesus Christ that all things are seen by its light. All of our "unreality systems" are exposed as antihuman distortions of the way to human flourishing. So the gospel of Jesus Christ discloses the Rule of God in which we truly find the flourishing of all creation. Without this conviction, Hartt's brilliant exposure of our lies plunges us into despair. But in the light of the good news that Jesus Christ has overcome all that we fear, all that we deny, all our anxieties, all Sin, we are now free to confess the truth of our sin because the grace of God is greater still.

This double-edged truth makes Hartt's theology an invaluable witness to our age. We seem to combine cynicism about intentions in the exercise of human powers with a fatalism about the inevitability of misguided optimism that "this one time" we will achieve our intentions, which, when achieved, turn out not to be our salvation but our continuing damnation—and that by our own hands. In the midst of such darkness and despairing, the light and hope of Christ announce God's salvation for a damned humanity.

Hartt's perceptive and profound witness to this good news illuminates our world, penetrates the armor of lies, breaks the chains of sin, and sets us free to follow Christ. For these reasons, his work equips us for the mission to which the Lord and Savior of the church has called us.

A third reason for reprinting and reading Hartt's work is his impact on North American theology. Although Hartt is not well-known, during his twenty-nine years at Yale and ten years at Virginia he exercised enormous influence on a whole generation of theologians. Hartt himself had relatively few doctoral students. Many suggest that his high standards and fierce rhetoric put many students off. Hartt was a skilled debater who appears to have seldom adjusted his style according to circumstance. During Hartt's years at Yale, the school produced a majority of North America's theologians for a generation. Many of these theologians have acknowledged to me in private correspondence that Hartt's influence upon them is strong even if they do not consider themselves to be one of Hartt's students. (There is also the untold and controversial role that Hartt played in a struggle over control of the graduate program in religion.)

But there are also many who trained or taught at Yale and Virginia who have publicly acknowledged Hartt's impact: Diogenes Allen, Stephen Crites, James Gustafson, David Bailey Harned, Ray Hart, Van Harvey, Stanley Hauerwas, Gordon Kaufman, Walter Lowe, and John Sykes. Anyone who knows the work of these men (and most of the graduates in those days were men; one notable exception is Sallie McFague who was a student of H. Richard Niebuhr but who also served as teaching assistant to Hartt) will be intrigued by Hartt's role in their work. Two of Hartt's greatest fans are James Gustafson and Stanley Hauerwas, whose theologies have developed along quite divergent paths. For Hartt to be acknowledged by such influential and wildly diverse thinkers means that his work deserves careful attention.

Moreover, Hartt's work has received attention from contemporary Anabaptist and Baptist theologians. John Howard Yoder references Hartt's work briefly and appreciatively. James Wm. McLendon, Jr., gives Hartt sustained attention in developing the last volume of his "baptist" theology, *Systematic Theology, Volume 3: Witness*.

Does this diversity mean that Hartt is hopelessly incoherent or so obscure that he can be taken to mean anything? Not at all. Rather, this diversity means that Hartt's thought is rich in depth and generous in its embrace. Hartt seemed to many of his peers to have read and assimilated everything, or almost everything, of importance to the work of theology. At the same time, he did not lose his creative powers. Thus, through the assimilative and creative power of his intellect he produces seminal work that contains the seeds of many fruitful theological endeavors.

Finally, we need Hartt's work available to us today because he wrote as a theologian for "America." Hartt grew up on the American prairies with Hubert Humphrey as his childhood friend. Like many he returned often to those wide-open skies that represented for him the possibilities of American culture. But given his clear-eyed perception of our lies and illusions and his apprehension of the truth of Jesus Christ, he also saw the cultural embodiment of anxiety that distorts and corrupts the flourishing of life in the human creation that we call America. Today, in the midst of the rise of "the American Empire," Hartt's prophetic and subtle analyses are more desperately needed than ever.

So, for these four reasons, at least, we need Hartt's witness to the gospel of Jesus Christ in our midst. In the seven volumes that make up "The Julian Hartt Library," a new generation of readers will have available to them the major works of this seminal "American" theologian. I have written the Introduction to this present volume. I wrote above about my first encounter with Hartt's work. I had set it aside by the time I arrived at Duke for graduate studies in 1986. In the course of preparing to write a dissertation on Austin Farrer under the guidance of Tom Langford, I discovered that Hartt had used Farrer's work in his classes at Yale. One evening, prior to the start of Stanley Hauerwas's Theological Ethics Seminar, I asked him if he thought that Hartt would be open to a visit from me to talk about Farrer's work. "Sure," he said. "But you know you should think about writing on Julian. No one has taken a close look at him." With Tom Langford's encouragement, that's what I did. Writing on Hartt and continuing to draw on his work for my own vocation has been a wonderful adventure. I am grateful to Julian Hartt for the work he has done, to Stanley Hauerwas for his insight, to Tom Langford for his guidance, and to Wipf and Stock for their impetus to republish these works.

Jonathan R. Wilson
Acadia Divinity College, 2005

Volume Foreword

Julian Hartt's *A Christian Critique of American Culture* is a major constructive theological project focused on the perennial "Christ and culture" question. However, for theological reasons to which I will return later, Hartt reframes it as a "Christ and civilization" question: Given the Gospel they proclaim, how should communities of Christian faith relate to the civilizations in which they are set? That is an issue in systematic theology, not culture theory. You will be misled by the book's title if you infer from it that the book will offer theological ruminations on some of the more or less specialized sociological, ethnographic, political, and culture-critical studies of high and low American culture that the academy and the higher journalism generously generate. Rather, in this book Julian Hartt proposes fresh formulations of Christian beliefs about God, human being, Jesus Christ, sin and redemption, grace and faith, providence, the Church, and human culture that stress the implications of each of these doctrines for the "Christ and civilization" issue. As the book's focus, this issue serves as an original way in which to integrate a Christian theology into a certain kind of systematic whole.

Of course, features of American civilization do surface repeatedly in Hartt's discussion. The book was first published in 1967, and it is mid-twentieth century America that appears in its pages. Here "contemporary" American culture shows traces of the impact of a tense cold war, the civil rights movement, the "sexual revolution," and the economic and social problems that prompted the "great society" federal programs. In certain ways this is a dated picture of American civilization. However, that datedness does not imprison Hartt's theological project in an American cultural era now sealed in the past. His dated cultural references serve as cases-in-point of Hartt's doctrinally grounded contentions about how communities of Christian faith ought and ought not to engage that culture. It does not take a great deal of imagination to find analogous cases-in-point of the same contentions about theologically appropriate terms of engagement of any subsequent culture.

A Christian Critique introduced a unique and genuinely distinctive voice into the world of American Protestant theology in the 1960s. This is true in several senses of "voice." Hartt had already been on the faculty of Yale Divinity School for many years as a professor of philosophical theology when the book was published. He was already legendary among faculty and students for his rhetorical power in preaching, his dialectical powers in the classroom, his powers as a humorist, and his exquisite gift of timing. His style of rhetoric and humor give the book one sort of distinctive voice. This is one book of theology with which one can laugh out loud. While Hartt's style may not be to everyone's taste, humor and attention to rhetoric are so rare in theology that any sign of them ought to be honored as an occasion for gratitude.

In the world of modern theology, a book whose voice does not defensively fend off opponents or aggressively round up support from distinguished predecessors is a truly distinctive voice in a second sense of the word. Although Hartt is a formidable public debater—and in seminars a brilliant analyst of the structure and movement of the complex arguments of theological and philosophical texts—he scarcely mentions other texts or writers in these pages. There are no explicit polemics against theologians with whom he disagrees and no analysis of texts whose lines of thought he wishes to appropriate and extend. To borrow a distinction from Dietrich Ritschl, in this book the ratio of information about other theologians' views to fresh theological proposals is extraordinarily low.

In a deeper sense, it is *A Christian Critique*'s fresh formulations of doctrines and its implicit dissent from the reigning theological consensus in the 1960s that give the book its most distinctive voice. Without attempting to summarize Hartt's original and important constructive theological proposals, I want to bring out some of the book's key dissents by contrasting them to aspects of the American Protestant theological scene in which they appeared.

One major dissent concerns the genre of constructive theology. By consensus, the Protestant theological enterprise has long been structured by a division of labor well established in the academy: constructive or systematic theology, pastoral theology, historical theology, and biblical theology have been understood as distinct academic disciplines producing distinct genres of writings. Few were the scholars deemed competent to contribute to more than one of them. Hartt dissents. He insists that Christian systematic theology properly conceived is inherently practical theology. For Hartt the key practice is preaching. Preaching is the church's defining mission, and it is in the practice of preaching that the community of faith is constantly engaged when encountering its host civilization. The practice of preaching is where the "Christ and civilization" issue is joined concretely. That, and not the spiritual depths of culture itself, is why a systematic theology has to be a theology of culture. Accordingly, the criterion of the adequacy of a theological proposal, Hartt says, is its preachability (131). Unlike many theologians who assert that theology is essentially in the service of the proclamation of the Gospel, but then discuss almost everything except preaching, Hartt has quite a lot to say throughout this book about the actual practice of preaching and devotes Chapter XIV to it, and especially to the implications of the Gospel for the appropriate rhetoric of preaching.

A second area where dissent and constructive proposals conjoin in this book concerns the basic subject matter of theology. At mid-century there was a tacit consensus among theologians to frame the issue this way: Should theology be conceived as primarily the explication of God's revelatory self-giving in Jesus Christ? Karl Barth was the symbolic figure for this camp. Or should theology be conceived primarily as the explication of the subjective state called "faith"? Rudolf Bultmann was the symbolic figure for this camp. Hartt declines to frame the question in terms of these two options and proposes a third. The subject matter of theology is the church's preached Gospel. The preached Gospel is at once the good news of Jesus Christ and the actuality of the Kingdom of God that the church is sent to preach, on one side, and the human practices of preaching by which that Gospel is proclaimed on the other. Hartt sounds a little like Karl Barth in his insistence that theology is in the service of the proclamation of the Gospel. But he is very unlike Barth in holding that the theological task is to illuminate the Gospel about actualities God has realized in Jesus Christ, as narrated by Scripture, rather than to illuminate the Gospel as formulated in classical dogma. Although he develops a Trinitarian doctrine of God and a high Christology, Hartt holds that classical Christian dogma is formulated in metaphysical categories that ought long ago to have been retired to a museum. Hartt sounds a little like Rudolf Bultmann in beginning theology by reflection on the existence of persons in community who have faith in the Gospel and are called to preach it. However, he is very unlike Bultmann in insisting that the subject matter of theology is not the subjectivity of those persons but rather the Kingdom that God has actualized in Jesus Christ. That Kingdom is a subject matter that is "other" than persons' lives and, indeed, defines their lives. Accordingly, the conceptual framework by which Hartt's proposals about various doctrines are held together is a theological anthropology, an account of what it is to be a human agent.

A third consensus in mid-century American Protestant theology from which Hartt implicitly dissents was shared by a multitude of theological movements, some of them quite new, that were getting a lot of attention at the time, such as process theology, the "new hermeneutics," liberation theologies, death of God theologies, theologies of secularity, theologies of hope, and a vigorous theology of culture movement inspired by Paul Tillich. The consensus held that systematic theologians have to choose between constructing their proposals in conversation with "philosophy" (as Bultmann did in his reliance on Martin Heidegger) or steering clear of any such intellectual entanglement (as supposedly did Barth.) That choice was generally perceived in the United States to be an updated version of an earlier debate in Protestant theology between "biblical theology" as represented by Reinhold Niebuhr and "philosophical theology" as represented by Paul Tillich. Old and new theological movements introduced a variety of constructive theological proposals, but they all implicitly accepted the consensus that a key issue about how to do theology should be framed as a choice between reliance on or avoidance of a philosophical conversation partner. It was conventional in disputes about this question to refer to "philosophy" as though it were some one type of intellectual work whose task is to propose a comprehensive, systematic body of theory that accounts for all types of reality, or types of experience of reality, and describes the order that makes them into a single, coherent, lived world or cosmos.

As the chapters that follow will show repeatedly, in making his own theological proposals Hartt declines to accept the consensus terms in which this debate was framed. He rejects the philosophically grounded claims of several of the newer theological movements of the time that metaphysical beliefs and theories are either necessarily false or meaningless. In his view the Gospel makes cognitive and reality claims. Therefore theology cannot avoid the responsibility to draw out and analyze the epistemological and metaphysical beliefs the Gospel entails. That is properly philosophical work inherent in properly theological work. By implication, Barth is held to be profoundly wrong on this score. On the other hand, Hartt also rejects the equation of "philosophy" with philosophical system-building.

Thus, by implication, almost everyone else is also held to be profoundly wrong.

Implicit in Hartt's theological proposals in *A Christian Critique* is the judgment that it is perfectly intelligible, and a philosophically responsible move, to affirm metaphysical beliefs, draw metaphysical distinctions, and employ distinctively metaphysical concepts without either committing oneself intellectually to any one body of systematic philosophy from which they may have been drawn or undertaking to construct such a system oneself. Consequently, Hartt's theological proposals about theological anthropology, the person and work of Christ, God's providence, the church, eschatology, and above all, the nature of culture and human creativity all rely extensively on his use of a few metaphysical concepts. In particular, they include "actuality" and "ideality," "participation" and "essence," "spirit" and "body," and "form," "teleology," and "narrative" in relation to "action."

In Hartt's view, the central claim made by anyone who preaches the Gospel rightly is that in the resurrection of Jesus Christ God has begun to actualize God's Kingdom in history. The Kingdom is the actuality of the world in which we live. That given actuality, and not any set of ideal possibilities ("idealities") that people might "actualize" for themselves, defines the present actuality of human subjects. It does so by virtue of their active participation in the Kingdom by the exercise of their creaturely powers. Their vocation is to act appropriately to their actual context, the Kingdom of God. The overall pattern of a life of such action corresponds to the pattern of Jesus' life by which the Kingdom of God is actualized in history. Such life is ordered to the end or telos of witnessing to the actuality of that Kingdom. Human agents have their essence in the pattern of such teleologically ordered action. The pattern of such actions inherently involves them in the common life of their civilization, both in witness to God's actualization of God's Kingdom in the resurrection of Jesus and in judgment on the civilization's injustices and distortions of human life as they come into view in light of the Kingdom's present actuality. Hence the task of the church is not to attempt to realize in the culture a set of ideal possibilities whose actualization would morally improve contemporary civilization. That is to try to dwell in the realm of "ideality." Rather, it is to seek to live in that civilization in light of the Kingdom of God that is already actual. That is to dwell in the realm of "actuality." "Actuality" is always prior to "ideality." "Ideality" is always an abstraction from and parasitic upon "actuality," both in the order of reality and in the order of knowing. That set of claims is a set of metaphysical beliefs that lies at the core of the Gospel.

Finally, there was a consensus in mid-century American Protestant theology about how to frame an issue about theology's own relation to civilization: Either theology is an inquiry that inherently focuses inwardly on the authenticity or inauthenticity of persons' subjectivity and sees civilization largely as an enemy, the cause of subjective inauthenticity (as much existentialist theology like Bultmann's urged); or theology is an inquiry that inherently drives outward toward explicit engagement with issues in the public realm of social, economic, and political power arrangements (as the newer liberation and political theologies, the older Niebuhrian and Tillichian theologies, and, arguably, Barth all urged).

Implicit in Hartt's theological analysis of "civilization" is a dissent: That way of framing the issue rests on a false alternative. This brings us back to the focal theme of this book. Hartt declines to view civilization either as a power from whose threat to objectify and depersonalize human subjects the Christian Gospel separates and protects us, or to view it as the inescapable collective product of human subjects' creative expressivity, for whose justice and well-being the Gospel makes us responsible. Rather, civilization and human agents are inseparably related: "Civilization is a global organization of human powers and achievements," Hartt writes. "To call it global calls attention to its comprehensiveness and to its pervasiveness, its inwardly-constituting power relative to the individual . . . A civilization embraces both the outer structures and symbols of meaning, such as paintings, railroads, and policemen; and the inner appropriations of meaning" (15). Hence a civilization is the embodiment of a culture in both its "low" and "high" modalities. Civilization is as integral to human agency as is bodiliness. Indeed, because it is as corporeal as the human body its institutions are often called "bodies." Theologically speaking, both civilizations and bodied human agents are concrete and finite creatures of God. It is because civilization, and not merely the culture it embodies, is integral to human agency, that the central theological issue for Hartt's theology must be framed as a question about "Christ and civilization" not "Christ and culture."

Civilization, then, is not necessarily hostile to human agency. To be sure, it can depersonalize human subjects. Hartt takes careful note of ways in which "contemporary civilization is a triumph of unconsciousness and (therefore) of nonpersonality" (21). But civilization is not, as such, essentially inimical to human flourishing. Hart also takes careful note of ways in which contemporary civilization "has also produced a tidal wave of rebellion against itself. It is not merely deficient in coherence, it is full of self-contradictions" (25–26). It is as full of contradictions as are human agents and their subjectivities, according to Hartt's anthropology. This is a basically positive theological assessment of civilization accomplished by incorporating it into a theological anthropology. Because human agency and civilization are so integral to each other, and together reciprocally vulnerable to distortion, theology cannot be a type of inquiry that addresses either without the other, and it most certainly must explicitly engage issues in the public realm structured by social, economic, and political power arrangements.

Hartt provides further analysis of civilization's ambiguity: It is good because it is integral to human flourishing; but at the same time, it is problematic because, in its creaturely finitude, it is vulnerable to distortions that are hostile to human flourishing. The culture embodied in a "civilization is (and not just offers) a particular interpretation of ontological essentials" (71), i.e. such "root elements of man's being" as death, love, creativity, anxiety, and guilt (70). The interpretation assigns values to these "root elements." These interpretations may just as easily foster "illusions as shelter against reality" (6) as they reveal reality. They also underwrite humankind's propensity to self-justification quite as vigorously as they hold humankind accountable. In fostering illusions and self-justifications a civilization's interpretations of our "ontological essentials" cut against human flourishing. The danger of this ambiguous mix is intensified by civilizations' claims, with "presumptive absoluteness," that Being, or reality as such, "is disclosed absolutely in their particular histories" (69). Their capacities to critique and relativize their own interpretations of "ontological essentials" are few and weak.

This qualified but fundamentally affirmative theological assessment of civilization frames Hartt's sketch of an important theology of culture. In a theology focused on the church's engagement with its host civilization, preaching, not culture, is the central theological theme. However, when "civilization" is understood as the embodiment of "culture," such a theology cannot but include "theology of culture" along with other standard theological topics. Hartt understands a culture to be the collective name for all sorts of products of human creative powers. It includes, among other things, a civilization's art, politics, and mass culture (in the final section of the book Hartt devotes a chapter to each of these in American civilization). Unlike Paul Tillich, the most influential theologian of culture at mid-century, Hartt does not view the products of human creativity as expressions of the "depth dimension" of human consciousness, the point where human spirit and divine Spirit touch without mediation, as expressions of "ultimate concern" in which the absolute and the concrete are one. Hence they are not construed theologically as transparencies to transcendence. He regards works of art, for example, as expressions of the human spirit's power to concentrate meanings found in the temporal flow of experience so concretely that they (at least in a relative way) transcend time and change (359). "Art is religious only if any effort to deal with reality is religious" (365). Finite creations of human creatures, works of art are takes on how the finite, creaturely world is and what it may mean. Works of art do transform the world, but "[p]oetic [and other artistic] transformations . . . do not reveal a higher world. At best they reveal how this world is enmeshed in unique relations with God and Ideality" (28).

Correlatively, it is not the task of the church's preaching to spiritualize the culture of its host civilization by converting "the Gospel into the piety of contemporary culture" (59). That would merely "imbue the norms of this civilization," norms by which an incoherent and self-contradictory civilization already judges itself and protests against itself, "with absoluteness" and thus "embellish and adorn its idealities with holiness" (60). Rather, the task of a theology of culture is to learn "to discern and rightly to relate . . . to the good of this world," which requires learning "to distinguish what is real from the specious, what is true from the merely plausible, what is good from its counterfeits, what is beautiful from the merely pretty and ingratiating" (69) in a culture's interpretations of our "ontological essentials." That, in turn, requires a criterion that can give us some distance from and leverage on the "presumptive absoluteness" of civilizations' implicit claim that Being, or reality as such, "is disclosed absolutely in their particular histories" (69). Hartt's entire project is an unpacking of his proposal that "Jesus Christ is this criterion" (69). Reliance on that criterion will require both theological critique of civilization and the preaching it serves to mount sharp protests against features of the culture embodied by that civilization. However, such protest cannot avoid also being protest against features of the church that is part of that civilization. The church is in no position to scold the world and its preaching may not take that form, not even when it involves "prophetic" protest. For on careful analysis the "conclusion is forced home: the church is the reason why contemporary civilization can no longer be called 'Christian'" (310).

In short, "The aim of theological criticism is not to prove that the church is right and the world is wrong. To show forth the truth in which man may rightly divine who he is and to whom he belongs and against whom he sins and whither he is bound; and with whom there is fullness of life from everlasting to everlasting: the elucidation of this Gospel is the theological calling" (48).

David H. Kelsey
Yale Divinity School, 2005

Acknowledgments

This volume is dedicated to the person to whom I owe more than to any other living person. I am glad to own this indebtedness and I am proud to declare it.

I wish also to thank persons of the faculties of Garrett Theological Seminary and Hartford Theological Seminary who gave me opportunity and incentive to present some of the material of this essay to their respective constituencies. These occasions were long ago; and since these persons might not wish to be accounted among my benefactors I have not listed them by name.

Miss Eleanor Jordan of the publisher's company has rendered invaluable assistance in making the text presentable.

None of the foregoing persons can be held responsible for the shape of the argument. So far as I know, no one else can be held accountable for that except the author. The argument has developed slowly. I hope to give various parts of it much fuller treatment in subsequent volumes.

Finally I want to thank the directors of the John Simon Guggenheim Memorial Foundation for the opportunity to devote a relatively carefree year to intensive work on this volume.

J. N. Hartt

Thanksgiving Day, 1966
New Haven, Connecticut

Preface

The present volume is the initial part of a theological program that I conceive to be Dogmatic. This may turn out to be a conceit in more than one sense, but one must hope to be prepared to accept the consequences of one's premeditated acts. One of these may be the discovery that it is too late in the day to revive even the name of that venerable discipline, Dogmatics, to say nothing of bringing its great business back to life; either because Barth has already accomplished those miracles; or because he has proved that neither is possible. In the meantime I do not believe that it is theologically wrongheaded to be as systematic as possible. I hope to discuss later, and in some detail, the matter of the peculiar systematic requirements of Christian dogma. Such things pertain to philosophical theology. They are not the proper beginning of Christian theological reflection. That is not a good reason for dismissing them; and it is not a good reason for smuggling them in where they do not belong. I do not believe that there are clear or adequate reasons for throwing philosophical issues out of the theological circle, once the circle is in motion.

Introduction

An enterprise identified as "theology of culture" has been highly visible in contemporary Christian thought for the past quarter of a century. To be sure, some elements of this enterprise have been integral parts of theology from the beginning of the church. Once it had become clear that the apocalyptic appearance of the Kingdom of God was not imminent, the people of the church had at least to modify their concrete relations with the "world," if not their feelings and opinions about it. So already in the epistles of St. Paul guidelines appear for the faithful conduct of life in a world largely given over to works of darkness (cf. Rom. 12-16). This hardly makes St. Paul a theologian of culture. It does suggest how "world" might become a theological object of high importance once the power and prominence of the church in the Empire were clearly moving to a zenith no amount of prophecy in the first century could have anticipated and no kind of "theologizing" then available could have rationalized. But St. Augustine is a different story. The architect of so many theological enterprises in the church's history, he is also the great father of theology of culture. His *City of God* is a wonderfully seminal theological response to the catastrophes—not all of them dramatic—which announced the collapse of the Empire in the West; and to an epoch which had also seen the ascent of the church to great prominence and the promise of great power in secular affairs. St. Augustine's range of topics in *The City of God* is very large. He offers an account of the origins of society. The root principle of the Roman Empire is analyzed in great depth. He ponders the relations of power, love, justice, and peace to one another. He shows why the civil order can never attain true peace. He delineates the adventures of the ideal, *Romanitas,* and why it has come to grief. All of this, and much more, in connection with the announced intent of showing that the Christian people are not responsible for the collapse of the Empire!

Theology of culture is not a grand continuum running in unbroken splendor from Pauline inspiration in St. Augustine to Paul Tillich. What we are now likely to call theology of culture has some uniquely modern features; and these occupy such a central place in the contemporary enterprise that to speak seriously of such a continuum is out of the question. The most distinctive of these signs of historically uncorrupted modernity is the theological readiness to find at least as much "truth" in the achievements of contemporary culture as in the historical beliefs of the church. In this way culture (= "world") becomes a prime theological subject; and theologians accordingly may ask in all sobriety how, or even whether, Tradition speaks significantly to Modern Man; and this clearly on the understanding that if the Tradition fails here successes elsewhere will be pointless ecclesiastical gains accompanied by witless bureaucratic self-congratulations.

Thus the passion for relevancy in the proclamation of the Gospel has become very nearly all-absorbing where theology of culture reigns. For whatever it might be deemed to be worth, this passion can be given an apostolic backing: it is St. Paul who first says, "I would rather speak five intelligible words, for the benefit of others as well as myself, than thousands of words in the language of ecstasy" (I Cor. 14:19, NEB). And it is he who also first announces the grand evangelical policy of becoming all things to all men (I Cor. 9:22). But the apostolic context and temper have been left far behind in theology of culture. For St. Paul was speaking of his ministry in and for the church and thus of his prime responsibility to mediate the power and wisdom of God in Jesus Christ first to the household of faith and thereafter to the world. Today one can do theology of culture, and call it Christian, without making or soliciting the same absolute confession. Indeed the apostolic confession may well prove a hindrance in the relentless drive for relevancy, since modern secular man has access to truth incomparably superior to that granted to ancient man, religious or secular. On this the Modern Mind and theologians of culture appear to be in perfect agreement. Thereafter the only open question for both concerns the appropriateness of ancient symbol as a device for displaying contemporary truth.

There is still more to learn from and about the churchly passion for relevancy. Bad conscience has a boundless suzerainty in the church, and it is a many-faceted thing. One aspect is the feeling that the church has misled the contemporary world by its own commitment to archaic symbols and outworn attitudes. Another aspect of the church's bad conscience is its guilt feelings for continuing to endorse and defend a system of value that has been eroded almost past recognition. The heralds of the New Morality (itself closely related to theology of culture) have not been reluctant to point this out, and to demand from the church a fairly severe penance: a readiness to give up the ghost if it cannot secularize its Gospel without reservation or residue.

So theology of culture seems to offer effective and appropriate remedy for the bad conscience of the church. It updates the Message. It offers new and powerful leverage on the unending critical mission of the church. Last but not least of its virtues, it is a way of doing theology that does not require, although it may tolerate, technical theological language, analytical precision, or dialectical prowess. Theology of culture thus arouses the interest of people frustrated and fatigued by conventional theological disputations that never seem to bring the Kingdom of God nearer or incline the heart to sing the praises of mysterious Providence.

Moreover theology of culture has made a solid contact with the acute perplexity of the church as it has tried to discern the kind of relationship to contemporary civilization most congruent with the full demands of the Gospel. Itself a signal expression of the passion for relevancy, theology of culture appears to be decisively relevant to the problems of the Christian who really cares to know which world he is living in and what kinds of criticism of the actual world are called for and are likely to be effective. Thus churchmen who feel this concern surely need to know that the Social Gospel is theologically dead, whether or not the theologians of culture were in on the kill. Christian protest against the iniquities of the present order is not now obedient to the heavenly vision of a social order made seemly in all its parts by the grand concert of men of goodwill everywhere. That vision has given way in the church to things many of which defy inflation to historic moment. On matters greatly affecting the public world the churches commonly break guilty silence to utter vague platitudes. Surely at the moment they are not, and hardly dream of becoming, a potent spiritual consensus in the social struggles that continue to test the fabric and foundations of this civilization. Everywhere in the churches we see a profound uncertainty of the ground on which to stand to make relevant and faithful proclamation of the Gospel. But we should be shallow and irresponsible if we did not at once admit that this wracking uncertainty is an inevitable reaction to a world whose problems have assumed a complexity properly demonic. It is the part of wisdom to recognize that simple traditional solutions are not available, not even the solutions of a tradition so recently in our midst as the Social Gospel.

Bad conscience, objective uncertainty, and self-doubt may well then be presently unavoidable descriptions of the church's relationship to contemporary civilization. Theology of culture has been properly unsparing in the delineation of these facts and in its judgment upon them. They are not definitions of the church's essential being. Its essential being, its being in relationship to God in Christ, is the real, that is, the decisive, explanation for its renewed quest for adequate theological foundations on which to offer interpretation of the good-and-evil of the present world. Fiery valorous spirits urge the good people of the church to take up the sword of Christ against rampant evil and leave theology—any theology other than theology of culture—to craven academics. But the church of Jesus Christ has only the sword given to it by God: the Word of God, "active and alive." And this "cuts more keenly than any two-edged sword, piercing as far as the place where life and spirit, joints and marrow, divide. It sifts the purposes and thoughts of the heart" (Heb. 4:12, NEB). Victory over interior uncertainty and public vacillation can therefore be promised only when the church comes again into vivid awareness of its divine foundations. Neither tumult abroad nor bad conscience within can generate *this.*

Theology of culture has spoken to this need for a fresh foundation by seeking to make a deeper penetration into the genius of contemporary civilization, and into the meaning of culture itself, than the advocates or the opponents of the Social Gospel attempted. The advocates attacked specific evils in the social order without raising very clearly, if at all, the question whether these evils might express the genius of modern civilization in the Western world. For example, war appeared to the advocates of liberal Christianity to be a monstrous excrescence on the human order, a blight to be removed by correcting the economic and political abuses from which it springs. Given this conviction, pacifism seemed to be an inescapable inference and at the same time a policy that did not call for total disengagement from the social order. But this overlooks a salient characteristic of war in the Western world, if not in general: it has been retooled to meet the specifications of contemporary civilization. War continues —God save us all!—to express values that only the most intrepid visionaries—the uncorruptible revolutionaries—are ready to excise from the body politic.

So the advocates of the Social Gospel seemed to say, "The Christian conscience demands justice. Let us therefore unite to strike down injustice so that men henceforth may dwell in peace together. No doubt the fight will be severe because powerful men have a heavy investment in the chains with which the brotherhood of man is shackled. They must be overcome but only with the instrumentalities consistent with the Gospel of Love. So we work to bring in the Kingdom of God!"

So inspired the churches contributed much to impressive victories against specific social evils. Then world war ensued. American idealism and optimism, fused in the Social Gospel, suffered severe dislocation from these cataclysms. These noble attitudes were not extinguished, as the crystallizing of the liberal conscience into broad welfare legislation amply testifies. But the explicit Christian sanction for this remarkable social transformation has never again been so clear. Only now that this civilization has reached a pinnacle of corporate affluence never attained anywhere before has it become possible to launch a War on Poverty that surpasses both in conception and in power any and all privately financed philanthropy—to the acute unhappiness of those who still want to acquire merit by distributing largesse as they see fit. But this social program and the philanthropy of works righteousness have one great thing in common: neither demands any hurting sacrifice from the Ins for the sake of the Outs. In neither case does the church have a shining reason for feeling that at last the gospel of denial of self for the enhancement of others carried the day. In fact the day of *that* gospel seems to have closed, even in the church. But it is also true that hardly anyone in the church believes that even the most sagacious harnessing of economic and political power to alleviate suffering produced by the social order will bring in the Kingdom of God.

But is it enough for the church to have learned that it cannot remake civilization into the image of the Kingdom, in one generation or in a hundred? Is there anything in this discovery by itself that will instruct the church in how it ought to "ransom the time"—how, that is, it must endure both patiently and creatively the anguish of living in and for a world that will not offer up its heart to the Lord Jesus Christ? If for the moment we might presume to match pronouncements with theologians of culture we should say that the church must learn how to hold both apathy and cynicism at bay in her own life, or perish; for apathy, as well as a spiritually toned cynicism, is an encroaching disease rather than a trap for the feet of the unwary.

If the church is to learn again how to ransom the time she must achieve a deeper penetration of that tightly woven fabric of good-and-evil we call contemporary civilization. Theology of culture has spoken to that need, even when it has been launched from the intuition of the church's impotence to speak creatively to contemporary man. Even the passionate indictment of the voluntary servitude of the church to the lords and masters of the age has thrown some light on the actualities of the world in which the Christian must make choices and hope for grace to live with their consequences. But this illumination, fitful or steady, is very much by way of a side effect of theology of culture. We shall find at the heart of the enterprise a conviction that Christian theology is improperly done when it comes only at the end—or in homiletical forays into the arts along the way—to consider the cultural situation of faith. Theology of culture seeks to relocate and reestablish the very foundations and form of Christian theology. It is not enough for culture to appear somewhere in theological systems as a topic of high importance. Theology proper must begin with the analysis of culture, or it will prove to be systematically meaningless. The analysis, thus, is no longer conceived as a bid to attract the attention of the audience before doing the serious work. It *is* the serious theological work. Thereafter the fate both of dogma and of metaphysics—if the theologian of culture will admit any such distinction—is not hard to predict.

In Part I of this treatise I undertake to show how the acute anxiety of the church concerning its role as a divinely licensed critic of the world seems to prompt, if not to warrant, the radical reorientation of Christian thinking properly identified as theology of culture. I do not think we can deny that the sensitive and responsible Christian critic is driven to seek a more solid foundation for his tasks than tradition provides. In this connection it is to be noted that theology of culture finds this foundation in new (or apparently new) doctrines of man. Having discovered, and duly announced, that God is dead, at least for the time being, the theologians of culture are ready to make the most of the fact that man is still, if not very much, alive—at least for the time being. If it is not premature or presumptuous to speculate about a new liturgy derived from the New Theology, one might suppose that it might contain the prayer: we thank the Ground of Being that man is not like God—that is, dead.

In Part II the essentially practical character of Dogmatics is delineated. Thereafter interpretations of certain doctrines of the faith are proposed. In these I have not assumed that "relevancy" is a criterion of "truth." Surely it *is* an aim and an obligation, nonetheless. But neither the importance nor the urgency of Christian claims can be accounted for as "relevancy."

Part III consists of essays in criticism. They may have the single virtue of reminding the reader who is persisting to the end that the transition from the classroom to the world is fraught with perils, even if one has never left the world.

No doubt a word is in order concerning the absence of scholarly discussion of contemporary theological standpoints and systems. The only serious excuse I can offer for this will likely seem as arrogant as it is serious, to wit: Dogmatics must be engaged with the life of the church in its actual setting; and therefore Dogmatics is far less committed to the scrutiny and refutation of theological systems than most modes of theological discourse.

PART I

THE VOCATION OF THE CHURCH AS A CRITIC OF CULTURE

CHAPTER I

The Church as a Critic in an Age of Anxiety

I

As a form of criticism of culture the Social Gospel was lively, productive, and pertinacious. Reactions to it were remarkably diverse; and even its memory is execrated by people whose unyielding devotion to the King James Version is an integral part of a version of Christianity dedicated to the sanctity of private property, free enterprise, white supremacy, the segregation of the races, the gold standard, and the open shop. Others felt that the Social Gospel erred liberally on the side of utopian simplification of immoral society; it did not reckon sufficiently with the evil-in-depth of social existence, nor with the perversity of the ego. So even if we were still accustomed to singing the hymn that proclaims

> These things shall be,—a loftier race
> Than e'er the world hath known shall rise. . . .

a nonmetrical afterthought would shatter the mood:

> unless radioactivity produces a mutant species

There was another kind of treatment given the Social Gospel, and it is still being given to the residual elements of liberal Christianity in the churches. Indifference is its name, indifference, that is, to every kind of criticism of contemporary life, except, perhaps, for mild rebukes for the more popular immoralities. At the present moment more rigorous and fundamental criticism seems to be at a very low ebb of interest in the church. Here and there some of its people are wholly preoccupied with issues of social justice; but these dedicated souls seem to find it bitterly hard work to arouse the conscience of their fellow believers. The unaroused, for their part, would have but little difficulty in showing that the prophetic zeal of these who are seeking to disturb the peace of Zion is anything but a strict inference of the Gospel—if they cared to. Elsewhere in the church the priest has replaced the prophet, only to be replaced himself by the ordained purveyor of homespun secular wisdom. But it is also the day of the administrative specialist; and of the personal counselor; and of those upon whom the apostolic charisma has descended for no other apparent purpose than simply to keep the people together.

So in this time many voices and many silences proclaim a Gospel indifferent to the serious criticism of culture.

This is not the whole story. Professional faddism, apathy, and reaction are present and voting. But this is a time of acutely anxious groping for the authentic foundation upon which the church may confidently stand to preach the whole Gospel. In all of its distracted behavior and behind the bland resolutions of life's problems the church is haunted by the possibility that in all its ways it has become superfluous. Granted, "irrelevancy" is immediately the judgment of man upon the church. But might it not also be the judgment of God? Perhaps if the Revelation of St. John were to be brought up to date it would include a denunciation of the irrelevant church as a fit companion of the church that is neither cold nor hot (Rev. 3:16).

So life in the church does not seem to be more merry or more healthy for having made so little of its critical function. The fact is that the church is no longer so sublimely sure of itself that it can assail the evils and follies of the age in joyful indifference to the real risks of being poor and despised for its efforts. But it is not so supremely well-adjusted that it can cheerfully accede to what the age wants from it, though it would gather honor and treasure if it did so.

These anxieties point to fundamental problems in the present life of the church. Decline of popularity is not one of these problems. As an institution among others the church is doing reasonably well. But this success is a terrible failure; and that *is* a problem. Many people are drowsily comfortable in the church, having parked their day-to-day problems outside. But even if the pressures of the everyday world have followed them into the church, the chances are pretty good that they will be anesthetized. They who look for something to deaden the terror of the ultimate questions ought not to overlook the church from sheer prejudice.

If readiness to take the plight of the church with deep seriousness is a mark of theology in culture, we ought to welcome so much of its program if not its label. It is meet and right for us to believe that the Holy Spirit is working in the distress of the church over its own popularity and in its anxiety about the foundations of its own life. Surely God is bringing it to a fresh grasp of the gifts of faith, hope, and love. But theologically some chances must be taken and some bets must be made. Dogma is not a proper substitute for personal piety or for public conscience; and it is surely no panacea for the anxieties produced by the failure of either. But for the Christian who intends and prays to be more than a statistical Christian, dogma cannot be blithely dismissed from piety and conscience as the dead hand of the past God. What the church needs is more chance-taking in the constructive interpretation of its dogmas rather than to get into some wonderfully modern religious enterprise that transcends its past life and present commitments.

Theology of culture makes its big bet on a reinterpretation of man's being in the light of what he now knows rather than what he once believed. So the constructive program of theology of culture rests upon, or more properly is an extension of, an analysis of the human situation. But how is this analysis to be done? What materials will it draw upon? Does one need to be a philosopher—or know one, at any rate—to be able to bring off the analysis? These are questions we must ponder but not before we see how one human datum leaps out to meet the inquiring eye: resistance to a deep interrogation of human being sets in early and stays very late because a great deal of happiness rides on keeping conventional outlooks and estimates intact. This is attested to by the fact that people generally expect the real truth about themselves to be bitter medicine and so they are likely to resort to it only when everything else has failed. Since the contemporary world is well stocked with palliatives—not all of them religious by any means—the moment of truth can be indefinitely postponed, with luck. Even scientific lore confirms the everyday anxiety about facing up to the truth. Which is to say that psychiatrists too believe that truth is dangerous stuff and use the utmost care in bringing their patients to face it. For many, healers and sick together, the truth cuts and stings; and they hope, but cannot promise, eventually to be the better for it. Until that great day what can one do but nail the truth-policy flag to the mast? Better to know that one hates one's father (or mother, but surely one or the other). Better to know that man is all alone in a silent and dark cosmos and must will to be "god" to himself. Better to know that other creative spirits have also been homosexuals. Better to know that one longs for immortality because of one's unfulfilled ego needs. In all cases, whatever they are, better to know than—to what? The alternative is not always crystal clear. Indeed the turbulence into which we sail under the truth policy makes us all wonder sometimes whether the unconscious souls are not the truly blessed in the world here below.

So part of the truth on to which we stumble is this: The human spirit has a natural and humanly inextirpable propensity for creating illusions as shelter against reality. The love of illusion is one of the fundamental factors in the human equation. To be is to be self-deceived—there's an axiom for you.

Surely then we cannot fault the theologian of culture for contending that the first step in the Christian criticism of culture is a determined quest for the right understanding of the human situation, love of illusion and all. To criticize means to judge, to evaluate. It means to determine what a thing really is and not merely what it appears to be. It means to evaluate claims upon attention, desire, and emotion. So criticism of culture is concerned to discover how human life and spirit really fare in an actual human world. This concern demands a concrete distinction between the realities and the pretensions to finality of truth, beauty, and goodness with which every civilization abounds.

Even so sketchy an account of the critical task makes us aware of another element of man's make-up: his propensity for self-justification. A propensity in us all, self-justification is the most formidable occupational hazard of the Christian critic. As a man of faith he believes that the ultimate wisdom available for the judgment and guidance of man's life is wisdom that transcends human creativity. But he also believes that such wisdom is really given to man, it has been communicated to him, it is in the world as the absolute meaning of the world. Wisdom infinitely above the wisdom of the world is nonetheless imparted for the judgment and redemption of the world.

Then what would be more inevitably human than to use—or at any rate to be tempted to use—this transcendent wisdom of God for the aggrandizement of the Christian and the church? How is one to resist the urge to claim absoluteness for one's own judgment, even though one professes in towering sincerity that only the judgment of God is absolute since only He is absolutely righteous?

Secular man and his spiritual advocate—the theologian of culture—know very well and loudly proclaim that the churchman does not steadily or predictably resist these temptations. But in the church we ought to be bothered by something more serious than these indictments. That is our failure to make an honest and steady habit of confessing this sin to God and thereafter to the world. Far too often, and in ways that elude our own attention, we act as though the wisdom of God had been turned over to our exclusive administration and for this sublime purpose He has made us immune to the deadly sin of Pride.

So the churchman may indeed fail properly to thank his secular brother and the secularizing theologians for their fearless advertisement of his shortcomings. Without their help he is already where the Gospel of Christ is a constant threat to comfort and self-love. From that Gospel alone he knows that God's judgment is pronounced upon mankind as a whole. He also knows that as a man of faith he must proclaim that Gospel, be he priest or layman. He also knows that he must not glorify himself for preaching the Gospel of holy judgment. So if the Christian or the church boasts, neither ought to boast of anything but the transforming power of God's Christ in the Gospel. None can boast faithfully of swelling membership lists or of earthly treasure or of power in the courts of the mighty or of the sweet smell of respectability in the haunts of respectable people. (Cf. II Cor. 10:7-18.) Better by far than the secular brotherhood the church knows how wonderful it would be if for even the briefest moment we shared heaven's uncalculating joy in the redemption of one inconspicuous soul!

In the church, therefore, the occupational hazard of coveting self-justification must certainly be acknowledged with honesty beyond mortal comfort. But this is also to say that the risk must be embraced as courageously as possible since the faithful soul cannot offer the risk as a reason for avoiding or scamping the tasks of criticism. A readiness to come to terms with the full actuality of human life, and thus with every bid for self-justification, is an earnest of intent to live wholly under the command of Jesus Christ.

II

Theology of culture operates from a position well behind the full actuality of human life. This base of operations is now generally identified as ontology, a designation that does very little for the man in the pew and puzzles the man in the philosopher's study. So to both let us say that in the context of theology of culture, the ontological inquiry seeks to disclose the essential being within the rich variety of human activities and of suppositions concerning human being. Originally "ontological" is that which pertains to being as such. Philosophers of Existence and theologians of culture now use "ontological" in primary, and perhaps exclusive, application to man's being. This restriction of "ontological" is a reasonably strict inference from the conviction that man has no cognitive access to any other ranges of Being. It might also be a hunch that really man has no interest in any other being—and certainly no religious interest. Indeed we may now hear that modern man has no religious interest in the being of God.

The reduction of the scope of ontological inquiry is an interesting story in itself but it certainly is not our major concern here—not, that is, as a chapter of intellectual history. It is of lively concern to us so far as we can see in this arbitrary and provincial restriction of ontology a significant symptom of anxiety so pervasive and potent that we can treat it as being constitutive for modern man: the anxiety that he has lost, or is about to lose, his real being.

We shall have to ask eventually whether this anxiety is realistic, given the conditions of contemporary life. But we shall not pursue this question until we have seen how other modes of thought about man are open to the charge of being inadequately ontological or, perhaps, ontological by accident rather than on clear purpose. Specifically, what can be made of the phenomenon of social science in this connection?

The question is hardly arbitrary, given the marked interest in society and culture exhibited by so much of contemporary theology. Specifically, theologians of culture would be among the last to welcome the charge of being obscurantist vis-à-vis any kind of science; and, I suppose, least of all vis-à-vis social science. Why should they —or anyone else—reject or denigrate the knowledge attained by these sciences simply because it is difficult to square with pre-established religious dogmas and commonsense opinions?

So we are agreed that theological tension properly develops only when science claims that it has or will give the world a definitive and normative understanding of man's being; for then and there science has put itself flatfootedly into the ontological business. So far as human life can be objectified in a scientific way, the scientific study of man is fertile; and one may invoke a kind of providence to back one's belief that whatever is cognitively fertile *must* be true—until scientific cognitive fertility turns the world into a desert. This is to say that human life can certainly be inspected as mere (no slight intended) things are. Moreover a human being can be treated as though he were simply an instance of a general rule, as in actuarial tables. But there are dimensions of human existence that are not open to that kind of inspection and that kind of generalization. A human being has interiority—an insides for which the spatial-bodily image is thinly useful. In his interior being a person resolves to take one direction for his life rather than any other one; and by that power commits himself, that is, makes a concrete and binding decision; and in the light of that resolution he makes judgments concerning his value in and for the world. Obviously, human action in the public world can be analyzed, measured, and explained with ever greater precision. For such purposes we may all say, Let science flourish! But should we go on to say that man—who in our time again vaunts himself as the measure of all things—merely is the analyzed, the measured, and the explained? Hardly! If we were to say that, we should be making a judgment, we should be engaged in appraising, assessing, and evaluating. These are activities which cannot be treated normatively in scientific discourse. It is one thing to say of a scientific theory, It is true. It is quite another to say, Science teaches us what "true" means.

So far then the value of "interior reference" is to call attention to essential human activities. The place-where, the seat, of such activities has at best a secondary importance. The Old Testament Hebrew may have localized it in the heart. Our contemporary neurological scientist may locate it in the cortex. Hebrew, scientist, and the man in the street must all know what "it" refers to, or the game doesn't start. So when we say that to be alive as a human being one must act from the inside outward we are really saying being human means to participate in activity that no amount or kind of description could intelligibly signify without that participation. The import of all such activities is that to be human is to be a subject which cannot be reduced to an object (even grammatically!) even though some aspects of subjecthood can be treated objectively. The norm of all such objective treatment is available only to a being who is and who knows himself to be subject. No standard of truth itself has any meaning apart from the self-conscious assessments of a subject.

This is more than a matter of saying that only man can decide what to do with the achievements of scientific knowledge. That is obviously true, and it is the germ of a profound discomfiture of the contemporary spirit. We have also to see that the recording and acknowledgment of an item as being scientific knowledge are themselves achievements of persons whose interfiliations to constitute a community are in no respect scientific, that is, an outcome of scientific investigation. Man as scientist participates in the life of a community the values of which are presupposed by scientific activities. Here too he cannot avoid being a real subject.

But the contention with science for ontological honors in the treatment of man sweeps on to include his most remarkable dimension: his concern over and with—and under—life-giving and death-dealing powers beyond the scope of effective and rational human administration. Primitive intuition—a child's wonderment at the immensity of the sky—has been crushingly confirmed by cosmological science. Now we know rather than merely intuit that man lives in a world of implausible magnitude. The world is immense beyond his terror and his comfort. Through it powers range on their own, without his knowledge or consent; and make it to be a world, a real cosmos, a unitive enterprise in the remotest detail. But now man also knows that these far-reaching powers determine whether man lives or dies; and whether his little globe survives through one more turn or a billion. Consciously to acknowledge and reckon with these powers mysteriously adds dignity as well as pathos to human existence. It is the part of the philosophic life to acknowledge them. It is the part of the religious life to reckon with them. And for both the decisive question is, What are the cosmic powers up to, touching on human life and the Good? The question, Across how much time and space do they range? is incidental both for the philosopher and the religious spirit. The reason for this summary judgment is an analogy drawn from the political life: the reality of a government has very little to do with how much territory its agents must cover; it has everything to do with what authority they exercise, and to what effect, when they arrive.

Ontology must deal nonreductively with this cosmic concern of man. No matter what our own predispositions—whether, i.e., we are ready to believe in an unfriendly or in an essentially enigmatic cosmos—we must concede that man's being is in many ways a function of the cosmos (though no doubt some will say, rather, of being as such). We do not learn this from science. We do not learn it from philosophy as an academic affair. We learn the cosmic lesson through the most elementary reflection on actually existing in a world where the mighty powers do not obey human commands or give off unmistakable hints of their concern for human good.

So the ontological inquiry is ultimately serious about this being concerned with the powers of the cosmos. The motives that precipitate man into this concern can be investigated scientifically. But whatever the results of that study, it is not a firm platform on which to assess the meaning and value of the cosmic concern itself. Science may help to cure man of that concern—a drug here, a couch there. The pathology of human self-deprivation inflicted in the name of truth and the good is not *our* present concern.

So far we are happy to make common cause with theology of culture. Man should not blink at the mystery of his own being as the subject rather than the object of ontological reflection. But a certain restlessness begins to blossom when we turn our attention to the religious reckoning with the ultimate powers of the cosmos: that singular activity called worship. Theology of culture has given considerable support to the contemporary readiness to denigrate religion as an inveterate enemy of creativity and freedom. Indeed, so often as we hear "religion" we are likely to hear about "idolatry," "mythology," "irrelevance," "institutional self-aggrandizement," etc.; and we begin to wonder whether the great leadership for the forces of secularization might not find its most inspired and dedicated candidates hereafter in the ranks of Christians delivered from bondage to the church and the faith. But perhaps one might dare to ask who has authorized theologians (to say nothing of scientists) to preside over the dissolution of the church and to read religion out of the portfolio of significant human activities? Can they seriously believe that the people of the church will be moved to renounce their corporate folly and follow theological leaders out into the rich nonreligious life? Or are the analysis and the strategy of theology of culture best understood as moves to make the proper distinction between the true faith, still authentically derivable from Jesus, and a religion of culture?

Such a distinction is our concen, too. But it does not dictate the rejection of religion as such, whatever that might be. Ontological inquiry ought to take this "whatever it might be" very seriously because the religious element is incorrigibly intrusive in the human scene. Man persists in worshiping something. That is a commonplace even when it is expressed in the language of "ultimate concern." But what is he doing when he worships? He is celebrating something. But what? In worship man celebrates the "godliness" of God. In worship man is making the maximum effort to see beyond creaturely existence and to catch intimations of the Good exactly where in creaturely striving they would be unheard and overlooked. So in worship man is aware that any need or desire to reckon with God must await a sign of how God has decided for him. This does not mean that worship is pure expectation. Remembrance in gratitude is there also: God has given a sign; and therefore man knows what to expect. God has been present; and the greatest expectation is that He will be here again. When God is present man is most fully himself—yes, even if the divine revelation sweeps the human subject far beyond the last twinge of self-concern.

Thus religion reveals man, whatever claims a specific religious community may make for the revelation of a God beyond man and cosmos. So we have returned to a truism: what and how a man worships reveals what he is, both his actuality and his ideal life. But we have returned to it in the hope of making a correction in the ontological account. How man really worships expresses what he really is. But this does not mean that all of this can and must be explained by something nonreligious so that worship becomes an effect of psychological-sociological causes. It is easy to assume that people descend to bestiality because they worship Moloch—perhaps religion is sometimes also a cause? In our time it would be more natural to suppose that people worship Moloch because they seek an ultimate expression, and very likely an ultimate justification, of native cruelty. Neither supposition ought to obscure a fundamental fact: people worship Moloch because they believe Moloch is in charge. So religious practices may be cruel, obscene, and degrading when judged by some secular moral code or by the ethical norms of another religious community. But unless religion has become a mere pretext for libertinism, the religious practices pronounced repugnant to proper sensibilities must be seen as following from a vision of the ultimate powers. The ultimate powers have given a sign to the faithful; so what the faithful now do religiously is to enact the prescriptions for a life of divine creative power. The ways of the gods are indeed mysterious: it is practically guaranteed that these prescriptions will offend proper sensibilities early and late, pagan and Christian!

Other explanations of religious aberrations from decency and sanity are plentiful. In our time the most persuasive of these explanations is likely to be scientific or scientifically inspired. Ontological interpretation, nakedly performed, is likely to come off a poor second. Since theology is certain to finish as a third and a very poor third too we can see why some theologians want to come in under the colors of ontology; and why a late generation in the academy dreamed of making theology scientific.

So the theologians' lot is not a happy one. They feel the pressures of nontheological explanations for everything human and therefore everything religious. The pressures can drive theology off its native ground and make the first responsibility of the theologian seem frightfully backworldly. But if theology is already marked for a loser, is there not some virtue in proposing to lose with style? If the efforts of the theologian are not likely to be more joyfully hailed when they come in under fraudulent colors, why should he not candidly—or even merrily!—admit that he is committed to dogma as his subject matter but not to dogmatism as the life of faith?

III

Christianity is the religious reckoning with God revealed as the Father of Jesus Christ. The task of the Christian life is to discover oneself in the depths and heights of God's creation, it is to find oneself in the "particular providence" of God. This cannot be done by pooling all religious reports and theological interpretations with a view to drawing off a cup of pure essence contingently expressed in Christian symbols. Human life is in fact dispersed across an incredible spectrum of religious behavior. The whole spectrum of life thus engaged with the ultimate powers is important for Christian self-understanding and for Christian praise of God's righteousness revealed in all creation. It hardly follows that only the erudite student of religious history can be a faithful Christian. But readiness to reject so odd a notion ought not to induce theologians to make a matching error, to wit, failing to acknowledge that the religious (and not merely the Christian) reckoning with reality is itself an ontological disclosure, in the restricted sense of ontological to which we have provisionally agreed. This does not mean that the Christian theologian must be able to track the human spirit through every religious labyrinth of history with a view to showing that the Christian labyrinth is the sole dwelling place of the Holy One. What is to be acknowledged is that the religious reckoning expresses a specific sense of the perdurability and value of human life in the cosmos. This sense is much more than a belief. It is the animating power in commitments of faith, hope, and love understood as responses to the demands of the governing powers.

The specific sense of the perdurability and value of human life has many ramifications. "Civilization" is their inclusive name. Accordingly Christian criticism has a natural focus upon civilization. (This is a partial explanation of the rise of theology of culture to prominence.) But criticism as "judgment" in the form of pronouncing a sentence (or at least filing an indictment) is premature until criticism in a more fundamental sense has been undertaken. That is, first the ontological roots of civilization must be laid bare. Wholesale rejection of a civilization is, for the Christian, bad faith. It announces either that the pious have discovered a hiatus in the providential ordering of history or a revulsion in heaven against earthly corruption. The first announcement denies the wisdom of God. The second denies His mercy to the impious and immoral. One wonders whether the wholesale rejection of religion by secular spirits—theological and other—may not be the dialectical twin of this "Christian" criticism of the world.

So in good faith Christian criticism is committed first to discovering what civilization is up to, that is, what the key structures are through which human energy must flow in that time and space—or against which it must recoil—if the human spirit is to reach significant expression. The critic of civilization must also inquire into the life expectancy of such structures, that is, how—or even whether! —an adequately disciplined intelligence is at work to modify them or, if necessary, to conduct a decent funeral for them, in the interest of concrete existence and aspiring spirit.

Seen in this light both the Social Gospel and its reactionary critics were highly vulnerable to criticism. The Social Gospel invested its great hope in the reconstruction of institutions. Reactionary critics made a counteremphasis upon the private individual. The tried-and-true slogan of revivalistic reaction was and is: convert the individual to true Christianity and the institutions of our civilization will be transformed, if they need it. But both the institution of the Social Gospel and the individual of evangelistic reaction are sterile abstractions from the concrete civilization. The actuality upon which Christian criticism ought to be trained is the life of persons in the complex structures of the social order, together with the value claims made for this life. Society is not a suprapersonal system with a life of its own. The individual is not a human atom whose being and value are self-contained and self-defined. The real human individual is an integral person living in a complex order created by human energy directed by the human spirit. (By "spirit" nothing explicitly theological is intended but only something ontological, i.e., one of the real powers of being.) That order is what we mean by a civilization. There are good reasons for calling it a world, as I shall now try to show.

1. A civilization is a global organization of human powers and achievements. To call it global calls attention both to its comprehensiveness and to its pervasiveness, its inwardly-constituting power relative to the individual.

2. A civilization embraces both the outer structures and symbols of meaning, such as paintings, railroads, and policemen; and the inner appropriations of meaning. Nature, artifacts, and sensibilities all fall within its suzerainty. Such is the ideal of a civilization.

3. A civilization has depth in time and a spread in space. It unites the living and the dead; and the near and the far.

4. A civilization is an embodiment of a culture. Sometimes "civilization" is used to denote the ways and means adopted by a people to get the day's work done and the daily bread into the pantry, etc. Correspondingly "culture" is sometimes used to denote the higher and finer achievements of the creative spirits in an era, none of whom can get far without bread. These commonplace distinctions are unnecessary and unhelpful. Ways and means have no real significance apart from the larger and more distinctive human ends for the sake of which they are adopted and refined. So also the higher life of the spirit becomes diseased when the bond with corporeality is denied. Thus when preachers attack contemporary life for its materialism

one supposes, somewhat charitably, that they refer to the blurring of the proper ends of human industry and aspirations. But unfortunately the attack upon "materialism" is often made in the interests of an equally lopsided spiritualism. But perhaps the first mistake is the key: Why should we take seriously at all an indictment of Communist Russia which begins with "godless materialism" and concludes with a smiling announcement that the leaders there would drive Cadillacs if they dared? Or a criticism of America's materialism which is but part of a financial drive to put air-conditioning in the sanctuary as well as in the ladies' parlor?

5. As an embodiment of a culture a civilization is one way of reckoning with ideality. High civilizations are prone to claim that their connections with ideality are normative for man as such. "Romanitas est Humanitas" is easily translated into German, English, American, Chinese, *ad infinitum*. Perhaps there is something to becoming civilized, i.e., to becoming human in a specific way, which automatically inflates the balloon of cosmic pretension. But perhaps this happens only when one is born on the winning side.

6. Because a civilization is concrete and finite it does not have the perdurability that man longs for. Even the most powerful, majestic, and coherent of such worlds is but one realization of the ideal it acknowledges to be normative. If the drive for coherence is paramount the conflict inalienably linked with contrast is likely to be repressed. If the drive for power is ascendant, the structures of law, always teetering on the edge of conventionality, are subverted, and coherence no longer functions even as an ideal.

So civilizations carry the seeds of tragic self-defeat everywhere and always. The progress of a civilization is bound up with the realization of novelty. But by a kind of Law of Entropy ideality is progressively reduced to the ghost of past achievements. The Ideal is contemplated religiously, its great realizations in the past are repeated and copied endlessly, its great moments are given lamination upon lamination of nostalgia, its great men become abstract avatars of traditional righteousness. And from time to time the most pathetic of heroes come into view—the men who try to turn their civilization back to ancient loyalties, e.g., Julian the Apostate. They may be dangerous as well as pathetic. This depends upon whether they will stop at nothing to recapture a past whose velocity of recession seems to be directly related to the violence expended to reinstate it in the structure of the present time.

7. Thus as a world—a global achievement of power and value—a civilization is an object of continuous and inexhaustible concern. Much has been made of the feeling of primitive wonder when one looks up into the starry heavens. Surely much of that wonder is disciplined by one's civilization. It does not seem likely that on his own (if he ever were purely on his own) it would occur to a person to fear the heavens, that is, to suffer the corrosion of his wonder by anxiety. Something very different must be said of the human world. To be consciously a member of a human world is to endure anxiety about it because any human world is essentially problematical. A human world inevitably provokes fundamental questions about itself. No civilization is more stable than a sandbar in the torrents of a mighty river. Therefore how can men avoid asking, When will our world be swept away? The great civilizations lay claim to a sufficient if not absolute realization of the Good. But who knows when the human spirit will reverse itself and say of that good, "Be thou my evil"? A civilization necessarily advertises itself as a world, a real if not an absolute unity. But who knows when it will fly to pieces as the result of an internal explosion, or collapse from external pressure?

This human world is the first world encountered as problematical. This is human being in its creation of and as a public world. So it is not the sun that makes us feel insecure. The deep night does not question our being. We do not begin by fearing remote impalpable gods. First we fear the near ones, of human form and utterance. In the human world a question mark can always be put against our existence. Later we learn that cosmic powers press home that question mark, straightening it into a steel shaft with which to probe the vitals of the spirit. Oddly enough, by the time we have begun to reap the terror of the cosmic powers our civilization seems to stand between the naked and powerless soul and the cosmic powers to protect it against the winds blowing up from the depths of the world beyond. These protective barriers owe much of their plausibility to the offices of religion; which is to say that for its own preservation every civilization gets into some kind of religious business. Indeed a civilization may get into religious business so successfully that for the time being the fundamental questions about itself and about human life at large are pushed into the background. In retrospect that moment may seem to have been the happiest of all, since the questions concerning man, his world, and the cosmos were dealt with in equanimity and good cheer, if they were consciously dealt with at all. Such are the times when priests, poets, seers, and philosophers are all deeply pleased with the human scene before them; and one feels that the observant gods share their pleasure. It is a moment when high aspirations and optimistic vistas seem cosmically encouraged.

The golden hours of a civilization are not without men who see the canker, invisible to others, in the rose; and who hear the subterranean forces, unheard by others, accumulating for the hour of destruction. But in the golden hours the happy many are not troubled by the acrid auguries of the tormented few. The prophets of doom mutter unintelligibly backstage, and they are explained as creatures inexplicably disaffected and disoriented. A fall from a horse, an unfortunate love affair, a sadistic governess—how little it takes to account adequately for the No! sayers in an age when Yes, Yes! fills the earth with happy sounds!

Then the time comes when the asking of the fundamental questions on the heart of every civilization brings on severe chills and men do not know whether the earth is trembling or only their own members. Now the values and the prospects of the beloved world come under questions loaded with anxiety spreading out to embrace the whole civilization. Finally the significance of the human enterprise as such falls under a heavy shadow. Bleak answers do not make a clean sweep. There are dusty corners where people try to warm their hearts with the embers of nostalgia. There are pulpits from which men say that there have been dark days before but it is always darkest before dawn. But unfeignedly joyful affirmations become scarce. The Yes! sayer shrivels into a banality, and the No! sayer becomes the hero and maybe even the saint. The scene is strewn with the corpses of genial sentiments. Half-buried in the detritus of their civilization people now have good cause to wonder whether the foundations of their world have been shattered; and where to look to see men of courage, wisdom, and hope laying new foundations. Yet the false prophets continue to chant: "The wrath of God is quickly appeased, soon He will smile on us again!"

What shall we say of our age? It has already been named the Age of Anxiety. There is very little that suggests that contemporary civilization has grown out of it. The question mark has been put against everything that once gave coherence and direction to human life in the Western world. Here we can agree with theologians of culture that this anxiety is ontological, it reaches, that is, into the depths of contemporary life. People continue to worry about success, but the worry goes deeper than the fear of not having it or the fear of losing it; now many are deeply uncertain that success really matters. A society hitherto overwhelmingly goal-oriented, and until now pathologically fixated upon success as the all-commanding goal, is now fundamentally uncertain of the value of the purposive life. But in this society we are also uneasy and uncertain about the value of mere enjoyment apart from purposive striving. The gospel of enjoyment is shouted from the mercantile housetops, everyday all day, and no time out for Christmas. But these evangels are too strident, and the receptors are already too stressful, to permit this gladsome message of Enjoy! to be much more than a gimmicky counsel of perfection or a sleazy excuse for a moral holiday.

So the sense of the past is infected by a sweet sickness of longing for the simple goodness of the old ways. What a sanctuary of happiness and health was the old-fashioned family! Who was disturbed that houses were large, ugly, and triumphs of inconvenience? The life within them was warm, stable, and sustaining. And remember the village church, and especially the Sunday nights in it! Who was disturbed, or even knew, that it was architecturally beyond salvation? Or that the "order of divine worship" was liturgically inexcusable? The Spirit was all that mattered, because the Spirit created a lovely warmth of heart, and a blessed security of righteousness; and these were the signs of divine election. If these signs were ratified either by worldly success (discounted up to 10 per cent for the missionary enterprise) or by sweet patience in meritorious poverty, who could then honestly doubt that God had created a new People of Promise in a new land?

Except for recitals in the harmonics of nostalgia, those days and nights are gone forever. When the anxious day is over we huddle in front of the TV, bemused and immobilized by its endless banality, and wonder whether sons will come home with the family car, and daughters with their virginity, intact; and take cold comfort from the fact that the car is covered with $100 deductible and virginity is no longer what it was cracked up to be. No wonder the tears start when we hear the sweet old hymn, "Blessed Be the Tie that Binds": weep for the ties that used to bless, weep for the blessings that no longer bind.

Behind the tears we know that the past is falsified in the litanies of nostalgia, but present anxiety will not admit this. A past steeped in illusion is summoned to hold at bay a future steeped in terror. Anxiety for the present life and the threatening future compel us to remake rather than remember the past. The past, real and imagined, is loved ever more dearly as what-is-to-be feeds consternation and confirms terror. In the world now taking shape people will be lonelier than even we are. The premonition of this leads many to cling desperately to the dogmas of individualism as the last and least affirmation of personal worth. For that matter it does not greatly concern our world whether we come or go—everyone is expendable. Friendship is daily sacrificed on the altar of social and economic advantage—whatever our doubts of success. Love is mastered by private and public imperialism: divorced from pledge love becomes freebooter and cannibal. Old institutions no longer afford the warmth and security without which life for man becomes a hell of tedium or terror. Emerging institutions cannot yet command great devotion. Wherever we look or sit, our world is under fire. In our time the torch is a weapon rather than a beacon.

Thus the Preacher, updated, the spokesman and warrant officer for galloping nostalgia. His message is narcotic, anaesthetic in fact: listening we glorify the fleshpots of Egypt and forget its slavery and heathenism.

Nostalgia is only one response to the problematical nature of civilization. It is only one of the moods in which the question of the meaning of the present human world is pursued. It is a mood which we do not properly understand until we see that the desire to penetrate to the heart of this world is one of the mastering passions of the age, finding expression in art, science, philosophy, and religion. The essence of the passion is not curiosity, the desire to "figure out" something and store the answer away for future reference. The essence is anxiety. It is anxiety that animates the asking of the ultimate questions about the world. But anxiety is still too vague a diagnosis. The inclusive anxiety is centered on the "everyday world," that common life which we commonly feel as the massive reality to which everything must somehow be assimilated.

Here again I must mark a break with the tenor and tendency of theology of culture. Theology of culture very generally places an honorific meaning on culture: culture is the proper name for the really creative dimension of the human spirit (if not of God the Spirit). A doctrine (or perhaps we ought to say an attitude) of this sort is naturally complemented with a denigration of mass culture. Mass culture thus emerges as the proper name for the everyday world. In this way a very important aspect of contemporary civilization is unduly minimized if not badly distorted. I mean the astonishing way in which the everyday world contin es to operate both as a dialectical necessity for theology of culture and as the actuality to which every creative advance must be assimilated, at the least an object of reformative zeal and at most as the massive reality of which every specialized activity, such as science or art, is an abstraction. Indeed we are tempted to overstate the case thus: the everyday world is the civilization to which culture bends; and it is the actuality in which alone modern man feels real. If the latter clause turns out to be true we should have to brace ourselves for an inference as inevitable as outrageous: contemporary civilization is a triumph of unconsciousness and (therefore) of nonpersonality. So weaponed we should be emboldened further to diagnose these conditions as the effects of acute ontological anxiety, that is, as a systematic effort of man to conceal the secret of his own being from himself. And if this is so, we should not be able to exculpate the creative spirits in our civilization from participating, in their own ways, in the general conspiracy.

If, then, the creative spirit today bears witness to the "death of God," he is testifying in adverse interest, since in this he is saying that the actual world in which he stands is irredeemable as well as nauseating. If God is dead, if the actual world *is* irredeemable, then the creative spirit is merely a master illusionist; and he can expect a fate worse than stoning or boiling oil: success.

Now we must see what the everyday world is. It is the taken-for-granted organization of human life which seems to be as plainly and firmly there as the world delivered to sense experience. In fact "everyday" (our familiar name henceforth) enjoys a certain priority over sense experience, a fact suggested by the folk maxim, "seeing is believing." Seeing correctly is seeing (and not merely reporting) in agreement with prevailing social expectation, a common belief, a constitutive prejudgment as to what is there to be seen. One is expected to see what everybody sees; and to believe what everybody believes; and to do what everybody is doing.

So everyday is made up of things people in general must do, feel, believe, and say if they are to function as an actual enduring and inclusive society. Everyday is therefore a minimal and indispensable state of affairs, a world constituted by habitual responses.

Right here anybody—and not just theologians and other creative spirits—can make a mistake, viz., supposing that "habitual" automatically rules out high-grade aspirations. Our everyday incorporates a feeling that there is an optimum and maximum world divulged only to profound reflection ("deep thought"), creative imagination ("great poets"), and—this with a diminuendo of conviction—pure piety ("the saint"). Moreover everyday feels that this higher world is always and necessarily in tension with the commonplace and habitual world. Every civilization acknowledges the pressure of the ideal in unique ways. This pressure is an element of man's being as man. Therefore the critic of culture, whatever his religious inspirations and commitments, must try to discern what is unique in contemporary civilization in this regard before he dismisses everyday as a snare and delusion.

Everyday is comprised of broadly inclusive and fundamental values and value convictions. Society aims at a rough-and-ready coherence of these values; and the achievement of the same is one of the things meant by saying that a social order is healthy. So when that coherence disappears, or when it becomes more rough than ready, trouble prowls in the land like a raging lion. Then every man does what is right in his own eyes (Judg. 21:25), and in his philosophical moments he calls this chaos freedom. Then man's world becomes a mere sum of disparate parts, and any addition to my being means a subtraction from the being of others.

Our everyday seethes with anxieties and agitations. Its human parts discover that they are nullities in it—unless you are somebody you are a nobody—and the somebodies must be few and far between since the mass media are always talking about the same ones. The nullities get by, eking out a little pleasure here and a little numbness there to deaden the emptiness. Minimal satisfactions are still available, though the price is never right. The world of enduring optimal satisfaction has become a distracting fantasy; and this is to say that the goal-oriented common life has been stripped of any teleology that is both inclusive and profoundly personal. People are pulled to pieces by demands and desires that defy coherence.—These are some of the things that happen when everyday does not have a durable humane unifying principle as its center. Lacking that, civilization becomes an absurd jumble. Its elements can be coerced into the semblance of a working order, but a comprehensive and coherent pattern no longer meets the eye. And if this is so, the failure is decisive, because everyday depends heavily on what meets the eye, on what is obviously true, for its operations.

So the prophets of our time decry the absurdity to which man's being has been reduced, and affirm the absurdity of the cosmos itself into the bargain. The sequence is important, but not because it is a convenient opening for a sociological explanation of Existentialism. It is important as a clue to the way in which everyday functions as a baseline and norm even in the most furious and lucid rejections of it. The prophet certainly pulls on his trousers one leg at a time even as irredeemable mass-man does. The prophet may be just as concerned with the proper crease, or noncrease, whichever the fashion gods decree. Perhaps he hates himself for this ignoble compliance. But the self-hatred is itself irredeemable unless the prophet is justified in his prophecy—not necessarily in his trousers—by the breakthrough of Ideality. The breakdown of everyday justifies nothing.

But we have not yet heard the full indictment of the everyday world. "Fragmentation" and "depersonalization" have not yet been properly attended to. "Fragmentation" signifies the demands for total loyalty made by powerful conflicting forces in contemporary civilization, rather than the simple fact of multiple goals and standards. Every-day is a scene of augmenting confusion, and in the confusion it may be cut to pieces and the pieces thereafter are likely to be ruled by a breed of petty tyrants each of whom claims to be a humble servant of the public. In the process of fragmentation the public becomes a mere name for a capricious and unstable consensus organized and manipulated by petty tyrants for their own ends thinly disguised by protestations of undying and selfless devotion to the high ends of civilization.

The fragmentation of civilization gives a greatly inflated impetus to the disposition of the natural man to dedicate himself to the pursuit of the minimal values. We cannot imagine a civilization in which it would be impossible for people to make a god of their bellies (Phil. 3:19). Indeed we may wonder—unfaithfully—whether the genius of man as the subject of civilization is not to set his mind on "earthly things" (*Ibid.*). But we have a much stronger and clearer hunch about contemporary civilization: the Belly and the fabled Erogenous Zones compete ruthlessly for deification. Today's woman is summoned to an all-out campaign to remain (become!) sexually attractive from pre-pubescence through interment. Today's man is assured that the right hair oil or bath soap or shaving cream will pile overpowered women at his feet, from whom he can then choose the one (why only one?) whose Erogenous Zones have been most successfully tailored to his exquisite taste. So the Belly—to say nothing of presumptively higher gods—is bound to suffer; unless he is willing to settle for gourmets rather than gluttons. But if he suffers it will not be at the hands of imperious spirit, demanding and enforcing sacrifices of the flesh. The petty tyrants slash at each other. And that would be all right, it would be fine indeed, did not the common life suffer greatly in the conflict, and feel itself being dissolved.

Depersonalization is also overtaking and undercutting everyday. The individual is losing any potent sense of significant personal value. At work he is a unit of production that is easy to replace, easier to replace than to repair. In fact as a worker he is being rapidly replaced by superior machines that require far less pampering and can be scrapped without its becoming a Federal case. In his leisure the ordinary man is the Slob, the anonymous mindless consumer computed on Ratings, the scepters that rule the entertainment and, increasingly, the political, world. But he cannot count on being computed even here. Only a few are called, enough to satisfy the statisticians who are therefore more nearly *vox Dei.* Everywhere mass man looks the prospects are roughly similar: he is going to be engineered, manipulated, slickered, flummoxed, and cut to standard measurements. All the while his spiritual leaders assure him that he is a free man and a being of infinite value. He is reminded that a civilization is healthy and wise, and not just wealthy, when everything human in it is grasped by a transcendant, unitary, and unifying meaning.

If he could really hear this message, if he could distinguish what is really wise in it from the cant, the everyday man might begin to see what it would mean to do all things for the glory of God. In such a world the shoemaker and the king could both believe, without either having to be a pious fool, that their respective work and lives had unique significance for the whole enterprise, not necessarily an equal place but a real and personal place. In such a world the contingent details of human existence would hold together as well as the great central commitments. It would be a world in which the first concern would be how well a thing was done, how well things were made; and thereafter a sensible price would be arrived at. It would not be an unjust world merely because only the few could afford the best of some things, so long as a poor man might eat his bread and drink his wine at a table so simply and yet elegantly and sturdily made that tomorrow a rich man would pay a small fortune to have it and point with pride to the ancient knifemarks and liquor stains.

A civilization is sick when its life is split into many independent provinces and the contingent details add up to nothing except so many sociological—and eventually archaeological—facts. In time each province will claim eminence rather than mere autonomy. So even today the real man is the man at his work, or the man in his leisure, or the man at his prayers, or the man at the polls, etc. etc.

Where are we? What are the prospects of our everyday world? If the prophets (rather than the priests) are right the sweetness in it is largely gone and it is endurable in direct ratio to the number of flights into unreality one can afford. For the time being enough people manage to return from these flights on any given workday to keep the wheels turning. (One is tempted to compare the picture drawn by today's theological prophets with the long-popular picture of the Roman Empire as one continuous orgy from top to bottom. If the indictments of Juvenal et al. were wholly true—to say nothing of the fulminations of the church fathers—the persistence of the Empire for so long is a very great mystery. Someone must have been tending the store while the orgiasts sported. Actually even the monstrous Nero spent a fair amount of time at his desk and away from his richly iniquitous bed. This may come as a jolt to our own orgiastic fantasies. It would not play in Hollywood.) But also for the time being the tenders of the everyday world may well be asking themselves such pointed questions as, "Was it smart to come back, to wake up, to sober up, to take the cure? Have I really come back or have I left the best part of myself elsewhere?" The everyday world seems to be populated by absent-hearted people who can give only marginal attention to a world that has made them fractional beings. Because the values that make for coherence are breaking up, contemporary civilization is becoming a desert of love, a dimly lit and uncertainly desirable illusion, a place to be haunted rather than lived in.

IV

So runs the word of the prophets. Whatever its other virtues it serves to reinforce the feeling that everyday is now vulnerable, acutely, to the most searching questions. But more remains to be told. Contemporary civilization has also produced a tidal wave of rebellion against itself. It is not merely deficient in coherence, it is also full of self-contradictions. These are so numerous, fundamental, and inclusive that we are tempted to believe that the age is possessed by a demon urging it on to self-destruction.

The rebellion is not uniformly conscious, organized, and controlled by affirmative purpose. The anxieties generated by the confusions of this world are very acute; but many people—perhaps everybody part of the time—have no other place to go. "Whither shall we go if the everyday world casts us out?" The only other world to which one might escape is unreality. Where anxiety is so acute the passionate interest in the roots and the prospects of this civilization is itself threatened with extinction as more and more people withdraw into the reality-canceling womb of apathy.

Elsewhere, however, the rebellion is highly conscious and it is being waged with great intensity of passion. A world so full of negativities must be negated, whether or not a fairer thing can be created in its place. Creative spirits form a common front on this point. Therefore they are generally a great puzzle, if not an active affront, to the unrebellious denizens of everyday.

Such is the realm of art. Much of contemporary painting, poetry, sculpture, fiction, drama, and now and then the movies, is deeply disquieting, when it is not sheerly unintelligible, to people still rooted in the values of everyday. When something does get through, it is likely to be an uncompromising rejection of the everyday world as unfit for human habitation. Thereupon everyday is very likely to complain, often with a very sturdy self-righteousness, that artists are interested only in the dirty side of life and they are pessimistic, negative, and perversely committed to distorting everything they touch. Everyday may even hint that artists behave so disagreeably because they have learned that dirt pays, a motivation he can respect even if the performance is shocking.

The response of the artist also has a high degree of predictability. As an artist his business is not to comfort, beguile, distract, and lie for the sake of public acceptance. He has bad days when he writes simply because he must eat (or, more likely, to keep up the payments on the XKE-150). If he has become used to living well he may become used to writing badly, but this is hardly axiomatic, and so there is not much comfort for everyday in that—especially since he may not know a really bad artistic performance when he sees it. Moreover, the artist continues—or the theologian says in his behalf—the artist as artist has a profound commitment to truth. This commitment accounts for the severity of the rebellion against everyday because there is so much in the latter that corrupts the joy and freedom of creativity and without this truth descends to the level of mere fact.

In this way our attention is directed to essential features of art in its prophetic relationship to everyday. The artist does not report what he knows. What he knows is transformed in the creative process so that mere fact becomes luminous truth. Whatever the state of civilization this luminosity is likely to prove discomfiting. Today it may easily repel the denizen of everyday and send him hurrying off to find something clearly and decently affirmative. But when everyday is confused and riddled with negations, what truth-loving spirit will affirm it? So whither can everyday man flee to find honest comfort? The artist may affirm the splendor of a past that cannot be reinstated in the present world; and this of course may be his reason for celebrating departed glory. Or he may distill a vision of heaven and hell, the one full of unearthly beauty and the other full of present evil; and both may stand, in the vision, as a condemnation of the trivial and tedious everyday world. Or if the artist is tired and subject to uncontrollable whimsies, he may affirm the importance of creativity alone and in itself, which makes him a grown-up Jack Horner, his cleverness dedicated to the immortalization of his own triviality. But when the artist is in command of his powers and has the courage of his vocation, he discloses (creates) a world that may well be read as a prophetic judgment upon the minimal satisfactions and standardized tastes, the incoherence and self-contradictions, of the everyday world. Then the possibility of a rapprochement of art with everyday is shattered. Everyday does not have the price of an effective peace. Tortured by powerful presentiments of its own doom, it reads in burgeoning dismay what art is writing so clearly on the walls.

Yet something is missing from this picture and we must try to identify the missing element. To be a prophet is a great thing. To be an artist is a great thing. To wear both crowns at once is not so happy a fate as all that, and theologians of culture are therefore warned not to expect enthusiastic and heartfelt thanks for insisting on it. Moreover—and the missing element may be here—prophets, artists, and theologians alike must live somewhere and this somewhere will have many of the features and qualities of everyday. For purposes that cannot be reduced to mere dialectical necessity they too must participate, both willy-nilly and by pledge, in the structures and activities of an actual everyday world.

This is not the full story, but what remains to be told is not likely to be better news. None of us, so far as he is still living, has any other world of reference than poor bedraggled everyday. Quite properly, we make many appeals to Ideality, in sickness and in health. Religiously we may invoke the Holy Spirit. But these appeals and invocations necessarily refer back to the world here below. If we despise it we are despising something man has made just as surely as the prophetic spirit has fashioned his superb denunciad. The poet has come no closer to slipping beyond the network of this actuality than the mechanic at his bench. Poetic transformations—whether or not they are achieved in prophetic fury—do not reveal a higher world. At best they disclose how this world is enmeshed in unique relations with God and Ideality. To do that in purity and power is a great thing. As for the prophet, at best he can recall his people, the denizens of everyday, to their proper destiny, and bid them throw off their superstitious servitude to Fate. To do that in purity and power is a great thing.

Prophetic insights and poetic transformations are important data for theological reflection, whether or not they attain greatness. Indeed, ambiguities and ambivalences of attitude toward everyday, prophetic, poetic, and what-not, are important for the theological understanding of civilization. Today the air is full of theological exhortations to look beyond the faith of the church for the criteria (as well as the proper motivation) with which to interpret rightly such data. I believe these exhortations spring from theological mistakes. They encourage the people of the church to do one of two things, both of which are theological errors: either to elevate themselves into the self-conscious elite of creative spirits; or to make individual drafts upon Ideality in support of a private rebellion against a world in which we must all manage to live together under a common destiny, or revert to the jungle.

V

Ambiguities of mind and heart concerning everyday are also a significant aspect of science. Indeed science and everyday appear to be engaged in a wide range of devastating conflicts with each other. In the camp of science prophets to inflame the ardor and ambition of its protagonists are not lacking.

Science itself has cooperated in the formation of popular stereotypes of scientific life and thought. These may have helped to elevate the image of the scientist above the image of the artist, in everyday. Nonetheless the image is a distortion and it creates confusion in many quarters. Consider, to begin with, the general representation of scientific objectivity. We have become accustomed to thinking of this as an essentially passionless state of being: whatever the scientist looks for, he looks for it with a detachment so profound that it passes for an actual transcendence of all interestedness. This spiritual achievement, real or fancied, is often supposed to be distinctively modern and the indispensable condition for the advancement of the true understanding of man and the cosmos. Why then should we not conclude that the scientist might well be the man to direct the human future?

Before we answer that question a prior one clamors for attention. How is it possible to get so much out of objectivity as a fundamental requirement of scientific discourse? As an ideal, objectivity has a great deal to do with the way in which the scientist reports his findings about what he is interested in as a scientist. One must be objective in trying to find out what things really are and what really happens, whatever one's personal investment in having them come out one way rather than another. But there is nothing uniquely modern or scientific in this, this is a requirement of reason as such. So to be objective one must try to state one's real findings in ways that make it possible for others to examine these reports and accounts, and make judgments of their truth, without having to dig into the personal history of the reporter, or wondering whether anyone in his social station could be trusted. And again this may be taken to be a requirement of rational discourse as such: in order to be rational one must be able to manage one's feelings when facts are to be ascertained and truth is to be judged.

But perhaps a third specification of objectivity does carry us beyond the requirements of reason as such. Scientific objectivity demands that cultural differentiations be bracketed in the formation of scientific theory and the prosecution of scientific arguments. That is, a theory cannot be true (though truth appears with diminishing frequency in scientific discourse) for Americans and false for Russians. This would hold as firmly for a theory of cultural differentiations as for any other scientific theory. As a theory cultural relativism must escape the condition it accounts for, or fail to pass muster as a scientific theory.

So this third specification of objectivity is a promising advance beyond the general requirements of rationality. It strongly suggests that "science" is the proper name of an actual community that transcends national and ethnic and perhaps ethical boundaries, a community with distinctive structures, values and sanctions of rewards and punishments. Here the seeds of conflict with everyday are sown in prodigal abundance, even though the conflicts actually reaped are remarkably ambiguous. On the one hand everyday is very suspicious of a serious appeal to an actual community which is supposed to transcend everyday, both as an object of loyalty and a realm of truth. Indeed everyday may well be more suspicious of the scientific appeal to a transcendent community than it is of the artist's appeal to Ideality. The artist may be a kook but scientists have refined the practice of treason.

Ambiguities are also launched from the side of science. "Science" may be the name of an empirical community transcending the everyday world of political structures and values. As such science makes its own drafts upon Ideality. The scientist may have become a traitor not because the enemy paid him to do so but because he believed that his nation and civilization have betrayed mankind. But let us put the issue in somewhat less dramatic terms: scientists believe that truth must be served whatever its repercussions on public policy. Far from being a passionless creature the scientist emerges from the stereotypes as a creature of great commanding passion: love for the truth. And with him, therefore, we ought to say that love of truth is the first passional component in all knowing of the actual and of the ideal. Let us go even further and say that possession of truth is a fundamental requirement for the achievement of life that is distinctively human. Man lives by truth as well as by bread; and perforce he judges that a lie is as deadly as poison, and a witting half-truth bespeaks a meaner spirit than the giver of a half-loaf or a stone.

But the community of science has as part of its unique structure of value and not merely as one of its bundle of unique mental activities something called publicity; and this means more than meets the eye. What meets the eye is the great store laid by the massive reality attested to by normal sensory experience. What does not meet the eye in scientific publicity is the self-referencing criterion of the scientific community. The imaginative application of this criterion has produced both a meaning-policy (rules for determining when discourse is meaningful) and a view of the cosmos and man in it. Neither of these achievements can be assimilated to everyday. Both of them must be assimilated to everyday. The meaning-policy has been generalized (admittedly by philosophers rather than by scientists, but in advocacy of scientific ideals) to cover all significant human discourse. But the world picture collides more immediately with the world pictures and sensibilities of everyday. For example, the massive solid physicality of the everyday world has long been viewed by physicists as a biocultural illusion. Matter has been dissolved into energy patterns, oddly geometrical; with the result that everyday is confronted with puzzles and paradoxes galore whenever it tries to reconcile the scientific picture with what still appear as plain facts. So the scientific appeal to the public world is obviously not an appeal to the common world.

Yet everyday has been greatly enriched by the practical technological applications of scientific lore. Thanks to science people in the West can confidently expect to live longer and far more comfortably than their fathers could have dreamed of doing—or, probably, would have thought compatible with divine ordination. For everyday this is the decisive verification of scientific thought. The man in the street does not know or care very much about philosophical-scientific arguments about verification. He is a pragmatist: the truth is what works. And science has worked a practical revolution of the human prospects.

It is reasonable to suppose that no one, at least no mortal, could have planned to have this come out the way it has in fact come out: scientist and everyday are now infected with a virulent anxiety. Dedication to truth has put man in the saddle of destiny and the question now is whether he can remember where he was supposed to go. Obviously he does not need a prophet to tell him what he wants. He does need to know what is really good for him. But is this not entirely beyond the jurisdiction of science? Scientist and everyday are alike haunted by the possibility that that need lies beyond knowledge altogether; but certainly beyond knowledge riveted by principle to sense-experience and utility value. So wisdom may come too late or too feebly on the scene to redeem civilization from its self-destructive impulses.

Therefore we ought not to be greatly surprised by the concern of scientists to demonstrate their social responsibility as scientists. They do not want science to be represented and feared as a Frankensteinian creature about to get out of hand and destroy the world. Since Hiroshima how could physicists fail to be anxiously interested in the political implications of nuclear power? After all, they dedicated themselves to fill the order for an absolute weapon, they harnessed the elemental energy of the cosmos to destroy human life temporarily disguised as the enemy. This is not quite the same thing as fashioning the longbow that defeated the French at Agincourt. No doubt the man with an arrow in his heart dies as surely as the victim of the A-bomb: dead is dead. But no one ever made an arrow that could put the curse of death on the earth and the sea and the air. Quite naturally, then, scientists are acutely anxious to show that the scientific expression of the generic love of truth does not promise the end of the human enterprise as such. Just as naturally the untutored piety of everyday sees cosmic and even divine penalties levied against scientific presumption in unlocking secret after secret of nature and the gods. Droughts, floods, hurricanes, pestilence, and worse yet to come, are all read as indications that man has at last gone too far for his own good.

There are other signs of anxiety in the realm of science. The hope (not yet a program, thank God) of using science to solve all human problems is a symptom of an acute anxiety with marked eschatological overtones. "Use science to reconstruct human life before it is too late—it is later than you think! Too long man has been deluded by metaphysical-religious myths, and now these myths may destroy us. So after them, science! Smoke them out and destroy them. Do not let them retreat into the realm of finalities, of ultimate ends and inclusive purposes invulnerable to (scientific) reason. For there is no teleology except the pursuit of truth. So prove that science can legislate ends and means alike. Preach to all the acceptable year of science. Proclaim the beauties of an order in which all of human life is predicable and controllable. Pour sublime rational contempt upon all backworldsmen and religious obstructionists, shame all who cannot live by the computer, and save the finest lightning for those who ask, 'But who will run the scientists?' "

This is a caricature of a real hope looking for policy and program. It is a position that cannot be said to be deficient in ambition: the world, or nothing. But the ambition is scored by the acids of anxiety: "nothing" is possible, thanks to science. "Nothing" may be only the destruction of civilization, rather than the destruction of all human life on the globe. For everyday the difference may be left to metaphysicians to ponder and worry about.

Retreat or abstention from imperialistic designs for the scientific salvation of the world surely ought to bring real release from the eschatological anxiety from which it springs; and especially if it is retreat into a cheery and sensible pragmatism. So let us say that it is enough to make science properly obedient to the high ends of civilization in the Western world.

This seems to be a step in the right direction. It reduces the temptation to paint science and scientist in demonic colors. It brings the moral responsibility of the scientist within manageable limits. When the nation is at war, the scientists do not call a conference to decide scientifically whether the cause is just and how far they can underwrite it as a group. What they can do as scientists for the common good, in peace and war, they will try to do. If the nation is at war, they teach the mechanics how to build the weapons. They tell the nation's leaders what the weapons will do to things and to people. They study the results. They make the necessary improvements for the next round. What they confess in their prayers, and what haunts their dreams, have no cure in science.

Sensible and sane as this attitude is, it is harrassed by the difficulties every pragmatism encounters. The paramount difficulty is precisely the point at which anxiety finds an opening into the center: the thinness of critical resources for grappling with the putative ends of the national life and of Western civilization. The everyday world holds together so long as its ends are not seriously questioned. Today these ends are under ferocious fire, and only hardy souls are ready to predict that these ends will survive the fire. Science itself has helped to build and stoke the fire, apparently convinced that science as an international transcultural community would be able to withstand the terrible traumas of world wars and the resultant social disorganization. This very conviction has been drawn into the maelstrom of the fire consuming traditional values. So the scientist has sound ground for his anxiety. No better than everyday man, than man himself, can he serve two masters each of whom demands the highest devotion.

The physical sciences do not have a monopoly on anxiety about the shape and course of civilization. Social science has not been dramatically successful in producing death-proliferating devices, but it has made its own contribution to confusion in everyday. Since the subject of the social sciences is man himself, rather than man as a member of a biological genus or man as a biochemical complex, social science can reasonably expect that its subject will begin by claiming that he already knows himself as he knows nothing else, that is both inside and outside. So the social scientists have a subject of unfailing interest to human beings, even though what they say about it may lack sometimes charm and transparency, e.g., economics.

Ambiguity and tension vis-à-vis everyday appear very quickly in the social sciences. First of all everyday learns that social science is not at all interested in his insides and in fact means to treat him as though he did not have any. So he must learn not to consult his interior being, even if he has one, if he really wants to know what he is. He must find the Why of his behavior in the all-inclusive causal nexus which itself has nothing distinctively human about it. But now a peculiar question comes up, namely, why he should exist at all, i.e., is there any point to it? A related question is not far behind, and that is whether he might live better than he is now living. The causal nexus is rigidly silent on such matters. Everyday must either give up on these questions or ask for reference to something else in order to live with them for another round or so. But this is a rather untidy state of affairs. People with tidy heads are not going to like it, and they are likely to feel morally obligated to vent their displeasure upon a civilization that wants to use truth rather than to understand it and reform along its lines.

Social science is also making a great impact upon everyday through the practical application of its findings. Advertisers, politicians, evangelists, bankers, butchers, bakers, and candlestickmakers (though probably not old-fashioned thieves) all utilize scientific discoveries of what people want and how they can be made to want something else. Scientific resources are exploited to measure the success of these campaigns, because it is important for future campaigns to know who was captured by which appeals. This is called the engineering of consent and it is a sterling scientific contribution to contemporary civilization.

This contribution does not make everybody happy. Some people are made so unhappy that they begin to talk of the prostitution of science, almost as though it were available, if the price were right, for any kind of exploitive enterprise. But is it fair to hold science itself responsible for such corruptions? Surely not, if social science has any real independence from the behavior of social scientists. If it does not, then each must answer for himself rather than for an ideal program mysteriously gone astray.

Protagonists of the ideal are not lacking. They ask why the social scientist should have to be satisfied with an instrumental role only.

Why should he not, as scientist, venture opinions about the moral quality of civilization? As scientist, since as a member of society he is entitled to make moral judgments anyway. The question is whether he has as scientist the proper intellectual tools (or should we say spiritual?) to assay the moral quality of human life in a given society? If his domain is as wide as man himself why should anything human be exempt from scientific determination?

Is this a proposal to subsume the interests of the human community as such under the interests of the scientific community? Or is it simply a plea for the application of rationality to all human interests? The scientific community, the community of actual working scientists, does not seem to have a monopoly on rationality. It might make a nice empirical study to see whether scientists are habitually more rational in the management of human affairs than nonscientific people. We should guess—nonscientifically—that scientists, social and otherwise, draw as heavily on the resources of everyday as anyone, in the management of private and public affairs.

If this is the case it is not very reassuring, it does not greatly reduce the anxiety of everyday. If anything, the social scientist is likely to become the source and object of exacerbated anxieties. We say this because we live in an age of overt and multiple clashes between civilizations as well as between nations. When civilizations are isolated from one another the issue of cultural and ethical superiority is an academic one for scientific observers. When their own civilization is in direct conflict with another one the issue is imbued with anxiety and ceases to be merely academic. Then the scientist must feel that the question of the relative value of a civilization, or even of a society within it, cannot be managed until a prior question is settled. The prior question concerns the meaning of the human world as such. If, for instance, we were able to identify the constants in human behavior would we not then be able to determine what constellations of these factors would be most meaningful? That question is ontological as well as ethical and scientific. Behind and in it there is a proposal to learn the good from the proper scrutiny of man's essential being. The Good and Being are not scientific categories. Where they speak as scientists only there is no need for them to try to assimilate these categories into their special language. Anxiety drives them beyond the possibilities of science as a special language for coping with the actual human condition; and leaves them with the need to talk of science as basically an attitude the values of which for the enhancement of the human community certainly cannot be scientifically demonstrated.

Finally, social scientists share an anxiety about presuppositions. Philosophers have discovered that presuppositions are as non-demonstrable as they are indispensable. Only in Euclidean geometry, if there, does a conceptual system really follow from its presuppositions. Even there the presuppositions might yield alternative results.

So presuppositions seem to be mental habits for which nothing very respectable in the line of rational certification is available. The important thing therefore is to take on presuppositions trailing the least suggeston of mystery, such mysteries as are suggested by such words as "freedom," "purpose," "the inner world," etc. But suppose that when social science is played back to everyday it is accepted as ontologically true and ethically illuminating; and people begin to say they have learned from sociologists and psychologists that man is not really free and purposes are illusions and the individual is always an effect of social conditioning and never a cause in his own right? Science itself as an achievement of creative spirit cannot survive and is not entitled to survive such a harvest. Accordingly the scientist is well advised to look with direct foreboding to the day when his presuppositions are accepted as true or as the necessary foundations for anything true. Perhaps he needs them for his technical work. As a human being he cannot afford to believe that they are true.

VI

Anxiety has made a dramatic entrance onto the stage of philosophy. In the popular imagination philosophy's best lines are questions about the meaning of civilization and of human life at large. I refer of course to the philosophical views which have had the best press in recent years and are commonly therein identified as Existentialism. Theology of culture has been profoundly influenced by philosophy of this sort, and is hardly conceivable without it. We have sufficient reason just in that to make a sketch of the chief components of a philosophical attitude and program that have at last displaced the philosophical-cultural idealism of the nineteenth century.

1. Existentialistic thinkers sternly reject the pallid spiritless categories that reigned for so many centuries over the metaphysical mind, Substance, Cause, Essence, Mind, Matter, Soul: these are not the concepts with which to understand man's being. For this purpose we must think in terms of Anxiety, Guilt, Death, Nothing, Decision, etc.

In this way philosophy is brought back into focus upon man's being after the long ages of wandering among the stars and the gods.

2. So the nonpersonal, nonhistorical, and scientific orientation of modern philosophy gives way to thinking centered upon the historical and the human; but upon the human as the actually existing individual for whose being neither scientific nor metaphysical explanations (including the theological) are valid; and upon the historical as a dimension of man's being.

3. Tragedy, Nausea, and Ennui assume ontological significance. Tragedy is an inescapable component of the human condition and therefore it must not be viewed as an antiprovidential accident. Job knew that "man is born to trouble as the sparks fly upward" (5:7, RSV), but this lesson is corrupted by the ending of the Biblical book of Job, and by Western religion generally. The result of this corruption of the tragic sense is that everyday believes devoutly that the right relation to God will bring an end to suffering or at least reveal its reason ("Sometime we'll understand why"). But of course everyday is wrong. Tragedy is part of destiny.

Nausea and Ennui are not far behind. The discovery of the real lineaments of man's situation produces a deep and powerful revulsion. Nausea is a recoil against the laying bare of life's meaninglessness. But man is also subject to Ennui, especially if he sees himself defined by the everyday life in which a person is merely a reflection—of other persons. If man's being were a good joke, he might properly laugh and even suppose that he could overhear laughter in heaven. But his being is a bad joke, or a merely tedious one. So he experiences either nausea or ennui, or both in alternation. The threat of either makes tragedy wither, because tragedy presupposes the possibility of momentous encounter. Perhaps everyday feels this and therefore welcomes triviality as its substance in the hope that the range of spirit will shrink to companionable dimensions.

4. Man's fate is not exhausted by meaninglessness, however. There is also alienation. The world is a strange place and no one is or can be really at home in it. Man came from nowhere and he is going nowhere. The man of courage must carve a significant existence for himself between the two blanks, popularly conceived as beginning and end. He can do this only if he is prepared to come to terms with death, the most potent of all alienating powers. Death is lord of alienation for a reason that goes beyond everyday's anticipation of the day when something happens and "I" shall be no more. Such a day

is surely coming. But in the meantime, in the only real time, the courage to exist authentically now can be corrupted by anxiety. The individual really exists, he becomes a real integer between Nothing on both ends of his time, only if his courage is equal to his awareness of his real situation.

5. Man creates everyday as a protection against ontological certainty: Death, Alienation, Guilt, Tragedy, Meaninglessness. Everyday is a fabric of illusion. This fabric assumes the properties of a massive reality. This is something of a miracle because the tissue is very flimsy and a patchwork. Man knows this is the case: his anxiety is the proof. The anxiety at the heart of contemporary civilization is not the dread that good people may soon be outnumbered by bad people. How long will man continue to live and die for illusions created to obscure the demands of authentic existence? There's the heart of the matter.

6. The thinnest and least plausible life for man is one committed to everyday, a life that denies the powerful solicitations of being to live beyond the specious surfaces of the world. Richness of spirit, largeness of vision, noble assent to the inevitable, these are available only to persons who will respond to such solicitations. They must not be afraid to be alone in the world and contemplate the finality of death and acknowledge the guiltiness of existence. Civilization, for these free spirits, ceases to be an overworld in which one can find genuine meaning: it is the last and greatest illusion standing between a person and a free creative existence.

Theologians of culture have found much of their work already done for them in these philosophical programs for laying bare the fundamental elements and dimensions of man's being. What they have had to do on their own is to show that the New Testament Gospel comes out at the same place, or, at least, moves miraculously into a place prepared by this philosophical John the Baptist. Yet dedication to this sole remaining task has produced remarkably varied readings of the Gospel, running from stern rejection of contemporary civilization as the demonic enemy of spirit and Spirit, to enthusiastic endorsement of the secularizing powers as the instrument of salvation from false gods. I doubt that the true lordship of Jesus Christ over all philosophies will strike a deeply responsive chord in this situation, but the attempt must be made, sooner or later. In the meantime we ought not to suppose that philosophical anxiety for the present age is limited to thinkers who rebuild categorial schemes around anxiety. Existentialism is not the only philosophical expression of a passionate concern for contemporary civilization even if it is the most dramatic.

This concern can be felt in the effort to reconstitute philosophy on the sure foundation of a new methodology. So reconstituted philosophy might then untangle ancient snarls in man's intellect and thus benefit the whole man. This means that philosophic therapy is again with us, a very old and honorable philosophic spirit reincarnate in tweed jacket rather than in toga. May it be spared the hemlock this time!

Other philosophers passionately reject this methodological passion as a trivializing of philosophy and a technical refinement running uncontrollably toward sterility. It is not enough that people should think clearly, though this does not threaten immediately to become a mass addiction. They should also think out an account of the world and of man's being in it and for this be prepared to leave behind parochialisms both of method and of outlook. The crisis of contemporary civilization, East and West, must be met not only with a fresh acknowledgment of the ontological foundations but also with a conceptual scheme applicable to the cosmos.

And other philosophers seek an ideological foundation on which a world community can be created. This is something that methodological refinements cannot offer. Speculative conceptual systems will not do for this purpose, either, though their largeness of vision is a virtue. The technological mastery of the West and the spiritual mastery of the East must be synthesized for the wellbeing of the inclusive human community. Must be! It is no longer an interesting possibility or an intriguing ideal. It is the affirmative arm of an ultimate either/or. The negative arm is exposed in the headlines everyday.

These are some, a random selection, of the philosophic expressions of an acute anxiety for contemporary civilization and for the human world altogether. Taking them all together we may say that everyday must be understood before it can be reformed. It must be understood before it is written off as irredeemable. Philosophers differ from one another on the latter question, as do we all. Some continue to believe that philosophers ought to do something about the shape of the world. Others view the philosopher as the one who reflects civilization's moment of acutest self-awareness. Here the philosopher vies with the artist in registering the Age of Anxiety most clearly.

VII

The quest for essential human reality is a thing of many aspects in contemporary civilization. It is a quest born of anxiety rather than of objective curiosity. It is engaged in with unmistakable passion on all sides. This passion expresses an ontological intuition: if man is to be fully himself he must have the truth. The intuition has a corollary: man has a humanly incurable propensity for creating illusions and thereafter a preference for illusion over reality.

The anxiety about this world is greatly exacerbated by the discovery of civilization's global character. The critic of civilization has no place to stand to do his work, to speak his piece, except within the object he is judging. He has no critical appliances except the values of the order he wishes to appraise. What then becomes of the time-honored distinction between appearance and reality, a distinction with which religion first, and philosophy thereafter, begins? Reality threatens to become merely the cultural consensus, and appearance a merely plausible denial of that consensus.

What is responsible for this strange and unsettling situation? The philosophical-scientific "historicizing" of man's being has played a very important part in bringing this about. The historicizing of man's being means that concrete human existence is fully absorbed into the fabric and process of the civilization in which persons appear and live. It seems to follow from this (though actually it is part of the viewpoint) that man has no history as such; and so ceases to exist as such. Essential human being is thereafter parceled out to the multitudinous particular human communities and their cultures, each of which is called human for purposes of cataloguing.

Existentialistic reductions of history to historicity are not really a cure for this condition. For that matter, they are rarely advertised as such, since historicity is a dimension or quality of the actually (presently) existing self rather than a time sequence in which the position of selves can be plotted. So the historical-relativistic outlook is ontologically confirmed; and theology of culture celebrates the timely passing of still another God.

In this situation the Christian Gospel is wonderfully strange and full of unseasonable demands. On the one hand it makes a great deal of a particular history: Israel, old and new, is the history of Revelation. But on the other hand the human subject of the Gospel is man himself, his whole being and history. The Gospel is thus self-represented as the clear, firm, and definitive foundation on which every false particularism and vacuous if not deadly universalism is to be judged: every program in which man's being and history are subsumed under a provincial destiny, and every program in which man's being and history are subsumed under categories of abstract inclusiveness.

Given and bound to this Gospel the church is called to a life at once proud and humble. It has something of which to boast, "Jesus Christ is the same yesterday, today, and for ever" (Heb. 13:8, NEB). Therefore the church has not the slightest excuse for being swept off the course "by all sorts of outlandish teachings" (*ibid.*). But the church does not have this Gospel as a reward or as an adornment for its own exaltation. Indeed, ought we not to confess that it is the least among all institutions since there is none which it is appointed to master? Yet it is also true that all of the powers of the world—and not merely the earth grubbers—shall one day bow the knee to Jesus Christ and "confess, 'Jesus Christ is Lord,' to the glory of God the Father" (Phil. 2:10, NEB).

The grandeur of this vision may momentarily blind us to the practical hazards daily confronted by the church in the proclamation of the Gospel. These hazards are self-justification and irrelevance. The power of the Gospel may be used to exalt church and Christian above the tarnishing and corrupting evils of the hour. The truth of the Gospel may be translated into esoteric self-referencing religious lore. So on the one side we have the church behaving like all of the other empires of the earth. On the other side we have the Gospel reduced to a Kerygma whose meaning is available only to persons of philosophical-theological sophistication, who are probably already well beyond the reach of any Gospel everyday would be able to recognize.

So the actual situation of the church seems to be very bleak. The church often delivers a message firmly wedded to everyday. But it is everlastingly and antecedently bound to a Gospel that will not permit it to accept everyday at its face value. In fact the Lord of this Gospel obliges the church to attack both the actualities and the idealities of everyday wherever they obstruct the vision and love of the Kingdom of God! The church carries on a fitful and illicit love affair with the world; but because of the Lord of the Gospel, it is liable at any moment to be sued for desertion and nonsupport by its worldly lover, or be itself deserted because it is incurably absent-minded in the very act of love.

What has just been called a fitful and illicit love affair with the world can be discussed in language not so indebted to the prophet Hosea. We can simply say that the church is taken for granted as a feature and component of everyday, of the present world, rather than as the ordained herald of another world. As a component of everyday the church acts as the guardian of the ideals of civilization.

The import of this can be properly appreciated only when we remember that civilizations tend to create an aura of ultimate meaningfulness around themselves. Being human means to feel some dissatisfaction with the present scene, whatever it is. Worldly wisdom turns this constitutive discontent to some positive account in the preservation and enhancement of culture by providing a space for the expression of discontent. The space of permissible dissatisfaction is measured by ideals indigenous in that civilization. Rome leaves room for a Roman to express his discontent with what Rome is at the moment. Rome and the Roman may be improved as a result. But the possibilities of a man becoming a better Roman do not include his becoming a Parthian. Really to be human one must be Roman or Parthian or American or what-not. One must be a constituent of a global enterprise. The divine urge to become a better human being is domesticated in every great civilization, to the point where becoming better is enclosed in becoming a better Roman, a better Parthian, a better American, etc. Absolute idealists in the ethical sphere generally overlook this in making their appeals to the good of humanity as the all-inclusive community. When great conflict demands a sharper definition of his loyalty the idealist confronts these options: (1) Revolution against the established order but without direct aid and comfort for the visible external enemies of the order. (2) Treason, in behalf of a humane revolution being staged by visible external enemies of the order. (3) Symbolic non-participation in the chief iniquity of one's civilization; without expectation that things will change in response to the symbolic gesture; and with realization that one cannot in fact disengage oneself from the massive everyday world. (4) A liturgical invocation of the rights of humanity as the norm of ethical-political judgment and the goal of history toward which civilization moves asymptotically. (5) Suicide: better to exercise personal decision in protesting inhumanity by destroying one's own being than to participate in inhumanity.

The idealistic strain in the American spirit is now held in a momentous tension with the religious thrust of American civilization. When a civilization successfully creates the illusion that it has captured the ideal possibilities of man, it proceeds with relatively clear conscience to exact absolute loyalty from its people. Such a loyalty is compounded of gratitude for what the nation has been, dedication to what it is now, and expectation for what it is certain to become; and all with divine approval. Thus civilizations take on a kind of religious quality, a quality that will surely seem the nobler, and the more necessary, as it is more closely linked with ideality. Such is cultural piety, the religiousness of civilization as such.

Cultural piety may find it very useful to borrow from particular religious traditions within civilization. When the borrowing is accomplished with intelligence, urbanity, and imagination, cultural piety effectively displaces the worship of the God who lives above all civilizations. This God may be saluted on solemn occasions, such as the opening of a session of the Congress of the United States, or a Cotton Bowl game, but all that His worship signifies has been gathered into the piety of civilization. Nothing of that piety is compromised or diminished by the most moving acknowledgments that our civilization owes its greatness to the will of God. There are liturgical moments in the nation's life when God is reminded that He too has profited from this historic association, e.g., presidential inaugural ceremonies.

Contemporary civilization has achieved a great deal in the elevation of cultural piety above every other. We expect religion to have practical effects. We habitually value religion because we value the practical effects. The piety of civilization obviously has more desirable practical effects than any other. Q.E.D.

The common name for this piety is "the Judaeo-Christian tradition." This tradition is presumed to be the synthesis of the great and enduring values of several particular religious communities. It is used to justify, though hardly to direct, the principal structures and processes of this civilization. Whatever the cultural elite may make of this situation, this tradition has been woven into the fabric of the everyday world. It continues to provide the spiritual warrant for keeping on the job, for manning the ramparts when foreign enemies threaten, for extending the helping hand and for hallowing the memory of all who have died for freedom and justice.

But now the piety of civilization is experiencing travail. On the surface things are going very well. Preachers declare that all is well; or that so little is wrong that a return to nonalcoholic sobriety, sexual purity, tithing, and a vote for the conservative candidate in the next election will put things in fine order. Indeed the name of Jesus is often invoked in this cause and rarely in any other, except by theologians. In the name of Jesus (who apparently is thoroughly at home within the Judaeo-Christian tradition—why not? he was a Jew and he started Christianity) we are warned against going any farther down the primrose path to materialism and license. But the same preachers who use their great histrionic gifts to make these warnings vivid do not sense anything fundamentally wrong with the piety of civilization; and they are as ready to discover its roots and justification in Moses as in Jesus.

The travail of this piety has not been brought on by theologians of culture, but they have not tried to soften the blow. Its spokesmen are all for contemporaneity—they too want to live fully in the present. But they want real piety to be seen in what is really creative in the contemporary world. Everyday including its famous preachers, be they bland or accusative is something to be diagnosed with the perceptual instrument of art rather than with the dogmatic norms of particular religious history. Everyday's anxieties are to be exposed as well-grounded, with the conceptual instruments of an analytic or existentialistic philosophy, and with some help from a theological Freudianism.

Anxiety is here, whatever we are able to make of it theologically. It can be felt in the reluctance of cultural piety to tolerate any serious and unambiguous gesture of loyalty to any other order, not even to an order presumably divine in its own right. The piety of civilization cannot permit the issue to be drawn in such terms. In the American setting it allows for the change of heart, provided that the change is essentially emotional and is geared for the reinforcement of the moral conventions. In this providential way people are given an opportunity to discharge the feelings of guilt generated by failure to meet the demands of everyday. But it is not so easy now to confuse those demands with the demands of the righteous God. It is possible that God demands something much more drastic than public confession of sin against middle-class moral conventions and a readiness to join a comfortable WASP congregation. Some hint of this may have begun to filter into the consciousness of everyday and make it dissatisfied with nineteenth-century revivalism as the grand ecstatic moment in the piety of civilization.

Nonetheless this piety achieved some important things, and the depressing triumphs of mass-media evangelism ought not to be allowed to obscure them. Religion in America has allowed a strong sense of personal unworthiness to find a bounded home within the space preordained for discontent and other negative feelings about the human world around and within. This sense of unworthiness is produced by breaking posted moral rules. Moral sensibilities are (or were) preconditioned to expect personal shortcomings of this order. So when they occur—when, not if—one is supposed to know what to do to reduce the guilt, even if one has had no explicit religious instruction at home and church. Revivalism was simply the ecstatic mode of this preordained resolution of guilt feelings. To the extent revivalism persists it all but invariably reinforces anxiety, even if it reduces guilt momentarily; because everyday threatens to erase the value the individual has been religiously coached to believe God has given him.

So the internal mechanism by which the piety of civilization achieves its eminence is also the one by which it is now threatened: the image the person has of himself. So long as he is adjusted to the demands and rewards of everyday the self-image is an effective lure and monitor presiding over actuality and possibility. The image instructs him in his duties and it points the way in which his aspirations, and even his fantasies, ought to run above and beyond the call of duty. So according to the piety of civilization there is no acceptable expression of his spirit but what everyday is the sole licenser. As for unacceptable behavior and dangerous thoughts, the piety of civilization has its most potent weapon against them also in the self-image. Why does the campus prostitute one day become a respectable matron? Hardly because the beauties of a life of sexual propriety become miraculously overpowering. The change comes when she begins to see herself in a new way. In her imagination she begins to play a different role. If she gets a break, she may play the role convincingly in real life, and not only receive the appropriate applause (from other matrons, not her erstwhile clients), but also come to be the part she plays.

But if the self-image is confused or repugnant, everyday ought to begin to be very anxious for itself. The unconscious person and the self-hater may stay on the job indefinitely but neither is the ideal of cultural piety, for neither is a good carrier of cultural values. The one is useless when routines break down. The other is committed to self-destruction and the explosion may bring down part of the world —how much of it depends on how much of it he has learned to include in his hatred.

VIII

The piety of civilization, one eye fixed upon the actualities and the other upon the idealities presumptively bounded by that civilization itself, embraces truth, goodness, and beauty transcending the order of present realizations. Only so far as this succeeds can a civilization hope to bind human time and human loyalty. This appeal to the bounded ideality requires a priesthood to make it fully effective.

The church has provided such a priesthood, both lay and clerical. The church has done this so generously and devotedly that it has taken on the guise of crown chaplain to contemporary civilization. For this it has been rewarded with theological commendations and theological abuse. But now even in the church we hear the question whether it is not too late to save everyday. Everyday is beyond the reach of symptomatic medicine. It needs deep surgery and reconstruction rather than spiritual aspirin. But would the patient survive the operation? No one professes seriously to know. We do know that everyday struggles desperately to maintain a pallid semblance of health, unity, and power. But we also know that if everyday collapses even the most intrepid spirits will be hard pressed to find a substitute father, mother, and God. The fate of the timorous and little-asking defies contemplation. (What a shocking irony that the innumerable millions of the new countries should be pressing so vehemently toward the day of personal reality at a time when the masses of Christian civilization are being herded toward the night of anonymity! What a pity that as a new everyday is being created in the one case and the old one eroded in the other, men of wisdom, power, and courage cannot conspire to direct the one and amend the other! Who would pay such a price to become like us if they knew how much we pay for gin and other wonder drugs to endure it?)

So culture-Christianity is bound to suffer as everyday suffers. Everyday is balanced precariously between being and nonbeing. Heroic endeavor is called for from great and small to keep it there. But is it worth the effort? Is it not so thoroughly honeycombed with the lie that lovers of truth can only wish it were dead? Is it not so essentially humdrum and repetitious that creative spirits can stay alive only by spurning it? Is it not so inevitably idolatrous that prophetic spirits must call down upon it the holy wrath of God?

Theologians of culture are able to return affirmatives to such questions. Whether they can point convincingly to higher and more certain ground on which to dance an executioner's jig is another question. But at least we can agree that the Christianized piety of civilization has failed to offer a meaningful interpretation of the creative aspects of contemporary culture. The upper ranges of ideality of this civilization are largely lost on culture-Christianity. So disaster is foreshadowed in the readiness of spokesmen of the church to use everyday as the decisive criterion for judging art, science, philosophy, and religion itself. Art is good if it confirms the perceptual and feeling values of the everyday world. Science is good if it makes life more comfortable. Philosophy is good if it leaves illusion on the throne. Religion is good if it goes on saying that all is well in the cosmos, in the nation, in the West, on the hearth, in the heart.

Even some of the critics of the order are still firmly enmeshed in the value nexus of everyday, though they may be a generation or two behind in its evolution. We hear pulpit-thumping proclamations of the opposition of revealed truth to indecency and immorality. Then it turns out that the critic has taken a firm stand on the everyday standards—of fifty years ago. His criteria do not transcend the present world. They fall behind it or below it. "Be good!" cannot be reduced to "Be as decent as your grandmother!"

These are some of the results of the church's love affair with contemporary civilization. The risks of disengagement from this affair are very great, but no serious, faithful, and creative criticism of the world is possible for the church unless it commits itself to that disengagement. That alone will not guarantee that the Gospel of the Kingdom of God in Jesus Christ will emerge clearly in the preaching of the church. That is one of the risks. The church could easily alienate its erstwhile lover and keeper, and still not be judged to have done so out of faithfulness to its true Lord. It can be hated as well as loved for the wrong reasons. This is to say that disengagement can be motivated by an unfaithful desire to appear untainted by the unrighteousness of the world, as though the Lord might return and find it in *flagrante delicto* unless it watches its step! In fact disengagement may be the wrong word and image for the distance necessary for relevant and cogent criticism; unless it be understood to signify only the giving of the church's heart to God's Christ and the will thereafter to resist the self-deifying propensities of civilization.

IX

The quest for the fundamentals of man's situation in being and in the world is much more than an exigency thrust upon the church by the constitutive anxiety of civilization. God demands that His church stand out against the world and yet be prepared to sacrifice itself for real human beings in the real world. The church is under a divine obligation to so preach the Gospel of Christ's Kingdom that the native love of illusion and fear of truth will be understood in their intimate interrelatedness. This interrelatedness is part of the fabric of everyday. This does not mean that the church should despise everyday as inane or demonic. Rather, everyday is to be offered up to the redemption of Jesus Christ. This offering-up occurs in the faithful praying of the church. That is the beginning and the end; but there is much for the church to do in the middle.

Criticism of contemporary civilization ought to occupy high priority in the theological business of the church. The aim of theological criticism is not to prove that the church is right and the world is wrong. To show forth the truth in which man may rightly divine who he is and to whom he belongs and against whom he sins and whither he is bound; and with whom there is fullness of life from everlasting to everlasting: the elucidation of this Gospel is the theological calling.

If this is really the aim of theology of culture we can have no serious objection to it. The church has a great need for the practical reorientation of its theological work. If theology of culture has helped to stimulate that need by dramatizing the predicament of the church in contemporary civilization, it has done a good thing indeed.

CHAPTER II

Is Civilization Itself a Religious Enterprise?

I

We have seen that civilization has intrinsic religious aspirations, such as permanency and all-sufficiency, whatever the variety of historical religious communities within that civilization. The needs of a civilization are certain to force it eventually to co-opt or coerce some of the services of these religious communities. The Christian church has responded to these demands and solicitations with remarkable alacrity, industry, and cheerfulness, almost as though its whole heart were in this response.

Now two considerable dangers descend upon this particular argument. The first is that civilization *per se,* having been given a kind of personal quality and power, will pass as a religious enterprise in and for itself. The second danger is that the church will appear to be two churches: one, the large pious mistress of civilization; the other, the small holy bride of Christ, obedient through thick and thin to her Master.

These dangers are so considerable that we must make a closer inspection of the situation, beginning with the religious dimensions of civilization itself.

II

When culture is used as an undifferentiated and unqualified noun it can hardly mean more than the world of human meaning. In our earlier discussion of this we did not pause to note that thereby man lives in two worlds, the other one being nature (which earlier we called cosmos). Nature is the world of things, powers, and events manifested first of all in sense experience. Man discovers early enough and painfully enough that this world has its own ways which he cannot alter significantly and which he cannot ignore, such as being born and dying. Culture is the world of man's creation, and as such it answers to human control. Culture is the creation of man's mind, heart, and hands; and it must obey him. But this marvelous human creation is in considerable part a response to the powers he encounters in nature. Culture does not appear simply because man must eat, find cover, and multiply. The birds and the bees are under the same compulsions of nature; and I think we must regard the generosity as misplaced which would credit them with culture. Culture appears when natural necessities are imbued with meaning having little if any clear relation to the strict necessities of survival. Food may have symbolic value rather than mere subsistence value. The dwelling place may be adorned with symbols of various sorts. The sexual act may be given a meaning only faintly related to the biological appetite.

These are of course hardly more than random samples of the way man creates a world of his own by infusing natural forces, entities, and events with the values of ideality.

A civilization is a historically concrete and distinctive embodiment of a culture. A society achieves civilization when it successfully applies a tradition (or complex of traditions) to the demands of a particular situation in space and time. To say "successfully applies" means that the members of that society, as a result of such efforts, achieve a significant measure both of stability and spread of satisfaction. This is why we have said that a civilization is a complex but reasonably coherent (when healthy) solution thrust upon man both by nature and by his own spirit. As a child of nature man has a powerful desire to go on living, even under the most hazardous and painful situations. He is also the subject of a peculiar inner desire to live well, to live nobly, courageously, joyously, generously, peacefully, rationally—the procession of adverbial expressions for man's desire to live well is itself one way of telling the human story in the cosmos.

The point of the distinction between a civilization and its culture is simply that the values of a civilization can be abstracted from the historical particularities of that civilization, beginning with a temporal segment called an epoch, and continuing until the abstracted values are free altogether of the flux of time and subsist in the realm of ideality. This abstractive operation is surely an expression of one of the most remarkable human powers. It makes possible a generic all-inclusive human community and history, an ideal at once the most potent and with the saddest adventures in time, as though it were a Ulysses forever losing but forever forcing his enemies into new prodigies of ingenuity and violence to overcome him.

Now if we may risk putting some of these matters in Freudian terms, the culture of a society is its superego. The conflict of superego with ego is our only warrant for running the risks of personalizing either society or civilization (or both). If we let ego = the individual member of a macrocosmic society, and superego = its culture, we shall see that society must subsume ego under the norms of culture, if society is to survive. A society has a civilization only to the degree that the inevitable conflicts between its "will" and the ego are resolved in its own favor. There can be no doubt that religion is one of the institutional powers used to produce an outcome of conflict favorable to society and its civilization.

But now things seem to have become thoroughly confused. Traditional Christianity calls man to worship and obey a God who transcends all of man's creative powers and achievements. How therefore could people who accept Christianity ever accept the total subjection of their religious life to the needs of civilization?

The confusion is not really very deep. Christians accept this subjection because their deepest concerns and dearest hopes have been already commandeered by contemporary civilization, and this so thoroughly that anxiety over one's stake in society and for the future of that society takes the place, insensibly, of the fear of the Lord. This does not mean that civilization itself has become a prime religious object, a god. It means that certain features of society have been elevated to such a level of value and pitch of power that they have become objects of the deepest concern. Such concern may bear some comparison with the devotion the Christian owes to God alone. We must now ask just how serviceable the comparison is. We shall seek to do this by asking whether to have a very deep concern for something is what it means to be religious. Then we shall ask what those elements of our civilization are which seem to elicit an ultimate concern.

III

It is often said that a person's real religion is whatever he takes more seriously than he takes anything else. So alcohol is the god of the alcoholic, even though he may not feel that his drinking is a sacrifice offered to a god. In the same vein, apparently, St. Paul says that the pagans have made a god of their bellies. But if "religion" is simply the name for the central and dominating interest of a person's life, we begin to wonder why the word is just as likely to stir images of mighty powers, some of them supernatural in power and dignity, who have some kind of concern for man. Perhaps we are much too prone to call any behavior "religious" which is simply a case of a person's bearing down very hard to get something. We ought to say that he is not really religious unless he feels that some power is bearing down on him, unless, that is, he believes that he must do something about divine powers who have done something about him. These powers may not have done it on purpose (there is not much point in denying the existence of nontheistic religions); but their having done it or their readiness to do it, is the difference between life and death, being and nothing, good and evil, joy and despair. Accordingly, to say that atheism is really a subtle form of religion makes about as much sense as saying that voluntary starvation is really a subtle nutritional program. It is true that some religious people are fanatics. It does not follow and it is not true that all fanatics are religious.

So far we conclude that a civilization is itself not a religious enterprise simply because people are greatly concerned about its goodness and its prospects.

But now it seems that there are some aspects or qualities of civilization which provoke a concern that is very deep and stimulate an expectation that has a religious quality.

One of these aspects is the unity by virtue of which a society can be called a community. The elemental human power in which the unity of society is grounded, is feeling. A society exists only so long as its people are bonded together by fellow-feeling, which alone makes the moral reality of loyalty possible.

Feeling has two kinds of objects: (1) concrete persons; (2) values. A society achieves a civilization, it becomes an embodiment of a culture, only if both kinds of objects of feeling are vividly apprehended. But (2) has a kind of primacy: to be embodied a culture requires (2); and in fact it is embodied where (2) obtains, even if (1) comes in a relatively poor second. Unless they are apprehended in vivid feeling, values subside (or evaporate) into the realm of ideality. Through the power of feeling values become a way of life, they become sentiments able to furnish a visible pattern to the members of a society. Even so, we have not left (1) very far behind. Granted that the bond of unity is a concurrence and consensus in value, we have to add at once that consensus is impossible without the element of fellow-feeling, the feeling that has concrete persons as its objects. A concrete system of values (a society with a culture) appears and endures just so long as its people are held together by fellow-feeling, as well as by appetitions and aspirations having a common focus.

These observations about (1) are not a substitute for an explicit ontological decision on the question, What is a "concrete person"? In the Christian West, the conventional answer is the individual human being. In the East an equally conventional answer is a larger social unit, such as the family in traditional Chinese society. The disparity between two such answers greatly perturbs us whenever a meeting of East and West is projected. Accordingly we may be induced to slide over a fact of equally formidable proportions: the breaking up of the conventions in both East and West. In the West (especially but not exclusively in America) the flight from the concreteness of individual responsibility is well under way, both in actuality and in fantasy life. In the East the conflict between opposing forces—the absorption of the family into much larger collectives and the thrust for individual meaning—is becoming acute; and this is a consequence of encounter with the West.

Perhaps this is a sufficient indication that any sort of catalogue of cultural differences, whether or not it is supplemented with scientific causal explanations, is not a substitute for ontological judgment concerning concrete personal existence. The biases of religious traditions, East and West, cannot be allowed to decide this question by themselves.

The unity of civilization may well become a subject of religious concern. Christians ought to feel a religious obligation to pray that the spirit of brotherhood will abound in the nation and everywhere.

This, however, does not mean that this unity, this coveted and blessed sense of community, has so far become a religious object. We pray *to* God *for* the unity of all mankind in love.

But let us suppose that the unity of civilization is threatened by very powerful enemies. Let us suppose that there is a very generally held feeling that "the axe has been laid against the roots of the tree" on which the nation in its present life is but one of the fruits; so that the principles of the nation, its values, its ideal aims, are under powerful and determined attack. Is it not likely that a crisis so severe as this will convert the unity of the beloved community into the prime object of religious devotion? I think this is not likely unless that unity is endowed with mutually incompatible characteristics, specifically, vulnerability to destructive power, and invulnerability to destructive power. Therefore it is a mistake to speak of even the most fanatic expression of nationalism as a religion, unless the fanatic has endowed his nation with a mysterious power to withstand all enmity forever, which he has not, of course, or he would not be a fanatic. He is a fanatic because he is far from sure that his god is absolute. His feeling is absolute and invincible but his god is but one among many.

This is not to deny that the anxiety produced by the severe crises in Western civilization may be so acute as to be nearly indistinguishable from the fear of the Lord, if we suppose that the fear of the Lord has any element of negation in it. The cultural crisis is above all threat to superego rather than to ego. Ego knows that he must die, he would rather not think about the fact but he knows that the fact remains. But must our civilization also die? If superego is also mortal, perhaps it ought not to reign. But when superego falters, ego's world collapses into chaos, even though the momentary and precarious "freedom" may seem very delightful. When superego falters, people continue to acknowledge values, but these values have lost coherence and power. The life of ego thereafter assumes a haphazard character; and whether he twitches or just sits still forever hardly matters, even to him. So in an age of anxiety concerning the permanency of this civilization the teachings of traditional piety are heard as a threat rather than as a reassurance: "from everlasting to everlasting, thou art God" (Ps. 90:2). The deathly fear of facing a cosmos and a civilization in which only God is everlasting, is one of the most telling symptoms of the disease of Western civilization.

So we are introduced to another candidate offered by contemporary civilization for religious honors, the hunger for everlastingness. This affliction has a variety of expressions. We shall begin with one of the more pedestrian, one affecting the transmission of truth from one generation to the next.

The truth transmitted by the teaching generation is indeterminate relative to the future, because the truth is timeless: "These things are so, they have always been so (we learned them from our fathers), and they will always be so (you must teach them to your children)." Ancient piety declares that all "flesh is grass, and all its beauty is like the flower of the field" (Isa. 40:6, RSV). But the piety of civilization cries, "Beauty, truth, and goodness shall endure forever!"—our truth, our beauty, our goodness. Men may come and men may go, but our civilization shall stand forever because it has caught the ideal.

Here knowledge and hope collide; and anxiety broods over the ruins. Men know that civilizations wither and die. Before the face of the Lord God the nations arise and pass away, and it is as though they had never been. But men also extract a precious satisfaction from the belief that they have not lived in vain and have not spent their lives for a foolish thing; their beloved community will endure forever. But when the lights of civilization start to gutter out in the wild storms man himself brews, and the smell of death is unmistakable, that precious satisfaction is gotten only by vain repetitions and ritualistic gestures aimed at the evil spirits. Hope becomes desperate: only God can save, but God is silent. Then it is all too clear that time is not bound by the hunger for everlastingness. Every creaturely thing must face its time to die, whether it is superego or ego. So ego makes provisions to be remembered, not as the one from whom the everlasting truth was first heard by his children, but as the good provider who reaches up from the grave to bestow good things, the benefits of his insurance policies, the harvest of his time-binding love. The beneficiaries may take the fruit thereof and waste it irreverently in riotous living, but in some far-off idle moment they may drop a grateful memory into the well of time; and in the tiny splash ego shall live again!—This is bad religion but it is good for the insurance business.

So it comes about that the hunger for everlastingness becomes fixed upon powers and values which cannot be advertised as holy. This does not mean that civilization becomes a religious object in itself. It may mean that a religious quality is added to the essential anxiety with which man confronts both cosmos and civilization.

Moreover a civilization, either out of vaulting terror or pride, may seek to deify its values, if not its powers. But to call this religious we should have to look beyond the ritualisms of patriotism in which the national life is, or ought to be, celebrated. It takes more than ritual to make religion. Songbirds and honeybees are remarkably ritualistic, but there is no evidence that the rituals implicate the higher powers of the cosmos.

IV

We have concluded that neither the unity nor the mortality of a civilization renders it an object of religious veneration. At the same time we have to admit that a perfectly obvious complication awaits this negative answer to the question whether civilization is a religious enterprise in itself. The complication is that Western civilization is presumptively Christian. Even at first glance, then, the church is not the pious mistress of contemporary civilization, she is its tender loving Mother. Whether or not this cultural epoch, or any other one, can seriously be called Christian is not the present issue, since we have in any case to concede that the present epoch is still seriously involved with historic Christianity. We have already contended that this very involvement, this persisting engagement, renders the reality and the role of the church both precarious and confusing. Some Christian ethical concerns are still a ferment in the contemporary world. It is beside the point to argue that these Christian concerns have themselves been the products of a complex historical development, since the consensus is that they are Christian and that they are part of the foundation of our civilization. Take, for example, the sentiment of justice. There is a consensus that our society must evolve in the direction of greater justice; and that justice means equality of access to the rights and privileges of our society. Other civilizations have not interpreted the sentiment of justice in this way, and many people—I hazard the guess that a consensus—believe that this is the Christian reading of the ideal of justice; and perhaps, even, that God long ago commanded that men should be just in this way and in no other. Thus this reading of justice is understood to be part of our national destiny. Americans have spilled blood in this belief, and have professed that in doing so they were obedient to the demands of the righteous God. This is why we say that the historical correctness of the interpretation is an issue beside the point. People accept this as the Christian value of justice. This is what the church itself claims. The claim is part of the problem of the contemporary church.

Let us take as another illustration the marked emphasis upon the value of the individual person in Western society. This individualism is an offshoot of Christian personalism. Traditional Christianity accords high ontological rank and high value to the human being, because God has put something special into His creation and continues to make man the direct object of His wholly righteous love. If the point of historical accuracy were allowed, we should have to grant that Jesus nowhere says of man, "You have an infinite value." He says that people are vastly more important in God's sight than sparrows (Matt. 10:31).—This has encouraged some people to shoot every sparrow in sight.

Modern individualism is an offshoot of historical Christian teaching; but the church has made a very heavy investment in the offshoot. Here it has had bad philosophical counsel, but it has also had a faithless heart. As a result the contemporary world, and the church with and in it, labors vainly to achieve a sentiment and actuality of community which is at once more than a mere aggregation of atomistic persons, and a moral reality in which every person is affirmed as the potential if not actual creator of unique values for the common life. So in the reigning sentimentality the individual is endowed with magisterial splendor. In actuality the individual person is fighting for his very soul against the superorganizational techniques and aims of the contemporary world. Perhaps the behavior of the church would be excusable if it simply dozed through this conflict, this Gethsemane of the person in contemporary life. But on Sunday it preaches the individualistic heresy. Throughout the rest of the week it uses the soul-crunching superorganizational methods employed everywhere else.

A third illustration of the meaning of "Christian" when used as an adjective of contemporary civilization comes from art rather than from morality.

Art has drawn very heavily upon Christianity for much of its subject matter. To this day Christ is still a subject for painters and poets. Novelists return repeatedly to Biblical themes if not to Biblical characters. Musicians still compose music for the Mass. Perhaps in quantitative terms this is not very impressive as compared to the Middle Ages. Quantitative criteria are irrelevant when it is a matter of the flow and power of creative expression in civilization.

That is just where our most acute anxiety over the church comes to life. The once plentiful and commanding ties of Christianity with civilization have been weakened and blurred, where they have not been severed. Christian elements—I mean the Christian realities, not the sentimentalities—float haphazardly upon the running tide of civilization, whether our interest is in morality, or art, or politics, or what-not. The tide is running in irresistible force in directions in which the church cannot travel without giving up the service of Christ and taking on the service of Antichrist. The logic of history may be moving civilization toward pinnacles of megalomania and self-sufficiency which tower over the pride of Babylon as Everest over an anthill. On those heights, the soul communes with Antichrist; and forgets that Antichrist's appearance always marks the end of the world. The moment in which illusion achieves its greatest triumph, when it seems to have become the world rather than its shadow and imitation, is precisely the moment of its greatest vulnerability. All of its specious glory can be shattered by a childish slingshot observation: "The emperor is naked."

V

It is time to remember that the subjects of megalomania and self-sufficiency are human beings in the concrete and not civilizations in rhetorical abstraction. The fear of being a concrete person and the incredible growth of superorganization are two sides of one coin. The coin is a counterfeit of essential human being. It is in some respects a demonically clever counterfeit. In other respects it is a fool's bungling job. But a counterfeit it is, in any case.

So let us see somewhat more closely how the tide running toward megalomania and self-sufficiency is to be understood.

No civilization can arrest time. Man in civilization creates the illusion of being in charge of time: present greatness will not endure forever, but the future will be familiar, we have it under option and commitment. This expectation can be so firmly schooled that people come to think of God as an ideal entirely congenial to that civilization, if not an ingredient of it. In this way reverence for the ideal takes on an aura which people in our day take to be religious. This disposition must not blind us to the fact that civilization must make an appeal to ideality. Man must look beyond mere fact and the present state of affairs to an ideal order of ideal persons who may or may not be gods, they may merely be saints and heroes.

The thrust toward megalomania exposes itself as an absolutistic claim upon the ideal and thus upon one great human capacity for devotion and loyalty. Under the power of the megalomaniacal delusion men claim that their ideals, if not their achievements, exhaust the possibilities for man as such. It follows from this that the nonsubscribers are heretics, atheists, servants of Satan, etc. From this it is but one short fatally easy step to the most brutal contempt for rival civilizations. Given provocation (if any further is actually needed) violent aggression is the next development. But even if that step is never taken, a terrible defacement and violation of the human community has already occurred. Reaping the whirlwind sowed by this sin may be stalled or softened by historical accident. That is in the hands of Providence. It is up to man to discover the point at which his own creations and creative powers become objects of obsessional love, become, as some theologians prefer to say, idols.

These obsessions (and human history reeks with them) are more commonly the creations of anxiety than of fierce unheeding pride. This anxiety is the recoil of an ontological and theological disaster of the first magnitude, namely, the isolation in the human spirit of ideality from God transcendent.

From this disaster modern civilizations have drawn the illusory sense of inexhaustible possibilities and illimitable power. Nation after nation has attempted to create an empire which would be invincible in perpetuity against all enemies. This megalomania adopted the disguise (the illusion) of simple, clear, and highly moral national self-interest; and committed the human world to the holocaust of world wars. Which means of course that we have *not* been spared the whirlwind's grim harvest, after all.

VI

To say that the church is the pious mistress of Western civilization is merely an offensively vivid way of saying that the church has accepted a solemn responsibility to convert the Gospel into the piety of contemporary culture. It is much too easy to be cynical about this, as though the church had become in this a crass self-server, a very apt student in learning the arts of success in the world, and thereafter a pious purveyor of the gospel recipe for success, happiness, and a clear conscience. As usual, the cynic misses or perversely distorts the truth. The truth is that the people of the church—and here there is no important difference between laity and clergy—seem to believe earnestly and sincerely that the essential mission of the church in the world is to spiritualize civilization. This spiritualization happens to imbue the norms of this civilization with absoluteness by identifying these ideals as the whole meaningful content of divine Revelation. So to spiritualize civilization is to embellish and adorn its idealities with holiness. Thus the really good man of moralistic piety is one who does his duties in the world as though they were assigned to him by God. He is therefore in an excellent position to thank God for his good character and good works; and to believe that he is forgiven for his moral failures, few and far between as these are, because of his favorable credit balance on the books of divine righteousness. And the really good man of theology of culture is the man who lives courageously beyond the specious comfort of obligation. After the manner of the real Jesus he is all out for openness and creativity in interpersonal relationships.

But for both the practice of religion becomes a way of developing spiritual resources. This is nicely compatible with the wisdom of the world because spiritual resources are necessary for the richness of civilization. Human existence without the spiritual dimension is a travesty. A nonspiritual person is a human being still submerged in biological routines which are humanly meaningless without the idealities and idealizations of memory and of anticipation. Human life achieves its proper fullness only when these idealities are synthesized and directed by a sense (however dim to understanding and impervious to criticism) of transcendent powers whose approval is the difference between life and death for that civilization.

A spiritualizing church does not strictly need a belief in and commitment to powers beyond and above contemporary civilization. Indeed much of the behavior of the church suggests that such a belief and commitment would be embarrassing. They would embarrass the standard preaching of the spiritual world as lying within the private individual, perhaps as a divine subconscious awaiting the nod to come forth in glory.

The spiritualizing church, in other words, takes as its grand vocation in the world the development of man's spiritual capacities by rightly relating him to the ideal world, which in turn rightly relates him to the world here and now. If the church does this job well, the destroyer will not knock at the door of our society, he will pass on, seeking a materialistic victim. Everybody in the spiritualizing church knows as well as the destroyer does where he can find such a victim.

If the church accepts this spiritualizing function as its real life and the real gospel, what will its critical function be? What will it say about its relation to the historic Gospel?

The answers of the spiritualizing church are in the record. Its criticism becomes an attack upon materialistic values, and a rejection of every kind of pessimistic and realistic reading of the contemporary situation as a betrayal of the Christian heritage and of the Christian nation. The historic Gospel is reduced to a simple moral preachment, the right acceptance of which makes for personal respectability, success in the world (or a graceful and humble acceptance of failure), and the triumph of our civilization over all its enemies, present and future.

But does the church actually commit itself so absolutely to the spiritualizing of civilization? Has it forgotten entirely that God Transcendent is the only God, and that no man and no civilization can stand before the perfect judgment of His righteousness?

The church is not a very good mistress because she cannot forget that this God created her and sent her into the world to preach the judgment of His righteousness. So she brings a bad case of heart trouble into her love affair with the world. This heart condition greatly complicates her life as a divinely ordained critic of the world. These complications are as severe as those which confuse and limit her career as mistress in the world. In less whimsical language the people of the church know that they have not obeyed God and are therefore sinners in His sight. Can they preach the righteousness of God from a ruptured conscience? Can they preach the hope of glory in the holiness of God's Kingdom, when their own powers of hope are diseased?

If contemporary civilization has in any way become a religious enterprise in itself, the church has a greater responsibility for this than any other institution. But to be a serious and effective critic of this development the church must first be a self-critic. It cannot be such a self-critic unless it stands squarely on that foundation which is established in Jesus Christ. If it stands elsewhere, if it holds any other mirror up to itself, it will fall away into self-loathing and thereafter into the death of despair; or into that very self-love upon which the judgment of God falls in the word of Jesus Christ: "whoever would save his life will lose it" (Matt. 16:25, RSV).

It is evident, therefore, that our next task is to discuss what it means for the church to stand on that foundation which is established in Jesus Christ and to stand there without apology to the present world or fear of the next.

CHAPTER III

The Authority of the Christian Critic

I

The revelation of God in Jesus Christ is the absolute authority upon which the Christian must stand as a critic of the contemporary world. What he accepts and proclaims as the purposes of God for human life, he accepts and proclaims because it is revealed in Jesus Christ. What he apprehends of human being and human destiny, he holds up to Jesus Christ as the absolute norm. "Behold the Lamb of God . . ." (John 1:29). "Jesus of Nazareth, the son of Joseph" (John 1:45). In Jesus Christ we know who God is. In him we see what man is to become. Through him we are apprehended by God the Spirit who works in us until we have become at last what God has created us to be.

From the beginning of such testimony we can see that "Jesus Christ" is both the name of a historical person, the one called Jesus of Nazareth, and the name of a community, identified as that condition of being in Christ (cf. Eph. 1). Jesus Christ lived as a man among human beings, he lived as a man in every way. Because he lived as he did, and because he was who he was, something indestructibly actual is now properly identified as Christ: power and a range of powers, a relationship and a pattern of relationships. Jesus Christ is a person in history. In the person he is, God the Father reveals His holy Kingdom as embracing in actuality the entire human story. In Christ we are able to say that God is Alpha and Omega, the Beginning and the End (Rev. 1:8).

Man is called to enter this holy actuality, the Kingdom of God, by faith in Jesus Christ. To be in this faith means giving up all projects and dreams of unholy advantage for oneself and all regrets for the failure of such advantage to materialize. Being in Jesus Christ the man of faith dies to every desire for aggrandizement of himself at the cost of other people. In the same Jesus Christ the man of faith rises from that death to rejoice in the beauty of God's creation; and to find particular pleasure in the diversity of man, this creature upon whom God bestows a particular love.

Jesus Christ is God's power of forgiveness of sin and of promise that the sinner is accepted, indeed is embraced, by the purposes of the divine Kingdom. Forgiven and accepted by God in Christ, man no longer needs to justify himself or to pretend that his creations are ultimately valuable. Now he can peer into the deepest recesses of his own life, and into his own vital center, without despair and without illusion.

The human spirit is created to be led by truth to a love of being; and this is why the lie is an ontological disaster and not merely a social error. The joy the spirit in us feels in having the truth (better to say "being in the truth") is the joy of home-coming, the condition in which every native power is oriented upon the good appropriate to it.

In Jesus Christ God shows man once and for all that his longing for home is the seal and signature of the Creator: what the essential spirit in us seeks as the good really exists, because God exists, and He does not lie.

The spirit caught up in the life of faith lives therefore in a great essential tension. God assures man that the love of home is absolutely authentic; and He judges every human longing for that home, and every claim to have found that home, by His Kingdom revealed in Jesus Christ. But this means that otherworldliness is as treacherous an orientation for the life of faith as worldliness is. Otherworldliness can betray the Christian into hatred of the world. Worldliness can make him think that an attractive chateau is the mansion prepared for him from the foundation of the cosmos. In between these two false poles of orientation the man of faith must find the faithful relationship to real time and to the Eternal God.

Jesus Christ is the beginning and the end. Apart from him (so far as the person of faith can imagine such a state) man is a pilgrim here: out of the very roots of our being springs a pure necessity to interrogate every ostensible reality, to learn what it can tell us about being and the good. In Jesus Christ we see that this very necessity bears witness to the good of being: the end exists in the beginning and is not postulated by man to mask the terror of being in the world.

II

We have begun this phase of our argument by offering certain propositions taken from the great storehouse of Christian reflection on Jesus Christ. The intention in the selection is to indicate the kind of reality upon which the Christian stands to understand and to interpret the world, so far as he is faithful. Before we continue in this direction we must pause to consider a kink in the mind of the present age, a condition we have already recognized as the preoccupation with presuppositions. Unless this condition can be remedied, Christian criticism will be confounded with criticism in general; and criticism in general will continue to be understood as "civilization becoming conscious of itself and in the process rising to new levels of value." We have seen that the preoccupation with presuppositions is one of the deepest and most formidable anxieties of the age. As an anxiety it is the emotional dimension of the quest for the ontological foundations upon which the castle of truth may be erected. As an anxiety it is also an expression of helplessness in controlling the direction and the momentum in which contemporary civilization moves.

Let us begin therefore with two elementary questions.

1. What is a presupposition?
2. What would be added to a presupposition by calling it an absolute presupposition?

1. We have said before that the present age has become acutely conscious of presuppositions because it has learned that all thought, and probably all significant action, is determined by assumptions the validity of which cannot be vindicated except in a very loose way by the value of the thinking and the action they make possible, i.e., make intelligible. This is a very loose vindication indeed, since the criteria of such value are either the original assumptions or other assumptions smuggled into the operation. A presupposition is therefore something necessarily taken for granted as valid and taken to be valid in such a way as to defy every rational effort to prove its validity. Thus a curious relationship emerges: if something really is a presupposition, its validity can only be asserted (or postulated), it cannot be proved. And so people often say today that presuppositions must be taken on faith.

Accordingly, as principles both necessary and arbitrary presuppositions are a cause for uneasiness in sophisticated minds, and on both counts. Sophisticated relativists are worried about the necessity which a presupposition has. Sophisticated rationalists are worried about the arbitrariness of presuppositions. As relativists we know too much about the relativities of culture seriously to believe that any claim for real necessity can be anything more than cultural pride. As rationalists we find it hard to credit the claim that the fundamental principles of reason are arbitrary.

The ontological quest is therefore not likely to provoke enthusiastic support from either camp. The pursuit of truth amid plausible appearances presupposes the value of truth. To recognize the value of truth is to confess something about man's being, namely, that man is created to know *what is* (simply another way of saying Being), and to govern his life accordingly. Thus the value of truth is ontological rather than psychological or cultural. The force of this seems to carry us toward the identification of this ontological value as an absolute presupposition.

2. What would be added to a presupposition by calling it an absolute presupposition? Two possibilities occur to us.

a. There must be a principle which is the foundation for every legitimate exercise of man's rational-cognitive powers. This possibility is immediately threatened with being driven back into disposition or attitude rather than formal logical principle, for suppose we say that truth is just such a principle, or that reason is clearly a better thing than nonreason. These proposals sound very much like recommendations of certain dispositions and attitudes as being more favorable to serious inquiry and honest communication than others. I am sure that this is the case; and I am just as sure that so far we do not have a logical principle on our hands. But if we try to formulate a propositional principle concerning truth which is presupposed by any and all other propositions, what will emerge? "Truth is ascertainable," a proposition the denial of which assumes its truth. Or, "reality can be known," again, a proposition the denial of which assumes its truth. But surely the fact that such propositions cannot be denied without suffering the pangs of self-contradiction does not make them the absolute formal condition of all thinking. They are appeals to a state of affairs in which human thinking goes forward productively. It is this state of affairs which is a necessary condition for productive thought and, for all we know, for sound and sensible behavior.

b. There is a less ambitious interpretation of the claim that some presupposition is absolute, and we shall illustrate this from our own necessities as Christian critics of contemporary civilization. Christian criticism (such is our argument) owes its essential quality to its being derived from faith in God revealed in Jesus Christ. Remove, or even seriously qualify, that presupposed faith, and what remains is not consistently and authentically Christian (although it might be interesting and useful on some other grounds). So we should not expect a Christian to deny that his faith in Christ is the necessary disposition and attitude (commitment, the theologians generally say now) for his work as a critic of the world around him.

This conclusion seems to return us to the (a) sense of absolute presupposition, with the single addition: the necessary state of affairs for Christian criticism is that one should be a Christian.

It will surely seem quixotic to quarrel with such a clear, consistent, and compelling conclusion, but quarrel with it we must, because it has been very widely taken to mean that Christian faith and criticism make sense only to a Christian, that is, to someone afflicted with those peculiar presuppositions. Christians today have found it very easy (and very persuasive, they hope) to reply: "But *all* presuppositions are peculiar (i.e., arbitrary) to the people who do not share them. So you (the nonbeliever) have your presuppositions, and we Christians have ours."

In this way, along this route, many sophisticated Christians have come to praise God for the arbitrariness of all presuppositions, and for His wisdom in making every expression in the interest of truth an expression of a faith which cannot be rationally validated except by good works of one kind or another.

I do not see how the Gospel of Jesus Christ can be preached to the whole world on such a basis. On this basis the Gospel can be preached to the whole world only by doctoring the grand principle of election to fit the situation of historical-cultural relativity. The tragic consequence of this theological (more nearly, sociological) surgery is that the unity of man is again dismembered, this time into cultural units, civilizations, perhaps even further into epochs of a civilization, which jabber meaninglessly at one another across the chasms created by—presuppositions!

We must therefore have a further look into presuppositions which manage to be both absolute and culturally contingent.

III

It has been said that the absolute foundation of every civilization is a value judgment which cannot be evaluated but must simply be taken for granted. Such a value is the absolute presupposition of a civilization. When such a value is finally exposed to evaluation, when it is vulnerable to criticism, it loses its absoluteness. When this happens civilization has entered another epoch; or it has ceased altogether to exist as an effective synthesis of human interests and energies.

The English philosopher, Collingwood, has made much of this view in his interpretation of history. Some Christian theologians have adopted this kind of relativism for the interpretation of a faith rather different from Collingwood's. Back of Collingwood looms Hegel, who of course would have been appalled, if not refuted, by this relativistic reduction of the Absolute. But it was Hegel who taught his time, and ours, how to absorb history into the human subject, without remainder. And this is another momentous ontological disaster. In Hegel the absolute Subject transcends but also incorporates the ego, but this does not really soften the blow. In fact, this is part of the disaster because it means that civilization (the superego) now becomes all the God there is. The consequence is man's self-deification. Collingwood's merit, if such it be, is to have shown that there are many gods, that is, as many gods as there are civilizations each having its own absolute presuppositions.

What could be more appealing to the present necessities of Christian thought? Christian values are the foundation of Western civilization. These cannot be effectively modified by evaluation without destroying the fabric of this mighty cultural achievement. So Christian values are the absolute presupposition of our world; and the Christian, above all others, ought therefore piously to accept these values and valiantly defend the civilization erected upon them, not only against external enemies who have their own presuppositions, but also from internal criticism. This is the route along which God and the American Destiny become two names for one ideal.

This view assumes a total lack of access to culture-transcending actuality. Man must be guided and judged by what his civilization offers as its best wisdom, because he has no access to the demands of the good, and of being, otherwise. From this it follows that changes in a civilization must be determined by subrational powers, which together constitute a biological and sociological fate. People within a civilization have (or may have) a certain transcendence of aspiration, that is, they may desire a better life than they enjoy now; but this transcendence is simply social ideality. Civilization draws heavily upon such ideality because it alone seems to yield the decisive answer to the question, Is life worth living? The present condition of man must be graced with reflection upon what he may yet become within the boundaries of that social order, or at the very least upon what he might have been but for cruel chance. The latter is the ideality of the subjunctive contrary to fact and to historical likelihood; but it is not without its comfort. The former is the ideality held within the iron boundaries of the presuppositions of that civilization; and it is much more likely to satisfy the imagination if not to modify behavior.

Moreover this historical-relativistic view overlooks one of the most salient aspects of Western civilization, and that is the persistence in it of the will to learn and obey the will of God who is infinitely more than the internal spirit of this civilization. Superego as well as ego must answer to the righteousness of God, The Holy One, The Almighty Father. Before Him all other fatherhood, real and specious, benign and vicious, must bow into the dust. So the Christian should be the last to give his assent to the view that human existence is bounded by civilization and culture. The human possibility can be realized only in a society, to be sure. As constituents of a society people may be viewed as so many instruments designed to carry out its functions. In this sense it is intelligible to speak of persons as being products of a civilization. But essentially man is not an instrument and he is not a product. He is a person, and he comes to be a person in a pattern of relationships itself personal, that is, in a community not created by nor limited to any concrete social order. The responsibilities of life in family, clan, race, church, nation, etc. are real enough. The reality of these responsibilities rests essentially in personal decision. The actualities of these, or any other institutions, cannot make human life personal. The creative powers of personal existence can transform all of these duties to the praise of God and all of them can be infused with love of mankind. Creativity of this kind (or of any other kind) cannot be reduced to that quasi-reality, the social constituent who wears the many masks of social necessity and permissibility but who has no soul of his own.

The Christian must be even more alert than others to the threats to freedom and creativity posed by a civilization ostensibly Christian.

Even if it were the case that the fundamental values of this civilization were indisputably Christian, it would not follow that the Christian could only accept them rather than judge them. It is one thing, as we have said, to recognize the continuing influence of historical Christianity upon the value systems of western society, even though these systems have in fact included strongly conflicting elements. It is another thing to recognize that Christian values are now often vestigial sentimentalities with very little power either to illuminate or to direct the course of contemporary civilization. These sentimentalities are often invoked to disguise the real conflicts in the value systems of contemporary society. As such they belong to the realm of illusion. Once this is understood the only serious question to be considered is whether they are illusions necessary for the preservation of this civilization.

So far as he is faithful the Christian believes that the demands of the righteous God revealed in Jesus Christ transcend every value system. Criticism of the values he shares with the age in which he lives is part of his service offered to his Lord. It is the will of God that he should accept and rejoice in whatever is good in the world around him. To discern and rightly to relate himself to the good of the world he must learn to distinguish what is real from the specious, what is true from the merely plausible, what is good from its counterfeits, what is beautiful from the merely pretty and ingratiating. Contemporary civilization, indeed any civilization, is a mixture of all of these. Therefore he preaches, and not merely to his fellow Christians, that man is not a mere creature of the social order in which he finds himself.

These demands of God assume that there is a criterion at hand to make their acceptance intelligible. Jesus Christ is this criterion. The anxious confused quest for absolute presuppositions seeks a way through to Being so massive and so insistent upon its own rights that every human concealment comes to grief against it. This quest, characteristically modern, runs aground on the presumptive absoluteness of civilizations claiming that such Being is disclosed absolutely in their particular histories.

IV

The revelation of God in Jesus Christ is the disclosure of such being. Here God discloses structures and powers which are not created by man yet in relationship to which man finds the fulfillment of his possibility. The Christian accepts Christ's commandment of love because he knows in Christ that reality is ordered to this end and ruled by this power. The Christian is not obliged to love because "Christian" civilization recommends it as a high value. "We love because he [God] loved us first." So "he who loves God must also love his brother." (I John 4:19, 21, NEB.) To love others as God in Christ loves us is to be rightly related to being and the good.

This is just the point at which we have to admit not only that there are things we know about being and human being apart from Jesus Christ, but also that some of these things are essential for the right interpretation of the knowledge we have in Jesus Christ. Not to admit these things, or to refuse to develop them, is to make the wrong assertion of the absoluteness of Jesus Christ. The mysteries of being and human existence are not silenced or cleared up by shouting "Jesus Christ" as loudly as possible.

This does not mean that we know adequately what we need to be saved from (or what questions to ask) before we lay hold of salvation. It means only that we must consider some of the root elements of man's being with which knowledge must cope whether or not one is religiously oriented. These are:

1. Death.
2. Love.
3. Creativity.
4. Anxiety.
5. Guilt.

Civilization has a great deal to say about all of these. But each of them has its own brute reality. None of them is really mastered by civilization. The failure of a civilization to concede this is a very decisive failure indeed.

1. *Death.* I know that I am mortal. Essentially I do not *judge* that I am mortal, "I feel it in my bones." This ontological intuition does not tell me all that death means, of whether it is good or bad, or whether I shall somehow surmount it to live again. Intuitively death is a direct encounter with powers which cannot be escaped or conquered. This encounter is not merely eschatological: everyday I die a little because something I cherish and something I am perishes.

2. *Love.* I know that I live by, in, and from love. I sense an essential kinship with humankind, and I give assent to what I am kin to. I desire another human being with so great a desire that if the

other is not there to respond, I am beside myself, I am less than myself. I sense that another desires me; and if I am dead to all such sensing, I am less than human. Without the appetite called love, and the power of enjoyment called love, and the policy called love, I am dead to the world, I am a lost cause, I am a nullity accidentally clothed in human flesh.

3. *Creativity.* I am a radical thrust seeking expression, not to be free of unbearable tension but because I am one with the creative thrust of life; but I am also one with the creative lure of spirit. So to create a world, to make a thing, to think a thought, I must harness a hand, a voice, a brain to a teleology which life alone does not know. I can not only become what I am not; I can create what has never existed before.

4. *Anxiety.* I know that my creative thrust, my essential hunger for expression, may misfire. Endowed with imagination (the power of entertaining reality as image alone), I people the present and the future with threats not only to life but to creativity. I am able to anticipate evils which can destroy me. I am able to anticipate good which may not befall me. Thus anxiety is one of my essential relations to time.

5. *Guilt.* Of all the creatures of the world, man alone is the guilty one. Laws and their systems of penalties and rewards work because I am a creature of guilt. Society can make me feel guilty for all kinds of things, from pinching my baby sister, to not doing something about hungry Hindus, to not having done anything (what could I do?—a question beside the point) to prevent the murder of six million Jews. But unless I have, as an essential component of my being, the sense of disparity between Is and Ought, the moral instruction society lavishes upon me (or ought to) is wasted effort. The moment in which I grasp this disparity, this raging inextinguishable conflict, for the first time, is the most shattering moment in my history. It is the fall from innocence into moral complexity. And there is no return. So guilt is one of my essential relations to time.

A civilization is (and not just offers) a particular interpretation of the ontological essentials. The interpretation assigns values to these brute intuitions of human existence. For example, "death is preferable to dishonor." This value does not deny that death is an evil, it says that there are greater evils, specifically, alienation from one's community because one has betrayed it. "Death before dishonor" can become a cliché. There are many people who would still be living, after a fashion, had they not believed it was true.

Human existence would be unbearable without some such system of interpretation, without some such ordering of the human essentials by a system of value. This is why it is nonsense to talk about "primitive" and "instinctive" wisdom. The intelligible interpretation of ontological intuitions, that is, rendering them somehow coherent and oriented upon a stable good, is a desperately hard, unbelieveably advanced spiritual process. The basic elements do not fall into pattern by themselves. Man must puzzle out and piece together a comprehensive pattern. In some ways the most shocking dispensation of providence is the freedom man has to kick all of this achievement to pieces and revert, not to barbarism, but to nonhumanity, to become, not a beast of the field, but a wantonly destructive simulacrum of man.

V

As the Son of Man, as fully human, Jesus Christ reckoned with the realities with which every man and every civilization must reckon. He came into a human world, not into a howling unbroken wilderness. Christian thinkers began very early to say that this same Jesus Christ is the very being through whom the cosmos was created; and that his history includes the whole history, the whole historical being, of man (cf. Col. 1:13-20). Such claims are made with a view to establishing Jesus Christ as a being who exists in preeminent dignity and power before as well as in and over time and the world. These are grand claims. Our interest in them has a narrower focus than the cosmos, namely, man's essential being. Here the Christian claim is that the power and purpose Jesus Christ reveals in the reconstitution of human existence are precisely the power and purpose by which human existence is originally constituted. No one, no matter how unbearably splendid the burden of inspiration, could know this to be true from personal observation. God's question to Job, "Where were you when I laid the foundation of the earth?" (38:4, RSV), is just as decisive for St. Paul, Plato, Einstein, and John Doe. It is known to be so because of the grasp Jesus Christ has on the essentials of human existence, a grasp inexhaustibly creative. Neither a man nor a god has any right or power (their unity: authority) to reconstitute man's being unless he has a perfect mastery of the ground plan. Jesus Christ himself puts his followers, in every age, on guard against false messiahs and pseudo-saviors; and we must include in that wretched company our own contemporaries who talk so glibly, and when given the power, behave so abominably, in the interest of modifying man. Every moral man, but Christians especially, ought to be supernaturally dubious about saviors and rebuilders of man who plunge in and hope for the best—for themselves.

So, to take but one case from the human essentials, Jesus Christ does not bring to man for the first time the knowledge of human mortality. As a man he also contended with the sense of mortality, he had the taste of death in his mouth, he drained the cup, "and in obedience accepted even death—death on a cross" (Phil. 2:8 NEB). This same Jesus God the Almighty Father brought forth from death and has established as the everlasting Lord of Resurrection. This is to say that the reconstitution of man's being begins with this absolute mastery of mortality. The mastery of Christ has not extinguished mortality—in case this fact had eluded attention!—but he makes possible the right expression of our mortality in the two prime modes: (a) "Fear him rather who is able to destroy both soul and body in hell" (Matt. 10:28, NEB); (b) "If anyone wishes to be a follower of mine, he must leave self behind; he must take up his cross and come with me" (Matt. 16:24, NEB).

Such mastery of the essentials of human existence comes only from the perfection of God's love. This is the power by which all things are created. And this is why Christian faith teaches that God the Almighty Father has done all of His creating through Jesus Christ.

We shall not undertake here to give an account of the work of Jesus Christ relative to all of the prime elements of man's being. The moral of the story of redemption is our present interest. In Jesus Christ God affirms man unqualifiedly; and He who so affirms man is the one to whom man belongs. No root element of human existence is alien or forbidding to Jesus Christ. He does not thread an anxious way through the City of Man like a fastidious Christian dreading (expecting?) to have either his virginity or his sense of smell outraged, or—O fate harsh beyond all endurance!—both at once.

So the question whether there is a human world already existing when Jesus Christ appears, turns out not to be very helpful or very important, except, perhaps, as a way of putting the affirmation of the Incarnation in a proper setting. If there had been no real world already existing there could have been no real Incarnation. The more telling question is what we learn about our being in the revelation of God as the Incarnate Lord. The faithful answer to this is that the Incarnate Lord, Jesus Christ, is the absolute norm of human existence. He is the sole and sufficient authority in the Christian criticism of civilization.

VI

Christian criticism is founded on the presence of God transcendent in the actual world. Let us note at once that "transcendent" has nothing essentially to do with being apart from other beings. To say that God is transcendent is to say: (a) He surpasses all other beings in richness of power and value; (b) His action springs purely and freely from His own purpose, His own inner life. Thus neither sense of "transcendent" has anything to do with the primitive question, "Where does God live?" God revealed in Jesus Christ is wholly present in the world, He is in the world but in it everywhere and always as Himself, the Lord of lords. For this He does not have to vacate some other place. When we say that He is wholly present in the world we mean that He is here dealing with us as He is in Himself; and He is here permitting Himself to be dealt with. He is a presence. He can operate as easily here as from the throne of heaven. He is entirely and absolutely Himself in this attention.

The terrible and beautiful power of Jesus' glance is a striking analogical expression of this presence of God. Jesus gives nothing a mere sidelong or veiled look, there is nothing merely casual in the way he looks at a person, there is nothing distracted or fractional in the attention he gives. In everyday encounters undivided attention is as formidable as it is rare. Just a taste of it is unnerving, quite enough to make one wonder why it was ever asked for and how soon it will end. In Jesus Christ this formidable power of attention is augmented to the nth degree. The disguises of small talk and of ingratiating mannerisms dissolve before that power; and the parties of the second part, the persons caught in this power of attention, begin to wonder whether they will ever be the same. The question is the right one. Really to be known is a very wonderful but also a very chancy thing: will there be anything left to know, and to love and be loved by, if all disguises are dissolved?

The norm of Christian judgment of the world is then God transcendent revealed as wholly present in Jesus Christ. The things of the world, the world itself, are to be judged as grasped by the power and truth of His presence. Is this not to say that things are to be judged as they are seen by God? Yes, but the way this is understood is important. The righteousness of God has been made known and therefore it is not necessary to guess what God demands.

Christian criticism is therefore different in principle from every effort to win divine approval for the achievements and aspirations of civilization. It is different from every kind of effort to have our own way by claiming God's authority for our ego purposes.

Nevertheless we must admit that the differences in principle are much easier to confess than the concrete differences are to trace. But the latter must be undertaken. We shall do so by considering again the ideality of civilization, that transcendence which is a familiar and indispensable component of civilization.

VII

Christianity came into a world in which the transcendence of ideality in and over the empirical order had already achieved formulations of immortal beauty. The most powerful minds of pagan culture had represented truth, beauty, and the good as not only absolutely and eternally valid ideals but as the highest reality. Some Christian theologians (ever since called Apologists) responded to this situation by asserting that ideality is a way of talking about the same God whom Christians worship as the father of Jesus Christ. Truth, beauty, and the good are fully realized in this one living God. So it is by no means unseemly for the human mind to ascend to Him who is *ens perfectissimum* by contemplating the imperfect realizations of the ideal in the empirical world. Other theologians, early and late, have insisted that any such apology is a capital error because it attempts to make a synthesis out of strictly incompatible components, paganism and Biblical revelation.

This controversy is important for us because it concerns the very heart of the Christian criticism of civilization. I contend that the rejection of apologetics is itself an error. The rejection of apologetics is very likely to convert the purity of Biblical faith into an ideal that cannot be compromised because it cannot be realized. But the rejection of apologetics is itself to be rejected for a more serious reason. It makes an adequate interpretation of the dialectic of the Kingdom of God impossible. Without that dialectic the world of divine creation and of divine redemption splits into two unreal and mutually hostile parts. Even pagan minds were uneasy about such a view of the world.

Therefore we must suggest why the dialectic of the Kingdom of God does not demand the outright rejection of the archetypal idealities of culture.

1. To say that God is Truth ascribes to Him both (a) truth of being and (b) truth of witness.

a. Truth of being is the identity of intention and power in God. God is what He purposes. He is therefore simple, a perfect unity, where man is composite and complex.

b. Truth of witness is the identity of promise and performance. What He reveals of Himself is so, He is what He says He will do. He says of Himself that He does not go back on His word. His word is His bond, His self-disclosure is His covenant, by His word He binds Himself to the world to the end of time. *Veritas Dei*: of the faithfulness of God there is no end.

Thus on both counts, (a) and (b), God as Truth is His absolutely personal being. Truth is not an ideal subsisting in timeless splendor.

Accordingly when the church assails the sins and shortcomings of an age relative to truth, it does so because truth is an ontological requirement and not merely a social obligation or a philosophical puzzle. Society must have truth in the (b) sense, in order to exist; and this is a way of saying that truth is an essential requirement of man's being. Man has the gift for creating illusions and deceits; but his attachment to counterfeit violently distorts his being. This power to create counterfeit, and to love it more than reality cannot carry man beyond the Kingdom of God. The distortion he so forces upon his own being is an aspect of the dialectic of the divine Kingdom. With the ethical idealists the Christian believes that the moral order is inviolable. But the Christian does not believe that the moral order is self-administering. It has too much "give" either to conform to the classical image of an immutable order, or for the peace of mind of the moral agent. If crime did not pay there would be no criminals. If crime always paid there would be no society and, again, no criminals. The criminal in his projects if not in his performance presupposes law but not punishment. The vigilante presupposes the right of punishment but not law. In between is the great mass which knows that policemen rather than logic catch criminals, and bad judges are better than good vigilantes. The moral order is so flexible, in fact, that one can get away with a good deal in this life, with a bit of luck and a sufficient concentration of stupidity and/or good faith in others. But the figure of speech, "getting away with it," is oddly wrong. Where do you go? The intelligent rule breaker or plunderer or what-not does not even try to "get away." His best chance is to disguise himself and stay put for the duration. The immoralist's best move (unless he is a mere *poseur* hoping to tell all in his memoirs) is to adopt the disguise of a moral man.

This is but one illustration of the propensity ingrained in man's life in civilization to live in illusion. The lovers and doers of truth seem always to be a tragic elite, the heroic few, the prophets without honor. And how easy it is for them to be corrupted by cynicism or by self-righteousness, and in either condition to fashion the Great Lie or withdraw in disgust or madness from the lying world!

Contemporary civilization cuts a rather graceless figure in the matter of truth. On the abstract intellectual front this is the age that represents itself as tracking the truth with unflagging zeal. Yet illusion and deceit are stock-in-trade in the everyday world. For the sake of a place in the sun of this world many are ready to credit the lie that appearances matter above everything else and that the highest necessity is to make a good impression on the right people, who in turn are trying to make a good impression on even righter people, and so on all the way to the top of the pecking order. Presumably the man at the top has only God upon whom to make a good impression, which perhaps helps to account for the "in" status of religion among the people at the top. So people keep up with the arts (and to a lesser extent with the sciences), in order to make the good impression. They express fine opinions, even where they have no knowledge, in order to make the good impression. Men use a particular after-shave lotion to attract and inflame desirable women—a risky kind of good impression. Whether men are really taken in by such appeals, or women by such anointed men, no one really seems to know. But the pitch sells the goods; and the pitcher makes the money; and if he makes enough of it he at least does not need to worry about his after-shave scent.

If one can believe some of the economic theorists, the fast-pitch artist, the huckster, is very nearly a metaphysical necessity in our economy, because this economy requires an ever-rising productivity and an ever-rising productivity requires an ever-rising level of consumption. For these lofty purposes taste and desire are controlled by the system. The buyer does not know what he wants, or whether he wants anything he does not have at the moment, until the huckster hits him. Thereafter he is not encouraged to discriminate between what he really wants and needs and what he appears to want and need. Of course he cannot really have everything he may want, but if only he could!—That would be heaven, for the producers and advertisers.

It is hard to avoid the conclusion that to live responsibly in the Affluent Society is to be a consumer so suggestible, indeed so voracious, that the ancient bugaboo of bankruptcy is impotent to call a halt to the ingestion of the goodies being produced in ever-increasing volume.

But this is one of the less taxing tensions between illusion and reality in our world. A much more formidable one is the conflicting demands to be at once a useful member of society and a real person. To be useful means to play well a whole repertory of roles. To be a real person is to have that core of personal reality once called the soul. A person is said to be shallow or superficial unless he displays that core. But the tides of contemporary civilization run strongly against this hard-core soul, this center of personal reality. The Image is more important by far than the Soul. The everyday world's biggest rewards go to the person who plays his roles most adroitly and manages to present to the world a smooth-textured, carefully composed image. The greatly admired image is the useful and harmonious person, the real teamplayer. The everyday world pays off on face, not on soul, on image, not on substance, on playback, not on creative expression. Blessed are they who have no souls out of which harmony-wrecking thrusts might come, bringing disorder and confusion to the brightly polished brassy mirrors!

There are other symptoms of the disease of untruthfulness, and again our diagnosis must be ontological. In our world we are compelled to struggle with false readings of the distinction between actuality and possibility. Frustrated, if not ruined, by the social demands we have just railed at, we find specious comfort in the contemplation of the counterfeit possibility of what-might-have-been, the subjective contrary to fact and historical likelihood. Thereby possibility is detached from an organic relationship to what is and is to be, and becomes a sterile sentimentality.

Contemporary civilization has created a subworld out of this specious mode of possibility. Entertainment is the proper name for that subworld. Entertainment as a subworld has an absolute presupposition: a fundamental need to be distracted from engagement with the actualities. A fabric of sterile but glamorous sentimentality is spun from this assumption. The harassed, confused, and frustrated housewife (troubled as much as anything by the feeling that being a "mere housewife" is a dismal failure), is given an ideal life by the entertainment world. She is given an ideal lover in ideal surroundings (out of *Better Homes and Gardens*). Magically she becomes the ideal woman she might have been if the actualities had not been so uncooperative. As for her husband, entertainment has something for him too. It gives him a dream world populated with luscious creatures from whom every unloveliness of scent, sound, touch, and familial demand has been thoughtfully removed. He may not be good enough for his real wife but in his fantasies he is the ever-ready inexhaustibly potent male animal, the stag rampant, equal to every demand of the love-queens fed into his imagination. Jane and John Doe did not get this way without help. They are the triumphant creation of unreality. Their descent into idealized implausibilities of sensibility and action was carefully prepared. Passion, wit, and cunning went into it. Entertainment is a great, expensive, and productive business, and it is run as such enterprises are generally run in this civilization. So that is why we say a great deal of thought, passion, and money went into the corruption of the sensibility and imagination of the Does. It will take more than hope and holy water to get them out of unreality, even on bail, because sentimentalized possibility exacerbates every hurt inflicted by actuality. They now judge the real world with fraudulent criteria. Their motivations and performances are coated over with film upon film of self-justification and self-excuse.

We must take care lest rhetorical excess in the judgment of entertainment blind us to its therapeutic values. Surely escapism is to be preferred to neurosis. People must get away from everything once in a while, if they are to keep the wheels of the everyday world turning. But neurosis is possible only when the reality principle has not already been severed. Escapist entertainment does not strengthen the reality-principle directly. We might cheerfully admit that escape may restore vitality. Reality without vitality is a great affliction, almost as great as reality without purpose. On the other hand, prayer, fasting, sleep, exercise, and aesthetic creativity are restoratives of proven efficacy. Unlike entertainment they do not in principle split attention and devotion between two sets of value.

Real possibility, as distinguished from its sentimental counterfeit, is a potentiality in the relation of an agent to an actual situation. The realization of such a possibility would increase the value either of the agent or of the situation or of both. Real possibility therefore is not the mere projection of wish or hunger uninstructed either by actuality or by ideality. (Poetic fancy is very different from fantasy, since the poet infuses richness of value into actuality by the power of a disciplined imagination. The real poet has a great hunger for being and no interest in sentimental possibility. He sings what is and has been and is to be. The rhythm of the song tells us something about being which mere factual reporting could not.)

So when we say of someone's fantastical project "It is impossible" we may not mean "It cannot be done." I say "That is impossible!" to a man who has just announced to me his intention to run away with his mistress, leaving wife, children, job, and mortgage to shift for themselves. But of course he *can* do it, as he may prove before lunch. What he cannot do by that action is to increase the value either of himself or of the actual situation he is fleeing. He is intrigued by the vision of a new life, as well as oppressed by the actualities of his present one. But he shall have to become a new person to make much of anything of that vision; and, Devil take it! the vision will not make him the new person because he must make the vision an actuality. He wants to be an effect of the vision, but the vision is his creature. So if he does silly and immoral things on the strength of the vision, he is still the cause. (It is possible that his wife, children, etc. will eventually be better off without him; but if that is the way it works out, it is no fault of his.)

So, again, nothing or nobody ought to make us more wary than promises to make new creatures of us. Mere men and half-gods are certain to botch the job. They may make something new, to be sure, but it will have less value than the old. In the human line only God can be trusted to make something really new and really good of the old human stuff. Being not only all-wise but also everlasting, God can both anticipate the consequences and endure them!

We summarize as follows: the demands of truth are built into our bones, they are of God. We can lie and cheat, and we can build a house, a world, of lies. But since we cannot lie to God we must be lying to ourselves, each to himself, each to his fellows. Thus God puts us in a very awkward spot: we lie and we know that we lie, we make counterfeit and we know that it is counterfeit. We are not the creatures and victims of a lying civilization, we are its creators. But we are absent-minded creators.

VIII

2. The good is another form of the ideal to which Christian thinkers have made affirmative responses. The general pattern of apologetic theology requires that the good be understood as the goodness of God. Thus again the appeal made by civilization to ideality is not simply wrong but is something that requires correction by acknowledgment of the revealed God. This God is without defect of purpose, His will is righteous altogether. His righteousness is the absolute perfection of love. So His goodness is supremely transitive: it proceeds from Himself as Subject to the cosmos of objects, all of which owe their being to the perfection of His goodness.

Natural man can only find it outrageously implausible that so sublime a being would or could lend Himself to communion with so absurd a creature as man. The sense of this absurdity is one of the triumphant religious achievements of high paganism. It probably deserves more respect than halfhearted Christianity. The high-minded pagan believed that a real God would not compromise his perfection, if it were a perfection of the good, by hobnobbing with men; man is only man even when he suffers a divine *afflatus*. High-minded pagans looked to the ideal world for their principles but not in any expectation that the ideal world would look back at them.

The Christian believes that the perfection of goodness, the living God, has indeed looked at him; but not as an object to be pitied from afar, rather as a subject, a living spirit, with whom God has chosen to have communion. The immediate consequence of this seems to be an aim and criterion simply impossible of entertainment and application by mere creatures: the goodness of God. In this situation the idealism of paganism becomes very attractive once again.

The immediate consequence, so drawn, is a mistake. In the community God has created in Jesus Christ man is not rebuked because he is always and necessarily less than God. He is rebuked because he is less than an adopted son of the Kingdom ought to be. Man is not rebuked because he is finite but because he clutches at moral ambiguity as though it were the rod of his salvation.

This ambiguity is itself distorted by the moralism of the contemporary religious life. Moralism is more than the reduction of moral imperatives to conventional morals. Moralistic reductions are geared into a view of Providence and of divine rewards and punishments. Inevitably moralism becomes a basis and a justification for splitting the human community. The sheep and the goats, the righteous and the unrighteous, must be separated here and now; and the goats are not to wait until the last Judgment to be penalized. The separation cannot always be physical, of course—in the actual world the righteous are always being breathed on by the unrighteous (which Providence must sometime justify). The separation is a spiritual-ethical alienation, which is far deadlier. The righteous man does not have to love the unrighteous man. The righteous man loves the community of the righteous, he loves his own reflection. So the Outs, the unrighteous, the unworthy, are objects both of human rejection and of presumptive divine disapproval. This follows both from the simple fact that they *are* Outs and from the feeling of divine approval that the Ins enjoy.

When moralistic piety is combined with the aims, principles, and rewards of a business civilization, the distinction between the Ins and the Outs becomes as simple as child's play. There must be something spiritually amiss in the wretchedly poor. There must be something spiritually sound in the man who succeeds.

Christians do not have a monoply of the moralistic heresies. Moralism has permeated our civilization. This is not something for which the church needs to congratulate itself. Quite to the contrary, there is something demonic in the reduction of the demands of God's righteousness to simple rules for all occasions of moral decision, great and small; and in teaching that conformity to these rules fulfills the will of God and qualifies the conformer for happiness and prosperity on earth and eternal felicity thereafter. But it is too early (or too late) to reach for the demonic. For the moment we must be content to insist on the failure of moralism to do much of anything for the contemporary world except to administer self-righteousness to people rapidly losing the sense of self-existence.

The Gospel is the criterion of the church's judgment upon moralism. The attack upon moralism is pressed by other critics for other reasons. Here and there Christian critics join in the hue and cry against any ethic of rule as an immoral infringement of freedom. This zeal may carry the Christian critic far beyond what the Gospel requires the church to preach, namely, that the perfect righteousness of God cannot be reduced to copybook rules. God in His righteousness is infinitely unlike the self-righteous man. He does not hug His perfection to Himself. His being, His love of being, are transitive, communicative, creative, other-creating, other-loving. Thus God is infinitely more than the ideal to which every other being looks as to the perfect good. In the power of His goodness God is the one absolutely actual everlasting being.

Does it follow that God has no truck with rules (law) and that He cordially despises—almost as cordially as do the antinomians early and late—all rulekeepers? The question is a time-honored theological battleground. We shall take a detour around it, for the time being, because the dialectic of the Kingdom of God is our present concern. The righteousness of the Holy Kingdom is disclosed in the fact that the human image but not the human substance can be transformed and revalued downward. The substantial reality is not and will not be canceled by counterfeits. It can be obscured, but it cannot be canceled. It is God who decides this. If man were alone in the cosmos, if his history were an episode in cosmic time interesting and valuable only to himself (and even to himself only intermittently), there would be no limit to what he might attempt to do to his essential reality. By one device or another and for various purposes he might modify it. He might transmute his being into an unrecognizable horror, a horror *he* could not recognize or properly name and could live with only so far as he could forget what he had been. But—thank God!—this is all in the speculative mood contrary to fact. Despite all of the beastly scientific experimentations with the human substance, man is called to account before he seals himself into a hell of his own creation. He is called to account by the righteousness of the living God and not by a presumably immutable moral order. The sin of attempted transmutation of human being is not that it goes against the moral grain of reality. It is a violation of a personal trust. Any kind or degree of betrayal tends to infect the order of personal trust, but the massive structures of the social order can absorb many betrayals and many lies. This is a sign of their partial unreality. But on the other hand the order of personal trust is so strong that Death and Hell do not have even the strength of a babe in arms against it. Ah, yes: the drama of the Crucifixion requires a Judas. Alas for Judas! He could not endure the crucifixion his betrayal assured. Suppose that he had waited around for the Resurrection?

IX

3. The third archetype of classical cultural idealism is beauty. Let it be said to the great credit of classical culture that no epoch of Western civilization has ever taken with greater seriousness this demand of ontological perfection. Greek art from Homer through Plato owns a first and highest obedience to the world of ideal forms rather than to actuality. It cannot therefore be seriously charged with representationalism, naturalism, etc. Homer is not a historian, he is the mightiest of epic singers. Thanks to virtuosity of the highest order the ideal essences of mankind take on the verisimilitude of actual human beings and concrete entities. There is an amazing richness of contingent detail in his epics, but the contingent detail is of two kinds, each remarkably ontological: (a) the essential quality of a weapon or of a man: the "blood-thirsty spear," the man of courage, the man of sagacity, etc.; (b) the contingencies of Fate, the way things break, the situations and circumstances in which essence (Destiny) is revealed.

Idealism of the aesthetic mode is still a significant element of Western culture. The ideal lives on in the everyday world as a cherished sentimentality, but the creative spirits of the age seem to have rejected altogether the ancient worship of beauty. Thereby the situation of Christian criticism of contemporary civilization is considerably complicated. Of all of the grand avowals concerning God, the avowal that He is beautiful (or that He is beauty), is the one likely to communicate the least to this age. Among the sophisticated, beauty is a doubtful ideal (except for the worshipers of classical culture). It is an ideal which has been badly strained and torn by the conflict of sentimentalism with extreme realism. Sentimentalism reduces beauty to mere prettiness and exploits prettiness for the purposes of ornamentation. The realistic recoil scorns beauty as irrelevant to the expression of the brute actualities in necessarily distorted forms. (An aesthetic idealism of geometry rejects both parties of the conflict, and achieves its own rejection of beauty as an instructive ideal.)

What, then, is being neglected in this sad adventure of beauty in the contemporary world? Our answer must depend heavily upon our understanding of the ideal of beauty. If we agree that the ideal is a demand for balance of contrasts in the realization of a form, we shall properly conclude that beauty is a judgment upon prettiness. Prettiness is ingratiating precisely because of the absence of the tension created by contrast. The pretty gratifies easily and quickly, it does not stir or order the powerful emotions. The beautiful arrests attention and elicits powerful emotion. Beauty offers a gratification that may very well upset the "normal" scheme and flow of life.

How could we fail to think here of the parable of the pearl of great value (Matt. 13:45, 46)? The great value of the pearl is its beauty. A man who really perceives this will gladly trade away everything he owns in order to have so great a treasure. Beauty prompts us to do strange things. This is a similitude of the Kingdom of God!

Beauty is a demand of the divine Kingdom. It is a unique demand rather than a restatement of ethical and intellectual demands (the demands of the good and of the truth). God demands the fullest expression of human creative power in the realization of forms delightful in and for themselves.

But the dialectic of the Holy Kingdom is disclosed in the fact that these escapes from beauty carry man into sterile illusions. Nothing can prevent his seeking contentment with the merely pretty. He can extract perverse pleasure from the ugly. Yet that I can make my bed in hell (Ps. 139:8) is no indictment of heaven; and even in a chintzy pit the demands of God seek me out.

But the creative spirits, and not just the masses, seem to be in full revolt against the demands of the Holy Kingdom. Repelled by the sins committed in its name artists in the many realms of art reject beauty. Appalled by artful harlotry parading as beauty, serious artists prefer to honor truth, or function, or the integrity of the material—anything but beauty. So art becomes personal testimony; or form warped out of proportion by the brute "power of being"; or form released from all accountability to actuality.

This is not the whole story. It is an important part of the story because the flight from beauty has been dictated by a civilization remarkably successful in alienating consciousness from reality. This world makes it easier all of the time to fall in love with low-grade attainments of consciousness. Thereby ego comes at last to deny the richness of being beyond itself. What remains thereafter except to fashion a world out of the stuff of dreams and populate it with phantasms?

Fascination with abstract form is a very limited therapy for people bogged down in obsessive love of consciousness for itself. The divine therapy brings renewal both of the appetite for the richness of being and of faith in the processes of formalizing this richness according to the canon of beauty. But the Kingdom of God is always in our midst as judgment upon escape from the demands of beauty which counterfeit realizations seem to provide. This judgment is part of the divine therapy.

IX

God with man in Jesus Christ is an unqualified demand for the transformation of the human world into the likeness of the holy Kingdom. What man is by God's creation is thus quickened by what he hears in Jesus Christ. Apart from Christ man knows that he has an essential capacity for living beyond himself by relating himself to ideality. To be human is to grasp the essential meaning of one's being by relating it to a perfection of being beyond one's existence, even if the reality of this relation is seen in a fleeting irrecoverable moment of ontological disclosure. The anxious interior inspection of consciousness is not sufficient for this purpose, neither is the scanning of the past, nor the inspection of the auguries of the future. Rightly to grasp this relation of my being to a perfection of being beyond but not alienated from me, I must see myself in the life of another being. This indispensable other being cannot be chosen arbitrarily out of personal preference. That other being must meet the highest (indeed the absolute) standards of perceptiveness and judiciousness; and he must therefore infinitely surpass any mere reflection or projection of my own being; but not infinitely surpass in the mode of alienation. The infinite viewer of my being must so embrace my being in his that I can see myself through his seeing. If he were simply and purely apart from me, and even if I could see him truly, I should have only his word as to what he sees in me; and this would come to me as something external, alien, and threatening to my being. And the profit from this would be ultimate despair.

Thus we are confronted with ontological demands. As we struggle to meet them we learn that there is no real middle ground between joy and despair. Joy is the mode of Christian response because the Christian knows that he who sets these requirements is also the one who has communicated to man the power of his divine life to meet them. God has done this in Jesus Christ, who is therefore our good cheer. In communion with God in Jesus Christ, we may look upon our own being in the spirit of utter truth, and live to tell it, because in him the truth is mediated in perfect love. We truthfully see ourselves as weak, foolish, corrupt, and perverse. But we are redeemed from having to hate all that we are. What is saved out from the wrathy fire of that hatred is surely not an infinitesmal core of unsullied goodness. That soul is the central illusion which the flame of divine love, not of human self-loathing, burns away. The illusory soul burned away, we know that the reason for our existence is God's love only. As subjects of God's love, we cannot any longer hate ourselves with a hatred which is but the recoil of a self-love upon which the blazing sun of truth now bears down implacably. The love of our own being thus restored to health, power, and joy, we know that every other self-love is born of despair and withers in the fury of hatred. That flame burns most savagely when a man discovers that both in his interior inspection and in his reflections of himself in society he has made himself a god which is no-god, a pseudo-being as cruel and insatiable as it is illusory.

God is our judge and our redeemer. The unreality systems created by man threaten to throttle man's created possibility, or at the least to disfigure it. When therefore God speaks as present with us in Christ, our essential being stirs in drugged sleep and begins the struggle to welcome its true Lord. In this sense the essence of man is struggle, conflict, tension: man is an *agon,* a momentous contention with God. The end of the contention is disclosed in Jesus Christ: that we might become, in the whole circuit of our life, and in the vital center, what we are in the creative seeing of God. "Be transformed" is the imperative of the righteous God communicated in Jesus Christ. The essential struggle is the work to free "the original plan of creation," the created possibility, from the dead weight of character and institution produced to block or distort the full realization of the creative spirit. Victory in this struggle is impossible without the power of God. The name of Jesus Christ is also Immanuel: God with us.

CHAPTER IV

The Strategic Aims of Christian Criticism

I

The calling of the Christian is to obey the will of God revealed in Jesus Christ. The Christian obeys by seeking diligently to interpret the righteousness of God for the actual situation in which he lives. Christian existence is itself interpretation of the Gospel demands and promises of Christ's Kingdom.

Criticism is part of this life of interpretation. Its objective is the freedom of the human spirit to find the richest enjoyment of being. Only thus is God, the author of all things, properly praised and obeyed.

The calling of the Christian throws him into conflict with the negativities of civilization. He lives amid structures and powers that depress and distort human creativity. Accordingly, the first strategic aim of Christian criticism is rightly to identify these negativities. By God's design, man is a subcreator, a created creator. For such a creature no prayer is more fitting than the words of the psalmist: "establish thou the work of our hands upon us" (Ps. 90:17, RSV). Not all of the work of our hands, because some of it is evil; but the work in whose beauty, truth, or goodness God Himself, the Creator, rejoices.

It is evident, therefore, that the faithful person must do his utmost to prevent the interpretation of the gospel of God's Kingdom from being invaded by a spirit of negativity directed indiscriminately against the world. Jesus Christ is God's assurance that he has not rejected the world of human creation as though it had become so vile a thing that he could abide it no longer. Yet faith seems always to be vulnerable to corruption by the spirit of negativity. It is never more vulnerable to this corruption than when the Christian and the church have been treated badly by the world. Then it is very easy to remember how Jesus instructed his disciples to shake the dust off their feet as a judgment against the city that would not receive them (Matt. 10:14); and very hard to remember that this same Lord prayed from the cross, "Father, forgive them; they do not know what they are doing" (Luke 23:24, NEB).

II

Faithful judgment of the world requires a right understanding of it. We have contended that the right understanding of contemporary civilization rests on a penetration of its formations of essential human being. A civilization is a formulation of man's essential being as a community creature. "Man" (mankind) is the proper name for an indestructible commonalty expressed in richly variegated fabrics of social structure, character formations, aesthetic creations, religious objects, and cognitive achievements. Bantu hunter and Wall Street broker alike are masters and slaves of economic process. Medicine man and archbishop alike are masters and slaves of religious traditions. Jungle drummer and symphonic conductor alike are masters and slaves of rhythmic patterns engrained in the nature of things. This does not mean that these culturally diverse creatures enjoy the same mastery and offer the same obeisance in each case. No healthy interest is served by any attempt to minimize or to lament the immense variety of human creation and obeisance. But it is just as wrong to so maximize the variety that the sense of the human community is diminished. This is why we have begun by saying that it is part of the right understanding of contemporary civilization to see it as one particular systematic solution to the essential questions expressed everywhere in the human community, everywhere in human being. A civilization is a complex and often confusing dialogue between man and God, man and cosmos, these men in this time and place and the essential human community. The essential human problems and questions always have a concrete historical context, a civilization that modifies their thrust in one way or another. The Roman Empire in the third century and the United States in the twentieth alike struggle with the problems of economic stabilization. Diocletian struggled valiantly with the problem (he took only a little time off to persecute the Christians), and failed. We do not know yet whether we shall succeed. We do know that the problem is at once the same and very different; so even if he (Diocletian) had succeeded, it is not at all likely that his solution would have any concrete value for us. Drawing historical parallels may be an interesting intellectual game, but one wonders whether the men who have to make decisions are greatly instructed by it. Historical reality bristles with novelty. Conservatives in American life seem always to be forgetting this in their anxiety to find somewhere in the past an everlasting valid realization of an eternal ideal.

The virus of self-righteousness finds an opening in a certain generosity of concession that the human community is infinitely variegated in its concrete realizations. This seems strange only until one begins to reflect upon the need for a criterion of value with which to make the human variety intelligible. Thereupon one's own civilization becomes the most obvious candidate for the high office of concrete criterion. Using contemporary American civilization as the criterion we discover, not altogether to our surprise, that the Bantu hunter is a barely human creature wrapped in the densest superstitions. The Wall Street broker, in his rationality and enlightenment, seems hardly to share the human commonalty with the primitive. The archbishop is the culmination, the climax, of a spirituality that seems to have nothing in common with the medicine man, except in the abstractions of the social sciences. And who in his senses would put the urbane many-splendored symphonic conductor in the same spectrum with the jungle drummer?

So what is strange to us, especially if it is primitive, becomes the negative. What is familiar to us, and cherished by us as the adornment of spiritual process, is the positive.

Many things are happening now which make the simple-minded application of a self-righteous and simplistic criterion of value increasingly difficult. Christian criticism has hardly been as aggressive on this front as it ought to have been, because the Christian has a particular point to make in this situation. Value distinctions ought not to be obscured by the increasing awareness of cultural variety, or by the growing political necessities of doing business with primitive people. The aim of Christian criticism is to reinforce and clarify human solidarity. One way of doing this is to insist that judgment of value must first be vertical before it becomes horizontal: let the right criteria of judgment be applied all the way from the bottom to the top of our own civilization before we use our achievements as the criterion for judging others.

In judging others the Christian has another and related point to make. Each person is one with all, for better and for worse. Therefore a man ought not to judge another, near or far, friend or enemy, strange or familiar, as though he had no part in him. There is an essential human community. Each man must seek it in himself, each man must love it for all others. Persons can be together in many wrong ways. There is no right way in which they can be alienated from one another.

Self-righteousness is a spirit of alienation that wreaks terrible havoc upon essential community. It is therefore one of the negativities that Christian criticism must unsparingly expose. Christians will suffer in this exposure, whether more or less than others is a matter of no consequence. Our plight as Christians would then be wretched past all endurance if the church were sent into the world to preach its own righteousness, or the righteousness of Christian civilization, rather than the righteousness of God.

III

If it can be granted that negativity can invade the preaching of the Gospel, we may be tempted thereafter to fall into a kind of spiritlessness in carrying out the mission of the Kingdom in the world. We may preach the righteousness of God without any hope and without any concern for the concrete efficacy of the preaching. This is the negativity of Jonah, the nonhero of one of the most edifying books of the Old Testament. Jonah knows that Nineveh is marked for destruction because God is mightily displeased with its nauseating wickedness (1:2). Therefore the mission to Nineveh is simply to advertise its early and total destruction because God considers Nineveh an abomination (3:4). But suppose that the wicked people of Nineveh, from the peasant to the emperor, heed God's warning, advertised by Jonah, and proceed to do something about their situation, such as repenting and giving up their wicked ways? This is what happens in the Biblical story (3:5-9). It happens because the Ninevites do the unexpected: they credit Jonah's preaching as the authentic disclosure of God's righteousness. Thereby a splendid and soul-warming disaster is averted;

and this "displeased Jonah exceedingly" (4:1). He had hoped for the worst for the unrighteous. But God had used *him* to bring about their salvation. Suspecting from the beginning that the gracious God might trick him, he had tried to run out on his assignment (4:2). So now he is angry enough to die (4:3).

Jonah is an unwitting and reluctant realist. He knows that people, the wicked as well as the righteous, are unpredictably moved to do what God demands, once they are able to credit the preaching of God's righteousness. The objects of disaster-loving judgment may not behave according to the hopes of the self-righteous judges. The unrighteous may have a greater readiness to respond to truth than the preacher does to proclaim it. The Jonah spirit finds no comfort in the truth that God does not think as man thinks. To God Nineveh penitent, sober, and determined to mend its ways is an infinitely more pleasing sight than Nineveh roaring off to a gaudy doom, drunk and obscene to the bitter end. Not so Jonah. He went to see justice vindicated and saw conversion, instead. So he is the unhappiest man in the Bible.

Surely the Christian who steadily believes that his witness is bound to effect nothing but his own sense of relief in having carried out a hard assignment is a very slight improvement upon Jonah. Hard assignments have no merit in themselves. They are endured in good faith and meaningful courage only when the people saddled with them believe that a great and common good could not otherwise be realized. Those who take up crosses only to join the company of the wearers of the cross, and flaunt a spirit of self-sacrifice to the world without any knowledge of the enormous cost of expiation, and without any love for a great and lovely thing secured to man by crucifixion alone —these need the prayers of all faithful people everywhere.

Christian criticism of this world is made in the interest of health, truth, creativity, and freedom; and with a view to making such criticism as practically helpful and concretely meaningful as possible. The church was not created to be a passive mouthpiece of supernatural wisdom. Since the criterion of Christian criticism of the world is an actuality, God in our midst, Christian judgment cannot be made in despair of all concrete, historical efficacy. A sick longing for martyrdom is a peculiarly grotesque expression of spiritlessness and despair. Men have died heroically for pernicious causes; but the mischief of an evil cause is not thereby undone. Many a saint has embraced martyrdom to keep faith with Jesus Christ. This ought not to inspire us to convert the Cross of Christ into a symbol of martyrdom. For faith, the Cross is the completion of the ministry of Jesus Christ in the days of his flesh. Since for him the Cross was not a substitute for a life overflowing with creative efficacious goodness, it cannot be that for us, either.

IV

The absoluteness of God's judgment does not confer infallibility upon human judgment. His judgment is revealed in Jesus Christ. If therefore we speak of God's wrath we must already have spoken of God's love, because divine wrath, either considered by itself or as the negative function of righteousness abstracted from love, is a falsification of the Gospel of Jesus Christ. The wrath of God is holy beyond any mortal analogy. The love of God is terrible in its brightness and it alone is invincible in its demands. But consider how petulant and self-justifying human wrath is, how anxious it is to destroy all evidence of general complicity in the evil done by wicked men! Consider how easily dimmed, corrupted, and distracted human love is, and how often irresolute and thereafter treacherous! In the light of the Gospel of Jesus Christ it is sinful folly to call upon the wrath of God to explain this or that dreadful calamity; and to speak of God's love as though it were this or that dreamy cozy fancy, alighting daintily for a moment in a human heart. Does the lovely child die under the wheels of the tractor because God is angry with her booze-loving, woman-chasing obscene father? No one has the warrant of the Gospel for making such outrageous explanation of human tragedy. Whatever we profess as Christian to know about the wrath of God we know only in the life, crucifixion, and resurrection of Jesus Christ; and not in the descent of Assyria upon Israel as a ravening wolf upon an innocent lamb, nor in the abominations of Nazism, nor in the scourge of Communist aggression. Or does the anxious banker find a moment's easement of his burdens, a fleeting but delicious peace of mind, because God loves him and bends the whole machinery of heaven and earth to this fantastic end? No one has the warrant of the Gospel for making such an outrageous explanation of the banker's peace of mind. Whatever we know of God's love we know in the life, death, and resurrection of Jesus Christ. This knowledge often quarrels fundamentally with what we would do it we were God and with the things, for weal and woe, we would ordain in complaisance or compassion.

In another context we shall need to discuss the meaning of theological explanations of historical and natural events. Here we must be content with but one observation concerning the kind of doctrinal-religious explanation just considered. These everyday appeals to God's wrath and to God's love are more often than not proposed in the interests of the institutional church and its righteous constituency. The booze-loving, woman-chasing father is an offense to the righteous: therefore his child must die. I doubt that the righteous in the congregation are quite ready for the strict formality of this argument, but they have already embraced the sentiment, it is part of the hard case and steel core of their righteousness. What they have forgotten, what in some moments the whole church seems to have forgotten, is that God alone is the wholly righteous judge, and His judgment expresses the perfection of His love. As the child born of this love, the Christian must exercise his own responsibility in deciding what concrete and practical interpretation to make of the love of God. This is the perilous and wonderful freedom of the Christian. In any literal sense God does not put words into his mouth—God seems to have decided that since he uttered his own Word, Jesus Christ, we have in him all that we need in order to learn how to speak the divine language of love. So as a beneficiary of God's grace, the Christian sets himself to learn and use the vocabulary of grace, in the school of the Holy Spirit.

The Word of God, Jesus Christ, is the ultimate criterion for distinguishing the positive from the negative in the world. In the abstract we know that alone is good which comes from love of being and that alone is evil which comes from the hatred of being. In the actual world, as in himself, the Christian finds love and hate interfused. He knows the power and beauty of love, and he knows the sterility and horror of lovelessness, and beyond that, even, the searing flame of hatred. But he does not know clearly and distinctly which of his actions is the expression of love only. He does not know whether the love he does express is corrupted and distorted at the source. Harrowing ambiguities leap out at him wherever he looks, within and without. He may have moments of transcendent clarity: being lifted beyond pleasure and pain, beyond anxiety for self and world, he is penetrated most exquisitely by love. Then he is neither body nor mind but a living spirit. These moments do not last very long, perhaps because we are not able to endure them very often or for very long. Thereafter the soul and the world again clutch each other in perfervid embrace, each having for the other a necessitous and greedy love, each seeking alternately empire and self-cancellation.

Wherever the Gospel is preached in the spirit of faithfulness the light of God's truth falls upon these dense ambiguous actualities of the world and the self. This light of truth is not alone the salvation of the world, but it is the beginning of salvation and a supernaturally uncomfortable beginning at that. It does not miraculously unravel the ambiguities for the faithful. It does give him the indispensable clue in his task of distinguishing the negativities from the creativities.

V

Faithful criticism of the world is pursued under the auspices of the Kingdom of God. In preaching the Kingdom the church must make clear that the Kingdom of God is not a religious name for the spiritual achievements of our civilization. These achievements are not thereby depreciated. The wisdom of the world is not the wisdom of God. The real wisdom of the world is not thereby undermined. Gnomic expressions of this sort are calculated to remind the church that the Gospel must not be preached with the aim of convicting the world of an alliance with Satan and proving that "worldly wisdom" originates in hell. Faithful preaching in the church is necessarily differential, in respect to the Kingdom and civilization, but the intention of this preaching is essentially affirmative. The Gospel is the astounding good news that God is in the world in saving power and for the sake of salvation He demands repentance for all unrighteousness. This demand is all-inclusive precisely because it comes from God. Therefore no element of our civilization is exempted from it, whether of actuality or of ideality. None of the things signified by the big spiritual-sounding words of our civilization is passed over by the holy demands of repentance and transformation things such as love, justice, peace, etc. The power to love must be reoriented. Justice must be pursued not to save face but to save persons. The inequalities springing from love of advantage must be surrendered in good will, or they will be wrenched away in violence that destroys good as well as evil and is no respecter of innocence. Our world must learn again what it means to walk humbly before God: renouncing self-deification, both private and corporate. Ego is no god, neither is superego, and we shall say nothing of the abysmal id.

Authentic preaching of the Gospel does not create false expectations of an immediate and dramatic about-face when God's demands are really brought home to the world. The world does not respond as Jonah's Nineveh, not so quickly, not so fervently, not so inclusively. Before conversion, even before repentance, there must be self-examination. This takes time as well as truth. Revivalism was eager to administer the truth but insisted that it had to be taken immediately because the time of God's patience had run out. To which it must be said that God has been patient with the church for a long time and it is not unreasonable to suppose that He has some patience left for the sinner. So the time for self-examination and self-recognition may not be used until the party is over. Reformation does not automatically follow the miseries of the hangover; but reformation never comes until a person has faced up to his real condition; and for that he needs to be cold sober. He also needs sustaining grace, so that he will not relapse into self-excuse, or slip away into the self-cancellation of despair.

One does not need to be a historian or a theologian to know that the church does not always preach authentically. Historical range and theological acumen may help to recognize distortions and to put the right names on them. "Moralism," for instance, is the name of an imposing spiritual achievement with which many generations can be credited rather than middle-class nineteenth-century modernity alone. Contemporary propheticism has launched and maintained a ferocious attack upon moralistic spirituality. (Indeed the attack may have convinced many that the faithful Christian does not really bother about morality any more.) But are we so sure that propheticism has given the *coup de grâce* to moralism? Granted, the old-fashioned moralistic eschatology is not often heard in the evangelical communions until the evangelist shows up. Then again the guns of righteousness pound at riotous living and the reckless pursuit of immoral pleasures is represented as the road to hell. But something has happened to our world: this assault on unrighteousness does not mean much to people whose souls are pretty well eaten out by boredom and self-loathing. That is the hell that drives people into riotous living. It is the same hell that opens to receive them when they are burned out. The age is not hell-bent in the gaudy old-fashioned way. It is rattled, frightened, confused, and frustrated; and in this condition it seems not to have the energy, the nerve, and the courage for the all-demanding and strangely exhilarating work of repentance. We learn early to say "I am sorry," and just as early we learn that this is a magic formula to restore us to good favor and to bring down the goodies. "I am sorry" has very little to do with God's demand for repentance. He demands the straitened life, the reorientation of the vital center, the clear eye for the good, the readiness to accept the disciplining of energy for the sake of creativity. Such are the fruits worthy of repentance.

The demands of this higher righteousness, and the communicated power to obey, have been given in Jesus Christ, "the power of God and the wisdom of God unto salvation." This Gospel endures in all of the distortions imposed upon it by the church.

VI

The strategy of Christian criticism is to put before the world the demands and the promises of the Kingdom of God. Only in obedience to these demands is there health for the spirit of man. Only in these promises is his authentic destiny disclosed.

Whatever problem it creates for the doctrine of Providence, the fact is that the human spirit is everywhere susceptible to disease. Some of the medicines recommended by contemporary civilization, and often enough available in the church without prescription, do nothing but temporarily pacify the patient and further conceal the real infection.

The strategy of Christian criticism is to focus attention upon the organism that is the seat of the infection, a figure of speech for the essential ontological element of man that is suffering specific infection. In Jesus Christ the power of God is focused upon man's being so that he may recover health and creativity. Since the Lord so conceived and enacted His own ministry (cf. Luke 4:18-22), the church created by the Holy Spirit is called to minister to the world for its restoration rather than for its rejection.

So the Christian critic has no warrant in the Gospel or from the Holy Spirit to reject the contemporary world as though it were a saint-trap of satanic invention. Jesus Christ is God's absolute affirmation of man's being. He is the everlasting Yea and Amen uttered by the Almighty Father to the entire human community (cf. II Cor. 1:19-22). In the light of this triumphant confession what are we to make of a church whose heart is pitted and darkened by a defeatist and negative spirit? Negativity may be a reaction against the religious attempt to turn

God's Yea and Amen into a blanket endorsement of human achievement. A protest against this is always in order, since disease lurks even in the sublimest human achievement. But religious attempts to domesticate the righteousness of God do not justify a negative spirit in the proclamation of the Gospel. So let us agree that premature and uncritical endorsement of this or that aspect of contemporary life is not a legitimate part of the program of Christian criticism. But let us also confess that the church is here to preach the righteousness of God, who is gratified neither by the death of a sinner nor by the self-congratulations of the righteous.

It does not follow that Christian values are to be derided and rejected. They are part of a heritage that Western man will jettison at his own grave peril. Nevertheless God has not created and licensed the church to be the conservator of these values. It is here to preach—to show forth, demonstrate, illustrate, and exemplify in every way it can command—the grace of God in Jesus Christ, the same being the mightiest of all powers and the most vital life of all that lives. He is the living God, and He will be obeyed. He has willed that man should create a world; and man has so far obeyed the will of God. But he has also disobeyed because in every world he has created there are evil things which have sprung from his own heart, and he has loved them; but he has also created good things, and these have sprung from the love of being in his own heart. Therefore the Christian has a particularly burdensome, and even dangerous task: to distinguish the good things from the evil ones. But he has also a particular joy: to thank both God and man for everything good offered to him in his time and place.

CHAPTER V

The Deployment of the Principles of Christian Criticism

I

The revelation of God in Jesus Christ is the foundation upon which the being of the Christian rests. Nothing else can be the absolute authority governing Christian criticism of civilization. We must now ask how the Christian critic proceeds properly from revelation to the concrete judgments he must make as a faithful Christian, faithful at once to the revelation in Jesus Christ and to the affirmative aspects of the culture in which he lives? This question is as old and persistent as the church itself. How, for instance, does St. Paul derive from his sublime encounter with the Risen Lord his rule requiring women to cover their heads in the sanctuary? (I Cor. 11:4) We can hardly suppose that rules concerning millinery were divinely communicated to him on the Road to Damascus or that they were any part of the divine wisdom disclosed to him during the years of preparation in the desert. Moreover there seems to be no good reason for supposing that St. Paul's extraction of this gem of wisdom from the Gospel is in method radically different from various other extractions and deductions employed by the church throughout the Christian ages. The great evangelical churches in America continue to claim revelational sanction for prohibiting the use of alcoholic beverages—a rule enforceable only against the clergy in any case—and for restricting the use of tobacco to the laity alone. The Roman Catholic Church for a long time has created the impression that its rules about birth control, divorce, and celibacy are all derived from the Gospel of Jesus Christ.

Obviously all such practical derivations from revelation have complex histories. Each particular history is like all the others in one interesting and important respect: at the beginning, there is far more tentativeness, and a much clearer sense of the contingencies that shape particular occasions, than at the later stages. John Wesley felt badly about the rum-sodden masses of eighteenth-century England but he seems not to have quarreled with St. Paul over the virtues of wine. Latter-day Methodists seem to have learned since Wesley that alcohol is bad for man as such; and they are officially convinced that the man who succumbs to the temptation to drink his first cocktail will land on skid row. Wesley could not rely upon Methodism as an authority in the moral-religious realm. Methodists do rely considerably upon Methodism, hardly upon John Wesley, and in this particular, not at all upon St. Paul. Thus a particular history emerges as the medium through which authoritative moral counsel and criticism of the world are made available to the believer. Something like this, something like the general process, seems to be the common story for the whole church. Historical factors are certainly involved in the actual deployment of the ethical principles of Christian faith, but these historical factors are moved around in many remarkable ways in order to give religious backing to practical judgments required by unique circumstances. The Christian critic must finally show how these judgments are demanded by the revelation in Jesus Christ.

This is not to say that revelation must be proved to be revelation. It does mean that when the revelation of Jesus Christ is offered as the warrant for a particular practical judgment, we must ask how and whether it *is* such a warrant. The claim may turn out to be a sound one when so tested. That would not make the testing irrelevant or improper. Rather, it would show that the Biblical advice to test all things was being taken seriously. Indeed the apostolic counsel to test all inspirations and prophetic utterances (I Thess. 5:21) is itself the inspiration of this maxim: when one appeals to absolute authority one had best be very clear about the kind of appeal one is making. The wrong kind of appeal to that authority may ruin one's argument, and also, perhaps, one's right to hold forth on high and holy matters. Even a sound appeal to absolute authority may fall on deaf ears. This ought not to depress the faithful nearly as much as the modest success of false appeals to true authority and the stunning success of appeals to very dubious authority, e.g., plausibility.

II

There are four principal routes by which the supreme principle of holy revelation has been deployed. If the metaphor is unhelpful, let us say simply that there are four kinds of appeal to the absolute authority of God in Jesus Christ as warranting particular judgments of good and evil:

1. *Logic.*
2. *Inspiration.*
3. *Good Sense.*
4. *Intuition.*

We shall examine these in the order given.

1. *Logic.*

The principle function of logic is to determine whether statements follow from (or are otherwise compatible with) certain antecedent statements. Implication is the proper name for the relation of following from. It is not necessary to appeal to fact to learn whether this relation is there in any given instance. The relation must be perceived mentally only, it must be thought, it cannot be experienced. This is merely to say that logic has a heavier commitment to formal validity than to truth. To put it more dogmatically, an appeal to logic cannot establish something as true. It can only show that B is true if (1) A is true, and (2) if B really follows from A. Logic cannot tell us about (1). It can tell us a great deal about (2).

(Here we are working with a narrow view of logic, in which it comes out much smaller than reason. Logic is one of the weapons of reason, but it is only one. There is nothing in logic itself that would elevate it to the throne in reason's kingdom. But I do not seriously suppose that this mild observation will slow down—let alone head off—the stampede to invent a thinking machine which will take the place of man's bumbling rational powers.)

It must seem very odd that so coldly formal an instrument of intellect as logic should be used to deploy the wisdom of revelation for the faithful criticism of the world. Actually logic is not always warmly received and highly honored in religious circles—a demand for straight hard thinking seems to unsettle some pious souls. On the other hand they may have been upset by claims that logic is at least the prime distributing agency of divine wisdom, if it is not one of the Persons of the Blessed Trinity. But the pious are sometimes a puzzle to the logician, especially when he is a philosopher with a view of his own about the nature of things. Piety seems to thrive on illogicality. Theologians may blanch when logicans say Boo! to them or when their beloved hermeneutic is treed by hard-running clean-living sharp-toothed implication; but piety acts as though it had no stake in these alarms and excursions. Yet piety too makes its own demands upon logic as a device for deploying the wisdom of revelation. This device may be primitive. It is certainly indispensable. Some illustration of this is now in order.

Jesus Christ said some things which all Christians believe to be true; and their believing them is a hallmark of their being Christian. From these truths other truths follow. Jesus Christ did not teach everything that the faithful Christian now believes; but in uttering the absolutely primary principles, Jesus Christ seems also, by logic, to have bound the Christian by the derivative or implied truths. Christian people have had to work out the implications. Once they have done so they have often proved as ready to accept the implied truths as they are to accept what Jesus Christ himself said. Sometimes they have been rather remarkably more ready to accept the implication than the antecedent principle presumably enunciated by Jesus Christ.

An instance of high confidence in the authority of implication is provided by the historical elaboration of what Jesus Christ said about loving our enemies.

(1) Jesus says: "Love your enemies" (Matt. 5:44).

(2) This means: If anybody is your enemy, love him.

(3) Or: Love the man who is your enemy.

(4) It follows: You are to love the Romans if the Romans are your enemies.

(5) It does not follow: You are to love *only* your enemies.

(6) Or: An enemy is (by definition) someone you love.

(7) Or: You must love Romans only so far as they are your enemies.

The possibilities eliminated by logic (5, 6, 7) might of course be restored by experience. The point is that the Christian would not be justified in saying that these logical rejects were implied by the Gospel command: Love your enemies.

(8) Or: Someone will become your enemy if you love him.

(9) Or: If you love someone he will cease to be your enemy.

These are also logical rejects. Piety has often insisted upon (9), as somehow implied in Christ's teachings. There is no somehow about implication: it is there or it is not. So, again, if one believes (9), one must have some warrant other than implication for believing it.

So far, then, we have no serious intellectual difficulties with the application of logic. The difficulties descend upon us when we ask, What does love mean? What is compatible with love?

Let us make some trial runs, as follow:

(10) If you love somebody you will try not to hurt him.

(11) It follows: if you love somebody you will not try to kill him.

(12) From which follows: War is wrong.

(13) And: the Christian cannot conscientiously bear arms.

(14) And: a civilization that makes war part of its life is evil.

Some important steps in this implicational process have been elided, so we must insert them.

(11A) You are not being good to a person when you try to kill him, to say nothing of when you succeed.

(12A) The purpose of war is to kill people, your enemies, specifically.

(13A) The Christian cannot justify his having done wrong things.

(14A) There is no greater evil than inflicting death.

These are important, in fact decisive, omissions. None of them is implied by anything Jesus Christ said as a matter of record. In response to this people sometimes say that after all Jesus really meant to say them, and would certainly say them now. Unfortunately these are factually unsupportable assertions. Moreover they carry us into a very different method of extracting from revelation specific principles for judging and directing human behavior. We cannot allow ourselves to be carried thither until we are sure that logic has nothing more to offer. So let us revert to the working example.

(11A) Hardly anyone denies that killing a person injures him in a significant way. At the very least it seriously impairs his prospects for continued earthly and bodily existence. Yet it is conceivable that worse things could be done to a person, such as totally corrupting him; or, if you believed in a future life in heaven, allowing him to destroy his prospects for that life by continuing to do terrible evil on earth. If a person had an immortal soul destined for eternal happiness in the life to come; and if the prospects of his enjoying that life were really imperiled by his present and presumptively unalterable conduct here; then, given opportunity to recant his heresies and to throw himself on the mercy of heaven, he is better off dead. Logic is obviously at work in such explanations. Heretic burners never recognized the ifs in the logical sequence, and here they shared a vice with their victims. Heretics and heretic burners do not seriously entertain the possibility of being wrong at the outset; and so it becomes merely a question of which one gets to the blowtorch first. The winner can always (history is the witness) work up a plausible theological explanation of his barbarity. The loser, unfortunately, can hardly console himself by saying to himself, "Better luck next time."

Furthermore it is conceivable that a person's not being willing to commit a wrong may directly support a wrong greater than the one he cannot conscientiously commit. Perhaps I ought to put my conscience in jeopardy if the life of someone within my reach is in jeopardy, if, that is, he has put his life in jeopardy by attacking an innocent person. It will not do to say that in the sight of God no one is innocent. If we took this line consistently no one would ever be punished for anything. Poland did not attack Germany in 1939. Belgium did not assault Germany in 1914. The Jews did not attack the Gestapo. Let the relativities be what they may, they cannot be permitted to blind us to the asymmetrical relationships of good and evil in human affairs. If A assaults B, A is the aggressor, B is the victim. B probably has his own faults, but they are beside the point of whether I ought to prevent what A is doing, or punish him if it is not possible to prevent his crime.

Let it be said again, therefore, that we are prone to use the complexity of civilization as a moral justification now of its faults and then of our own refusal to become personally involved with a particular wickedness. Even so, it is a shocking thing that Christians, whose Lord loves the world with all of the love of God, should look for some holy excuse for disengagement from the world that has so much evil in it. The fact that this habit is as old as Christianity itself does not lend grandeur to such self-excusing. Prostitution is an even older institution, but hardly anybody supposes that it has acquired nobility from its longevity.

So far, then, we conclude that while logic can offer only a limited service, its legitimate service ought not to be rejected. It can provide a clear passage from primal truth, so far as such truth can be expressed propositionally, to its proper (propositional) consequences. Such clarity ought not to be rejected by the Christian critic, even though he ought to admit that logic cannot clear the tough tangled jungles of the human world—it has no power to work miracles. It can teach us how to string "if" statements together properly (with results which will please some people and horrify others), but logic alone has no way to remove the ifs. Logic can keep an argument aloft but it cannot get an argument off the ground. Logic is a splendid instrument for the ordering of human reflection; but it is not the instrument with which to probe the depths of human existence nor to plumb any of the mysteries of being. Logic is not a prime instrument for the laying bare of being and existence. It is an instrument for the communication of truth antecedently and certainly apprehended.

III

2. *Inspiration.*

Somehow it seems more fitting for the Christian to rely upon inspiration to deploy the right principles for the judgment of the world. Not a word is said about logic in the Bible (certainly the things said about Logos cannot be so construed!), but much is said about inspiration. So much, in fact, that many people are thereby encouraged to lump revelation and inspiration together, as in familiar notions about the authority of the Bible. This confusion of revelation and inspiration has far-reaching consequences. Perhaps the most notable of these is the supposition that inspiration is the continuation of revelation. From this a readiness to claim divine sanction for particular judgments made about the good and evil of the world is a short step.

So men come to believe that specific and concrete judgments are presented to them by God the Holy Spirit, revealing to them in this present moment that mind which was also in Christ Jesus.

People who believe this probably do not believe that the Holy Spirit has privately disclosed to them what Jesus Christ really had in mind when he said what he said and did what he did. They mean to say, one would rather suppose, that the Holy Spirit plants whole-bodied in their minds what they are to say about the world. Imagine, for instance, a person deeply concerned about the obvious injustices in the distribution of wealth and aroused by hearing the poor assured that God loves them despite their poverty. Perturbed, he opens the Bible. Like a bolt from heaven the word of the prophet Amos strikes him. "Hear this, you who trample upon the needy and bring the poor of the land to an end!" (8:4.) Moved by this, he turns the pages; and another word leaps into flaming life before his eyes: "Woe to you rich!" Now his indignation burns with a new intensity and clarity; and he becomes a divinely inspired critic of capitalistic civilization.

Malice prepense is of course visible on the face of this illustration. Nowadays it is the critics of the Social Gospel (simply called Liberalism) who claim divine inspiration for their defense of what they call Private Property. In their view the Commandments of Moses are clearly opposed to the income tax; and the Apostle Paul, if not the Lord Jesus himself, would have been scandalized by the niggardly 27 per cent depletion clause. But whether it is social liberal or conservative who claims inspiration directly from God, we must say that there is something doubtful about the claim. Something is amiss in the nature of the appeal to inspiration, though the content of the view so authorized may be so repugnant that we have little patience left to consider how the appeal to divine authority has been made. It is a doubtful appeal because it starts out as one thing and concludes as something else; and it does not seem appropriate for a Christian to offer the Holy Spirit as his warrant for this kind of procedure. Inspiration starts off by imputing responsibility to Almighty God through the Holy Spirit both for the occurrence and the meaning of certain ideas in the mind of the Christian making a particular judgment. The appeal to inspiration concludes, however, as a way of characterizing human states of mind. Inspiration, therefore, designates certain meanings and characteristics of human states of consciousness as having the value of God. We often say, "Thoughts great and noble come to us from Beyond." Beyond what? To say that such thoughts are inspired does not offer an explanation of their occurrence, it merely calls attention to their greatness. It may be that such thoughts are dropped down from heaven into minds preordained to receive them. The supposition cannot be used to support the appeal to inspiration, even though a person's readiness to believe that all of his best thoughts are heaven's gifts may be credited to him as proper humility.

This first difficulty with inspiration can be put in a somewhat different and perhaps more forward-looking way. The appeal to inspiration combines the meaning of a providential occasion in which to "testify" with a sense of immediate and providential delivery of what to say in that situation. The situation may be inspired, that is, of providential provision. The message, if it be faithfully Christian, has already been given, it is the Gospel of God in Jesus Christ. A powerful imagination may make a novel and striking combination, seeing how to make the most of the situation God has delivered into his hands. In that case the performance is inspired, not the message. The message is revealed, not inspired. The message, if it be the authentic Gospel, does not belong to the preacher, it is not his. The performance, on the other hand, is certainly his. If he is a great man, his performance will be memorable; and it may come to modify the tradition—not all of the men who have made significant contributions to the theological life of the church have been Professors of Systematic Theology. But one may criticize the performance, nonetheless, without the slightest hint of *lèse majesté* to Almighty God. Thus Savonarola mounted a smashing performance, in which he very likely felt inspired. We may well believe that the message was wrong, though (one would hope) not for the reasons his destroyers advanced.

Thus the claim of inspiration is entirely manageable when it is understood as an appeal to God's providential ordering of a situation in which to make a particular witness. It is not manageable at all as an appeal to revelation to justify absolutely what one has said. From this vantage point we can consider a better-known objection to inspiration, namely, that the Holy Spirit seems to communicate mutually contradictory messages concerning human affairs. The liberal prophet claimed inspiration for his attack on the evils of capitalistic society. The conservative critic of the prophet claims inspiration for his rejection of the prophet. Perhaps some of the counterclaimants are as cynical as some of the prophets were hallucinated, but both of the charges are beside the point. The point is that when inspiration is so used it precipitates a deadly regression into absurdity. A is inspired to proclaim that B's claims to inspiration are false. B is inspired to contend that A's claims to inspiration pertaining to his (B's) claims are false, etc. The Holy Spirit is thus caught in the middle of a power play, and the suspicion grows that people have confused lung power and the ability to stay with the many involutions of a logical regression with the gifts of the Holy Spirit.

On the other hand it is sometimes said that God has not made any commitment to the laws of logic. Are we to infer from this that God values incoherence above coherence? Or that all human discourse must finally die away into adoring silence before the mystery of the Holy God? How can we doubt the latter—? How can we believe the former? So long as man may speak of God, and is encouraged to set a modest store of confidence in his so speaking, we cannot recklessly spurn something that pertains to the very essence of human thought, i.e., to look for coherence. Coherent thought does sometimes disastrously overlook reality; and incoherent thought does sometimes miraculously hit it. But it is patently absurd to combine these two factual statements in such a way as to make disorder the *sine qua non* of truth, in the religious realm or elsewhere.

Inspiration seems to acquire greater dignity as it becomes a communal claim rather than a merely individual one. So far the shift of focus from the individual as inspired to the community as inspired has the witness of the New Testament on its side. There God the Holy Spirit takes the community of the faithful as the locus of His operations, not the individual psyche, and certainly not the individual psyche atomistically understood. In the community of His own creation God the Spirit administers revelation in order to guarantee the unity, power, and health of the community in whose midst He dwells. Unity, power, and health are broad criteria indeed; but no unmanageable mystery is suggested by any of them, since these are conditions reasonably accessible to knowledge. When, in other words, people are living and working together for a high common purpose, when they are, as it were, but one life within the compass of such a teleology, the well-being of that community need not be a matter of mere guesswork. Even if one is not a member of the community, one can still see how memory, aspiration, imagination, and the daily routines as well are disciplined into creative power by that common spirit.

There is much to be commended in this kind of appeal to inspiration. One reason for commending it is partly negative: it applies a brake to the confusion of individual eccentricity with the gifts of the Holy Spirit. But there is a more positive reason: it sets great store by the continuity of the community, that great value greatly wronged in the everyday longing for everlastingness.

The applications of these social criteria nonetheless brings us to the beginning of the end for the distinctiveness, and perhaps even of the intelligibility, of the route of inspiration. Surely in the New Testament the appeal to the sure presence of the Holy Spirit in the church is an appeal to the qualities of the common life thus manifested, rather than to the power, supernaturally infused, to endure forever as a community on earth. Any great concern for the sheer perdurability of the church must therefore be a lapse into worldly anxiety; and this is the wrong way to share the suffering of the world. Through the power of the Holy Spirit the members of the faithful community have the mind of Christ, by virtue of which they love their essential unity, not because this will make them the equal of Rome in worldly power, but because this is the way life is in the eternal Kingdom of God.

Moreover the communal interpretation of inspiration in our time merges the power of the Holy Spirit with the power to create and sustain a cultural heritage, it makes the Holy Spirit a great believer in tradition. Indeed the Holy Spirit is systematically offered as an explanation of the particular interpretations of Holy Scripture proposed and adopted by certain councils of the church. Thus tradition emerges as the mediator of revelation.

This use of inspiration makes it extremely difficult to distinguish it from any social-historical process by which a community becomes aware of the values perfectly and timelessly contained in its tradition, perfectly and timelessly according to that tradition itself. Nothing of substantial alteration, enlargement, or diminution can happen to tradition, so long as the Holy Spirit is on the job. The Holy Spirit opens the eyes of a given generation upon the changeless truth, thereby teaching new duties for new occasions; but the novelty is only in the human understanding.

We shall discuss later the metaphysical errors embedded in this view of inspiration, errors such as the confusion of the immutability of God with the timeless truth of a proposition. Here we conclude discussion of inspiration by indicating another kind of trap into which it falls when the church's intellectual traditions are made the peculiar and especial objects of the Holy Spirit's activity. In this way revelation is made to stand to the church in the same relation in which absolute ideality stands to civilization. The analogical relation makes it possible for the church to conceive itself as being a worldly empire, at the price of ceasing to be the church of the Gospel. Thereafter the perdurability of the civilization the church has embraced becomes the most important question to be asked of Providence both inside and outside the church.

Self-aggrandizement and self-justification on a community scale have certain advantages compared to individual projects. Individual schemes for ego-aggrandizement require social discipline to prevent the community from disintegrating into chaos or from being corrupted into a loose and precarious mutual benefit association. But social discipline itself requires continuous criticism, and not less so when the instrument of discipline is appeal to tradition. Unless the Holy Spirit manifests essential independence relative to the tradition, some uncompromised free-play, some primordial power and readiness "to blow where it wills to blow," it is reduced to being an accessory to the will of the community to be absolute, to be itself divine, holy and everlasting. We have deliberately said "it" for "He" in so stating the option: the reduction of the Holy Spirit just sketched here, and realized often enough historically, reduces the full personhood of God to a nonpersonal social process.

One of man's most remarkable dreams is the dream of infallibility. Not to be able to err in matters of the highest importance would surely be an exaltation of the human spirit beyond the boundaries of creaturehood. The historical career of this dream, both in the church and in the secular world, is rather more instructive than edifying. It shows where communal inspiration leads. Thanks be to God that in His wisdom men are emboldened to hold every such claim to infallibility up to unblinking scrutiny. This is providential for the human community as well as for the church.

Criticisms made of such communal appeals to inspiration have been made sometimes on the strength of counterappeals to inspiration. They have also been made on the strength of appeals to good sense.

IV

3. *Good Sense.*

Less grand than inspiration and less neat than logic, good sense is more sturdy, plain, and livable than either inspiration or logic. True, it is sometimes invoked and applied under their names rather than under its own, but this hardly matters so long as its essential work is done.

When a person says that as a Christian he must "feel his way" into a situation before he passes judgment upon it or upon anybody in it, he is probably following good sense as the route leading from the revelation of God in Jesus Christ to concrete situations and specific solutions.

Good sense is first of all the desire to take into account the specific actualities of the situation in which one lives as a Christian: It is up to good sense to make out the distinctive features of the present situation. In every situation the Christian works with broad principles he shares with faithful Christians everywhere. As an obedient servant of Jesus Christ, he accepts the obligation to love all of God's children. But when he asks, "What does the love of Christ require of me in this concrete situation?" he must use good sense to make out the answer, because what that principle and Lord of love required in that situation may not tell us how they are to be served in this situation. What the Lord demands here must somehow be learned here. The answers good sense makes out will have therefore a roughhewn, rough-and-ready quality. They will have some loose ends. They may have a certain air of contingency, and even of provisionality. This means that good sense at its best will produce enough to work with today, but when the day is over there will be very little left to put in the bank for someone else to draw upon. Good sense does not set itself to solve today's problems with yesterday's solutions; and it makes no effort to solve tomorrow's problems today. Its policies are projected over only so much time as a situation actually embraces, because realistic policies are not understood to have transcendence over all time and all persons. Good sense therefore is idealistic only within the boundaries of practicality. Its policies are not blueprints kept on file in heaven and loaned to properly certified Christian agencies.

Let us take a commonplace illustration of good sense at work upon a New Testament commandment that has perplexed (and irritated) many people: A faithful disciple must dispose of all his worldly goods and concerns if he is to take up his cross and follow Christ in a really authentic way. It does not appear that Christians in our time are generally tempted to put this into actual operation. But ought we not to feel guilty about our disobedience?

Good sense, either with or without scientific Biblical criticism to back it up, says that this demand cannot be interpreted as a comprehensive commandment, a program for everybody in the church. Jesus Christ demanded this of a particular man in a particular situation—and it met with a refusal and an excuse then, too. No wholesale condemnation of private property or of wealth or of worldly callings is implied. In fact some people in the very early church got rid of all their holdings because they believed that the world was going to end very shortly. It is likely, too, that some people got rid of their holdings, as they joined the early church, in order to share the wealth, such as it was, with the many poor in the fellowship—a somewhat more exalted motive, surely, than the simple calculation that you can't take it with you.

So good sense must decide when and where love of property, prestige, and power threatens to choke off the spirit of Christian love, both among the Haves and the Have-Nots. Perhaps property arrangements, property values, and property ideology are all grave liabilities in contemporary civilization. This cannot be learned by comparing this age with some other age. It cannot be learned, either, by asking, "What would Jesus do?," a question which merely opens the door to sentimental speculation. Whatever the moral issue where Christian principle has application, the faithful Christian must do his best to discern the actualities of the situation; and then determine what principles are applicable; and then work for an effective consensus in support of the policy most relevant to that situation and most congruent with those principles.

Consensus strongly suggests that good sense cannot be counted upon to be good so long as it is limited to private judgment. Good sense must test itself in the world. It must solicit and receive support from right-thinking men of goodwill. Good sense that is not a consensus, a sensing together, is likely to be a mere pretender to good sense. And since consensus can easily be misunderstood, we must stop to consider as carefully as we can what it means.

First, then, let us note that consensus is not to be confused with majority opinion. A majority opinion may be an effective consensus; but a consensus is not necessarily a majority opinion. Consensus is reasonable consent to a policy framed by certain principles; and it is the consent of persons qualified to make a judgment about the matter in hand. Majority opinion is a mere fact: where there is a constituency of ten people, six of them in agreement upon a matter is a majority. The agreement may be quite fortuitous, it may owe more to the laws of chance than to principles of reason. Accordingly, to appeal to this fact, this majority opinion, as a serious reason for doing or for believing anything of importance, is absurd on the face of it. Opinion, simply as opinion, is hardly more intimately related to truth, beauty, and goodness than the larger colon is.

Consensus, then, is reasonable consent, a consent arrived at by rational process. Consensus requires a man's best judgment dealing with a situation in which he knows the pertinent facts and has a grasp of the principles relevant to them. That is why we say that consensus is the consent of persons whose judgments matter. This qualification has nothing to do with social and economic status. It has everything to do with the appetite and the capacities for rational deliberation. The appetite is very important. One must believe that rational deliberation is a good and necessary activity; and that things bear looking into; and that the practical significance of the commands of Jesus Christ most certainly requires looking into with all of the powers of the mind.

Persons whose judgment does not matter may yet have claims which require due consideration. For example, children ought to be protected against exploitation even though their opinions concerning the issue may be worthless. Weighty claims and valid interests do not of themselves argue a full voice in the determination of policy.

In passing we ought to take note of the fact that democracy is sometimes said to rest on an illicit inference, namely, that to have a stake in the administration of a society implies having a voice in its government. In place of such a howling absurdity people quite sensibly express a preference for what they call republicanism, a political system in which only the properly qualified govern and participate in the selection of those who govern. But democracy does not rest upon such an absurdity; though as absurdities go it is hardly more fantastic than the republican assumption that ownership of property is the qualification for political responsibility. Democracy (we are talking about our own history) does assume a very broad distribution of rationality in the populace at large. Since the eighteenth century this rational power has been all too often represented simply as the ability to calculate one's economic profit from investment. This is a grotesque limitation of the life of reason in man; and fortunately practice has been better than the ideology.

Consensus is effective when it is the basis for concerted actions affecting the body politic. Preservation of this consensus may require the marshaling of majority opinion to support it, but, as we have already noted, majority opinion does not make it a consensus. Sooner or later in a democracy policy must be submitted to the judgment of the people. The objective in this is not simply that the people will vote for it but that they will know why they are voting for it, having given due consideration to that policy and to the other relevant options. This is not too much to hope for, but a prudent man might hesitate to bet his shirt on its happening in any particular instance. On the other hand the political cynics are as wrong in their own way of supposing that "the people" is made up of idiots and blind self-servers.

Good sense is interested in getting things done. Even if it moves but a handful they aim at something larger than pious and noble gestures. No matter how confused and perilous the situation may be, good sense whispers that it contains the seeds of a better future within the reach of people of good sense. Sometimes these seeds yield great benefit. When this happens the wisdom of good sense is confirmed: the tree is known by its fruit, the good tree brings forth good fruit.

Good sense is so free of the eschatological dimension that we begin to wonder how plausible it is as a route leading from revelation to the judgment and direction of human affairs. It is Martha rather than Mary, to be sure, but a Martha who really keeps the show on the road rather than one who calls attention to herself by rattling dishes in the sink. Good sense does not produce many saints, though some saints have had a large supply of it. But it does guarantee, so far as merely human resources can do so, that there will be church on Sunday morning because somebody patched the roof on Saturday. It is a kind of worldly mind, investing, perhaps, more in prudence than in self-sacrifice, more in justice than in charity, more in deliberation than in mysticism, more in reasonable and proximate solutions than in absolute judgments; and investing nothing in ecstasy.

Yet, having said all of these things about good sense, we feel some uneasiness with it as the chief route from revelation to the particular situation in which the Christian finds himself. This uneasiness springs to life when *good* sense, *right* choice, *reasonable* solutions, are so steadily reiterated. What makes sense *good*? we are prompted to ask. The very looseness of good sense, its intensely practical and particularistic orientation, opens the door to expediency, which is a cheap counterfeit of wisdom. Consensus, for that matter, can be organized for purposes inimical to the public good, such as the power of a particular group or person. The loftiest principles can be invoked to create a smokescreen behind which drives for power and privilege scheme to go on to new triumphs over the public good. Even Christ's commandments can be woven into a fabric of ego aggrandizement and ego justification.

We are compelled therefore to conclude that good sense as a route from revelation to concrete criticism can be trusted only so far as the persons using it and appealing to it can be trusted, and no further. The instincts of the Christian man can be relied upon, when they can, not because they are instincts but because the Christian man can and must be held responsible for them. The man of good sense is right: the proof of the pudding is in the eating. But neither the pudding nor its good taste is a criterion of health.

We are saying, then, that much of the power of good sense cannot be adequately grasped by good sense alone. So far as good sense is healthy and productive, it points to another route.

V

4. *Intuition.*

Rather than being intimidated by the long and chequered career of this word, we shall run the risk of stating summarily what we intend it to mean in this context. Intuition is the immediate apprehension of the concrete truth of revelation. Taken at this, its face value, intuition rules that *no* route can be staked out for moving from the truth of revelation to practical corollaries available for the interpretation of the concrete situation. As intuition has it, God's revelation is a living word and it finds us out where we are in the real living present. The actualities of the Christian's situation cannot be deduced from doctrine or Scripture. Neither can they be pieced together by intelligence sensitized to the possibilities of creative (or at least reasonable) action. The real structures, the real powers, and the real demands of God in a given situation are seen through the real presence of Jesus Christ the Lord.

The kinship of intuition and inspiration is superficial and remote. Inspiration claims supernatural sanction for specific judgments, as though the inspired person knew God's mind from the inside. Intuition makes no such claims.

Moreover intuition does not take refuge in the common plea, "You would have done what I did if you had been in my shoes." Such a statement can be neither proved nor disproved; and it is generally entered as a plea in self-justification. The truth is, human places, the shoes, cannot be exchanged or even compared, except for nonserious purposes. You are in your place. I am in mine. If intuition is right, I know Christ present as God's judgment unto salvation. In Christ I see what I am. I expect you to say the same thing about your situation, namely, that God as well as the rest of us recognizes its uniqueness, and says the unique word to you in the uniqueness of your situation.

It would seem to follow that there are as many Christs as there are unique people claiming direct knowledge of him in the uniqueness of their situations. Such a consequence would put the scriptural testimony "Jesus Christ the same yesterday, today and tomorrow" in an odd light. It would become a theological interpretation not only after the fact of intuition but at odds with the report of intuition. If we generalize from this, all theological teachings become secondary and derivative truths, at best. Jesus Christ himself the absolute Presence, is truth, and as such he is known in intuition, in direct encounter, Being with being, Person with person. This does not mean that intuition is a matter of having visions or dreaming dreams, though visions are sometimes the "language" in which the content of intuition is communicated to the church and the world. The reality value of the intuition is in what the Christian sets himself to do and to be for Christ's sake. Therefore the Christian falsifies his existence as one called to live under the power of the Kingdom when he puts his problem thus: "Since God was in Jesus Christ, what follows as my responsibility in my world?" According to intuition this is the way the faithful Christian should put his problem: "I know Thee and love Thee, O Lord, but how can I do what Thou demandest of me?" Christ is known in these demands, such is the revelation of God. In that encounter He does not tell me what He is demanding of others; and He does not commission me to tell them for Him. When He has something for them He will tell them so. For the work of the Kingdom He calls and ordains whom He pleases.

On first hearing, we wonder how intuition as such accounts for the church as a real community. Then it occurs to us that there is nothing really astonishing in the appearance of a community of servants of God in Christ. If this is His good pleasure why should we be astonished? We are much comforted by this company and are proud to be part of it. But Christ also calls each of his disciples to walk a lonely road, where the temptations and perils allayed—perhaps even forgotten—while I was in the goodly company, smite now with doubled and trebled fury. In the lonely way (the *via dolorosa* every disciple is called to walk as he moves out to his own Golgotha) only Christ sustains me. Silent the joyful noise of the congregation, invisible the crowd of witnesses, barren the land, black the night; Christ alone is my staff, my shield, my bread, my light.

Beyond making one observation I do not intend to argue the theological adequacy of this account of Crucifixion given by intuition.

The intuitional account of Crucifixion does underline the unmistakable and inalienable solitariness of the experience of the Cross. But Christianity is also the faith in the Lord of the Resurrection. The New Testament is very clear at this point: Resurrection is communal in its human reference. Even St. Paul, who claims (or does someone claim for him?) an ecstatic experience of the Risen Christ, also acknowledges at once the community reference. The Lord commissions him to serve in the church; and this so clearly that we hardly exaggerate by saying that his apostolic service in the church is the meaning of his ecstatic experience of the Resurrection. So even if the moment of revelation itself contained no essential reference to the past—if, that is, we credit the view that Christ is the absolute contemporary of everyone who feels the call to serve him in love—we have still to ask whether revelation, if it be in Christ, does not always and essentially contain a reference to a community?

What then become of church, tradition, and history if intuition be accepted as the prime route from revelation? If community becomes secondary and derivative, what kind of check or test does intuition allow? What is the person of faith to do in between intuition events?

An intuitional account of church and history can of course be provided. We could say that church and history are occasions in which one encounters the living Lord. Neither church nor history is a medium of revelation, because revelation is an immediate encounter with the living Christ. Revelation is God disclosing Himself to a living spirit in an actual present moment. God speaks where He wills so to do. Man cannot make God speak merely by standing in the social-historical context in which God has spoken before and by using incantations of one sort or another. Perhaps God wills to speak as one participates in the Lord's Supper. The bread and the wine, the archaic elegant phrases, the thronging images, the solemn ministrants: any or all of it may suddenly and miraculously radiate the power and beauty of the Holy Presence. Whereupon the soul leaps in joy to greet the Lord Christ, "And on winged feet His errands run."

We cannot say in faith that the Holy Presence is produced by anything said or done in the Lord's Supper, nor by any air or sign of hungry expectation in us. Psychologically everything may come off handsomely, producing that golden inner glow which so many people take to be the Holy Presence. This kind of success may be very bad for the health of the spirit. It may induce the illusion that God the

Spirit can be commanded to appear by incantational magic. Not even the golden glow is a ritualistic sure thing, as many people testify in leaving the service by saying, "Nothing happened today."

But again the question arises: How does intuition know that it is Christ who appears? Intuition can only answer: Because he so identifies himself. His self-identification is (normally) not in visions, voices, and eerie feelings. He shows himself as the Lord of life and death in the very demands he makes, for these are the demands of one who masters the elements of human existence. Human life responds to him as to its Creator and Savior, as well as conscience to its absolutely righteous Judge.

The demands of God in Christ do indeed encompass the wide world beyond the threshold of the ego. The duties that Christ binds upon those to whom he appears are all in and of the public domain. Christ cannot be known privately because he cannot be served in secret. Indeed, under the impact of his presence, the conventional division of the world into the two parts, individual and society, begins to crumble before the reality of the integral human condition: because of Jesus Christ who is God-with-man, the human community, man really with man, becomes an actuality. This is what Christ came to do. He is known as Christ where people pledge their freedom for the glory of that Kingdom, of which man-with-man is surely a real dimension and not merely a portent.

VI

To put the matter this way is to say two things: (1) intuition cannot be the whole story; (2) some kind of verifying process is called for whenever one appeals to revelation as the absolute warrant for one's actions and judgments as Christian.

We must admit that (2) is currently a theological red flag. The very phrase "verification of revelation" is enough to produce theological fevers, tremors, and other symptoms of outrage; as though someone were proposing to put God to the test! Not at all. It is a matter of testing human, very human, claims, not to prove that somebody has made a mistake but to learn, if possible, what world a particular claim refers to, and whether there is general admission into that world, and if there is, how one knows one has landed in the right place.

So for intuition the "verification of revelation" is the course in the restored world to which the will is resolutely set by the coming of Jesus Christ. The criterion is not social approval. It is not even enhancement of the public good. The criterion is God having come in Christ, setting the course in which we are to meet him. He is the everlasting faithfulness in this course through time and space. "I will not leave you comfortless," "I will come to you, I will be with you": this is our bread, our rock, our shield, throughout the vicissitudes of this life.

But just as surely the Christ of God speaks a wholly personal word directly to me. He finds me where he has established me: in the community of his original creation, not the church, but essential mankind. The church has something to say about that community. The church has a history that says something about that wider community. The church's history is above all a narrative, not a chronology, not even a memory. The narrative is told in many ways but not least or last in being enacted. The obedience Jesus Christ claims from me is obedience in such enactment. In the will to obey this claim, and in the enactment of it, with as much of whatever unique power God has given me, Jesus Christ is present and is known as the Lord.

VII

How then can we venture to assign preeminence to any of these routes over the others? One must hear or see in order to obey, but does this mean that perception is more important than will? In a sense, yes, but not in an absolute sense, because hearing without the enactment of the will, hearing the Word but not doing it, is a curse, in the end, not a blessing. For me to exist as a Christian means that Christ's command has become my law, my purpose, my reason for existing, my very essence.

So in a sense this means that intuition assumes the ascendancy, because I see myself as seen by God's Christ, when I say God has revealed Himself. But first I must know who Jesus Christ is, I must learn why and how as a Christian I say that the criterion of all Christian witness, and therefore of every judgment of the world, is not so much a life as a living presence, and everlasting actuality. To be Christian is to surrender one's life to the interpretation of the Holy Spirit whose text is Jesus Christ. The Christian is not a mere passive object in this process. He too is a subject. He is an interpreter as well as an interpretation, he is a speaker as well as a word. He must know what to speak about Jesus Christ before he knows what to say about the good and evil of this world.

Many problems and perils remain to intrigue and frighten the Christian as he thus ventures in faith to assay the meaning of his world. He will not read out of heaven what he is to find when he judges this enterprise and himself in relationship to it. He knows that truth and falsity, good and evil, beauty and ugliness, are tightly woven together in this world, and in himself. Therefore he always prays, "Mea culpa, miserere!" But he also always prays, "Veni, Sanctus Spiritus!" and "Thy Kingdom come."

PART II

THE DOGMATIC CONTENT OF PRACTICAL THEOLOGY

CHAPTER VI

Practical and Systematic Theology

I

One of the great temptations of the Christian thinker is to represent the church as a subculture, a world within the world but also a society answering commands directly communicated to it, or to its leadership at any rate, by God in heaven. As a rebuke to the Christianity of cultural piety such a representation of the church may have some merit. Whatever virtue it has in that connection must not blind us to a serious deficiency in this representation. This is the tendency to interpret the faith of the church according to the analogy of philosophy in civilization, an analogy we may express thus: Faith is to the church as philosophy is to civilization. In the analogy the faith of the church becomes the ideological element of a given historical phenomenon called Christianity. As a subcultural phenomenon it properly comes under the overarching phenomenon, Western civilization, both for descriptive and critical purposes. In this way the ostensible virtue in the representation of the church as a subculture holding out stoutly for its own integrity is largely vitiated; and we are confronted with another engulfment by the world. The faithful person and the faithful church ought to resist this and all other forms of engulfment; but the resistance ought to be intelligent and knowledgeable as well as passionate. Specifically, we need to know the truth upon which a persuasive illusion trades. The first step in the pursuit of that truth is an examination of the theological life of the church, looking for the prime characteristics and divisions of labor of that theological life.

II

Christian theology is the intellectual interpretation of the revelation of God in Jesus Christ, as Scripture testifies. We call it an intellectual interpretation simply to distinguish it from dramatic interpretations: the theologian is not a poet, a dancer, an actor, or a priest. He may be any of these as an avocation, to be sure, but none of them qualifies him for his specific tasks as theologian.

Christian theology has several arms. To identify them let us use the more or less standard labels:

Biblical Theology.
Systematic Theology.
Philosophical Theology.
Moral Theology.

Even a superficial examination of the catalogue of courses offered by almost any Protestant theological seminary would disclose another arm of theology, very rarely, if ever, mentioned in the same breath or in the same part of the catalogue with the ancient and honorable sciences listed above. This is a poor cousin, generally labeled:

Practical Theology.

Pressing on, perhaps from mere curiosity, we learn certain things about practical theology which may strike us as odd specifications for anything called theology in the initial sense, such as the following.

1. The courses in practical theology are generally taught by professors without Ph.D's. These professors may have D.D.'s, which proves that they have been eminent preacher-pastors.

2. The courses are about church management, sermon preparation, parish visitation, and, perhaps, the organization of the church school. The courses offered as practical theology may explain in part why the instructors rarely boast Ph.D's.

If our curiosity or concern were to carry us into further examination of this situation, we should very likely discover:

3. A wide majority of seminary alumni agree that practical theology is not theological; and many question whether it is really practical.

Now let us turn our attention to the other part of the catalogue. Here we learn the following things about the nonpractical classical theological studies:

a. The instructors in all of these courses almost always have Ph.D's, in hand or in sight. (Some of them may also have D.D.'s, but this adornment is no part of their professional qualifications.)

b. These courses have as their subject matter the doctrinal content of the Christian faith, its history, and the methods for its authentic interpretation. These courses are therefore the core of seminary education.

c. Many students, probably a thumping majority, wish that they could take more of these courses and fewer (if any at all) courses in practical theology.

If we were visitors from Mars we might by this time be ready with a prescription for the elevation of the part of the curriculum called practical theology to real theological dignity: teachers of practical theology ought to have Ph.D.'s. Since we cannot claim that excuse for such a shocking nonsequitur, or for precipitating a revolution in theological education, we must settle for a somewhat less practical observation:

4. The opposite of practical theology must surely be theoretical, or "scientific," theology.

If this observation is correct, then the situation disclosed by this cursory examination of the theological enterprise is indeed astonishing in the highest degree, and we shall express our astonishment in the question: How is it possible for a religiously serious interpretation of divine revelation to be essentially theoretical and scientific? Surely the theologian organizes the propositional expressions of Christian belief with a view to exhibiting their truth. He is not trying to test theory as a scientist does. He is not interested decisively in the purely logical connections of one proposition with another. If he builds a complex metaphysical system, as in fact some Christian theologians have, he does it neither to satisfy an aesthetic appetite nor finally to see what he can learn and recommend about God, man, and the world. If he builds a system he must do it to show forth some of the remoter implications of the revelation of God in Jesus Christ.

We are therefore ready for a conclusion somewhat different from the one we might have proposed had we simply dropped in from Mars.

5. The distinction between practical and scientific theology is both unclear and injurious to productive reflection upon the meaning of revelation; and it ought to be dropped as well as repented of.

Since our interest is not in institutional reformation at the moment, we want to indicate what this conclusion means for the reformation of theology as the intellectual interpretation of the revelation of God in Jesus Christ.

The first thing it means is that the fundamental first venture of theology ought to be identified as practical theology because it is immediately and decisively engaged with those doctrines, those propositionally formulated beliefs, that are indispensable to the actual preaching of the Gospel of Jesus Christ.

III

This Gospel, the sole authentic message the church has at its disposal, must be distinguished from a philosophy of life for two reasons.

1. The Gospel is the one really radical criticism of man in civilization; and it therefore defies incorporation into a philosophy of life.

2. Systematic theology incorporates significant elements of one or more cultural world views. Therefore it cannot be accepted as the sufficient and ultimate criterion of the preaching of the Gospel. The preachability of a theological formulation is the ultimate criterion of systematic validity.

Because (1) may well seem to be a flat mistake, where (2) is more likely to seem a mere paradox, I shall take up (1) immediately, in order, naturally, to show that it is not a mistake. Thereafter I shall try to show that (2) is not a paradox. If it were it ought not to be accepted as being more than an innocuous entertainment.

(1) Here I assume that it is the latter part of this assertion which makes for unhappiness, since we must overlook the merely superstitious dislike for "radical" in the first part.

The great question about the second part of (1) is whether it does not effectively cancel the real immanence of God's Word, Jesus Christ, by making the Gospel a pure essence defying any actual embodiment. My response to this is that the Gospel does have embodiment but not as an authentic component of a "philosophy of life." It would be silly to say that such embodiments had never been attempted since this very fact has been allowed for in the first part of (2). What must be said is that the Gospel as proclamation of the Kingdom of God is indigestible as an element in cultural philosophies. To make good on this we must first see how these philosophies are constituted. Thereafter we may see why the Gospel is indigestible for them.

IV

A philosophy of life is an attitude toward civilization, nature, and Deity. It is an attitude that expresses concern for the values of particular human achievement and perhaps of man generally. It is an attitude expressed in a variety of forms and modes: poetry, moral sentiments, metaphysical arguments, religion, perhaps even science. (There might be some gain in simply using the term "metaphysical beliefs" for "philosophy of life." But metaphysics undertakes things not necessarily hostile to world viewing but not exhausted by it either. So all things considered I think that we would do well simply to stay with "philosophy of life" and world viewing.)

The use of such labels as optimism and pessimism has real merit in application to philosophies of life, precisely because they suggest the attitudinal dimension of human existence expressed in world views. Thus an optimist may have a carefully articulated set of propositional doctrines in which he expresses his confidence that the ruling powers of the cosmos will look after the good; but he need not have a propositional system in order to be an optimist; and the garden-variety optimist certainly does not have such a system at his command. As for the pessimist, he may have thought up some very impressive arguments to support his view that things are bound to turn out badly in the long run, even though his book sells well in the short run. But it is not likely that these arguments have ever made a pessimist of a man who just did not see the world that way, arguments or no arguments. This odd situation does not necessarily add to the despair of the pessimist since he may not expect much from people anyway; or he may have a theory about the limited value of logical demonstrations that helps to explain this odd situation, as the great pessimist Schopenhauer did. Moreover both the optimist and the pessimist may be quite content to express their respective views, and leave sophisticated attack and defense to people more interested in logic than in livable outlooks.

Now without turning psychological we can say that a philosophy of life expresses concern for value realizations, and perhaps for the fate of the good generally. This is not a psychological observation (as we have said before, it is much more nearly an ontological one), because all human value realizations are up against humanly unbrookable powers in the cosmos if not in the heart of man himself. The world-viewing expression of this concern presupposes values and value criteria. People already know what is important, and what is possible relative to what is important, when they begin to read the cosmic and historical auguries. They already know why blankness "out there" will be very hard to live with relative to some human interests, and very easy relative to others. They already know their actual situation before they express their hopes and fears for the future.

Thus a philosophy of life, a world view, puts questions to the ultimate powers on the basis of assured truth. For example, given the scientific view of things, what can we say about man's chances in the cosmos? Many persuasive answers to this question (that is, many world-viewing answers) seem not to have been proposed by people who had any misgiving whatever about the truth of the scientific view of things. From physics, astrophysics, geology, etc. they have learned the truth about man's place in the cosmos; even though no particular positive science speaks as such to this question. They have garnered a rich harvest for world viewing.

There was a time when Christianity was the principal support for some world views, and was often enough simply understood to be a world view shared with optimists and idealists generally, except for some doctrinal oddities left over from earlier uncritical centuries. Indeed, it is likely that optimistic and idealistic people still think of Christianity in this way; and we can be sure that many Christians do. These are reasons why we must understand that the Gospel of God in Jesus Christ is indigestible for world-viewing purposes.

The Gospel does have a great deal to say about man's prospects in the real world in relation to the ultimate powers thereof. But it calls in question (from the beginning and from the top to the bottom) the value assumptions indispensable to world viewing. This calling in question is not a simple No! to these value realizations, and it is not a simple Yes! either. The Gospel opens the fundamentals of man's being to a new evaluation and to a new perception. The power whereby this is done is the divine life itself, God present as grace and truth. This radical opening up of man's being to himself is not the accomplishment of ingenious (or even true!) theories and doctrines. In God's presence as Jesus Christ man learns what and how to represent authentically his situation as the creature summoned into creativity by God's invincible love. This is why we have said that from the Gospel man learns to think of himself as God sees him, as God loves him, as God judges him. And this is why we say now that through the Gospel God the Spirit teaches man how to evaluate human values as well as what to hope for. As creatures of a particular civilization we are not always able to abstain from consulting auguries. From the Gospel we know that the present is the now of repentance; but we naturally hope also to enjoy some of the good things of this world before we die or this world passes away.

So we begin to understand why both the cheerfulness and the despair of the natural man come under radical judgment in the Gospel. Apart from the Gospel we do not know what to be cheerful about; or for what we ought to despair, so far as our fundamental and ultimate reality is concerned. The Gospel fixes man's attention upon essential human being in its relation to God. The focus of attention and concern is no longer upon ego in relation to civilization; nor upon civilization in relation to ideality. The systematic illusions of ego and civilization are opened up to perception and judgment resurrected from the grave of untruth.

There is another reason why the Gospel is unassimilable to a philosophy of life. The Gospel is proclamation: it is presented to man and must be represented by him in the mode of unqualified assertion. It cannot be represented with an initial "I think it may be the case"; or "It has occurred to me . . ." Even more shocking to our natural creed-making propensities, we are not even allowed to begin the preaching of the Gospel with an "I believe that . . ." There are of course Christian creeds, and we must not minimize their importance. But none of them came from heaven, and it is very unlikely that any of them will take us there, or make it recognizable if we make it there otherwise. The Gospel begins and ends with an uncompromising declaration that certain things are facts, that is, that certain things have happened. The Gospel is just as uncompromisingly insistent that anybody who knows these things had better do something about his situation now. The Gospel is not a Delphic, or even a Socratic, oracle, which, once given, opens up deliciously terrifying options for interpretation. The Gospel is: "The Kingdom of God is at hand, so repent!"

Here we must pause to note one of the most formidable angularities of the Gospel which make it a ruinous member of any philosophy of life, namely, an odd stubbornness: If you have heard it of course you know that it is true; and since you know that it is true, why aren't you obeying it? It is almost as though the Spirit spoke to us through the Gospel in this way: You continue to thrash around, pretending the while that the sword of divine truth has not pierced your vitals, or at least hoping that other members of the club will not notice it or will be too polite to say anything except behind your back. You know that the Gospel is true because it has reached the depths of your being with that power identified in the New Testament as grace and truth.

No whimsy succeeds in diminishing or masking this astonishing stubbornness of the Gospel. Quite naturally we resist such inelegant presumption. But our recoil against it may very well deflect attention from something even more astonishing: from the very beginning the Gospel preachers assume that the Resurrection of Jesus Christ will make real and telling sense to people whose philosophy, or, in Israel's case, whose historical expectations, cannot possibly assimilate it! The philosophically-minded are told that the reality of man's being and situation has been opened up by a series of historical events. The historically-minded are told that the very thing they have been waiting for is true. So the philosopher asks for the truth, and is given some historical events. The watcher of history asks for *the* event, and is given the truth. With a vengeance, this is being all things to all men: a many-splendored offense.

In due time theologians worked out a theory to explain (or to justify?) this extraordinary behavior of the preachers of the Gospel: God in His perfectly mysterious wisdom appoints some minds to accept the absolute assertions of the Gospel; and persons who do not have this appointment cannot believe; and thereafter, of course, those who do not believe cannot be saved out from the total ruin of this world for the glory of the world to come. Election is the name of this remarkable doctrine. It is handsomely tooled for the production of self-righteous creatures. This does not make the doctrine wrong. Rather, it ought to remind us that it is a doctrine to be taken only on prescription; and the prescription contains a warning about the dangers of misuse.

There are many other things to be said about election but we shall be content to say here one of the more controversial: the doctrine is no part of the Gospel of Jesus Christ. The first preachers of the Gospel of Jesus Christ were convinced that people would believe what they preached because its hearers would see that it was true. As men called of God they were given the power of the Holy Spirit to open up this truth; but they did not speak of God as though He were a supernatural agent making (causing) people to believe it. Perhaps this was very naïve of them. Nonetheless people did believe what they preached as the Gospel, not all of them, of course; but those who did not believe were left with something to confess rather than something to charge off to the mysterious decrees of the cosmos. The apostles, for their part, certainly did not preach metaphysics disguised as theological explanation of belief and unbelief. They represent God as being adequate to every situation. He is not baffled or intimidated by rude unbelief. It does not follow that God is the cause of that pitiful condition.

The doctrine of election must be distinguished from proclamation of what God has done and is in His own right. The doctrine has drawn upon metaphysical systems for a conception of causality that is not at all compatible with the causality of proclamation. Later on this issue will be aired more thoroughly. Here our task is to see how preachability is the norm of doctrinal adequacy. If this can be established we shall be in a position to proceed to the doctrinal structure of Practical Theology.

V

Given the present state of the church the proposal to elevate preachability to a preeminent position must seem a lunatic aberration from the sweet reasonableness and scientific serenity of systematic theology. The actual state of preaching (there is no reason to exclude the Catholic churches from our generalization) seems to many to be deplorable; and we cannot derive much comfort from the observation that it may have been worse in some other time. Congregations Sunday after Sunday still hear a great deal of amiable psychological-moralistic chitchat from the pulpit, though here and there an intellectual-type preacher throws Kierkegaard or Barth or Bultmann at the iron heads of his congregation, and argues with Tillich about Picasso rather than about the Gospel. Occasionally a preacher moves up his popgun artillery to the defense of Liberalism against that foul scourge, Neo-orthodoxy. The Catholic churches are not really in better case simply because their priests do not need to preach and are not trained to preach in any case. The Roman priest can always fulminate from the pulpit against mixed marriages and birth control, the only heresies that really matter at the parish level. His parishioners may actually welcome this sermon, even the butts of his attack, after hearing the celebration of the Mass in a language that is presumed to be holy because it is unintelligible.

Anglican Catholics make a little more of preaching. In their preaching they are likely to attack heresies that have had a more distinguished history in the church, even though the issues are largely lost on the congregation. Since the first rule of the liturgy is that everything must be over on the hour, their sermonizing manages to be very brief without being very incisive. Wit is not the soul of brevity.

Conservative Protestant churches continue to have sermons that are heavily Biblical in a special sense: the Bible is cited as proof of many things which the preacher and his congregation believe although they are not mentioned in the Bible, such as the iniquity of the National Council of Churches. Preaching of this sort hardly reminds the congregation that in the Bible God judges all creaturely presumption. The Board of Publications might conceivably be included under that heading.

Moreover preachability at first glance promises the elevation of relevance to the king's throne. Surely in that direction lies the cultural assimilation of the Gospel! Above all to be relevant is to preach what people want to hear, with perhaps a clever jab now and then to remind the congregation that the preacher knows the score even though he has not the slightest intention of changing the game.

I am not prepared to defend the scientific adequacy of these generalizations, even though I doubt that they can be knowledgeably and conscientiously denied. But none of them, nor even grimmer tales of dereliction from apostolic responsibility, diminishes the authority of preaching as a criterion of theological adequacy. Indeed, the issue and the claim may be put even more uncompromisingly. The failures of the pulpit are to be measured by the demands put upon it by the Gospel, and not primarily by theoretical-theological norms.

This is the case because the Gospel is given to the church to be proclaimed just as it (the Gospel) is. "Just as it is" means that since the Gospel says one thing about God, the church has no authority to say anything else in its preaching. If the church says anything else, it tells a lie, not merely some other truth, even though the other truth (probably an optimistic view of man in the world) is told with every sign of pious sincerity.

The criterion of preachability is not at all an appeal to the actual performance of the church. The criterion is the one thing God gives in the Gospel to be preached by the church. To say that this is the only thing preachable by the church is not to deny that the church can jabber endlessly about many other things. It means, simply, that these other things are lies, when they come from the mouth of the church. They are not only things which God has not given the church to say, they are untruths because the church has said them. Apart from the church people may promulgate and believe superstitious nonsense with a curious air of innocence, e.g., that white men are better (and probably more human) than black men. When the church preaches anything which gives the smallest kind or degree of support to this rank superstition, it lies. To know that it lies in doing so one needs only to read the Gospel attentively, it is not necessary to do anthropological research.

The hunger for relevance so evident in the preaching of the church today is a wayward expression of something fundamentally sound. What is sound in it is illuminated by the Pentecost moment in the church's life (Acts 2:1-13). Then the Holy Spirit imparted the marvelous power to proclaim the Gospel in whatever tongue was required to make it understood. From this the church correctly concludes that the Gospel is always to be proclaimed in an intelligible tongue. The life of the church thereafter is committed to the translation of the Gospel into the idiom of the contemporary world.

Hardly anything else better illustrates the precarious and contingent being of the church than this divinely imposed obligation to speak intelligibly. For what can promise that the church will not adopt a persuasive world view in adopting a living idiom? Modernity as a religious passion assimilates the Gospel to the dominant world view of the age, even when that view is ambiguously affirmative. So to assimilate the Gospel to the mind of the age evaporates the church's message into a nonhistorical ideality, and it leaves the mind of the age free to swing irrationally from tedium to terror. Thus an assimilation undertaken to make the Gospel more meaningful historically (that is, contemporaneously) actually corrupts both the historicity of the Gospel and the meaning of history. In the mirror of an idealistically reduced Gospel, man can see only himself as the creature of a civilization. In learning how to think scientificaly or existentially or metaphysically about the Gospel, we ought not to suppose that we have learned how to think Christianly about God and ourselves.

But let us suppose that the church has been adequately warned of the dangers of assimilation understood as the divinely ordained translation of the Gospel. Are we now to suppose that such dangers can be averted and that the preaching life of the church can be amended by the right kind of doctrinal preaching?

An affirmative answer to this question may well derive from the antecedent conviction that the translation of the Gospel is theological interpretation. Given this conviction it is necessary and proper to seek a new theology congenial to the spirit of the age. For this purpose doctrine becomes the persuasive image and the intelligible concept. "Persuasive" and "intelligible" in turn signify variables of contemporary culture rather than any constants of psyche and reason.

The mistakes in this view are fundamental ones. Consider only the account of doctrine. We cannot pretend that "doctrine" means "teaching" only, as it is now frequently translated in the New Testament (cf. I Tim. 1:10, NEB: "wholesome teaching"). In the history of the church doctrine is teaching that has achieved formal expression and as such it is certainly more than a straightaway reading of the facts.

A doctrine may intend the Gospel. It ought to accord "with the glorious gospel of the blessed God" (I Tim. 1:11, RSV). But the Gospel does not intend doctrine. "The glorious gospel" is not doctrine in embryo awaiting the wonderful moment of birth into an intellectual system. Given the Gospel we can understand something of what Calvin is up to. Given Calvin we could not understand what the Gospel is up to. Calvin, for example, makes the Gospel intelligible to a cultural epoch. He labored mightily and brought forth Calvinism: the name of a moment in Western civilization as well as of a doctrinal monument.

We ought not to suppose, therefore, that the essential moves of the New Testament are implicitly doctrinal. Certainly theological minds are at work in the New Testament itself. This does not mean that they are struggling to achieve formal purity and formal normativeness. God has spoken the living word and this living word is the norm for all the ages to come. Human speech is purified and revivified in His service; but not without man's taking thought to this end. That taking-thought is theology in and for the church. From this, doctrine emerges. Is it therefore an excrescence to be explained as a religious-cultural phenomenon rather than as a serious bid for truth? Hardly! Then perhaps doctrines are to be understood as symbolic expressions subject to the mysterious decrees of the creative unconscious, arising out of deep psychic needs and dying out as the psyche feels its way into new worlds? Not so. Doctrines are bids for truth. They are bids made in a market that demands formalization. Styles of formalization change. The church must acknowledge this if it intends to make truth bids in that market.

There is nothing in the Gospel that stands over against such bidding as a divine prohibition. Many theologians now rail at it, but the historical methodologies now in the saddle make it highly unlikely that this attitude can be imputed to Jesus. St. Paul's disparagement of philosophy (Col. 2:8) does not make him a triumphantly clear model of the antimetaphysical disposition, either.

Nevertheless we too must insist that the relation of dependence runs from doctrine to preaching rather than from preaching to doctrine. Preaching is the representation of the Gospel as that one thing absolutely necessary for the interpretation of man-in-the-world and of the world-in-man. The preached Gospel is the opening-up of this life to the life revealed in Jesus Christ. To take a particularly bothersome example, the church does not behave faithfully when it tries to make the Resurrection somehow intellectually digestible, if not exactly palatable, for the refined sensitivities of contemporary man (who has buried enough victims of his modernity to have little stomach for the prospects of meeting them all face to face sometime). Rather, the faithful church interprets what man is and ought to become in the light of Resurrection. If someday we all must be confronted by every last one of our victims, many of whom we could not name if we wanted to, it is only because God who brought Jesus Christ forth from the dead loves them and loves us all with that infinite love which will prevail even over our mortal guilt.

Committed to this kind of preaching the church needs measureless support and comfort. Nothing creaturely can provide that. That is the pure gift of God. But the support and comfort of the Holy Spirit are not promised to a church that preaches lies and then pleads dire circumstances in the world as its excuse. Even a miraculous accession of sound doctrine will not bring such a church back into the right relation to the Gospel, any more than a course in Systematic Theology will set the preacher in the right orientation upon the Gospel.

VI

We come now to the second contention advanced on page 126, namely, that Systematic Theology inevitably incorporates one or more elements of worldly wisdom; and it is therefore invalidated as the prime criterion of the adequacy of the preaching of the Gospel.

Systematic theology is a formal achievement in two senses:

1. It works only with propositions.

2. It imposes an order upon these propositions that no single proposition itself requires.

1. A proposition itself is a formal achievement, both of grammar and of logic. (Not all grammatical forms are the products of reason, as every schoolboy knows.) Logical formalizations are presumptively rational in principle. Theological-doctrinal propositions are not simple statements of fact or of supposition. Certainly some theological propositions incorporate, or refer to, some factual statements; but some do not. It is legitimate to say, "It is a fact that Jesus Christ arose from the dead," even though nobody above ground at a given moment may believe it. It is not legitimate to say, "It is a fact that God is Triune," even though as a proposition it might be true and five hundred million Christians believed it. There is no fact that could make the latter proposition true. One fact would make a great deal of difficulty for the former statement: discovering the actual body of Jesus. The Resurrection can be so interpreted as to accommodate such a discovery. One could say that the appearance of Jesus Christ after his death is purely spiritual; and immediately brace oneself to resist the happy embraces of spiritualists and to refute psychological arguments about hallucinations. But there is another kind of comfort. No one in the New Testament appeals to any theoretical explanation of Christ's presence as the Lord of Resurrection as the warrant for belief in this Lord or as the ground for authority to preach the Gospel. For New Testament faith, and for authentic Christian faith as such, the Resurrection is an integral part of a recital in and over which Jesus Christ himself presides.

The doctrinal elaboration of propositions requires theologians to keep at least one eye open for the formal (rather than the factual) conditions of meaningfulness. Doctrinal propositions are certain to be assayed for their coherence as well as for their compatibility with the facts.

2. So an ideal order must be invoked to make the systematic effort in theology intelligible. This order must be obeyed once it is invoked. If in Part One of the system the theologian has said that God's perfection of being rules out His having passions, he cannot say in Part Two that God is really angry about anything; and he

must say that God's love is not really a passion.

So dramatic and complete a retreat from Biblical talk about God requires careful explanation and justification. Theologians long ago produced a theory of language and logic for that purpose: analogy. The traditional uses of analogy more than hint the predicament of theology as serving two masters, God revealed in Jesus Christ, and the creativity evinced in human culture. Surely some presentiments of the one true God must be forthcoming in the creativity of culture, unless we imagine that God did not learn to speak until Moses appeared, who taught Him Hebrew. But the very minute cultural creativity is endowed with divine meaning the specter of idolatry moves front and center from the wings. On the other hand God revealed in Jesus Christ stands forth as He who affirms all that is positive in being, no matter how frail or spotty it may be. So: granted that we cannot extrapolate from the God of the philosophers (ancient, modern, or contemporary) to God in Jesus Christ, are we therefore licensed to say that God in Christ cannot account for the God of the philosophers? I greatly fear that on this matter theologians have confused nonconvertibility with flat irreconcilability.

The theory of analogy may be the best human wit can devise to render tolerable a situation created by man. It might therefore be said to have the usefulness of truth—on loan. But the truth of the Gospel cannot be made dependent upon such a theory. This is not to say that the formal aspirations expressed in theology are a flight from the one thing needful for the Christian. Quite to the contrary, one of the things surely and sorely needed in the church today is a fresh understanding of the scope and the processes of theology. To this end we turn now to a further investigation of systematic theology.

Systematic theology incorporates material as well as formal instruction from the wisdom of the world: it borrows from metaphysics as well as from logic. This does not mean that systematic theology is merely a metaphysical system that has passed ordination examinations and received the blessing of a bishop. So far as he is a faithful Christian the theologian will give the chief seat of honor, in the world of ordered reflection, to Jesus Christ as the supreme medium if not the substance of divine truth. He may go even further and contend that there are truths of revelation essentially beyond the grasp of human reason, to which man's highest rational-cognitive powers dumbly look up; for such truths are the fulfillment, and not merely the despair, of man's desire to know.

What then shall we say about the towering intellectual systems created upon this distinction between the truths of revelation and the truths of reason (and experience)? The truths of revelation, to be accepted on faith alone, are remarkably similar to esoteric doctrines intelligible to mystic penetration alone. If this is the case, then the movement of faith elicited by the enunciation of such truths is a movement away from the Gospel rather than a movement inspired and equipped to penetrate the Gospel. I do not mean by this to depreciate the beauties of mystical theology. I do mean to say that it is Plotinus rather than Jesus Christ who makes them possible. What we who are not mystical do not know about Plotinus' system (or any other mystical system) is whether the mystical flight verifies it. What we do know is that it is a majestic metaphysical account of reality; and that as such its merits and deficiencies can be argued about. As a speculative, rather than a mystical, account of reality, it has been remarkably productive in the world here below. I mean, of course, productive in the realm of metaphysics, where his idealistic account of the world has had many reincarnations, including some in Christian theology.

Only in a secondary sense can the Gospel be said to be the cause of the metaphysical flights of Christian spirituality. Now, as well as originally, the Gospel comes into a world in which men endeavor to excogitate a speculative account of reality, animated in such endeavors by an unslakable desire to know. This desire, this hunger for the truth of being, leads men to take seriously many kinds of clues as to the nature of reality. So along comes the Gospel that promises truth beyond anything hitherto or otherwise available. Whatever the consequences, this is a promise worth testing.

Systematic theology is one of these consequences. At three decisive points systematic theology has taken into its own fabric doctrines from metaphysics, doctrines worked out to meet the logical-speculative requirements of one rational synthesis or another. These three points are:

1. The subject of action is a substance.
2. The subject is entirely within a causal nexus.
3. The meaning of time is exhausted by "periodicity" and "linearity."

1. Metaphysical thinking in Western culture long ago decided that action is the expression of a subject. On this both commonsense and speculative profundity agree. (One remembers philosophical dissents,

eg., Hume's. But Hume was also commonsensical, and he was proud of it, and he entertained therefore not a doubt as to the person who had written his books.)

Very well, but what is a subject? A subject is a being whose core (essence) is impervious to change. Speculatively we should say that not all subjects are in time; but those that are must have an unchanging self-identity; and the higher a subject is in the scale of ontological perfection, the greater its essential indifference to change; so the perfection of God's being necessarily puts Him beyond the least hint or shadow of change. The cause of all things is not subject to becoming: He eternally is.

Until very recent times Christian theologians have been more than willing to follow this metaphysical development all of the way, as though it were contained in revelation. Some of their efforts to elaborate this doctrine, on the assumption that it is Biblical, are in fact admirable speculative flights. Espousing the same doctrine of divine perfection, Plotinus is on sounder ground: he knows that speculation cannot accept any historical-textual norms, not even the texts of Plato and Aristotle, as being anything more than illustrative of rational cognition. But be that as it may, the prior question is whether Christian theologians ought to have accepted so unqualifiedly the classical doctrine of substance and thereunder subsumed *subject.* Saddled with this doctrine Christian thinkers seem to be in no better position to account for the world of change than the classical metaphysicians. But surely Christian thinkers believed that the cosmos is entirely the handiwork of the Creator who has therefore a great investment in the changeful world, quite unlike that honored by any pagan deity. Hence we ought to say that the Christian thinkers were in worse shape than the great pagan metaphysicians. For here is the world of change in any case. Commonsense, in the West, is rooted in it. Speculative minds, East and West, have been embarrassed by it because it puts to them the question, What changes? Commonsensically, life itself is change, change of varying times and rhythms. Commonsensically still, there must be something to which or in which the change occurs, because change itself cannot be the subject of change. (This is commonsensical; but it inspired a famous dialectical argument. It is now a philosophical custom to say that Plato was unwittingly victimized by mere linguistic habit or, even more sadly, by mere grammar. It seems a bit odd—only to commonsense, of course—to use pretty much the same old grammatical structure with which to say Fie! to poor old Plato.) But now the question does seem to be a matter of degree; for the change must make a difference in some subject or we would not be able to mark it or to discuss it concretely and practically. One can seek to evade the point by saying that a subject (substance) is (timelessly) all of its changes; and as such it is not subject to any (further) change. This sounds a little like saying that X is the sum of everything that has happened to X, including everything X has done. But it cannot really be this, because X must also be at any given moment the sum of everything that will happen to it but has not yet happened to it. In that case X is surely a very odd kind of sum, since if X is already what has not yet happened, the as-yet-not-happened will not in fact make any difference in X; which is to say that that change at any rate has no reality. If we generalize this objection we reach a result that quarrels rather drastically with commonsense: future time is really an illusion. This would be a very strange result for a religion that purports to take the future with uncompromising seriousness.

Classical Christian theology tries to live with these metaphysical problems by insisting that future time is real for the creature but not for the Creator. But if we grant this we are confronted with a formidable consequence: substance cannot be used properly to designate any creature; and the creature is an aspect (or mode) of God the one real substance; so that man is no longer a creature of freedom, able in any sense to stand over against God, the same being at once the source of his creaturely greatness and of his awful wretchedness.

These metaphysical consequences would be a great embarrassment to the proclamation of the Gospel. If one embraced them one ought thereafter to forswear any form of judgment except the judgment of truth, because the power of actual determination in every subject and of every event has been imputed to God's power; and is God. In fact, the preaching church has often gone one way, in respect to such consequences of metaphysical import, and systematic theology another. In the abstract it is better that the church should preach the truth of the Gospel rather than teach doctrine whose soundness is a linear consequence of metaphysical speculation. Concretely, neither church preaching nor theology is able to enjoy good health when they are alienated from each other.

2. The creaturely subject is wholly within a causal system; and the proper personal name of the system is God. This God has chosen (if

the language of choice can be so extravagantly extended) to accomplish His purposes through creating and synchronizing finite entities (improperly called subjects). This seems to say that God is not content to exist in solitary glory; but it does not say that His creatures have any power (any reality, actually) that is not derived from God. They can do only what He consents to. In essence what He consents to is His own determination; and it would be hard to give a cogent reason why He should not do so.

We are not interested at the moment in raising purely metaphysical objections to this view. Our contention is that the theological appropriation of this metaphysical doctrine creates insuperable difficulties for the proclamation of the Gospel. These difficulties have not always been acutely felt and clearly expressed in the history of the church. The most compellingly interesting reason for this remarkable insensitivity is the drive of the church to fashion a Christian civilization, in Byzantium, in Rome, in Geneva, in Plymouth, etc. Theological systematization is much more compatible with this drive than is the preaching mission of the church. It is therefore among the gravest misfortunes, visited alike upon church and civilization, that reforming movements in the church have either repudiated theology in favor of the simplicisms of monasticism and of Biblical fundamentalism; or have haggled over doctrinal issues without giving any serious attention to the norm of preachability. So Thomists and Calvinists have haggled over secondary causation without worrying whether the Gospel of the New Testament ever uses the language of causation; or whether a confession of sin which is even remotely the repentance to which Jesus Christ summons mankind retains any reality when it is an effect determined by God from eternity.

The metaphysics that absorbs the human subject into the absolute causal sytem offers a remarkably consistent account of the regularities of nature. There is nothing very remarkable about this, however, since the regularities of nature furnish the model for this kind of metaphysical explanation. But it is also an account that gives powerful expression to the human love of order: a place for everything and everything in its place. Which is to say it is a view that leaves no opening to chance; and the possibility of a misappropriation of human freedom is rigorously denied. I am not prepared to assert that the Gospel implies cosmological chance. I believe that it does imply a kind of subject power which the classical metaphysics of causation renders unrecognizable.

In passing we note that St. Augustine's famous doctrine of man "being free only to sin" is a confusion of classical stature and momentous consequences. If man is unable to choose his true good it must be either because he has lost all power of choice, or because the good ceases to be good when man chooses it. St. Augustine will not admit either, quite understandably. But he persists in the folly of assimilating substance-language and will-language to each other. Truly, Original Sin is a great mystery. But there is no profit in crawling toward it over the pitfalls of categorial confusions.

3. The Christian theologian must grant an adequate meaning to time, if for no other reason than that the creature must have some characteristics, and live in a world, essentially different from God the Almighty Creator. An even better reason is the *prima facie* reality of time, because the system of a Christian theologian can only suffer from any reasonable similarity with pagan views of appearance and reality. The latter bemean the perceptible world by calling it appearance. A Christian account ought to redeem the perceptible world from that poor estate, by calling it creaturely. How sad it is therefore to note that the metaphysical options open to the Christian systematic theologians seem to have been but two: (a) time is cyclical; (b) time is linear.

a. It is customary to claim that this view is incompatible with the Gospel (and with the Bible altogether) because it was held by pagan thinkers. This is an absurd, if commonplace, reason for rejecting a metaphysical option. It is roughly comparable to rejecting a criminal's observations of the weather on the grounds that the criminal mind is not to be trusted. But a more serious reason is not hard to find. The view that time is cyclical is essentially incompatible with Christian faith in the once-for-allness of God's work in Jesus Christ. The Incarnation happened once, and that once satisfies all of the conditions. This is to say that time itself is radically modified by it.

This is a promising start. Rightly developed it would cause a great deal of grief to the traditional theological account of God's relationship to time. For the view that God sees all time as complete is nicely compatible with the view of time as cyclical; and is not at all compatible with the view of time as linear.

b. To say that time is linear is to exploit cosmologically both the Gospel and the *prima facie* reality of the experience of aspiration (or end pursuit). As to the former, the Gospel sets forth Jesus Christ as the event for which all time has been making. As to the latter, we note that in pursuing an end one has the sense of moving from phase to phase, from moment to moment, for the first time; not squarely to the denial that any such things have ever happened before, but surely to the assertion that this particular concrete sequence is *de novo.*

In recent times systematic theologians have made a practice of saying that time is linear and the "line" has a terminal point; for otherwise time would be infinite and thus rival eternity. This view is wrong on both counts. It is wrong on the first count because linearity *per se* omits the factor of periodicity. It is wrong on the second count because if it is true that time has a last point in its line, then time is an illusion now. Each of these points demands some expansion.

i. Linearity ordinarily understood is not subject to periodicity. Yet human time is essentially periodicity. In more vivid metaphor, man's time is lumpy rather than a straight line or an even flow. His moments are not so many equal segments of a line. Some moments are cosmically inclusive, some are scrappy and thin. One moment is an eternity of ecstasy, and another is an eternity of boredom. Even the pace, the flow, is uneven: now time crawls, and now it races. Moreover moments overlap and can be pried apart only by the forceps of abstraction wielded by historians and metaphysicians.

ii. If the time line as such has a last point, a moment is coming which contains no reference to a future moment. But a moment with no future reference is a denial of time rather than a unit of it; so that neither experientially nor analytically can such a moment itself be said to be in time. On the other hand this ultimate moment cannot be lopped off without destroying the whole series in principle. From which it is reasonable to conclude that the consummation of time cannot mean a last moment on a line. It might mean a moment in which the value of the whole process is supremely actual. This is what the Gospel of Incarnation does mean.

The classical metaphysical options have then been a drastically oppressive burden upon the spirit of freedom Christian theology ought to express. Why should theology not have struggled against this oppressive burden, even if the struggle falsified seriously the theological task? Even, that is, if it led to the invocation of mystery in order to exalt and protect the truths of faith. There can be nothing properly mysterious about propositional truth. There is something essentially mysterious about the truth of actuality. Thus the greater the actuality the greater the mystery. From which we properly conclude that all the reasons given for crediting the proposition "God exists" cannot prepare one for the shock of His actuality. The Gospel administers this shocking mystery. Woe to theology if it provide metaphysical insulation against it!

VII

So it has come to pass that even theologians turn to faith as to a divinely created and blessed instrument of knowledge, an instrument with which to avoid, if not to reform, the most grievous theological sins. Men have begun to wonder whether the doctrines of theology are not so many fumbling efforts to express propositionally what cannot be expressed that way at all. They have begun to wonder whether the intuitions of faith must not be expressed in the dramatic mode rather than in the explanatory-descriptive modes of traditional theology. Perhaps the truth of the Gospel is most properly expressed in the Eucharist, or in the life of humble obedience to the demands of Christian love, or in the B-Minor Mass. Perhaps theology even at its best, even when it is most humble before the Gospel, is only a dim distorted reflection of truth.

The possibility will bear some examination. The examination will need to be conducted with some care, or the game will go over to the philosopher, to the psychologist, to the liturgist, etc.; and the only grace left to the theologian will be to liquidate himself cheerfully and neatly. The program for theology proposed here could not be further removed from this graceful deferential suicide.

CHAPTER VII

The Principle of Faith

I

Faith is the name of a supernatural virtue. It is also the name of a theological passion for which a supernatural explanation is not immediately necessary. As a theological passion faith lays claim to being a special kind of knowledge; and as such it is a response to the competitive demands of the intellectual situation. This is not a complete interpretation of the passion of faith but it is a plausible one. Theologians must contend with a situation in which knowledge seems to have been preempted by the natural sciences. If it could be shown that the unique claims of Christianity exhibit (and not merely presuppose) a unique mode of knowledge, the case for Christianity would be greatly improved in the eyes of persons of intellectual sophistication.

Faith as theological passion does not settle simply for uniqueness of cognitive power but must drive on to lay claim to primacy of cognitive station. The whole package requires further explanation; and this ought to be an explanation that does justice to the actual situation of the church in the world. The essential work of the church in the world cannot be faithfully done if the grand elements of its message are wholly vulnerable to the corruptions of illusion. Since the church exists to preach the Kingdom of God it must have a sure criterion for distinguishing the Kingdom of God from the kingdom of man. Jesus Christ is the revelation of God and he is therefore this criterion. We know already that Jesus Christ is God's "everlasting Yea and Amen," so we cannot suppose (to say nothing *hope!*) that God has rejected or canceled the kingdom of man. But we have to add at once that the Kingdom revealed in Christ does not stand in a simple dialectical relation to the kingdom of man. Accordingly the truth of the Gospel cannot be displayed in the correct operation of a dialectical method. A dialectical method attains certainty only in the negative mode. Any affirmations it generates must be contingent, unless the operator of the dialectical device is ready to admit that the device has now come to a predetermined end. In that case only one kind of contingency remains in the dialectic: the dependence of the whole operation on an unwarranted axiom.

The truth of the Gospel cannot be committed, therefore, to any dialectical device. The revelation of God in Jesus Christ is certain beyond all human certainties, whether they are commonsensical or dialectical. And yet this truth is open and responsive to man's spirit. This astonishing situation has been referred to as the "dialectic of the Kingdom of God" (pp. 75 ff.). Perhaps now we ought to admit that all of that boils down to the ominous paradox: the revelation in Jesus Christ is at once infallible and subject to development, at once definite and open, concrete and universal.

Theological paradoxes (if not all paradoxes) are programs for bringing and holding together notions that seem bent on living apart from each other, and perhaps wisely so since each threatens to annihilate the other. But in this particular case do we not have a fairly easy out? We can safely impute certainty to God and openness (contingency, mutability, corruptibility, reformability, etc.) to man. Ostensibly the true character of each is thus assured. God is protected from corruption; and man—especially theological man—is given the lumps he deserves. Theological interpretations of Jesus Christ are subject to all of the infections of worldly wisdom. So when the church claims absolute validity for a scheme of interpretation it is trying to make a human achievement absolute, it is trying to make the word of man infallible. Surely this is a very touching and instructive performance—it is so full of human need! Nothing is more human than the desire to master time and bind it in obedience to the desire to escape the limitations of creatureliness. And what could be more instructive than the refusal of the Roman Catholic Church so far to unify claims of infallibility with the possibilities of dogmatic development? If a dogma is infallible it cannot be modified. It might be forgotten, but it is not subject to correction.

A church really capable of dogmatic inerrancy would have to be substantially divine if one assumes that God Himself is dogmatically inerrant. The reason for this is, I think, fairly straightforward: the teaching church, rather than the dogma itself, is infallible. A dogma is a proposition, and it makes no sense at all to say that a mere proposition, no matter how lofty and momentous its meaning may be, is infallible. As a proposition a dogma may be certain or certainly true. It does not strictly follow that the institution (or person) promulgating that proposition must be infallible, since we have it on very prestigious authority that God has brought perfect praise "out of the mouths of babes and sucklings" (Matt. 21:16, RSV). But I suppose that the point is, again, fairly obvious: one cannot count on babes and sucklings to deliver when necessary. Children say wonderfully true things but *they* generally do not know what is wonderful in their speech and when they do they are insufferable. The church, on the other hand, can be (must be?) counted on to deliver the wonderfully true and to know what is both true and wonderful in such utterance.

Why should this strain or outrage the sensibilities of the non-Catholic? I suspect that it does not do so until the Catholic Church converts "wonderfully true" into "infallibly binding upon true believers" as something not to be denied if not something to be said. The latter distinction is profoundly offensive despite its innocent air, because it is utterly foreign to anything in the Gospel. The amazing bounty of God's grace is there set forth as wonderfully true; and in such terms that even the closed mind and hardened heart might well wish it were so. But what is so wonderful and exhilarating about an institution's pronouncement and self-advertisement as being incapable of error where error would be ruinous? No one denies that grievous and flagrant errors have appeared in this same institution. Thereafter what can the true believer in it do but deny that the real church made them, or insist that the errors were not made where it counts?

Our conclusion is modest: The first of the theological virtues is humility. The Christian thinker, whether he is a bishop or a mere professor, cannot ascribe absoluteness to the products of his own thought. If absoluteness appears in his work, it must be imputed to God's decisive intervention in the otherwise normally fallible operations of his mind. Inspiration is the wrong name and explanation of this intervention. So intervention may already have gotten us off on the wrong foot. In the gift of the Kingdom in Jesus Christ God has already, and once and for all, intervened. In God's own testimony about His own Kingdom there is the only infallibility that the Christian can accept in good faith.

Yet we have to allow the claim of faith, if by faith we mean now the "spirit of obedience" to the Holy Spirit. Jesus Christ promises the Holy Spirit to all who will be faithful disciples; and the Holy Spirit will make all things evident to them (John 14:15ff). Thus through faith the truth is mediated for "the healing of the nations" (Rev. 22:2). If we were to say "infallibly" mediated we could at most intend by the adverb to call attention to the efficacy of the preached Gospel. The Gospel has been immaculately conceived, it is the pure mind of God, the simple expression of His absolute freedom and righteousness. It must therefore be infallibly deployed, it is always present as the Gospel in the variety of languages in which it is proclaimed in the world.

The use of such figures of speech as "immaculate conception" and "infallibility" is here governed by a single purpose, namely, to call attention to the fact that the church everywhere is now haunted by the question whether the Gospel is a kernel of truth wrapped in the husks of cultural relativities. Ought we to conceive of the Gospel as the core for which faith probes? Is not faith summoned to discover the *real* Jesus by using the right historical-theological method to disentangle him from the layers of cultural interpretation?

These are the questions that animate the theological passion of faith. Faith emerges as the right relationship to the scientific-philosophical demands of the age, and the spirit of obedience to the demands of the Holy Spirit. Faith seems now to be both of these at once. If it is so we may be impaled on still another paradox: To be obedient to the Holy Spirit one must also (first?) be obedient to the spirit of the age; or, fleeing from the fallible absolutes of the church, we embrace—as though it were heaven's doing—the infallible relativities of the world.

Faith as the theological passion is confronted by two cultural phenomena of immense moment. These are: (1) the pathos of knowledge, and (2) the breakdown of communication.

1. The informed people of this age know a great deal more about the cosmos and about man than the people of any other time. This towering eminence is deeply tinged with pathos, because the people of this age do not know what this knowledge means, they do not know what it is they know. The pathos of knowledge appears also in a pervasive uncertainty about the proper ends of human life, human destiny, and the relationship of the good to the truth. This uncertainty is ineffectively screened by the dogmatism about science as the

only knowledge; because we are still waiting to hear what science is knowledge of; and what we ought to do with it. Naturally, then, many believe that the proper import of the scientific advancement of knowledge is that one ought to be skeptical of all claims to certainty. All of the absolutes are in disrepute. But all the while the people in charge of things have to make decisions. If they make the wrong decisions much of the world will be destroyed—there is certainty about that. So who wants to have a mere skeptic in charge?

And yet the tough-minded pragmatist in public affairs is widely admired and emulated today. It is not necessary to think of him as being a skeptic. Rather, he is the opposite and the opponent of the dogmatic ideologue who has only circumstance to blame if he does not become a red-eyed fanatic. The victims of the decisions made by both may find the distinction academic, but we like to believe that the victims of the pragmatist are likely to be fewer: since he carries a very light metaphysical kit he ought to be able to maneuver more adroitly in the tight corners. This must surely seem greatly advantageous to all concerned except the fanatical irredentist.

Nonetheless a commonsense concern is hard to throttle. How does the tough-minded pragmatical leader know which way is forward, which direction is up? When the ship is sinking the right direction in which to swim is toward land—if one can see it. If no land is in sight and the night is very dark, one ought to swim to hold despair at bay; but there is very little of the pragmatic about that. Then one struggles against death. Policy will have to wait on the outcome. This is to say that one can be pragmatic only when life options are plural. Then a poor choice may reduce life, to be sure; but death is not one of the choices.

Furthermore, not even the toughest-minded pragmatist is pragmatic about everything. I mean now everything in the land of the living. He is not able to put everything to the pragmatic test even if he is tentative in his endorsement of whatever he has not so tested. So soon as he acts—especially if he decides the fate of others—tentativeness may linger in his attitude but it is banished from the public world. His act may of course be irresolute; but he is on record with it; and for all he knows or now can do it may change the world. There would be great comfort in cowardice if it could disengage one from the necessity of acting at all.

How then can we avoid concluding that life-and-death decisions cannot be made pragmatically, or, at any rate, not just pragmatically?

The immensity of the stakes cannot but argue that the men in charge had better be right as well as tough-minded, or we shall all lose the game that allows no replay.

In such a time the "little man" is very reluctant to seek power and to admit to any responsibility for its exercise, especially in the political realm. After all if no one really knows what ought to be done, why should he expose himself to the very great risks, not of being wrong but of being a coward?

The church cannot fail to acknowledge the "pathos of knowledge." It is deeply affected by it. But it must pray for grace that it shall not be paralyzed by this situation. It is called to preach the Gospel as the truth for every age. Alas, it must also confess that this truth is to be accepted "on faith." Thereby the church is put into a very vulnerable position, and the good Christian sees new meaning in the scriptural testimony, "for the Lord disciplines those whom he loves" (Heb. 12:6, NEB).

"On faith" makes the church exquisitely vulnerable to either of two temptations, or to both in deadly rotation: (a) to say that faith is assent to a formal creed; or (b) to say that faith is the consensus of religious and moral sentiments prevailing at the moment in the church, the consensus of the truly spiritual people, the conscience of the righteous.

These temptations are ever with the church. Of the two (b) is the more attractive and persuasive because it offers a way of dealing with the pathos of knowledge: the church too can point both to the needs of practical decisions and to dominant moral sentiments by which these decisions can be guided. So why should the contemporary prophets flog the conscience of the high-minded consensus? Is this conscience to be condemned because it is the best in the moral fabric of civilization crying out for release both from servitude to the second-best and from the fearsome burden of corporate guilt? The Christian surely must try to deal justly with the conscience that is the faith of this civilization. It may well be an important part of his own outlook.

The life of the church is so very hard because the Gospel is implausible, if not fantastic, when it is preached as the divine truth and therefore as the criterion by which even the conscience of the high-minded, the deeply spiritual, must be judged. The Gospel declares that man can be for God because in Christ God is for man. To be for God is an aim, a teleology, which the conscience of the age accepts only when it is reduced to a sentimentality, to a graceful illusion in which man continues simply to love himself even when he must hold his nose to dim the stench given off by his behavior.

2. The breakdown of communication is a phenomenon closely related to (1). It is a phenomenon of many aspects. One of these is the inability of specialists in one area of knowledge to communicate meaningfully with specialists in other areas. Another aspect is the common inability of the specialists to get through to the masses hungering for the latest word from them. A rich common language is necessary for these purposes, but it does not exist.

A third aspect of this phenomenon has great importance for the church: the line of communication with the past is down, and perhaps it has been broken. Earlier generations accepted a heritage in good faith and thereby found history meaningful. Destiny was disclosed in that history, and the arm of the Lord.

Now destiny is presumption; and to whom is the arm of the Lord revealed? Now in Western civilization it is very easy for man to see himself carried upon a broad irresistible flood, where the meaningful is whatever he can clutch to himself as it is swept near him. This or that element of the past is snatched at and is flaunted as a cultural adornment or as a badge of moral earnestness. But everything is at the mercy of caprice. Here and there people cling to tradition, as drowning men cling to splinters and straws; but even they have little sense of doing anything more than arbitrarily grasping something privately meaningful.

Furthermore in the realm of everyday relationships we have grave troubles with any communication that threatens to rise unaccountably above the commonplace. In the everyday world we are therefore strangers to one another, for what do we share of fundamental and great importance? We have a confused awareness of a common but shallow history; and therefore we have a confused awareness of ourselves as really human. We have common habits but we do not have a commonly understood explanation and justification of these habits that ever threatens to break out of cliché. Of necessity we live together, but we do not speak a rich common language.

This impressionistic reading of the breakdown of communication in our civilization is very likely an exaggeration of the facts. It is justified only if it helps to illuminate the predicament of the church: it is charged with preaching the Gospel in a rich common contemporary language, a language rich not merely because it is contemporary or popular but because it gives creative expression to the truths upon which human life must be built. The predicament is severe. If the church does not find such a language, it will find itself speaking slangily to the ignorant masses and speaking in a very sophisticated way to the knowledgeable few. In the latter event it may pride itself on the eminence of its clientele. In trying to do both, the church creates the illusion that it has two gospels.

II

So far we have avoided the most obvious factor in the problem of communication confronting the church. This factor is the resistance of the Gospel to every attempt to abstract its truth from its language. The truth of the Gospel is not a kernel persisting in successive efforts to remove from around it everything that is merely timely, everything that expresses the essential mentality of a given age. So to view the Gospel is to work from (or to fall into) a very inadequate understanding of historical existence: to exist historically means that man is forever trying to extract nuggets of truth from the detritus of earlier epochs. In this process truth operates as a felt need of the present. This view in turn is a function of a metaphysics of time in which the present is the only reality, temporalistically speaking.

We are not presently concerned with the metaphysical inadequacies of such doctrines, though I think they are grievous. Our concern, rather, is with the fundamental religious affirmation of the Lordship of Jesus Christ in and over history, including Gospel history. Jesus Christ is the Lord of history rather than an object of historical pursuit. He is the judge of the multitudinous historical representations of his being: he, rather than the regnant idealizations (ethical, eschatological, and aesthetic) of an epoch, is the judge. Hence "the quest for the historical Jesus" is essentially a search for the translation-formula by which the Gospel and its Lord can be most satisfactorily adjusted to the regnant idealizations. This is the case unless from the outset of the quest the same Jesus Christ is acknowledged as being in full command of the language as well as of the truth—unless, in other words, the realm of idealization also does obeisance to God's anointed Son.

(When we speak thus of a language we refer to a mode of expression rather than to a linguistic system. The Gospel can be proclaimed in English [even in American], in Greek, even in German. The reason for this is clear. Every concrete language does some essential business with being and the good, every tongue has ontological intentions of one kind or another. But we must go further than this. A language lives so far as it enables people to feel that the way in which they express themselves in it is a proper response to the way things are. Every civilization claims that at least one mode of expression reaches the heart of things. If it does not do so, then that civilization confesses bankruptcy for the essential human purpose. May God have mercy upon the civilization that blithely elevates a nonexpressive sign system [such as mathematics] over every expressive mode and succeeds in stripping all expressive modes of access to reality; for thereby the human spirit is isolated from everything but itself and cannot even understand itself properly.)

The Lordship of Jesus Christ is therefore to be construed in this way: Jesus Christ and the Gospel cannot be separated from the language that God chose from the beginning, that God chose purely and simply because He is God, Jesus Christ himself exists in the expressive mode, he is the language in which God expresses himself. The same Jesus Christ opens for man an existence within the same expressive mode. Only thereafter and thereupon is it important to learn how to make correct abstract attributions to the divine being. It does not follow that theologians ought not to argue with metaphysicians. It means rather that theologians cannot expect metaphysicians to tell them how God is known to be what He is.

Viewed from this perspective the problem of interpretation that the church is always facing becomes the problem of faith, if now by faith we mean first of all the acceptance of a mode of expression wholly binding because wholly real. To have faith is to accept a pattern, a mode, as comprehending at once my being and the being of God. The pattern is the revelation of God in Jesus Christ. Given Jesus Christ we cannot say that God externally controls the pattern. We must say that God is the pattern. And then we must say that God not only gives Himself to be the object of faith's knowledge, we must also say that God gives the mode in which He Himself as object is to be interpreted. By faith, faith.

III

We hear it said frequently in the church that one of the great spiritual discoveries of the age is this very thing: man is the creature who lives by faith. Minds given to speculation raise a question about this discovery. Is this necessity of living by faith the manifest work of God's grace? Or is it merely the dismal combination of weakness of instinct and dimness of reason? Nonspeculative minds flatter themselves that they have come upon the essentially religious quality of human life: "A person must have something to believe in." It is hard to think of a sentiment any dearer to the spiritual heart of contemporary civilization. But it reveals a terrible condition of spirit compounded of arrogance and poverty. The arrogance is the dismissal of real history and the summons to Everyman (or is it just to the intellectual elite?) to make up his own object of faith. The poverty is the result, the candidates for transitory deification. To make up an object of faith is to endow some element of the world, past or present, visible or invisible, with power and value sufficient to redeem human life from both triviality and disaster. Thus summoned out of creatureliness the elected gods prove to be as capricious and untrustworthy as their creators; and go down with them into a common grave.

Nevertheless Christians are frequently enheartened by this pervasive sentimentality about faith, and take it to mean that the world is finally coming around to give the spiritual kingdom, the religious realm, its due. This is an illusion. The fact is that the subjective necessity of faith has been largely isolated from objective necessity, the private need to have faith has been largely isolated from the demands of a real Lord. This isolation and alienation of the "inner" from the "outer" confers upon the individual his sense of freedom to believe anything privately gratifying. This is now called religious liberty.

On the other hand we must acknowledge that serious and significant attempts are being made to deepen the conception of faith. Perhaps the most notable of these is the interpretation of faith as the decision to be rather than believing something to be true. This view is close enough to the argument I am advancing that it will be of some value to see what problems it encounters.

The first problem may well seem the least formidable. Outside of theological discussion we generally do not use faith to signify a momentous act of decision; and we do use it as roughly synonymous with belief. Beliefs are habits often acquired and retained without intensive reflection upon the nature of things or upon alternative interpretations of the world. (The wisdom of the catechetical churches is thus evident, since they attempt to establish patterns of belief, or at least propositional objects of belief, in childhood; and so firmly that these beliefs will withstand every assault from the unbelieving world.) Decision, on the other hand, seems to follow belief; and especially when we think of really momentous and telling decisions. A person finds that he believes one thing rather than another (we are speaking of religious options). Thereafter he decides to join a company of like-minded people. He decides on the basis of his beliefs; and the more adult he is, the more we expect this to be the case. So if a person cannot accept the beliefs of the church, we should expect him to make the appropriate decision to go elsewhere. He may, of course, decide to pocket his demurrers on the prevailing beliefs in order to remain in that church for the sake of its prestige or its good fellowship or its aesthetically satisfying liturgy, etc.

Nonetheless decision might be thought of as a component of belief. For example, I may decide to express my beliefs in a particular way. Again, I may decide to put a particular evaluation on my beliefs, that is, that they are strong or weak, clear or confused, important or trivial. An evaluational decision of this sort ought not to be confused with a judgment concerning the truth or falsity of these beliefs. Indeed, judgment in the sense in which we have used it ought not to be confused with decision in the sense of an act of the will.

We have not shown that decision is never more centrally involved with belief. But if someone claims that his beliefs are so many conscious decisions, we must ask him what he means. We must ask him whether he decided to believe; or whether he decided to say one thing rather than another. Suppose he says that he decided to believe in God. Does this mean that he willed to accept as true the statement "God exists"? If this is what he means to say, then we have a more general question to put to him. It is the question whether in the case of religion we ought to abandon the intellect as the instrument of truth and install the will in its place. The question does not presuppose the ancient faculty psychology that seems to be a rigid compartmentalization of the human spirit. Quite to the contrary, not only in religious matters but generally the condition of the knower affects his receptiveness of truth. Nevertheless to see the truth of a statement is not a matter of willing or deciding to accept it, whether we are talking about religious statements or others. Certainly there are other and better ways of making the ontological point, namely, that what a person wills to be determines what he is. In this sense it is meaningful to speak of the penetrating power of truth.

The ontological point is one we have tried to make throughout.

It says something true about man's being; and what it says cannot be reduced to the perennial controversy over the freedom of the will. Whether or not something nonvolitional (such as raw onions in the stomach) determines one's power of choice, one becomes what one has chosen. Brutus may say that he was undone by the stars rather than by his stomach (or by his oedipal problem), but he lies. He chose to be an assassin. A causal explanation which assigns his choice to anything or anyone else, is a *prima facie* absurdity, though it may be intelligible as part of a metaphysical system. (There are of course counterfeits of choice, such as reflex actions. And there are actions which were once initiated by choice but for which choice is not any longer necessary.)

When we speak of truth as having a power of penetrating one's being, we have begun to use the language of commitment, where commitment is understood to mean the decision to relate oneself in trust to what one finds to be trustworthy. So to decide reaches more deeply into one's being than to assent to the truth of a proposition. Moreover, finding something or somebody to be trustworthy is rather more than simply crediting testimony as to the reliability of the person or power trusted. Specifically, the Christian life is not devotion to supposition, it is loyalty to God who reveals Himself as absolutely faithful. It behooves us therefore to see whether trust in the absolute faithfulness of God is what we ought to mean by faith.

Let us grant, again, that I can will to do one thing rather than another, for example, to be kind rather than cruel. Faith does not seem to be involved in this until or unless I believe that God, too, wills (wants) me to be kind rather than cruel. If this is what God wants and ordains, then cruelty is faithlessness, it is disobedience to God. Put positively, we are saying that one's faith is his trustworthiness relative to God's demands, as unfaith is one's untrustworthiness relative to God's demands.

Very well. But there is in this an unanswered question: What are the acts of the mind by which God is known to be God? Surely the Christian recognizes the reality and the significance of such acts, or his believing that kindness is a divine demand is merely an effort to give his moral preferences as much weight and dignity as possible. We know that only the pure in heart shall see God; but we must not infer from this that God is a projection of moral purity. The eye of the soul must be clear and it must be properly focused if one is to know God. But no matter how clear that eye is, it cannot see what is not there. The inverse rule is just as valid: Seeing what is there is not finally a function of wanting or needing to see it. We cite the inverse rule here simply because some people seem to have learned from psychologists that all perception is conditioned by what the perceiver wants to see or has been taught to expect to see. But it is necessary to assume that perception is in principle a truthful instrument. If this is not so, there is no problem of knowledge; and no psychology, for that matter.

Thus faith is a word that is now stretched to cover three phenomena: believing, trusting, and knowing. If we omit the third, very serious difficulties ensue, as we must now see.

In human affairs one believes that certain statements are true because (in part) one trusts the person who has made these statements. But one does not credit these statements simply because one trusts their human source. There is some kind of check upon the accuracy and weight of his statements. If no such check is possible, trust is then "blind": one relies upon another person without any knowledge of *his* access to the truth, and therefore without any knowledge of *his* reliability in that particular. And this of course is exceedingly poor policy both for trustee and trustor.

Now it will be said that these considerations are canceled when we leave human relationships behind and ascend to the divine world. Must we not solemnly confess that unless we *trust* God, throwing ourselves without reservation upon Him, we will never learn the truth about Him? Here surely we cannot ask for an independent checkpoint from which to assay His reliability! In His case, what He says must be accepted as true simply and purely because He has said it.

Unfortunately the beauty and purity of this confession are corrupted in theology by the elevation of the reasons of the heart over the reasons of the intellect. This performance assumes thereafter (before, more realistically) that the "heart" is the instrument God chooses for His revelation. Thus the intellect is reduced to the status of Esau, it is thrust out to live in the wilderness of mere abstractions. The next step is inevitable: to question this interpretation of faith is the same as questioning God. This means that the proposition (propositional assertion) "God does not lie" rightly pronounced permits the person who says it to participate in the divine infallibility. In fact, however, an atheist could agree that "God does not lie" is analytically true, that is, is true if one knows what he has in mind by using the word "God"; but he could not agree that the statement is true of any actual world without giving up his atheism.

If then we look a bit more closely into the famous opposition of the reasons of the heart to the reasons of the intellect we shall find some interesting things. If, for instance, we mean by heart, emotion, impulse, and feeling, we should have to say that these are odd reasons at best. Sometimes they present themselves spontaneously, sometimes they are summoned by cerebration. Sometimes they drag reasons along as so many hostages. For example, a man says that he did something "because I felt like doing it." If this comes off, it comes off as an explanation of his action but not as a justification for it. To give a reason of the heart for what one has done is to relate the heart to an actual situation under the category of fittingness or appropriateness. But the right use of the category can be determined only by perception and judgment rather than by the heart itself. Thus we have this result, put as a paradox: One who says that a man ought to do what he feels like doing, is saying that he ought to do it whether or not he feels like it. Or nonparadoxically: Ought has no validity so far as it is a name for a feeling. The statement "I felt like doing it" is neither here nor there on the question whether you ought to have done it. We can assume that you wanted to do it, or felt impelled to do it, from the simple fact that you did it.

On the other hand the powers to trust and to love are certainly powers of the heart. The things to which these powers relate the self are the reasons that the heart gives. Accordingly the heart is intimately involved in faith, since no activity of the intellect can establish that kind of relationship to the object of faith. Trust makes demands both upon the heart and upon the will. It is a vote of confidence in another being, and a pledge of self to that other being. Therefore we say that faith in this sense of trust is an essential condition of revelation. It is a way to knowledge and not a way of knowing.

(There is an epistemological view expressed in this result. Facts are perceived, truths are known. Facts are given, truths are understood. One assents to truths. One apprehends facts. Reality is therefore both fact and truth. A world that was all truth would have no concrete existence. A world that was all fact could not be known.)

God can be trusted so far as one knows that God is a person. One cannot trust the world. I can trust one or more persons in a room but I cannot trust the room as such. In a burst of rhetoric, which may carry me out of sight of the shores of sense, I may say that I accept the universe. In love for the first time, or in such a way (with such a person) as to make me forget the first time; or after an unusually fine dinner and while smoking a very fine cigar; or lately returned from mystic communion with God: given any or all of these I may say, "God! it's good to be alive!" This is about all that universe-acceptance means. The greater the rhetorical feat therefore when someone vows to accept the universe, to trust the cosmos as such, who has never fallen in love (or never confessed it); or who has a poor or provincial digestion; and who habitually avoids mystic communion of any kind or degree!

Herein the wisdom of Scripture is shown forth: "I know whom I have believed" (II Tim. 1:12). This is not a case of saying, "I know *that* I have believed," a statement presumably incontestable by anybody else. Rather it is a case of directing attention toward (if not upon) the object of belief, the existence of the being in whom I believe. So again the act of trust follows upon a certainty of knowledge, it goes out toward a being "fixed" by perception and judgment rather than posited by exigent affection and clamorous impulse. It is not the heart which knows where God is to be found; but it is the heart by which I am bound to the love and service of the God who knows where I am to be found.

Man can give his heart to a false god, which cannot return the gift. He can give his heart to a false god because the heart of man has an inextinguishable desire to be mastered (as his will does to be a master). This hunger can feed on husks left by swine; and adore the porcine providence that so thoughtfully bequeathed them.

So the heart, endowed by its creator with this powerful flame of hunger, cannot be simply turned loose to seek its ordained food. It must be harnessed by some other power of spirit to seek what is truly good, what alone is divine.

IV

Let us consider once more that religious discovery of contemporary civilization, the universal necessity of faith. We have suggested that there are two ways in which this necessity has been described; and we must briefly review these.

1. The necessity of faith can be seen in the fundamental power of nondemonstrable beliefs.

2. But it can also be seen in the fact that man's being is actually constituted by his power of self-commitment.

1. Our return to the consideration of this view is determined by its acquisition of philosophical quality of a sort. The nondemonstrability of some beliefs may be supposed to be a clue to the nature of things. So it is not merely a case of these beliefs being both nondemonstrable and indispensable (the qualities claimed for presuppositions). What is added now is the claim that the world (or that aspect of it taken on faith) responds favorably to the bid of faith. But the world responds favorably to the bid of faith because reality has actually solicited the movement of faith toward its good. Thus faith is not merely a product of cultural-psychological conditioning. It is a response to a summons from the heart of things to the heart in us.

This view has both commonsensical and sophisticated modes of expression. Commonsense man (perhaps the real philosopher in all of us) has a very firm and thoroughly nondemonstrable belief that the sun will rise tomorrow. Obviously this belief cannot be proved to be true today. The sun has a habit of coming up, but we do not really know (commonsensically) that the habit is incorrigible. Some people hope as well as believe that the time is coming when the sun will set never to rise again. In the meantime, along with the rest of us, they get up in the morning because the sun has done it again.

There is a good bit of evidence, now collected by science, that this heliotropism is very deeply embedded in human life, and is not merely an odd habit of thought. Here human habit is predicated upon the habits of the world; and this turns out to be a good thing for man.

Science provides a more sophisticated account of things. The scientist cannot prove that nature is in all her parts a law-abiding lady. But things work out, for minds able to follow them, as if this were so. Things work out as if complex and elegant equations were the Open Sesame to all of nature's secrets. They work out so well, in fact, that every now and then a mystic of science reports that behind the curtain of sense phenomena there dwells (really, merely thinks) The Master Mathematician. But, again, there is no proof that nature is law-abiding in all her parts, unless we suppose the very fact that things work out is a kind of proof.

Why we wonder and how we wonder whether the working-out is not a kind of proof can be illustrated in a crude way. Flowers, fripperies, and bubbly wine may induce a woman to part with her chastity. The thing that unsettles the mind, as well as disrupts the economy, of her seducer is the possibility that she may not have had a price on it to begin with, so far as he was concerned. Perhaps his approach provided her with an opportunity and not him with an argument. So the poor chap may never know whether he was a seducer or a conquest. But does the distinction matter that much? Perhaps one day he will learn that she had her way too; or even that her way determined his. In any case the venture succeeded. So also of science. Working from beliefs that cannot be proved, it has had many successes. These successes cannot be written off as so many sociocultural achievements. They are that but they are also achievements of knowledge.

But now we have run into difficulty. Some nondemonstrable beliefs turn out to adorn and perhaps even instruct human life; but surely there are also such beliefs which harass and misdirect it. Do we really know whether belief in God is one of the former rather than one of the latter? Grant that belief in God cannot be proved. This does not justify the conclusion that the belief is necessary rather than merely possible. To show its necessity one must go beyond showing how profitable acceptance of the belief may be in terms of peace of mind, patience, courage in adversity, and large bank accounts. Beliefs about important matters ought to have practical consequences. But where evidence is produced by believing one thing rather than another, people exercise the greatest possible latitude in what they believe. So if we were to try to show that belief in God is a necessity, we ought to show that it is a belief solicited by reality as a response to an antecedent movement of reality toward man. This would be to show that the necessity of belief in God is grounded both in the being of man and the reality of the world; and, again, this is to speak of ontological necessities rather than of habits ingrained and enforced by civilization.

2. Perhaps we can see somewhat more clearly now why the view that man is naturally religious has taken such a firm grip upon contemporary religious thought. In the heyday of Pragmatism theologians and theistic metaphysicians were proving the truth of Christian faith by pointing to the human good produced by that faith. The current attempt to prove that all men are religious, at least in the sense of putting faith in something, is not so provincial, not so man-centered as Pragmatism. Now the point is to show that man by essential constitution is bound to commit himself to something in whose power and value he has an ultimate confidence.

In Chapter 2 we have discussed this view. There I contended that any program for making every man religious is bound to impoverish the meaning of religion. My object in bringing up the view again is to show that it is seriously deficient so long as it does not do two things:

a. show how the religious fundamental of commitment is related to the other ontological fundamentals;

b. show how the religious thrust is toward being mastered rather than toward world mastery.

a. We cannot be satisfied with the (2) program until this is at least attempted, because otherwise the religious fundamental may easily turn out to be a peculiar formation adopted by some other ontological element, such as anxiety, or love. The enlightened spirits of the eighteenth century (to say nothing of more recent illuminati such as Freud) were convinced that they had tracked religion home to fear. Quite apart from the empirical embarrassment inflicted upon this theory by people who do not fear their gods at all, there is the further, perhaps more abstract, difficulty: anxiety (to say nothing of a particular fear formation) is simply not the religious category. The (2) view is here an important corrective, if it would only show how the religious fundamental, whatever it is, is world-relating as well as self-expressing. Anxiety posits the value and the peril of the ego. Commitment posits the value and security of Deity. Thus a crippling limitation appears in saying that a man's god is whatever he fears *or* esteems above everything else. So Zola says of one of his fictional families: "The Gregoires had an unshakable faith in their mine. . . . God Himself was not more reliable. . . . It was their private deity whom they in their egotism extolled with sacred rites as the divine benefactor of their home." (*Germinal.*)

Our quarrel is not with such fictional realities. Presumably we all pin our hopes to one thing rather than to another, just as to act at all is to make choices in the hope that what we choose is right for us, and will be properly gratifying. Our quarrel is with the inferences drawn from these realities, namely, that such faith is a religious commitment, in essence identical with the Christians' faith in God. Zola has confused the unconscious reflexes of egoism with religion. It would be much nearer the mark to say that the Gregoire's real religion would have been their trust that some power other than themselves was at hand to justify their commitment of everything in them to the mine. If a man worships his belly (his stomach and/or his genitals), worships literally, that is, he is demented; and the world is never without such madness. But if he acknowledges a power ready to justify gluttony and lasciviousness, that is quite another matter. Then we may be tempted to say that the pagan worships Ashtarte to justify giving free reign to lust, going from bad to worse; and, conversely, that the Christian worships the Holy Mother of God to justify his sexual inhibitions. But the facts are difficult, in both cases. The worship of Ashtarte was much more than an open invitation to debauchery. It made debauchery an episode (strangely disciplined in its madness) in a continuous commerce with the mysterious powers determining human life. And as for the worshiper of the Virgin, we must say again that the facts are difficult. Sexual inhibition may be at work in such elevation of sexual purity; but this worship is, again, but an episode in a continuous commerce with a supreme being who has larger stakes in the world and in man than sexual purity, the parish priest to the contrary notwithstanding.

The reality of religious faith therefore is to be found in the powers evoked and pursued to justify, purify, and direct human life, rather than in the patterns and incidents of commitment. The miser becomes religious rather than merely miserly when he looks for corroboration and comfort from powers which he cannot master. He may behave ritualistically toward his gold, where his heart is. But his religious hopes are not pinned to the gold. His hopes go out to the ruling powers of the cosmos, that he may keep his booty and live to enjoy it. His religion is not his aim in life, but everything that he does (and dreams of doing) to wrest the consent of Deity to these aims. His religion is what he believes makes these aims possible and desirable in a world over which his control is minute and ephemeral.

Thus the religious thrust is in essence ego-transcending rather than ego-reflexive. The ego cannot refer to itself to justify itself simply because this self-reference is but another statement or expression of itself; and it already has on its hands an expression requiring justification (which is a mode of interpretation). The world already knows that ego has acted. The question of justification is, Why? The question of justification is not, From what cause? It is rather, For what envisaged good?

b. The religious thrust carries the ego toward being mastered rather than toward world mastery. To this we must add at once: toward being mastered by the good for which the self yearns in its essential depth. Without this, the desire to be mastered can all too swiftly and surely become a mortal sickness: the yearning for death.

Without the qualification, the desire to be master of the world can also become a mortal sickness: megalomania. In the fundamental depths of his being man knows that he is a creature, as well as finite. The religious thrust and the metaphysical appetite carry the self up and out to a communion in which his creatureliness is fulfilled rather than obliterated. This fulfillment in the divine community is precisely what we mean by being mastered. Faith understood as commitment is surrender to the power of such a community. It is the act of relinquishing an illusion of absolute sovereignty in order to obtain the reality of creaturely fulfillment.

V

Christian faith incorporates things known and things believed. The ontological fundamentals of man's being are things known. Chief among the things believed is: The scriptural witness to Jesus Christ is true. To have faith in God is to accept the sonship opened for us in the Gospel of Jesus Christ. This sonship, this condition of being, is the transcendent and triumphant affirmation of man's creatureliness, because it is God's word. To accept this new condition of being, this new state of affairs, this sonship, is no longer an expression of the ego looking for justification. Faith in God is acceptance of a justification which grasps the essentials of our being. The "I" is no longer ego, but Christ.

The theological task devolving upon us, accordingly, is immense and exhilarating. It is to show how the things believed do in fact grapple with the ontological fundamentals of the human condition. To succeed in showing this will not in itself be a proof of the truth of the Christian faith. It will be a proving, a putting to the test, a demonstration, a showing-forth, an opening-up, an explication, and an elucidation. It will not be a reason for becoming a Christian. It will be the reason why a Christian believes he must preach the Gospel of Jesus Christ as long as he lives and in every way he lives.

The next step must be to outline what a Christian accepts in believing that the scriptural witness to Jesus Christ is true. From the outset we must see in all such endeavors, that the being witnessed to, rather than the instrument of witness, is the prime object of faith.

CHAPTER VIII

The Gospel of Jesus Christ

I

The church has only one thing to preach: Jesus Christ and him crucified, "the power of God, and the wisdom of God" (I Cor. 1:24). Changing times cannot mean a changing Gospel because Jesus Christ is the same yesterday, today, and forever (Heb. 13:8). To every generation of every civilization no other name is given in heaven or on earth before which every knee shall bow in praise and obedience (Phil. 2:9-11).

The word given to the church to proclaim is at once a message concerning the Kingdom of God and an acknowledgment of a person. The duality-in-unity of this message has proved exceedingly difficult to sustain in the life of the church; and therefore it has been exceedingly difficult for the church to be the obedient servant of the Word. The church has preached the Kingdom. It has preached it crookedly and straightforwardly; but whether the one or the other the church has accepted the prime responsibility of preaching the Kingdom of God. The acknowledgment of the Person, the rest of the Gospel, has been turned over to the theologians for interpretation. The preaching church has always talked about Jesus Christ, but it has often acted as though the real meaning of this talk was known only to the theologians. The theologians for their part have made the most of an opportunity thus provided for metaphysical speculation. In this curious way the muse of metaphysics has been richly avenged for every stone hurled at her by pious ecclesiastics: for with every intonation of Chalcedon and Nicaea, the Person of the Gospel bows humbly at the shrine of classical metaphysics.

There is no way to preach these creeds that does not resurrect the heresies the creeds were designed to seal in the tomb of outrageous error. Moreover there is no way to preach the creeds that does not put the congregation to sleep. But this is not yet the worst. If the church preaches the creed it ceases, at least for that moment, to preach the Gospel. This is why we have begun by saying that the life of obedience to the Gospel is an exceedingly hard one. As the New Testament is our witness, the proclamation of the Kingdom of God and the acknowledgment of the Lordship of Jesus Christ are an individual unity. But as history is our witness the church tries again and again to divide the indivisible.

Thus the first task of theology is to show how the Christ of the Gospel and the Gospel of Christ are to be preached as a unity created by God, a unity that man must not sunder. This is the first task of any practical theology worthy of the name. Every other arm of the theological enterprise must return to this first task, it must return to see how practical theology has fared with this task, and to lend whatever aid it can. Just as the most sophisticated logician returns to the primitive grammar of everyday language when he buys his groceries, makes love to his wife, and buries his dead. (Everyday language is full of puzzles and nonsense, but these must be endured, so long as the day's work is there to be done—or until men talk like computers.) So also the most sophisticated speculative theologian must return to the primitive language of the New Testament in which the Kingdom and the Lord are preached as an indivisible unity.

II

We shall begin with the Gospel of Jesus Christ, that is, with what he preached, the same being the Kingdom of God (Mark 1:1).

This is no sooner proposed than we must brace ourselves to receive the frontal assault of Biblical historians and Biblical theologians. For together they ask: Do we really know what Jesus preached as distinguished from what the church puts into his mouth? Well, given the now dominant doctrines and theories concerning history, we should have to admit that everything Jesus Christ preaches is put into his mouth by the church, since there is nothing to suggest that Jesus Christ left his memoirs around somewhere. But on the theological side we have to say that the church of the New Testament epoch found in its mouth the thing Jesus Christ had given it to say. It is an agreeable conceit that the church made up or picked up some incredible yarns in the process, very much as any hagiolatrizing mentality always does. I shall not debate this conceit here, except to say that even the most incredible yarn in the New Testament (and we cheerfully permit the historian to take his pick) has a clarity, pertinency, and sobriety, relative to the Gospel Jesus Christ himself preaches, which make post-New Testament hagiolatry look like wildly hyperbolic, undisciplined, and even morbid exercises of imagination. This suggests very strongly that the imaginations of the preachers of the New Testament were under a very powerful and sure-handed discipline; and I take it that this discipline is the Gospel Jesus Christ himself preached.

Therefore we repeat: Whatever else Jesus Christ did, we can have no serious doubt that he preached the Kingdom of God; and that everything he did pertaining to his vocation, he did as a mode of Kingdom-proclamation. But we must be even more radical than this. Jesus Christ acknowledges the Kingdom of God as the sole and absolute warrant for his words and his actions. It is not too much to say that on every page of the New Testament the truth of the Gospel of Jesus Christ is proved by an appeal to the Kingdom of God.

But even in the New Testament there are interesting differences—out of which a good deal of theological confusion has sprung—in the way in which this appeal is made. Matthew, for instance, seems to take it as an appeal to the truth taught by the Old Testament prophets (beginning with 2:15). Matthew is therefore an inspiration to theologians who want to make the most of the eternal determination and ordination of Jesus' (and man's) earthly career. But even Matthew knows that Jesus Christ cannot be subsumed under the Law and the Prophets. He taught "as one having authority" in himself rather than as one who is wholly dependent upon a tradition (7:29). Certainly it is necessary to know and believe the scriptures; but it is also necessary to know the power of God, that living reality to which scripture is witness (22:29). The prophets spoke truly because they perceived the Kingdom from afar. The Kingdom itself now at hand is the criterion of all prophecy, old and new (12:28).

It is not our present purpose to delineate in detail the important differences in the ways the New Testament sets forth this criterion of all prophecy. We must rather consider the qualities of the Kingdom of God Jesus Christ proclaimed.

1. *The Kingdom is very near.*

There are three strikingly different ways in which Jesus Christ preaches the nearness of the Kingdom.

a. It is something about to happen.

b. It is something remarkably like human arrangements.

c. It has more certainty than even the most certain of the natural habits of the world.

a. The Kingdom is something about to happen (cf. Mark 1:15; Mark 14:30; Matt. 16:28; Luke 10:11; Luke 11:20). This teaching of the imminence of the Kingdom has from the start been very vulnerable to misappropriations, of which apocalypticism is the most dramatic and perhaps also the most resilient. History has nights black enough and long enough repeatedly to bring apocalyptic seeds to full flower. The twentieth century is a good case in point with its distinctive thermonuclear version of apocalyptic doom. But whatever the flavor and hue of apocalypticism in the Christian context, it is always a misappropriation of something really given in the Gospel: a very emphatic insistence upon the portents of an imminent occurrence. The Kingdom overhangs the present moment. Therefore, "Repent!" Even now a blow is being struck at the kingdom of evil from which it will rally but never recover. Therefore examine where your own loyalty is!

"Even now" is a clear reference to the works of the Kingdom Jesus did. The healing of the maimed, the casting out of demons, the forgiving of sins, these are Kingdom works. But "even now" refers also to the imminence of the Kingdom: Jesus Christ binds his own being to the proclamation of the Kingdom by announcing his death and resurrection (Matt. 16:21-28). In these events the Kingdom comes indeed, and they are about to occur.

Accordingly the religious business of gathering and trading on mysterious portents of the future is no part of good faith (Luke 11:29-32). Jesus Christ has forced the powers of evil into open engagement. Because of him the kingdom of evil is now gathering itself for a paroxysm in which it will receive its deathblow (Luke 10:18). (If there is any place where foreordination makes perfect sense it is hell, because the demons *know* that they cannot win but resolve nonetheless to oppose God to the bitter end.)

Imminence is no more than the beginning of what is intended by the nearness of the Kingdom. It pins down the meaning, terrible and wonderful, of the present moment; but it does not tell us what the Kingdom is. So if we were to stop here we should resemble theologians who make everything of encounter events but who say that they have no knowledge of the being encountered.

b. The Kingdom is remarkably like human arrangements, which is to say that it is near in its perfect recognizability. It is not created by man, but it is human. It is a Person, but it is neither you nor I.

Much has been made of the Parables of the Kingdom in the preaching of the church. Has enough been made of them as Christ's chosen vehicle for revealing the similitude, the perfect recognizability, of the Kingdom? It is like a political realm: it has a King, couriers, subjects, laws, courts, boundaries, and enemies. It is like a patriarchal family: it has a Father, sons (and even daughters), and servants. It is like a business establishment: it has an owner, hired hands, bosses, percentages, wage scales and complaints from workers, and assessments. It is like an army: it has a Commander, scouts, legions, standards, and deserters and traitors. In the preaching of Jesus Christ the Kingdom is like so many human arrangements and performances that we cannot help but sense and share the amazing joy that radiates from this divine freedom of expression!

The (b) meaning of nearness tells us a great deal more about the Kingdom than imminence alone can. Parabolic similitude does not tell us that human arrangements *de facto* are good but it does tell us, triumphantly, that the Kingdom is a community. As a community it is a common life; and it has an immense variety of members; and each member is loved, honored, and rejoiced in by all.

We have already noted that theologians have a formula that promises to make sense of the likeness of the Kingdom. The formula is called analogy. We recall it here because it seems to be so close to similitude but actually is far removed from it. Given analogy (a particular theory of analogy, in fact) theologians know that the Kingdom of God is not really like human arrangements because God Himself can be said to be like any creature only in a very special manner of speaking, a manner so special that only the trained and ordained metaphysician can understand it. Our objections to this overcoming of similitude by analogy are modest to the point of absurdity. One: given even the most astonishing unlikeness of God Himself that a theologian could (mysteriously) posit, God might nonetheless set up all sorts of humanlike arrangements either for fun (to "glorify Himself") or to achieve some business of cosmic magnitude. If a theologian were right at the outset, i.e., about God's total unlikeness (whatever in the world that might mean), he would thereafter have no very plausible way of deciding why God did anything God was charged with doing. Two: the business of analogy misses the essential point in the New Testament similitudes of the Kingdom, namely, that Jesus Christ so sharply and decisively delineates its quality and shape that a man is left without excuse when he is asked why he has not chosen the Kingdom. As an object of love the God preached by Jesus Christ is really the Father. As an object of holy terror the God preached by Jesus Christ is really Judge. As an object of absolute loyalty the God preached by Jesus Christ is really the Lord of lords. Really, in each case, not analogically. Standing at a spiritual distance created in part by theologians, we can easily and lightheartedly decide that "father," "judge," and "lord" (and all other titles and attributes of God) are symbols; and thereafter gather information to decide whether they are living or dead symbols. In this way theologians become amateur sociologists rather than subtle philosophers. But the moral is about the same: One must wait upon an expert decision about religious language before one can become a real Christian.

Nothing could be further from my intention than to depreciate philosophical and sociological prowess in theologians. Nevertheless I do think that these powers can be misdirected; and that they are misdirected when they are used to deter or deflect a Christian from recognizing the quality and shape of the Kingdom of God as set forth by Jesus Christ.

c. The nearness of the Kingdom is also expressed as the certainty of truthfulness. This is not the same as the inevitability of imminent occurrence. This is the certainty that "the plan of creation" will be perfected. The Prophets proclaimed the Kingdom as an unimaginably glorious fulfillment. The absolute faithfulness of God, rather than the substance of the Kingdom, is revealed to them; and Israel clings to this assurance as to a well in a dry and thirsty land. Now Jesus Christ adds an immeasurable joy to this. He testifies directly to the Kingdom because he is the first-born son of the Kingdom. The Promise is no longer just that the Kingdom will come. The Promise is his pledge: I will be with you forever. This is a perfection of faithfulness.

The truthfulness of the Kingdom has another aspect. In its proclamation man sees what he really is. Man is what the Lord of the Kingdom summons him to become. Why then is the response to the summons of the Lord not absolutely spontaneous? When it comes it is the response of the depths of our being to the "Day-Spring from on high," it is a tropism placed in us by the Almighty Father. Why then do not all persons respond promptly and in utter naturalness to the showing forth of the Kingdom? The question reveals our readiness to overlook man's membership in a counterfeit kingdom. Because of his voluntary contribution of himself to a counterfeit kingdom man now has access to the Kingdom of God only if he repents. He has wasted his inheritance by trading on it for his own glory. He has surrendered his creative powers to no-gods. But at least one tropism is left. And this element of the divine likeness, though crippled and defaced, is the rock upon which salvation is built. He can hear the truth and recognize it for what it is. Therefore once he sees how near the Kingdom is and senses its dearness, he may indeed repent and be saved.

2. The Kingdom is dear beyond all comparisons and beyond all possibility of successful counterfeit.

The dearness of the Kingdom is both (a) its incomparably great value; and (b) its costliness as an object of human desire and pursuit.

a. The incomparable and inestimable value of the Kingdom is set forth in the Parables of Jesus Christ. What does not at once meet us there can nonetheless be exhibited as a chain of proper inferences, as follows.

i. The supreme value of the Kingdom is expressed as the fulfillment of a promise so time-binding and historically essential as to be fundamental in man's being. Thus the mythological back-dating of the promise of the Kingdom to the original human pair is to be understood Christianly as the grounding of human existence in a promise for which history is the story told in time. The story begins with a promise made to Israel. The Promise is given to Israel purely and simply because God so chooses. Before God chooses Israel, Israel is a "nothing" (Hos. 2:23). So God is not Lord because Israel chose Him. He made Himself known to Abraham, Isaac, and Jacob as the Almighty. Now He reveals Himself to the people of Israel as Lord with Israel forever; and because they are His by His election, they are now the people of the Promise (Exod. 6:2-7).

Nothing in the New Testament denies this, no matter how vehement the accusations leveled at "the Jews." Rather, the Promise of the Kingdom becomes the presence of one who opens it to all who will open themselves to the love of the Kingdom whether or not they are "sons of Abraham."

ii. The supreme value of the Kingdom is not conferred on it by the greatness of human expectation. Expectation and aspiration are able to augment the value of their objects; and never more so than when they have been repeatedly tried and frustrated by great vicissitudes. But the Kingdom draws aspiration to it, and it disciplines expectation. The Kingdom instructs hope and conforms hope to its own transcendently blessed reality. So both things are true: we do not know really what to hope for until the beauty of the Kingdom is revealed; and we respond to the disclosure of this beauty under the deepest promptings of our essential being.

iii. Thus the Gospel is preached as news, as tidings the like of which have never before been published to the world. No one, whether Jew or Greek, Greek or Barbarian, has ever heard anything like this before. But whoever really hears it, no matter how wildly different his civilization from that of Galilee, has an inner and implacable assurance of the truth of the Gospel. His humanity leaps up in trembling fearful joy when the Gospel is preached, because the Kingdom therein disclosed is for his humanity. But the Kingdom is for humanity in God's own way. Man is created for the Kingdom, he cannot conform the Kingdom to his desires and achievements. He can have the Kingdom only in the spirit of obedience, not in the will to be world master.

iv. The Kingdom is therefore absolutely beyond all possibility of effective counterfeit. Man is created to seek truth in order to enter into the fullness of his inheritance as a creative spirit. The Kingdom is this truth. The lie cannot prevail against it.

Yet the certainty of the Kingdom does not prevent the lying spirit from having a go at cheating, for the simple reason that it *is* the lying spirit. And one of the lies this spirit peddles is that God made him a liar. (Perhaps this is the beginning of the heresy that society makes criminals. The devil knows better; but there is no profit for him in admitting it. Anyway, he plays for bigger stakes than an endowed professorship—for himself.)

So history abounds with false messiahs, the lying spirits who leap about in ecstasies of prophecy in behalf of one counterfeit kingdom or another. They have moments of success, too; and some of these successes are monstrously attractive and breed great disasters. They owe their success to human well-doing that blights the desire to do better; and to man's conviction that he is better off without God and thereafter without any obligations beyond self and tribe; and to innumerable other things that produce in us a great unreadiness to pay the price for the Kingdom of Truth.

b. For the Kingdom of God is unbearably costly. A wise man gladly gives up everything for it. Where does he get the courage to appear to be a fool to the wise of this world? Perhaps in this courage he is already the beneficiary of the Kingdom, a speculation somewhat shocking to our civilized conviction that God grants a headstart to no one. Be that as it may, the wise man *is* wise because he sees the value of the Kingdom, and he will not stop thereafter until it is his.

i. The Kingdom demands everything. This is the first aspect of its costliness. The Kingdom of God does not share its sovereignty, it does not distribute its value on loan to other realms, it cannot be incorporated with conflicting interests. We cannot have it unless we are prepared to do without whatever conflicts with it. And again our civilized sensibilities are outraged by the discovery that there are such things. We do not know in advance what things they will be for us, and this is another source of uneasiness about the Kingdom.

The multiplication or intensification of uneasiness about the Kingdom leads us to ask, in mounting fretfulness, why it is so terribly expensive. To have it why do we have to struggle? What is more appealing than the picture of ourselves loving, serving, and enjoying the Kingdom in perfect naturalness? And what picture is a greater illusion? It is an illusion rather than a pure fantasy. "Doing what comes naturally" must somewhere and sometime be the situation both *de facto* and *de jure*. But where and when? And what? One of the saddest little self-revelations of contemporary life, and one by no means limited to college sophomores, is the unquestioned assumption that the natural spontaneous good life would be one in which sexual expression is casual, free of responsibility, and quite unbelievably good fun. But why do we not dream as readily and happily of a society in which people naturally prefer the good of all to private good? Why do we not picture ourselves as naturally thinking first of the neighbor's welfare and then of our own? The sad truth is that man in the state of nature is everywhere in chains. His fantasies seem to spring from his latest (rather than his deepest) bondage to legalism.

We must return to the question why the Kingdom is so costly. An appraisal of our situation will provide some elements of the answer.

Each of us has a plethora of commitments and investments; and each projects his self-love into these expressions, distributions, extensions, and reflections of himself. This is called the well-rounded life. It is a life in which the person is canceled and comes therefore to love his own death with unwitting extravagance of ferocity.

So when the Gospel of the Kingdom is heard, nothing seems easier than to add the Kingdom to the list of commitments, assigning it a place and value under the category of the spiritual. This is easier than rejecting the Kingdom flatly. The flat rejection is not easy for one who believes that every cause has some value, especially if it is spiritual, and is part of the Tradition.

Unfortunately for our peace of mind the Kingdom cannot be added to the list of pledges now in force. It demands an unqualified first place. From that position it launches judgment upon all other commitments, which is not a very nice thing for it to do. The Kingdom must be loved above all other things, not alongside them. Acceptance of the Kingdom is therefore a kind of death, but it is not an unwitting and merely kind death.

It is clear, then, that part of the terrible costliness of the Kingdom is its manifest power to enforce a drastic simplification of existence. A remarkably large part of the history of Western civilization is the story of how this demand for the simplification of human existence has been interpreted. Monasticism is one such interpretation. Self-denial for the sake of aggrandizing the institutional church is another one. Economic frugality for the aggrandizing of investment capital is still another one. Hardly a single teleological suspension of the natural man has escaped being interpreted, and socially enforced, as the self-denial, as the radical simplification, demanded by the Gospel of Jesus Christ. Every civilization, as Freud saw in the peculiar half-light cast by his own doctrines, is a story of such teleological suspensions and repressions enforced against the ego. (The suspensions and inhibitions are enforced against the ego rather than upon the unconscious. The unconscious is the effect of repression, not a participating cause. The unconscious is not the primordial ground out of which ego arises. It is a fragment of ego, the connection—and in the most drastic instances, the identity—with which is now obscured in consciousness.) But Christian culture has given a normal structure of repressions a supernormal teleology. The astounding consequence: many generations in the West have believed it to be divine wisdom to suspect and despise life in this world altogether! This is why we contend that the Gospel can become a civilization only by deducing persuasive heresies from it, whether or not a church council denounced them or even discussed them.

The simplification of existence demanded by the Gospel of the Kingdom cannot be systematized as a social program. Any such program is an attempt either to universalize some precious feature of an actual society; or to incorporate a segment of ideality as yet unrealized —one or the other, no matter how piously Scripture is quoted to certify a social program as the clear demand of the Gospel, or to assure people that this is the way the Kingdom comes on earth. Thus even the most rational and humanely inspired schemes for achieving distributive justice take unto themselves the religious quality of works righteousness.

Such observations (dogmatic strictures!) take away nothing from the sincerity of the protagonists of systematic social reform or from the real social gains registered by such efforts. Nor does it give the game over to systematic opposition to social reform. Counterreformation systematic programs are hardly less vulnerable to judgment upon works righteousness.

c. The costliness of the Kingdom is also revealed in the Gospel of Jesus Christ as the crucifixion of death as well as of life. The Kingdom of God stands over against the kingdom of death. Man does not enter the divine Kingdom merely by dying. Death as an escape hatch from the travail and guilt of life is surely the most hideously bewitching counterfeit of all. It proves only that one can hope to die now rather than pay later. How drunk with disgust or with folly does one need to be to credit that lying hope?

The Kingdom demands that man acknowledge its supreme value even at the cost of his own life. Thus the Gospel clearly envisages and sanctions a metaphorical dying; and it may require an actual dying out of season. "There is a time for being born and another time for dying." The truth and wisdom of this is proverbial, and it directs attention to the broad appointment of Providence. These appointed times are subject to unannounced and ostensibly unscheduled interruptions. Awareness of this formidable fact is called ontological anxiety. Ontological anxiety occurs within the providentially ordered seasons of life and the world. This limiting power exercised by Providence over anxiety is hardly perfect, but it is real. Even in the moment when disaster strikes, the rhythms of continuity can sometimes be felt already to be asserting themselves.

What ought we to say about Crucifixion in this connection? Put sentimentally, Jesus dies "before his time," a young man full of promise and hardly begun on his mature life of leadership. In reality the time of Jesus Christ embraced the Cross. He was obedient to the Cross because he was first obedient to God to whom the Kingdom belongs. His readiness to die (thank God that he was not overready!) does not make him the first Son of the Kingdom. If that were the rule only a fool would hesitate to seek crucifixion. His obedience to the Cross is a pure expression of sonship. It expresses a sonship already established and otherwise expressed, a sonship about whose priority there can be no doubt.

So the Christian cannot hope to win God's approval by embracing his own cross. This would be tantamount to loving people for the evil they do. Being already assured of God's acceptance, the Christian accepts his cross as part of his total obedience. He does not seek to know from God what his trial will be or when or where. He can be very sure that it will come as a rude inexplicable interruption of the season. He will not be ready for it. His reliance upon the Spirit will need to be absolute.

3. After all of this it must strike us an anticlimax to say that the Kingdom is disclosed in Jesus Christ as the perfection of the plan of creation; and therefore the joy and peace of the Kingdom are already communicated to the life of faith. Joy and peace are aspects of life in the Kingdom of God that are even now made available to those who believe in Him. The time in which faith lives is always the acceptable year of the Lord.

a. The joy of the Kingdom is richly expressed in the Gospel. It is pure and perfect joy.

What emotion, what expression of man's being, is more precious or more fugitive than joy? Happiness is a random gossamer surface thing. Joy is internally related to the creative power of human existence. (Spinoza is certainly on the right track when he says that joy is the affective correlate of vitality.) All passion spent, and the energy of life depleted to the vanishing point, one may yet have a kind of contentment. "Let now thy servant depart in peace" is the proper valedictory prayer for this state of being. But joy is what a strong man feels in running a race. Joy is the divinely intended value of ecstatic union, sexual and otherwise. Joy is the sense of one's vitality being lifted to the point of confluence with whatever anywhere that is creative and athrob with life. Joy is what one feels when one's powers merge so superbly with the being of another that one becomes what is perceived and loved. (D. H. Lawrence was deeply confused about this. Here we might say, somewhat lightheartedly, that he was too much of a Christian for his own good. "Christian" attitudes, at any rate, show something of the same ambivalence. He frequently represents sexual union as the mystic ecstasy in which the ego dies an appointed death in confluence with the dark fecund powers of the world. But he also felt that the joy of right sexual love was a sure sign of the self's being raised to a fresh and unique level of creativity. To be caught up in this creativity is to be raised to the point where light begins to overcome the darkness, and the dark tangled primeval underground of the spirit is opened to the light. Lawrence, we may feel, is saved by this very ambivalence. What ought we to say of a Christian who persists in believing that the sexual power is linked firmly with the powers of darkness, so the joy of sexual fulfillment is unholy, if he has ever felt it? But perhaps we ought to be even more acutely distressed by the malaise now apparently epidemic among uninhibited youth: that blank-faced acceptance of sex as merely another pleasure of the body, a satisfaction hardly more significant than picking one's nose.)

The divine Preacher of the Kingdom, Jesus Christ, assumes that his hearers already know something about joy, brief and rare though these moments have been. He does not need to persuade them to believe that joy is a beautiful thing: they have tasted it and the taste is unforgettable. Their first draft of it may have been their last until now; but in that they had what every creator feels, from the nightingale singing his throat to a frazzle, to Almighty God who gave the morning stars something to shout about.

Yet the joy man has tasted before the Kingdom is disclosed has always proved transitory. From this he has learned crooked things: the joy was not pure enough or it would have lasted forever; and one would have had more of it had one earned more of it.

To this joy-doubting creature Jesus Christ preaches the Kingdom of God as the object and source of pure unbreakable joy. It is unlimited joy because in the Kingdom there is no limit to creativity. There joy is pure because nothing is available to adulterate, darken, confuse, or dissipate it. Indeed, the Gospel is "good news!"

Too, the joy of the Kingdom is *free*. How could it be earned? In this world the best we can earn is the pleasure of time off, a pleasure that dialectically preserves the travail of time on. But the joy of the Kingdom is free for a better and more fundamental reason. It is the joy attendant upon the release of the creative powers from everything that has oppressed and distorted them. This joy is therefore the authentic sense of being free to express what one really is. The war is over. Peace is at hand. Therefore, rejoice.

b. So the peace of the Kingdom is the peace that the world cannot give because the world helped to make the war. The world can offer a truce but not peace. It is a truce which always guarantees a fresh outbreak of hostilities.

This has not prevented the church from so preaching the Gospel that men are encouraged to assimilate the peace of the Kingdom to the peace of the world. Sometimes the church preaches the beauty of a peace obtained by withdrawing from the world, for the sake of one's soul. Sometimes the church preaches the beauty of a peace consequent upon the cessation of all desire. And we must not leave out of this account the peace made possible by an imperialistic sovereignty achieved by one power of the spirit over all of the other powers thereof, because the church sometimes preaches this as the peace of the Kingdom of God.

The peace of the Kingdom offered in the Gospel of Jesus Christ is like none of these. The Kingdom comes as the fulfillment of the world, and therefore the servant of Christ cannot have the peace of the Kingdom if he withdraws from the world. Again, the Kingdom comes to release the creativity of the creature, and therefore the servant of Christ cannot have the peace of the Kingdom by suppressing the power of desire. Finally, the Kingdom cannot be likened to any earthly empire, secular or ecclesiastical, because God rules in it and over it in absolute love; and therefore the servant of Christ cannot have the peace of the Kingdom if he accepts as ultimate in his person or in his world any other power or principle for the ordering of human powers.

But there is still another false preaching of the peace of the Kingdom. The church sometimes preaches the peace of the Kingdom as a purely private feeling indistinguishable from the feeling of self-satisfaction and self-approval. This is certainly a peace which the world can give; and it is a peace which the world can withdraw. It is not the peace of the Kingdom of God, not simply because the world can give it and can cancel it, but also because it alienates the interior man from the community of God's appointment. The peace of God is given in and for the life of that community.

4. Jesus Christ preaches the Kingdom of God as the perfection of unity. The Kingdom is that condition in which man comes fully to himself because God is there in the inexhaustible plenitude of his own life. Thus the Kingdom is the community actualized by God's condescension, that is, by God's proportioning Himself to the creature

whom He has created for Himself. The Kingdom is therefore the community, and the only community, in which no wall of alienation is possible. The principle of individuality is affirmed by the Kingdom without reservation. In the perfect unity of the Kingdom difference is no longer a threat to identity: you do not diminish me by your being yourself to the utmost of your power. We are more because each of us is an individual. Neither of us can claim to be greater in the Kingdom because he had a head start, such as being born a Jew or an American or a Baptist or rich or poor. In the Kingdom greatness is measured by the quality of love expressed, and not merely felt, for all; and all other claims to dignity and power in the Kingdom are null and void. "Let him who would be chief among you be the servant of all." This can be framed as a paradox: a man who aims to be the greatest will make a very poor servant, unless one can learn what the Kingdom really is only by being a servant! If that is the case, then the greatness open to human calculation pertains solely to the size of the investment of oneself one can make in and for the community. It pertains exclusively to one's power of love rather than to greatness of return and increment for self, such as the magnification of one's lovableness.

In the perfection of the unity of the Kingdom we have a sure foundation for understanding Christ's demand for self-forgetfulness: "whoever seeks to save his life will surely lose it." Obviously the avoidance of death is not at stake, since the avoidance of death is a pure ontological impossibility. Jesus Christ is talking about the death of the soul. He says that a self-protective, self-justifying, self-continuing soul is a lost cause: it is another ontological impossibility. To try to save one's life is an attempt to use life as it cannot be used, every illusion to the contrary notwithstanding.

"But whoever loses his life for my sake and the Kingdom's, shall surely save it." This can be read as a divine encouragement to martyrdom. One can become a martyr for bad reasons, and one of these bad reasons is the hope of thereby winning a crown in heaven. The plain emphasis in the Gospel of Jesus Christ is upon having the Kingdom in view in the exposure of one's life to mortal peril, rather than one's magnification. Martyrdom ought not to be a policy or a project. If one is so to die, one must hope and pray that one will see at the end the Cross of Christ rather than the obituary columns and the beautiful memorial window to be given by an admiring and grateful posterity. The martyr, in other words, must die for the Kingdom if he is to earn the highest accolade of the Kingdom: "Well done, thou good and faithful servant!"

The good and faithful servant is the one who has already "died to himself" before it occurs to some power of this world to hang him up for the instruction and entertainment of the general public, or from malice.

The unity of the Kingdom of God is a hard Gospel for the church to preach, even when the worldly powers are deacons. No existing human organization is the model actualization of the Gospel. Every empirical human community excludes or downgrades some elements of mankind. To be sure, the church does not make any such exclusions "in principle." The colored people stopped at the door of the church in Birmingham might have heard the preacher say that outside the church there is no salvation. Since they cannot enter that church, the preacher is either condemning them to hell because he has enough bouncers to keep them out of his church; or he is saying in effect that his church at any rate is not the church indispensable to salvation. We have of course overlooked what the preacher and his bouncers really mean, which is that these black people are really happier and better off in an all-black church, and white people are happier and better off in an all-white church.

(It is now considered a failure of Christian charity to point the finger of Christian judgment at any Southern city. Here the assumption appears to be that the Christian ought to occupy himself solely with his neighborhood iniquities. One can imagine that the sober citizens of Sodom felt that their home town got a bad press. After all, is it fair to call it sodomy when the foul thing also occurs in Dubuque? So Birmingham too has earned its ignominy. The fact that other cities may not have made it into that class does not diminish her disgrace.)

So the appeal to "in principle," in Birmingham and elsewhere, can be a naked exercise in self-justification. In the light of the Gospel we know that all such exercises are futile. In the Kingdom there is no wall of separation. Those who continue to build such walls on earth, or to cower behind the ones already existing, are still in the kingdom of darkness, and slaves and lovers of its lord.

Who then is within the Kingdom of God? What must we do to be saved?

5. Those belong to the Kingdom who accept and obey the law thereof. No other claim, birthright or whatnot, is enforceable upon

the Kingdom. Whatever one's history, there is but one condition of membership.

Here we must acknowledge that we have arrived at one of those decisive places from which divergent theological roads lead. Jesus Christ seems to have preached that this one condition of membership in the Kingdom of God is repentance. Yet very early the church posted another condition not reducible to this one: believe in the Lord Jesus Christ and you will be saved (cf. Acts 16:31). But there are also indications that Jesus Christ made acceptance of his word, his preaching, the condition of acceptance into the Kingdom (cf. John 5:24).

Divergence is not necessarily incompatibility. This general observation may not have any decisive bearing upon any particular issue of historical scholarship. It may have a bearing on the theological issues; but this remains to be seen. The theological contention I wish to propose is this: The distinction between faith in Jesus Christ and the faith Jesus Christ himself held, is theologically unreal and Christianly unimportant. Even if historical scholarship were able to uncover the "faith" Jesus Christ held in the same sense in which the historian might be able to tell us what faith Abraham Lincoln held, we would have in that alone an insufficient reason, if a reason at all, for making the distinction here rejected.

Coming back, then, to the repentance that Jesus Christ preaches as the condition of membership in the Kingdom of God, we say that this must be understood as the authoritative demand of one who knows directly and fully what the righteousness of the Kingdom is. He knows this by his immersion in the life and power of the Kingdom.

We need accordingly to note the following things about the demand for repentance.

a. Jesus Christ does not assume that the hearer of the Gospel already knows all that he needs to know about the law of the Kingdom. But since his first proclamation is "Repent, for the Kingdom of God is at hand!" he knows that the hearer has not obeyed so much of God's will as was already disclosed. The hearer of the Gospel already knows something about the righteousness of God, and he has not met the demands he already knows. In addressing the Romans, St. Paul makes the same assumption, though of course he does not hold them responsible for having known the righteousness of God as disclosed through Moses. Whether Jew or Gentile, therefore, man lives under condemnation: he is at enmity with himself and his creator. The Jew has not observed "the weightier matters of the Law" even though he may have been hyperscrupulous in observing its letter. The Gentile has set at nought the rudimentary knowledge of good and evil that God has imparted to all mankind.

Romans 1 is a great comfort to the protagonists of natural law. But too much can be made of this text for this purpose. Granted that St. Paul makes a great deal of the immorality of doing the things that arouse shame in the very people who do them. This is what it means to sin against nature: deliberately to do the shameful thing, whatever it is. No doubt St. Paul, as one who had been a strict Jew, was grievously offended by the sexual laxity he saw in Rome; and in respect to the demands of sexual purity he remained a Jew, except when he lapsed into suspicions or anxieties about marriage. But Paul's own moral code is not the issue at stake. The question is whether the Romans are perverse according to their own lights. He says that they are. In other words, natural law here is not a rudimentary code of morals. It is, rather, the feeling of condemnation, not just guilt but shame for moral perversity, sexual or otherwise.

b. Neither the law of the Old Testament nor the rudimentary moral sense is a premise from which the law of the Kingdom can be deduced: the moral experience of man is not an anticipation of the revelation of the righteousness of the Kingdom. For example, the Old Testament law makes common cause with many other moral codes against willful homicide. But Jesus Christ says that anybody who hates his brother is in danger of the everlasting fire. Some nice things can be done with this, such as making hatred the everlasting fire, the foul and fierce heat that destroys whatever it touches. Or, again, we can use such texts to prove that Jesus teaches an ethics of intention.

Certainly there is merit in such interpretations, but there is not much weight of truth. Hate is evil not simply because it may erupt into overt violence, but because it is the negative, indeed the ontological negative, of love; because, in other words, God has made love the first law of the Kingdom. When man breaks this law, he violates his own being.

But the first law of the Kingdom can then hardly be a law at all. No moral system can command a person to love his fellows. Obligation, as a moral phenomenon, does not sink so deeply into the fundamentals of human existence, it would seem. It is on the ground floor, yes, but it has no power over the deep passions.

In preaching the righteousness of the Kingdom Jesus Christ appears to ignore this plain fact of the moral life, much to the bewilderment and frustration of many highly moral people, to say nothing of moral philosophers. Many an honest good man has said, "Try ever so hard as I can, I am not able to love my mortal enemies." Is he therefore unworthy of the Kingdom? The answer of Jesus Christ is terribly clear: Yes. The reason is just as clear: If I cannot love my enemies it must be because I hate them. I justify my hatred by saying that my enemies are wicked, they deserve my hatred and the hatred of all righteous people. Truly, my enemies may be wicked—there is wickedness in the world after all; but I lie if I say that my hatred of these wicked people, my enemies, is but an instance of my hatred of the whole damnable species of wicked people.

So it would be possible to oppose wickedness without cementing myself to it with hatred of the malefactor. Jesus said, "Love your enemies. He did not say, You really have no enemies. He did not say, Do nothing to impede or arrest or reform your enemies. Jesus Christ himself exerts a power, and envisages a situation, in which evil is overcome. That power is love. The situation is the community of reconciliation. In the light of that power and of that community we begin to understand what is really evil in hate. It is a destructive force, it opens fresh wounds, and poisons old ones, in the body of mankind.

c. Accordingly the demand of repentance is a demand that the hearer desist from doing hateful things and begin doing the things in which love is expressed. The works of love are the things in which a person undertakes persistently and intelligently (one would hope) to be helpful toward any and all who need help. But the works of love are more than this. For the person who does the works of love in faith, these works are an "imitation of Christ," a following-after Jesus Christ. Thereby the works of love are a response to the righteousness of the Kingdom of God, disclosed in the mighty deeds of Jesus Christ, those good works of his that are the only authentic "signs and wonders" of the Kingdom of God in history, that same Jesus Christ who went about doing good, and who in the perfection of love was obedient even unto death upon the Cross.

Therefore through Jesus Christ the works of love bespeak a common membership. The doer and the beneficiary are members each of the other; and both and all are one in God.

Here we begin to sense the confluence of Christ's preaching of the Kingdom and the presence of the Kingdom in his own person. For the faith by virtue of which simple human kindness is now endowed with the portent of the Kingdom, is an act of obedience to Jesus Christ. The disciples are the first Christians not because they breathed the dust kicked up by his sandals but because they first heard the summons "Follow me!" and obeyed. They did not begin by sharing his knowledge of the Kingdom but by obeying his representations of its reality and of its demands upon them. Because of their obedience we can begin further along, that is, with a knowledge of the Kingdom with which they could not begin. But the demands of the Kingdom are exactly the same. For us as for them Jesus Christ is the author and pioneer of our faith and of our salvation.

d. Jesus Christ expects to be heard and to be obeyed as the one whose representations of the Kingdom are authoritative. These representations are both verbal and nonverbal, he preaches the Kingdom and he does the good works of the Kingdom. In this unity of his Gospel, and the unity of the Preacher with what he proclaims, the "acceptable year of the Lord" is made known. Thus the Kingdom has entered the body of mankind, beginning with Israel and running on, in "majestic instancy," to embrace all humanity.

III

Very early the church began to claim things for Jesus Christ which he did not claim for himself. Our only serious question about any of these doctrinal inferences is whether they serve to illuminate whatever Jesus Christ claimed for himself, whether, that is, any metaphysical expansion and propositional formalization renders our understanding of the authority of Jesus Christ more secure.

The question is not put this way in the interest of any kind of theological skepticism. The reason for summarizing the matter thus is already expressed in the New Testament. Jesus Christ spent himself without remainder to make the Kingdom of God man's primary object of perception and love. The New Testament itself does not let us forget that Jesus Christ preached the Kingdom and not himself. This is true even of the testimony of John, in which the question of the authority of Jesus Christ is of paramount concern; and where Christ answers the question by asserting his unity with the Father.

Since the church is called to preach Jesus Christ only, this must be the Christ who lived, died, and lived again for the glory of the Kingdom of God. It must be the Christ by whom the Kingdom is lodged in the body of mankind until the end of the world.

CHAPTER IX

The Identity of Christ the Preacher

I

The question of the being of the Preacher, the same Jesus Christ, is inescapably present in the New Testament. There it is obviously not generated by historical-scientific curiosity. Neither is it a product of philosophical skepticism. "Who is this Jesus?" is a call for the recognition of a personal identity as well as for an explanation of what he has been doing. In the latter sense the question has a certain similarity to the question, "who does he think he is, anyway?" ("Is this not Joseph's son?"), and this smacks more of outrage than of curiosity or wonder (Luke 4:22). In the former sense the question becomes, "Who is he *really*?—that is, ultimately or behind the appearances. The dialectic of the Kingdom of God is apparent in both senses of the question. Because God speaks as Jesus Christ human beings can now ask an ultimately significant question by asking, "who is this Jesus, that I may call him Lord?", whether they ask it in outraged human aspiration or in sure presentiment of peace and joy. Therefore we say that the question is raised providentially in the New Testament. It is the question in which the wisdom of God and the agony of good faith are simultaneously expressed. Jesus Christ himself asks his disciples, "Who do men say that I am?" The question is not designed to raise the issue of family or regional derivation. Neither God nor good faith asks it in order to set the wheels of metaphysical speculation in motion. What is at stake both in the historical context (Matt. 16) and in the human situation *per se* is the authority with which Jesus Christ preaches the righteousness of the Kingdom of God. If Jesus is Elijah *redivivus,* if his authority is that of a prophet (either a newcomer in the stream of prophecy or an ancient prophet of Israel miraculously reappearing), then men of good faith in the everlasting faithfulness of God ought to listen to him with respect and thank God for the renewal of prophecy. But if the authority of Jesus is the authority of Christ, Messiah, he ought to be obeyed; and to be obeyed is a very different matter from being listened to however respectfully and thankfully. So a man of good faith will seek to do what this Christ demands, because in these demands the Kingdom of God is addressing him. On Christ's warrant the Kingdom is something man must do as well as see and hear.

Now the great complication appears at once. Jesus is the Christ; but he is also a historical novelty; and therefore a certain kind of faith recoils from the revelation of this messiahship as though it were of Satanic inspiration. Such is the faith of Peter at Caesarea Philippi. In the power of the Spirit he detects the real identity of this Jesus. What is thus disclosed to him is at once filtered through a historical mesh that rejects real novelty.

So the great complication concerns historical novelty in an exceptional way. The question of authority is compelled to merge with the question of personal identity. Jesus does much more than proclaim the glory and the imminence of the Kingdom. In proclaiming what he knows directly and personally about the Kingdom he reveals who he is. His vocation comes from the depths of his being. His vocation comes also from on high. And the depths and the heights in him are one. Why then are we offended by the New Testament stories that are steeped in the "born to be King" atmosphere, and go to great pains to invent or borrow a philosophic apparatus that will scream "Myth!" whenever such stories come on? Is it because we simply cannot accept kings into our charming democratic outlook? Modern man is hardly as bedeviled as all that by consistency. In fact in the secular world men who achieve greatness are generally suspected of having been born with it (and scientists are now trying to track this preordination back to DNA). So in Luke's charming story (2:41 ff) it would seem that Jesus is out of his starting blocks, and almost out of sight, at the time when "normal" boys are taking the Boy Scout Oath. Luke's display of tender religiousness and poetic imagination has nothing in it to warrant offense, unless it tempts one into idealizations and romanticizings really pernicious in their effects upon the texture of faith. No such effect is more pernicious than the failure to grant to Jesus Christ the authority revealed in the full round of his life, death, and resurrection. Unlike us Luke does not linger either in morbidity or delight over these beautiful episodes. He has many other and much more decisive things to relate. Perhaps he knew also that any bright twelve year old can ask questions that a panel of theological greats could not field. By itself this proves only that he is difficult and not that he (rather than they) is somehow divine.

In the New Testament representation of Jesus Christ his authority and his identity are absolutely inseparable from each other. The church cannot in good faith try to separate what the Holy Spirit has joined. Jesus Christ is its only valid warrant for preaching the Kingdom of God. It has no one else to acknowledge as Lord on earth or in heaven. In acknowledging who he is the church is not merely offering a historical accreditation for its claims concerning the Kingdom. It is making an act of obeisance to the living Lord. The church confesses that Jesus Christ is the Lord in the Kingdom. This is a position of dignity and power in which he has been established forever by God the Almighty Father. The church acknowledges that the authority of Jesus Christ is the authority of the "only-begotten Son of the Father."

Drawing upon the speculative resources of pagan culture the church very early began to crystallize its confession as metaphysical doctrines of the relationship of the Father to the Son. Throughout the Christian centuries the church has tried valiantly to preach these doctrines; and even now the creedal churches appeal to them as to the rule of faith. I believe that this courage is misplaced, and for a categorically simple reason: The speculative mode has its own reward and it can neither be packaged for general distribution in an era nor bound upon the spirits of souls yet unborn as the content of their good faith. Gothic culture for example contains a great wealth of speculation. This metaphysical output is no more binding upon Christian preaching, or upon Christian speculation for that matter, than Chartres is normative for church architecture. This is not to deny that scholastic metaphysics is a marvelous intellectual achievement. Nor do I argue here that something has happened since to throw metaphysical speculation permanently out of gear (that would be a very curious argument on all counts). My contention is that the question of the being of the Preacher, Jesus Christ, must be lifted out of metaphysics, unless we can uncover a nonspeculative metaphysical account of man's being with which the imperatives of the Gospel make a natural fit. The question of the being of Jesus Christ is launched by the answer given to the question of his authority in formulating the demands of the Kingdom.

In Chapter III I have sketched such an account of man's being. The task now is to suggest how the authority and the identity of Jesus Christ are to be interpreted with the categories of this nonspeculative reading of human being.

II

The authority of Jesus Christ has an ontological ground: he is what he is from the depths of his being. He says what he says because of his command of the elemental powers of human being.

The ontological grounding of Christ's authority offers a sharp contrast to every kind of characterological grounding. The New Testament does not talk about the character or the personality of Jesus Christ, as we use these terms. (Indeed, we tremble at the mere prospect of a thoroughgoing characterological examination of Jesus, or of the personality-inventory test. Would he not surely appear to be an authoritarian personality, or a character in whom the drive for leadership produced messianic hallucinations? We must always remember that ours is an age in which the individual does not know who he is until someone else tells him.) Moreover the New Testament does not give us the comfort of grounding the authority of Jesus Christ in his moral achievements. His moral attributes are expressions of his authority. He was not called Son of God because he was a good man. His goodness expresses his Sonship and Lordship. In his full humanity Jesus Christ is in full command of the fundamental realities of man's being. He is in the human situation and in human life to the lowermost levels. But he is in the depths of human being as one from on high. His participation in human being is the participation of God. He is Son of Man and Son of God.

These venerable phrases must be brought into the context of the following broad characterizations of human existence.

1. *Power of Participation.* This is one of man's most distinctive powers. Of everything distinctively human it can be said that one participates in it rather than possesses it. Whatever it is, a concrete human person has it under the predicative rather than under the substantive mode. I am not Life, I am living. "I am living" identifies a subject ("I") with an enterprise, a state of affairs, which (both grammatically

and ontologically) will persist though I withdraw from it. This simple truth fills the unregenerate heart with disgust.

Now life may seem a very odd illustration of being-by-participation, since I had life before I chose it. In existentialistic terminology, I have been thrown into the world. In ordinary Christian language that life is a pure gift. In any case certainly our entrance lines are not very dignified or noteworthy. (This simple fact sometimes lends encouragement to false doctrines, such as the belief that we really do not begin as human at all.) But the beginning is only a part of the story. If the story has emerged at all, if it has acquired definition and aim as well as momentum, then the caterwauling entrance has only the meaning of the story as a whole; and otherwise there is no reason for mentioning it, either in the case of John Doe or of Jesus Christ. There is no point in telling stories about the birth of Jesus Christ unless the birth participates in the overarching meaning of that life. Even if we say, "*That* is where it all began," though in fact no birth narrative in the New Testament does say that, we clearly refer to a whole of meaning by no means visible in the newborn babe. So we have nothing but respect for the unconscious wisdom, as well as the aesthetic necessity, evident in clothing the whole cast of characters of the Adoration of the Magi in the culture of the time in which the Adoration is painted or hymned. The Magi could not have seen the whole story in the newborn babe or they would have been the first Christians. They could not see the whole story because it had just begun. The birth participates in the whole story, the birth is really the beginning, just so far as the process of interpretation can make a place for it. A human life with a story, an existence teleologically ordered, is already such a process of interpretation, a process in which in some real and significant sense the "end" is prefigured in the beginning. The necessity of grappling with how the end is prefigured has carried Christian reflection both into unbridled poetic fancy and metaphysical explanations that strip time and freedom of their reality; and thereby deny both deity and humanity to Jesus Christ.

An ontological perspective is therefore indispensable. And it must be a perspective which rightly draws both the distinction and the unity of essence and participative act.

2. The essence of a human life still under way (we must allow a place for historical essences) is the thing aimed at and not the thing

already achieved, unless the preservation of something already achieved has become the dominant end in view. So far, then, it makes a certain kind of sense to say that a person is what he seeks to become. But it does not make enough sense, because the "is" (the present tense) of a human life is its actual and active power of participation.

Given the fact of man's being in time, one could deduce an inversion of the relation between essence and participative act. One could predict that this ontological inversion would be attempted to explain away human freedom. If I am saddled with an essence from the beginning my participative act is nothing but my arm reflexively waving a banner put into my hand by an external maker (or causal order of some sort). And if this is the case then I, this creature who merely goes through the motions of freely determing his participation, am not responsible for what I do, my essence is to blame, or whatever being meted out this essence to me.

Another disaster could also be predicted. Poets, theologians, and speculative philosophers will interpret the duality of essence and participative act as that alienation from which all human mischief and misery spring. This is indeed a disaster because it beclouds an important truth: the actual process of human life falls into a profound self-alienation made possible by the ontological duality. But the alienation is the splitting away of essence from truth. This alienation works mischief upon participation: possessed by an illusion, a false essence, the course of life is bound to be deflected from its proper good. It will continue to function teleologically; but it will thrash around hurtfully to itself and to the world.

3. One of the essences, one of the aims of aspiration definitively and constitutively human, is a condition of being in which the alienation of essence and truth is overcome, and the act and the object of participation become identical relative to the good of each. We say "identical relative to the good of each" to warn against a forced option of one or the other of the classical alternatives: (a) the alienation is overcome by the absorption of all predicates into a (necessarily perfect) subject-substance. (b) Or the subject is now dispersed into an act pluriform to infinity. When the option is forced upon classical theology, the vote is for (a), which absorbs by implication the world into the perfection of God, rather than (b) in which God is diffused into the perfection of the world. Yet (a) leaves God with nothing to love in and for itself except Himself, a consequence

with which the Agape theology is saddled. Thus creation is reduced to an eternal process that is no process at all but an eternal relation. So if the option were forced here, we should vote for (b), which at least allows God to participate in the good of being other than Himself.

But the choice of either of these classical options is not yet necessary and is in fact premature. There are other aspects of man's being and situation that have a bearing upon the way in which the overcoming of alienation is interpreted.

4. One of these additional elements is a duality of consciousness that reflects the ontological duality of essence and act. Man is at once an actor and a role, as well as an agent and an enterprise. Consciousness doubles back upon the self; and thereby the human being becomes spirit. Given the reality of history, man becomes a sinner. (If it served any useful purpose we could then produce the axiom: only so far as he is spirit is man a sinner.) But how does this come about? I act, and I am aware of myself as acting. Thereby I am able to assign a value to myself as actor; and this is a value not necessarily identical with my value as agent, it is not necessarily identical with my real potentialities. But because I am an actor the enterprise, the human project, can be parceled out into roles. Society as a complex organization of role players already presupposes the duality of consciousness. But society as such a complex creates the illusion of being a (metaphysically) antecedent reality. Hence essence becomes a statable function in a social structure.

Now in fact I can be an actor, a role player, without being much of an agent. My whole life can be seen as a drama, an imitation of an action. I can lend myself to a teleology that cancels any real personal participation: I can accept a role which anybody can play, and which everybody does play.

But I cannot do this without paying the price. The price is so excessive that Providence threatens to become either sheer dogma or sheer mystery. If I accept the reduction of my being as agent to the status of being an actor, I will have to pay either of these prices: (a) Bad conscience, which is the self-infliction of a value so low that achievement of the good becomes a despair-producing possibility. (b) The suppression of the duality of consciousness which offers an escape from the despair of bad conscience; but it entails the renunciation of spirit. This is the most dreadful of human options. The participating human act is itself spirit. To cancel the duality of consciousness, to renounce spirit, is to accept the destruction of the human essence and to abdicate from the human enterprise.

When the I merges with the everybody, when the agent sinks without a trace into his role, the alienation of essence from truth is complete. There is nothing further that man can do to himself. There is nothing that he can do for himself to heal this mortal ontological wound.

III

What is impossible for man is possible for God, for with God all things are possible. Jesus Christ is God's Word to man in an impossible situation that is all too real, all too human. He is God's Word spoken from within the human condition. As such Jesus Christ is neither God talking to Himself, nor man talking to himself but each talking to the other, each "speaking the truth in love." Jesus Christ is therefore the reconciling word, the reconciling act of God. He is the word speaking from the flesh, he does not thunder out of heaven. Spoken from the flesh, he is also the Word spoken in the absolute power and invincible authority of God the Spirit.

It does not follow that the appropriate way to take up anew the question of the identity of Jesus Christ is with a speculative theory about the connection of his body and his soul; or with speculation about the relation of the three Persons of the Blessed Trinity to one another first and thereafter to the historical existence of Jesus. It is not necessary and it is not legitimate to base either acceptance of the Kingdom demands proclaimed by Jesus Christ or acknowledgment of his identity upon complex speculative theories. The metaphysics of body and soul is a long, fascinating, and tortuous chapter in philosophy and science; and late portions of it may eventually prove to be useful for Christian theology (such as reflection on the meaning of embodiment). I do not intend to disparage the domain of speculative metaphysics, and I do not believe that it is disparaged by insisting that Christian preaching is not in that domain and is not to be subordinated to it. Again, it does not follow that the hearers of the church's proclamation are beyond the need or the possibility of metaphysical instruction. But the Gospel is not a primer of metaphysics. Its proper acceptance requires its being understood. It can be understood only if the hearer is aware of what and where he is.

This awareness may be clarified and a curiously thin light thrown on it by speculation. It is deepened, purified, and made concretely coherent by something else. The "something else" is what is given through the church in the Gospel. The Gospel is the Word of God spoken to the concrete actualities of the human condition. It behooves us now to indicate how this living word is taken up into the being of Jesus Christ.

1. Jesus Christ is fully human in the expression of his powers of participation. He relates himself to objects and events in the mode open to man as such. This is the mode of predicational nonidentity: objects and events are not distributions of his own substance. Objects and events have their own ontological integrity. Jesus Christ fully acknowledges this, as something binding upon man, as man must fully acknowledge and as something that expresses God's freedom. If man denies the ontological integrity of beings and processes other than his own he denies at the same stroke the meaning of his own participational act. No such denial is even hinted in Jesus Christ. He does not act as though the actual world were his property. Therefore his Lordship must be seen in his participational power rather than in any antecedent essential identity binding the world into his "substance." "The Father saw fit in his good pleasure to give him all things" is exactly the decisive accent. The supreme expression of participational power in Jesus Christ is his obedience to the Almighty Father.

This same act of participation, in scriptural terms the obedience of Jesus Christ, is the "sign" of God's presence in and with man. The love with which Jesus Christ loves the world is precisely the love out of which God the Almighty Father created the world; and it is this love that renders Jesus Christ obedient to the Father. But we shall lose the track at once if we express this connection in terms of "substantial union" uniting either Father and Son, or God and Man; because this love, this power that generates and regenerates the world, is the perfection of predicational nonidentity.

One very important indication of this is the futurity of the Kingdom of God represented in the Gospel of Jesus Christ. The Kingdom is the "essence" upon which Jesus Christ focuses his full attention. In this he is not playing a role or acting out a part in a drama the outcome of which he must certainly know as "the man from heaven." Every such interpretation flaws the beauty and power of his participation in the human condition. The Kingdom is not simply future, but it is really future; and Jesus Christ relates himself to it as to real futurity.

Only in the romanticizing imagination and in the speculative flight does Jesus Christ have from the beginning of his earthly story what he has at its end. In either mode one can read into the Babe of Bethlehem a supernatural potency for absolute devotion to the Father in His Kingdom. In fact this immense power appears only when he begins to preach the Kingdom of God. In this preaching the Kingdom is that toward which he looks in absolute devotion. His power in this is the love he has for God the Father. In this sense, and for this reason, it is permissible to say that the essence revealed in the power of Christ's participational act, is God.

2. Jesus Christ overcomes the fatal betrayal of essence into the hands of illusion. This is the central message of Jesus' temptation by Satan. In his most plausible role Satan offers an object alternative to the divine essence. In his most plausible ontological counterfeiting, he offers this alternative to Jesus Christ in three forms.

a. Power over the world of natural objects. This is the temptation to assimilate the world to his own substance.

b. Upgrading his ontological status and value. This is the temptation to make of himself something so precious that the Almighty Father would save him even from any natural disaster produced by Jesus' own folly.

c. Subsuming every earthly power under his jurisdiction. This temptation is at once the most ingenious and the least plausible sleight of hand worked by the master illusionist. It is the most ingenious because it erases the futurity of the Kingdom in offering him perfectly manifest and absolute Lordship *now*. It is the least plausible because the condition is that Jesus may have all of this simply by bowing the knee (or perhaps making a more discreet signal of obeisance) to the Illusionist. The promise is specious because the kingdoms of this world are not Satan's to give; and it is bad faith to imagine otherwise. The signal of false obeisance could therefore only be a lie. So the enormity of this temptation very nearly eludes description. It is not primarily that Jesus would have been trapped into making a play for power. Rather he would have been trapped into swapping lies with the father of lies.

All of these proposals and projects spread before Jesus Christ are so many solicitations to embrace illusion. No one knows this so well as Jesus Christ. No one, not even Satan, knows so well how plausible each of these bids is. Nonetheless, we have an inkling or two gleaned both from the New Testament and from real life. For one thing the New Testament does not hesitate to impute to Jesus, even prior to the Resurrection, ample power over the natural world. But the New Testament also tells us that Jesus exercises this power only in relation to the holy essence, the Kingdom of his Father; and never to assimilate the natural world into his own being. It is very easy to overlook this qualification in Christ's exercise of this power. But when this qualification is overlooked we may be moved to accept his lordship merely because he did exercise that power. And which is worse? To believe that Jesus is the Christ because he walked on the water? Or to believe that Jesus is the Christ because his power was purely spiritual? Either way we lose sight of the purity of his devotion to the Kingdom of his Father.

The Temptation narratives also remind us of how naturally it comes to us to convert the Kingdom of God into a reason for devotion to ourselves. Whether the self is seeking empire or is merely running for cover, the Kingdom seems to invite incorporation into its design. For the Kingdom has been given to men, has it not? That one settled satisfactorily, we seem to be at liberty to treat humanity as something to which we can do anything we choose. The infinite distance between "with God all things are possible" and "everything is permitted" is miraculously shriveled to nothing. But the miracle is a fraud. Its author is Satan.

Therefore Jesus Christ attacks Satan as the father of lies. Satan (like some atheists) is forever talking about God. But he is condemned forever to tell lies about God, in the dismal hope of thus corrupting man's power of love, a power as splendid as it is vulnerable. But the father of lies is overcome by the love of Jesus Christ which goes unerringly to its proper object. His participational aim and thrust are perfect, so Satan has no lie at his command for the love of which Jesus Christ can be deflected. So both in his rebuke to Satan and in his commandments to man, Jesus Christ acts with the authority of the Almighty Father. The familiar Johannine expression of this is "the Father and I are one." This unity is visible in the perfection of devotion with which Jesus Christ attends to the works of the Kingdom. Speculative theologians have often enough proposed an invisible metaphysical substantial unity as the explanation of the sublime quality of this devotion. Any explanation of this participative power in terms of antecedent essential connection sacrifices in principle the very thing to be explained. In other words, if Christ's being is causally divine he cannot really participate in the human condition. He could then only act the part.

3. Accordingly human aspiration for unity of essence and act is both faithfully expressed and radically reexpressed in Jesus Christ. The unity he expresses as his own and the unity for which He works in us is purely intentional: He would that the love of God in the righteousness of the Kingdom should be at once the first and last love of our being, as it is of his. He would that we should love God for His own sake, for what God is in Himself, and no longer as the extension of our self-love to infinity.

Human existence is justified only in such intentional unity. To be justified is to be made straight, it is to be rectified in the sense of being given a radical reorientation. (It is this rather than being accepted. God is not a lover who accepts the sinner only when the sinner apologizes, or sends someone in his place to do so.) This correction of man's intentional being, this rectification of man's orientation relative to good, truth, and beauty, is the work which Jesus Christ has the authority to institute and to supervise.

But rectification is one thing and energizing is something else. Jesus Christ is both the truth and the power of God. The end in view in his divine work and person is the freedom of man's participative powers. "You shall know the truth, and the truth will set you free" (John 8:32, NEB). This is both the freedom of the eye of the soul from whatever lies have dimmed and confused its seeing; and the freedom of the heart to love God in undivided devotion.

4. The full participation of Jesus Christ in the human condition means that he participates also in the duality of human consciousness. His participative act is not merely a reflection of the human condition. It is the act of God in the person of Jesus Christ. "For our sake he made him to be sin who knew no sin, so that in him we might become the righteousness of God" (II Cor. 5:21, RSV).

This text is of course deeply implicated in the doctrine of the Sinlessness of Jesus Christ. The doctrine in turn is deeply implicated in the present agony of good faith. For this reason (rather than for any speculative profit) we must consider it.

In the first place it seems perfectly obvious that Jesus Christ is not Lord Incarnate so long as he has a merely external knowledge of sin. It is just as obvious on the other hand that he cannot be the

Lord strong to save if his knowledge of sin is interior, that is, if he knows himself as one who has actually sinned; for then he would stand alongside of us as one in need of rectification. Actually his lot would then be more painfully desperate than ours because he would know better than we do of our own sin how grievous his was.

I suspect that many sturdy believers have been comforted in this doctrinal embarrassment by the lofty spiritual wisdom expressed by Plato, namely, that the truly righteous man has a better knowledge of evil than the evildoer, because the righteous man is in command of the criterion. But Jesus Christ is much more than the righteous judge. In him God judges from the exact center of the human condition, where He has come to regenerate human life. The judgment of Christ is the divine power at work in the human center for the amendment of man's being. This amendment is attained by releasing spirit from the disintegration of duality into division. Release from this division and the reformation of the duality are achieved by the application of pure spirit from within the body. Here again the authority to represent the Kingdom, and the power to enforce the righteous demands of the Kingdom by energizing man's being, are unified in the person of Jesus Christ.

The New Testament represents Jesus Christ as being perfectly responsive to the leadings and promptings of the Holy Spirit. In the power of the Spirit Jesus began to preach the righteousness of the Kingdom. The Spirit led him into the wilderness of temptation. The Spirit assured him of his unity with the will of the Father in heaven.

None of this ought to be taken to mean that the Holy Spirit is an external agency applied to a passive being. The Spirit is God present in being perfectly proportioned to the condition of man on earth. So in Jesus Christ the presence of the Spirit is not properly interpreted as the presence of another subject (another person understood as subject). Rather, we ought to speak of a participative act which is one with another intentionally rather than substantively. Only if this distinction is enforced are we able to understand why it matters seriously only to speculative theologians when we use the phrases "Holy Spirit," "Spirit of God," and "Spirit of Christ" interchangeably. With the distinction between the intentional and the substantival in mind, we can say that the Spirit by which Jesus is led into the wilderness to be tempted is no heavenly invader of his own spirit. An external cause is still external, no matter how sublime. Rather, it is his own spirit, if we understand "his own" intentionally rather than either psychologically or metaphysically. To say that Jesus Christ was led by the Spirit is to say, again, that there is a perfect unity of essence shared by God and man in Jesus Christ.

This same power, this same Spirit, this same presence, in whom and to whom we say both "Lord!" and "Abba, Father!" is the one who heals the wounds in the duality of consciousness. Jesus Christ is afflicted neither with bad conscience nor with the unholy desire to stifle the spirit by diminishing consciousness. His consciousness of himself does not betray him into the alternation of self-aggrandizement and self-cancellation so familiar to us as the spiritual rhythm of our life. Jesus Christ does not see himself as an actor in a drama, as one who plays a role from which he holds back his "real" being. For this reason he will not accept the *role* of Messiah, as though it were a "part," a mask, which could be lowered and fixed upon a being already in existence in some other form. Jesus is Messiah, and he is Messiah in the depths of his being. His entire being is in his act of participation in God's purpose for man. He is the supreme agent of the Kingdom, agent both in the sense of one who acts, and in the sense of one who represents the interests of another. He holds nothing in reserve for some other role. His spirit does not recoil upon itself but leads him straightaway into the most solid and massive relationship with the actual world. The religious term for this massive relationship is Lordship. Expressed ontologically it is the participative penetration of man's actual condition in the real world.

Except for purposes of historical fictioneering there is no profit in trying to divine the "inner life" of Jesus Christ. His life, inner and outer, is in his act. His word is his substance. His essence is in his death on the Cross. He has no role to play, whether it be the role of Messiah, or Sinner, or Prince of the House of David, or King of the Jews, or Prophet, or Priest. He simply is what he proclaims: the righteousness of the Kingdom of God.

IV

Jesus Christ is the righteousness of the Kingdom of God incarnate. Jesus Christ is the tabernacle of flesh in which the Spirit radiates a perfect mastery of the powers of the flesh.

In our time (and perhaps in every time) the preaching of the Incarnation is infected with the desire to take some of the sting out of bodily existence. This is an age infatuated with "spirituality," largely because its heart has been invested in "material" values. The Incarnation is indeed a rebuke to the false spiritualizing of man and the world; but in its preaching of the Incarnation the church must not be carried away by a desire to take some of the sting out of bodily existence. Jesus Christ is not to be preached as one sent by God to attack heresies as his main calling. This is the peril at hand when the New Testament is interpreted as a rebuke to heresy, e.g., John as an attack upon Docetism. Unless great care is exercised such an interpretation of the New Testament will fall into a much more inclusive heresy: Intellectualism. We ought not to minimize the threat to the unity of the Gospel and of the church posed by the great historical heresies. On the other hand we must not interpret the New Testament either as an elementary primer in theology, or as a supernaturally sophisticated and definitive key to metaphysical puzzles.

So we say again that the church does well to preach the Incarnation as God's assurance of the goodness of bodily existence. The church does even better when it preaches Jesus Christ as the revelation of God at hand, God with us, to carry bodily existence to the perfection God purposes for it. Here again the example of Jesus Christ and his person are one seamless reality. He makes known the demands of God the Almighty Father; and he leads the way in responding to these demands. He is the "pioneer and perfecter of our faith" (Heb. 12:2, RSV). In him alone is our salvation.

As Savior Jesus Christ orders and ordains the flesh to the service of spirit. This does not mean that the flesh became etherialized under his masterly control. To etherialize the flesh until it becomes the diaphanous veil through which Eternity shines, is no part of his essence. For the purpose of making this clear the church might do well to give romantic imagination its head for a season in the encounter with the "spirituality" of the world to which it preaches Jesus Christ as Incarnate Lord. Let the world be reminded that Jesus had normal sweat glands; and that he might have been afflicted with hangnails, bunions, and falling hair! But the valid intention, in any such imaginative expansion of the Gospel story, is largely negative: it is to loosen if not to demolish illusions that block the vision of the essence of Jesus Christ. His essence, the sublime teleological ordering of his life, probably was not totally successful in bringing the cells of his flesh into perfect obedience. It is a pious whimsy to think otherwise; and the whimsy flies in the face of the Gospel narrative. According to the narrative, sometimes Jesus was tired; and sometimes he was hungry; and sometimes he was sleepy. These metabolic seasons were not perfectly synchronized with the seasons of the Spirit. A healthy man sleeps when he is tired, and if he is wise as well as healthy he knows that sleep is part of the Divine Providence which governs the world; and if he is religious as well as healthy and wise he therefore praises God before he sleeps and as soon as he awakens. But Jesus Christ on one occasion at least seemed too healthy for the piety of his disciples: he slept while they were all, disciples and Master alike, in imminent peril of drowning; and so of course they had to waken him to their common danger. Dominated by a realistic fear, they would have found it hard to believe that Jesus' metabolism was providentially synchronized with the rhythms of the world. But then what shall we say about their sleeping through Jesus' hour of travail in Gethsemane? Let us say neither more nor less than Jesus Christ himself said to and of them, and to and of all mankind: the flesh is weak, it does not respond perfectly to the demands of spirit. And let us remember that this word is spoken from within the flesh and not by a spiritual being to whom flesh is alien earth.

The man who said "the flesh is weak" bore this testimony about his own flesh. It turned out, in fact, that he was unable to carry the cross all the way to the top. By that time it had also turned out that Jesus was no stranger to fear. This is not the behavior of flesh harmonized in all its parts by the power of Spirit pursuing the grand design. Indeed, one might well question just how spiritual Jesus was as the master of his flesh. If he had been a great swami he would have had the flesh under perfect control. If he had been a master of Yoga would he have sweat globulets of blood? If he had been a true spiritual master would he have not won his ends by a hunger strike stretched out into years, into a little eternity of spiritual concentration?

As it turned out Jesus Christ even refused the pain deadener conventionally offered to the crucified: he accepted the last ounce, so to speak, of pain, as though it were ordained in the grand design. In the same manner he accepted the ultimate pangs of solitariness on the Cross, crying out, "My God, my God, why hast thou forsaken me?" And as it turned out, he did not live on the Cross for as long as many men had, his flesh did not set a new record in that grisly competition.

These are various ways of saying, on the warrant of the New Testament, that Christ's mastery of the flesh is revealed in the power of his spirit over his essence rather than over his cells and glands. So we thank God that Jesus was a Jew. He did not need to give a metaphysical explanation of the flesh or dream of bringing it under greater control than God had allowed for. He says that the flesh is weak, he does not say that the flesh is hostile. The difference is immense, and the church has not always remembered it in preaching the Incarnation. Therefore men have learned from the preaching of the Incarnation how to offer either the weakness or the hostility of the flesh as a metaphysical-religious excuse for the display of irresolute and ambiguous spirit.

V

So far we have spoken of the flesh of the Incarnate Lord as though it were perfectly synonymous with body. Now we must correct this supposition, and again we must correct it on the basis of something other than speculative metaphysics.

Body is more than flesh. By virtue of the flesh man participates in the world of matter (and here it matters very little whether by matter we mean energy or substance). By virtue of body man participates in the concrete human world. Human institutions, without exception, are made possible by man's corporeal nature (and are themselves often called bodies). The body is the only system of expression over which man has direct and predictable control; whereas the flesh is one in its tropisms and rhythms with matter everywhere. Accordingly, no matter how lofty the ideals of a person or of a society of persons, the living human being must make some perceptible signal of his membership in it and his loyalty to it: a kiss, a handshake, a verbal statement, a ten-dollar bill, etc.

The spirit's command of the body is therefore a humanly more complex affair than its command of the flesh. The body is subject to invasion by hostile powers, the flesh is not. Microbes and bacteria may be a threat to the health of the body; but the flesh is obviously their natural environment. Flesh knows nothing of health. Without health the body ceases to function properly, and may cease to exist. On the other hand the flesh is not the natural habitat of demons, but the body is, because it is the home of the spirit.

So when the church preaches Jesus Christ as the Incarnate Lord it preaches the perfection of his body. But it preaches the perfection of his body as a system of expression which is perfectly obedient to the leadings of the Spirit as the flesh is not. To say that Jesus Christ has the highest perfection of bodily existence is to say that he is the perfect master of his commitments. His Yea means Yea, and his Nay means Nay. He affirms what is really comprehended by his essence. He denies what cannot be comprehended by it. Both the affirmation and the denial are unambiguous. He uses his body to express who he really is, that is, what he really intends.

For this purpose he must of course know who he is, he must know infallibly what he wants to express through the body; and he must know infallibly the double connection of this essence, on the one side with the righteousness of God in His Kingdom, and on the other, with the actualities of the human condition. The possession of such knowledge is possible only when consciousness has achieved maximal clarity, only when spirit has routed the last shadow of ambiguity lurking in the last crease of the last involution of consciousness. In dimly illuminated involutions the lie germinates and finds nourishment and protection. From them the lie, full grown, launches its forays against the body personal and politic.

So when we speak of the simplicity of the being of Jesus Christ we must have in mind first this maximal clarity of consciousness. His cells have lives of their own. His body is animated with but one purpose, his life has but one essence: his full concrete being is trained upon the Kingdom of God. Duplicity can find no lodgment in him, because everything has been made straight, everything has been opened to the illumination of the Holy Spirit, there are no crannies or pockets or recesses where the lie can germinate.

Therefore Jesus Christ preached: "Blessed are the pure in heart, for they shall see God." And: "If your eye offends thee, pluck it out"! These are two sides of the same truth. He does not preach: "Watch out for the demonic tricks of the body"! He does preach: For love of the Kingdom be prepared to do without whatever cannot be subordinated to the righteousness of the Kingdom; because no unruliness will be indulged there. Obviously this means that lusting after harlots will have to go. But it also means that love of mother, and mother's love, will also have to go if they sap or distort the love of the Kingdom. Obviously it means that the miser's love of gold will have to be cut out. But it also means that a reasonable love for a reasonable standard of living may have to be sacrificed. There is no telling in advance, and there is no possibility of decision when the time comes by referring to a rule or formula. All we can say now, and always, is that the spirit in us can attach itself with humanly unbreakable grip to the body, and thereby lose the Kingdom. To the body, let us say it again, not to the flesh: that is, to creatures and creaturely things to which man may wholly pledge his life power. The result of such commitment is civil war in man's concrete existence. Born a creature, man is destined and called to communion with the everlasting God. So long as he gears his love and power of expression wholly to the creaturely, he will have no peace, no unity, no joy. He may have their counterfeits, but he cannot have their reality. So long as he lives for the body, he is always in imminent peril of dismemberment, of death by fragmentation; because the powers to whose invasion he is in that love of the body fully exposed, are themselves lying, rebellious, and perverse spirits.

If, therefore, the church could rightly preach the evils of carnality, and be rightly understood, it would be a triumph for the Kingdom. If, that is, the carnal life were described, in Pauline terms, as the life in which loyalty is randomly distributed among beings all of which are creaturely. But the chances are very good that the attack upon carnality would be understood, and applauded, as an attack upon harlotry, drunkenness, and gluttony; and every other divisive creaturely adoration would leave the church unscathed.

The alien spirits can find no opening in the person of Jesus Christ. His love of everything creaturely, including his own earthly frame, is proportionate to its true good. He freely gives everything creaturely its due: the body is mastered, it is not suppressed or denied in principle. We do not know why he did not marry. We do know that the standard reasons given in support of ecclesiastical celibacy are no part of and no proper inference from the Gospel. Indeed we must be even more aggressive. A spirituality which casts the shadow of ethical and metaphysical dubiety upon the body, or upon the enjoyment of life in the body, is a disease of the spirit. It is a disease made possible by the doubling-back of consciousness upon itself with a view to upgrading the value of the self considered as spirit alone.

Another modest burst of fictioneering would not be inappropriate when the church preaches Jesus Christ the Incarnate Lord. Let us conjecture that people generally took Jesus for a healthy and hearty man. He did not have a reputation for being an ascetic. To the contrary, in fact, some people seem to have found him too frequently in society too convivial. He did not make the grade of the preternaturally solemn. Quite to the contrary, some people found him guilty of unseemly merriment. The rigors of his spiritual discipline did not produce stigmata, visions, or levitations. The stigmata were produced by hammerblows on spikeheads, and there is nothing very spiritual about that. He was lifted off the earth, once he had been firmly nailed to the Cross, and there is nothing very spiritual about that elevation. The elevation of the Cross gave him an unusual angle of vision from which to survey the human situation, and there was no one to wipe the blood from his eyes; but even (especially) there and then he recognizes fidelity, courage, and truthfulness, and all of their contradictions, in the human scene below him. So even *in extremis* he is in command of his person, his spirit to the end renders his body a faithful instrument, he is a free agent in and with the body. He is where he belongs, even as he embraces death.

We do not know whether puppy dogs, starlings, lions, scorpions, and eagles recognized him, and gathered around him lovingly whenever he did sit beside the road. We do know that human beings heard him and followed him. Some followed him because they had not recognized who he was. Some followed him because they had recognized who he was. The recognition was far from perfect. It was not clear or firm enough to prevent betrayal of perfect trust. But the nonrecognition was not always perfect either. Some men, having heard the summons, turned sorrowfully away because they had many possessions, they were voluntary prisoners of their bodies and slaves of the no-gods. As for the demons, they heard him and trembled. The powers of darkness have no difficulty in recognizing the Son of God. This is where all *their* troubles begin.

VI

Man has his being in time. In taking humanity and the form of man unto himself God Incarnate comes into time. Jesus Christ is in the body of time. He is in the body of time as the Lord of time.

Mastery of time is surely one of the strangest powers revealed in the person of Jesus Christ. Commonsensically it is both true and false to say that Jesus Christ masters time. It is commonsensically true because Western man marks his own fleeting time as a Year of Our Lord. It is commonsensically false because Jesus Christ could not arrest the swift pursuit of day after day, or decree that henceforth Easter should come before Good Friday. Unlike the earlier bearer of his name, Jesus did not command the sun to stand still.

The contradictions of commonsense are not the first order of business for theology. They are important so far as they call attention to the impossibility of finding any appropriate criteria in the world around us by which to measure the Lordship of Jesus Christ. If subsequently we can explain away those contradictions, that is, show why they are certain to arise, that is a different matter; and we can attend to it only after we have apprehended in the person of Jesus Christ the power by which time is mastered without being ruined.

1. This power over time is expressed in the perceptual mode. Jesus Christ knows that "this is the acceptable year of the Lord," he perceives that the Kingdom is imminent. His knowledge may be likened (romantically) to that of a secret agent working in a foreign country. He knows exactly when his sovereign will attack, either because the agent has an infallible time schedule or a secret communication system with his home base open and alive at all times. Moreover the Gospel contains grist for such romantic similitudes, for instance, "Jesus, knowing that his hour had come. . . ." How does he know this? A romantic imagination can supply an answer.

But there are other answers. Jesus knows that the hour has struck because he knows his own plans. He knows how these plans have matured, what they have done to time and what time has done to them, and what must be done now to consummate them. He also knows what his enemies are up to. He does not know to the minute when they will strike, but he knows that they will strike when he is most vulnerable and they are most desperate. He knows how to render himself the one and them the other.

This is the knowledge of the time of purpose, both divine and human. Mastery of this time is precisely what we should expect in that person whose power of participation and power of essence-envisagement were of maximal clarity and intensity.

It does not follow, and it is not the case, that the other time ranges are equally under the command of Jesus Christ. Consider the time range of simple past and simple future. Would Jesus have known the answer if some impertinent tourist had asked him for the exact date of the Exodus, or the span of the XVIII Dynasty? But an even more embarrassing example is at hand. Did Jesus know when the Kingdom would no longer have a futurity reference? Classical speculative doctrines of the two natures do not help much at these points. If the Logos mind knew from eternity all such things, yet did not or could not put them within the reach of the human mind of Jesus, the Logos had not penetrated the human but towered beyond it, remote, inaccessible, and mysterious. This is an odd way to spell *incarnation.* But perhaps Jesus Christ does not answer such questions because he knows that the answers would be bad for the life of humble obedience. Or perhaps he does not answer such questions because he does not know the answers. If we offer the latter explanation we must give it a positive value: what Jesus Christ does not command of the other ranges of time does not have an adverse effect upon the time he mastered in his own person. Of what value is the knowledge of the exact date of the Exodus when the real question is whether Israel (how, rather than whether) is caught up in God's redemptive purpose? Of what value is an exact knowledge of when the glory of the Kingdom will be revealed if one is not prepared now to obey the demands of its righteousness?

Another time range gives the present age a great deal of difficulty. What command of cosmic time does Jesus Christ exercise in his own person?

Cosmic time is that unspeakably grand sequence and rhythm in which man's feverish life is but a wispy moment. This is the language astrophysicists, the modern hierophants of the cosmic mysteries, use outside of the observatory for the instruction of the masses. It is language that is metaphysically problematical in an extreme measure; but it is also a rhetorical instrument nicely calculated to arouse ontological anxieties. (The technical language of science reduces time to "t," a mathematical function with very thin commitments to the world of gross fact.) The rhetoric is much older than hieratic science. When has man not known that time is a mighty river sweeping through the cosmos, bearing away all things on its restless tides? Certainly the disparities between the mythologies of the first and the twentieth centuries are very great, but they cannot conceal this persistent constitutive intuition of time. Island universes as well as children at play are indiscriminately caught up and carried along on the river of time.

Jesus Christ has a clear perception of this time in his own person. He cannot arrest its passage, he too is carried thither on its floodtide to his destiny. He is its creature and not its Lord.

But to whom then does cosmic time belong? Rhetorically, it now belongs to the astrophysicists rather than to priest or poet. But nothing, in its rising and passing away, is determined by rhetoric, except human passion and voice. Therefore we ask again to whom cosmic time, the mighty river, belongs? Of whose purpose is it the beat, the measure, the rhythm? Good faith replies: It belongs to God the Father Almighty, and he has established the Son as Lord over all of the Kingdoms of the earth, in their rising and their falling.

It is part of the obedience of Jesus Christ as the son of God that he does not seek to divine the vast cosmic future. It is part of his obedience as the son of Israel that he steadfastly refuses to allow auguries into the acceptance of the Kingdom's futurity. God's all-seeing all-compassionate eye notes the falling sparrow, as well as the rising and falling of human life and fortune. All things are in his hands. Within his purpose, within his life, Jesus Christ has his own work to do.

2. The mastery of Jesus Christ in and over time includes the volitional mode. Jesus Christ orders his will to the pace as well as to the essence of the Kingdom. His devotion to the Kingdom has a place for everything which time can bring to him and every point to which time will carry him. So he is not merely a creature of time. Time itself obeys a teleology not visible in the moving hands of the clock. Jesus Christ acknowledges that teleology and he is wholly responsive to it. This is the reason that he feels no anxiety about the pace of the Kingdom. He does not have an anxiety criterion by which to measure its pace. Now is as much the time of the Kingdom as tomorrow and yesterday. Now is the only time in which the will of man can move to accept the offer and the demands of the Kingdom. Jesus Christ is content with this now, he embraces it with his whole being.

Thus the mastery of time in the volitional mode is expressed as the power with which the present moment is converted by Jesus Christ into the now of salvation. Accordingly the decisive question about the now concerns its content rather than its boundaries. What matters about the now is the way it is ordered rather than its length. Jesus Christ reveals the now as the moment to be appropriated for repentance. It is revealed in such a way (and this is part of what we mean by the content of the now) that the possibility—always real enough—of one's not having another now takes second place to the wonder of existing at this moment in this now. Neither clock nor cosmos determines the boundaries of such a moment. Its boundaries are internally determined by attention and participation energized by the spirit of obedience to Jesus Christ. True, in a certain sense Pilate puts an end to the now of Jesus Christ. In a much deeper and truer sense the now of Jesus Christ has no end. We and all men live in it until the end of the world. This means that the choice Jesus Christ offered to his first hearers is the same choice he offers to us today. The Kingdom has not changed its shape since it became visible in the person of Jesus Christ. Its demands have not been altered, and no new gateways have been opened. It is still true that this power of choice is released in us by Jesus Christ. It is still true that this power of choice is ours because in his own being essence and act, the thing to be chosen and the power to participate in its good, achieve perfect unity.

All such acknowledgments of the being of Jesus Christ may well appear to be so many ways in which time is absorbed into the mysterious fullness of eternity. We cannot complete our consideration of Christ's mastery of time without reflecting upon this prospect.

3. The easiest possible way of interpreting Jesus Christ's command of time is to represent him as having come into the temporal world with all of the knowledge of time's secrets that eternity alone allows. But that kind of solution draws very heavily upon metaphysical speculations concerning time and eternity that are incompatible with the Gospel. Nowhere in the Gospel is the now of salvation represented as a moment encapsulated in eternity. We may so speak to show that some decisions made in time have a world of meaning. But this meaning is displayed in time. We do not know from the Gospel how human decisions are evaluated in heaven, except that some occasion great joy among God and His angels.

Moreover, as we have seen in Chapter VI, if eternity is wrongly interpreted the meaning of the now of decision collapses. But the Gospel maximizes the meaning of that moment, the Gospel makes it the time that matters most. Therefore the Gospel identification of the now as the moment in which the fullness of time has come must be taken with the seriousness that questions the right of any speculation to dictate to it; and particularly speculation that reduces time to mere appearance. In Jesus Christ God has said the decisive word about the time of human existence. The Word in which God speaks "became flesh and dwelt among us" (John 1:14). Time was not a diaphanous veil nor a web of illusion. The story of God with man is a story about time. The story of Jesus Christ is the story of man's time.

Yet in a certain sense the story of Jesus Christ is timeless. Timelessness cannot be the heart of eternity so far as Jesus Christ is the revelation of God, unless it is this kind of timelessness: time bound but not distorted and certainly not canceled. Given Jesus Christ we know that time is not canceled by the religious-metaphysical hunger for the motionless perfection of abstract eternity. Given Jesus Christ we know that time is not distorted by an overweening desire to capture the essence in a time-when, either of beginning or ending. The story of Jesus Christ, the faithful representation of his being in history, has an internal time that expresses his mastery of time. The time internal to the story is the development of the theme of Christ's identity, it is the movement from event to event in which *who he is* is disclosed, once and for all. What is thus disclosed is generically true of the human condition. Thus Jesus Christ is the truth as well as the Way and the Life. He speaks directly to the generic conditions of human existence. What he says of the Kingdom is an embodiment of the Kingdom in his own person. In his own person he brings the powers of God into immediate application upon generic man. In this sense the essence of time is captured and the story is timeless.

Many Christians believe that when his work on earth was finished Jesus Christ returned to eternity. There may be a way of saying this theologically that does not depend upon speculation. For the moment we must settle for the acknowledgment of Jesus Christ as the Lord Everlasting whose seat of command is within the human realm. Command of the farthermost reaches of space and time and Lordship over all that has been created are his by imputation. His revealed Lordship embraces the realm of man. It is here, not on Arcturus, that the Kingdom of God is revealed. He took unto himself the time of man. He took it unto himself with such perfection of authority that he is the man for all time.

CHAPTER X

The Sufficiency of Christ's Work

I

Even though the theological distinction between the Person and the Work of Jesus Christ lends itself to artificial amplification and application, the abuses of the distinction must not blind us to its values. Properly drawn it reinforces the conviction that God acts in the work of Jesus Christ. The work of Jesus Christ is "the full, perfect and sufficient sacrifice for the sins of the whole world," because God is immediately engaged in the work thus performed.

This being our prime principle we shall have to reject any doctrinal formulation of the work of sacrifice and reconciliation that by implication divides God into a being whose offended righteousness demands satisfaction and a being whose sinlessness enables Him to meet this demand on behalf of the sinner. What we have had to say about the unity of the being of Jesus Christ we must also say about the unity of the being of God in Himself: rather than a metaphysical postulation it is in the first instance an acknowledgment and recognition of "truth and grace," power and wisdom, as a unity in all that God does. In Jesus Christ as the revelation of this God we have no legitimate way of dividing the righteousness of God's justice from the righteousness of His creativity and His mercy. At some stage in Christian reflection it may be necessary to introduce speculative distinctions, but the first theological task is to interpret the sacrifice of Jesus Christ as the work of God's righteousness in perfect self-unity; as work, therefore, anticipated in the plan of creation.

For this purpose we must see how the sacrifice of Jesus Christ is related to the generic elements of man's being, since what man is by creation and what he has become as sinner, are expressions of the righteousness of God. Thus the efficacy of the sacrifice of Jesus Christ is the power of the Risen Lord to transform the generic elements of man's being. Put negatively, this means that the Cross and the Resurrection are so integrally united to each other in the work of God in Christ that the authentic acknowledgment of Christ as Lord is ruined by their separation. God speaks through the Cross. God speaks through the Risen Lord. These are not two different gods. The One God does not say two different things. What He says through the Cross He ratifies, beyond all peradventure of doubt, in the Resurrection. Men know that they are dealing directly with the Christ of God because of the Resurrection. If therefore the Christian were confronted with the contrived necessity of choosing between the Crucifixion and the Resurrection, in good faith he would have to choose the latter. Speculatively we might have heard about the death of Jesus from some non-Biblical source. It is hard to imagine why this report would be any more important religiously to us than it was to Josephus. Christianly we have to say that the death of Jesus Christ receives its significance from the Resurrection: it is the Resurrection which certifies that he is Lord forever. Apart from the Resurrection, Jesus is entitled to election to the order of Religious Heroes, to be admired or not, depending upon one's taste in heroes. Given the Resurrection, Jesus is the Christ, the true Lord of mankind. He is therefore to be obeyed and not merely admired. We are to follow him and not merely praise him. In him God has done the thing impossible with man: he has reconciled man unto himself.

This transaction is called sacrifice when seen from man's side only; and reconciliation when seen as the unity of God in Himself and as the unity of man with God. In all events the transaction reaches into the ontological roots of humanity; and it changes everything it reaches. Thus the Resurrection produces the new man, the "man in Christ." Just as certainly the Resurrection reveals the unchanging faithfulness of God. God himself is the agent effecting that transformation of the old Adam. His is the love which in every change remains purely and everlastingly itself.

The righteousness of God is everywhere evident in the saving work of Jesus Christ. It is also evident in the demand that man must be what he is created to be but is not. Man has an inheritance. He has converted this inheritance into "futures" in order to do business with the powers of darkness. Therefore he lives in the kingdom of sin-and-death. His life in the dark kingdom is specious at best and bankrupt at the end, but he can do nothing in his own behalf. So it occurs to him that he could get out of it by dying. Actually he can get out of it by dying only if he is given license and power to die unto God. So here again man's dependence upon the unitary righteousness of God is absolute.

II

Man is in bondage to alien powers. In this bondage he is a deserter from his homeland and a traitor to his own household. He gives aid and comfort to invaders from the dark kingdom.

The invaders do not begin by fomenting outright rebellion against the righteousness of God. They begin by finding the right soil in which to plant the seed of the lie. The sprouting bed of the lie must be as dark as possible. With their own kind of inerrancy the invaders find the right soil in the involutions of man's consciousness. (Involutions, not stratifications.)

The strategic aim of the invaders is transparently clear. They hope to carry man off into slavery, they plan to make him a vassal of their own kingdom.

Today we have at best very mixed feelings about the validity and the wisdom of the dramatic metaphors with which the New Testament depicts the human condition. Even the conservative among us are not sure that the New Testament images will stand up under rigorous theological scrutiny. The busy hammers of the demythologizers raise a great clamor all over the place and perhaps a great cloud of dust as well. Conservatives are attacked for being backworldsmen. The enemies of myth are branded enemies of Jesus Christ. Mediators are (as usual) assailed from both camps as confused and irresolute. It is a brisk theological season that the language of the New Testament is having; but it may be its last. If it should turn out that way theologians could find something else to fight over. But what about the man in the pew?

There is little evidence that the theological uproar is reaching him. Even if it is getting through to the pew the fact would be at best a secondary cause for misgiving about the dramatic imagery in which the New Testament represents man's situation. A more forbidding fact confronting the preaching church is the unreadiness of contemporary man to think of himself as a member of any kingdom, unless it is the cosmos where "law" does not imply a king or lawgiver. (Cosmos is a system in which law is ultimate and is therefore automatic in its operations.)

Yet this same creature sets great store by his freedom. It is instinctive with him to question the reality of freedom under a king, unless the king is a mere figurehead carefully embalmed for use on state occasions. (We should do quite as well to question the reality of freedom in a cosmos where law functions automatically. We might wonder why we do not see more clearly the connection between having to live in such a cosmos and the confession of modern man that he has lost his self-identity as well as his self-confidence and self-esteem.)

Nevertheless the pressure of the New Testament is also very real. The power with which it discloses the diversity of the kingdoms will not be denied; and it is not the proper business of the theologian to explain it away. On the other hand he does have a responsibility to interpret, and not merely quote, what the New Testament discloses.

So we are constrained to admit that the kingdom of sin-and-death is a going concern. It has lords and slaves. The lords of the dark kingdom rule only by God's consent. God's consent is a grant of time rather than a lease of power or grant of privilege. The lords obtain their subjects by the arts of duplicity and counterfeit, of which they are past masters. They have no charter rights to the human spirit. Whatever they now enjoy of rights and privileges over the human spirit they have extracted by guile—from man, not from God.

These dramatic images raise questions that the images themselves do not answer. Perhaps they are not answered by anything else in the Bible, at least not directly. Where, for instance, do the powers of darkness, the lords of Sin and Death, get their license, their power, in the first place? Why should such a kingdom exist at all? Our hunger for causal explanation is not likely to be gratified by the Bible. Certainly "consent" cannot be understood as a causal explanation of the existence of evil powers. God's consent applies properly to the time these powers have in which to do their work. The source of their power, indeed of their existence, is a mystery. God can and will destroy them. Does it follow that He created them? The metaphysical appetite will not be satisfied until it has a direct answer to this question; and philosophical reason is not likely to be satisfied with any answer. This tension opens the way for the mythologizing imagination to propose its own answers. For example, the lords of the dark kingdom were originally good, because everything that God created is necessarily good. Mythological interpretations of this sort have sometimes been accepted as food for the metaphysical appetite; and have thereafter acquired the odor of theological sanctity.

All but the most philistine rationalists are willing to grant that the existence of evil is a mystery, given the sense of reality predisposed to the good. We can have no doubt that such a predisposition is visible as a very potent element of the Gospel (and of the Bible as a whole). But we have no doubt, either, that this predisposition is a singular one. Let us attempt to frame this "presupposition" thus: The purpose of God has been published as all-inclusive. No agent and no event lies beyond this teleology. Neither in cosmos nor in history is there anything which defies God's incorporation of it into His purpose. In this sense, and so far in this sense alone, do we have Biblical warrant for saying that all beings and all events are expressions of God's power.

I hope eventually to return to the metaphysical-speculative issues. My intention here is to note the way in which the mystery of evil is rooted in man's being. In his own being the mystery of evil assumes its darkest hues. St. Paul expresses this in great power and clarity in his confession: "The good I would I do not; the evil I would not, I do" (Rom. 7:15-20). The confession brings to light the "sense of reality predisposed to the good." But it also throws light upon the weakness of this sense; and upon man's propensity to make the weakness of this sense an excuse for wrongdoing. Habitually man signs up for causes the connection of which with other causes and other powers is very dimly perceived. This tragic dimness of perception is sometimes a fault (if such we may call it) of the insurmountable limitations of his rational-cognitive powers. But it is sometimes the result of the self-involutions of consciousness: we prefer not to peer into these depths, lest we be overcome by the rank growth and the foul stench of the Lie. So we do much weighty business with plausibilities. We say that we would have done better if we had only seen better; that we are the victims of circumstances; that the reasons for our actions are so very nice that they are wasted upon grossly factual minds; etc., to infinity. Having made commitments that have trapped us in a net of evil consequences, we take a resolute stand on mere plausibility, and defend ourselves stoutly against every attack of truth.

A further justification of the Biblical imagery of the kingdoms is within reach. Ontologically, human existence is concretely possible only in a kingdom. To be recognizably and responsibly human is to accept a structure of authority impervious to any single application of individual will against it, whether or not the *ethos* of that society is democratic. Concrete human existence is possible only within the boundaries of that authority. When it collapses, meaningful human life collapses with it.

The source of authority is a mystery very nearly as nice as the source of evil. And once again men have allowed their resistance to mystery to confuse them about the reality at stake. The democratic confusion is a sterling example of this law. Every severe crisis of the body politic demonstrates anew the axiomatic character of authority, that is, that it must be impervious to any single application of the individual will against it. Actually the full story is likely to be even more offensive to the conventionalities of the democratic spirit. Authority may have to withstand the application of *majority* sentiment against it. Like every other political order a democratic state will have to command men to do what does not come naturally when the life of the order is at stake, namely, to put their very lives on the block before a vote has been taken.

So, again, we have ample warrant for saying that the human realm is made up of kingdoms, some of which have sovereign authority over life and death. In some kingdoms we choose our membership, we participate in them voluntarily in order to enjoy benefits not otherwise available in that form and quantity, or at that price.

III

There is a kingdom whose sovereign lords are sin and death. They cannot offer life to their subjects, or any other great benefit. Yet their subjects are legion. Their constituency is as wide as mankind. Their term of office seems to be from everlasting to everlasting.

God comes into human life as Jesus Christ to redeem man from bondage to sin and death. The Cross is a stunning blow against sin, that spirit of faithlessness, that will to betray. The Resurrection is the *coup de grâce* to death. Since we have already indicated that the current agony of good faith with Resurrection puts a primary responsibility upon the conscience of the theologian, we shall address ourselves to the impact of Resurrection upon the sovereignty of death. Good faith can often see as far as immortality, partly because this lies comfortingly in the Great Future. But today good faith has immense difficulties with Resurrection. It has already occurred, and yet we are still subjects of death!

We have first, then, to see how death has seized the being of man. How is it possible for elements of man's being to have been misappropriated and expanded into so vast a kingdom?

Man is that singular creature who can create a "bad infinite" in his imagination and thereafter love this counterfeit which has an extraordinary variety of forms. The "bad infinite" is that realm in which life is just "one damn thing after another." It is that state in which each damned thing has no power except to guarantee that there will be another damned thing, to infinity. Endless continuity without essential value is the "bad infinite." This is the kingdom of death.

A mere paradox? To show that it is true, and not merely paradoxical, we must apply it to the ontological elements.

1. *Mortality.*

People today are too much given to talking about death as the moment and thereafter the condition of total annihilation. Despite our allegiance to these verbal and metaphysical conventions, we really know better than this indulgence in the rhetoric of total annihilation would indicate. There is nothing to fear in total annihilation, because there is no such moment and there is no such condition. These rhetorical unrealities are conjured by the sick imagination (one of the illnesses of the self-involuted consciousness) to conceal or distort the truth. I know that there will be something going on after I die (I know it, I do not merely "believe" it), and the going on, the continuity, is stripped of value because I am no longer an active agent in it.

The next stage in the dialectic of the sick imagination follows hard upon the first. This value-less continuity now reads itself backward from futurity into my present actuality. If I shall be a nonactual component in a value-less continuity, how can I avoid seeing that now I have only the value I give myself? But the movement of time is implacable. Self-value is therefore mortally precarious in every moment. I and Thou also become one damned thing after the other.

So I begin to understand the impossible heroics of the suicide. A despairing citizen (slave, rather) of the kingdom of death, he wants to enforce his value upon life to come, he wants someone in perpetuity to feel sorrow, remorse, loneliness, or admiration for him. The "in perpetuity" is an assignment of value to his own being, necessarily, because he knows that nobody lives forever. "In perpetuity" means that he craves a value for his death that his life could not have. This is true for the noble suicide, too, the person who lets himself out before the next dreadful increment of suffering tears away the last shred of dignity or of financial resources. Noble of mind or base-spirited, the suicide wants to make an imprint upon continuity with his death. (If there were no continuity, if he embraced total annihilation by his act, his act would have no meaning.) In the power and heat of this desire, he becomes a deserter and a traitor. And may God have mercy upon us all, because each of us carries with him at all times the seed of this treason; as though at birth this seed were placed as an amulet about the neck of each person by death's dread king, the counterfeit-god, the father of lies.

Thus our mortality is dragged down from truth into illusion. Only in illusion is death illimitable. In the everyday world the power of the illusion is inexhaustible.

2. *Love.*

Love is the first positive power of our being to feel the thrust of the rancid kingdom. When a person can no longer love himself adequately because that love, that value, is not adequately reflected by the world beyond him, the natural consequence is for him to withdraw love (except for uncontrollable spasms) from that evil nonreflecting world. Thus the order of creation is warped, since love is the first law of our being. The choices of the self are thereafter unduly and unnaturally reduced. (a) The self can hate the world because it has failed to reflect the ego's self-value. Only in the most severe emotional disorientation does the world as a whole become the object of this hatred. The normal pattern in the kingdom of death is a differential and discriminating hatred: this person and that person, rather than mankind as a whole, are the objects of this hatred; but a world magnitude of hatred is concentrated upon them. (b) The self creates a fantastic world in imagination. The essence of this fantastical world reflects the love ego has for itself. Again, this fantastical world wholly absorbs the ego only in the most severe cases of disorientation. The normal service of the kingdom of death is a life torn between the pleasures of the fantasy world and the pains inflicted by the real one.

The wretched plight of love when man is a vassal of the kingdom of darkness is a sufficient indication that this kingdom includes hell. It is surely one of the great oddities of Western civilization that in its eschatological visions and doctrines hell is represented as post-death and post-judgment. Whoever has experienced the disasters identified above as (a) and (b), has had a strong and unforgettable taste of damnation. He has felt the temptation to go all the way under into the kingdom of darkness. In the words of the psalmist, he seeks to make his bed in hell.

3. *Creativity.*

The corruption of love identified under (b) above is warrant for saying that even when a root element of his being is dislocated, man continues to seek creative expression and not merely to live. Under the providential ordering of time opportunities will arise in which a creative response is possible, when, in other words, the self cannot fall back upon tropisms and habits, if it is to live with any sense of positive value. This is why we have said that mere continuity is a metaphysical myth conjured by the diseased imagination. But neither time nor any other creaturely power guarantees that creativity will produce an enhancement of man and the world. Indeed, when the heart (the power to love) is in the grip of death, man's creative power is used to curse life and the world. This curse is not necessarily an imprecation, although a good bit of creativity may be invested in imprecations. By "curse" we mean an achievement of creativity that releases a train of evil consequences. By "imprecation" we mean a gesture of disgust provoked by some evil of the world. The imprecation is a rhetorical achievement. The curse assumes the form of historical necessity and forced moral options.

This distinction is drawn in order to call attention to the difference between science and poetry as expressions of creativity in the desert of love. Contemporary culture boasts remarkable lyric imprecations against the evils of life in a cosmos from which Providence has vanished. Such is the burden of some of Dylan Thomas' poems, and of Robinson Jeffers. They do not file whining complaints, they hurl imprecations.

As for scientific creativity, it has become a curse, not merely but surely a curse. It is customary to say promptly that the evil consequences flowing from scientific creativity have been accidental and are dwarfed by the wonderful practical benefactions of technology as well as by the towering cognitive attainments of science in its theoretical enterprise. Then Dachau, Hiroshima, and Dresden offer their horrid testimony. And we begin to wonder whether noisome rumor of human malefaction may not leak out of the earth's atmospheric envelope. Somewhat less fantastically we ponder how much good must be done, here below, to balance the accounts of scientific creativity. Improved carburetion and the prolongation of man's life do not seem overwhelming credits.

So this century has revealed new depths of servitude to the deathly kingdom. Nothing is any more nakedly and speciously self-flattering, on the part of this age, than the illusion that world war and the age of science are merely coincidentally related to each other. Scientific creativity has been successfully harnessed to the hellish projects of mass destruction. All parties have claimed, in this nightmare, the justification of national survival. Philosophers and theologians may argue the question whether this is an ethical justification. Policy makers are not likely to hold the phone until that report has been made.

Scientific creativity has produced a situation in which for the first time in history peace among the nations is precariously balanced upon the possession of weapons that can wipe out Western civilization, at least, and very likely make a large down payment on a rather more inclusive catastrophe. Given time and incentive scientists will learn how to convert other natural processes to incredibly destructive purposes. The next levels of creative achievement may well outstrip our present weapons as a nuclear bomb outstrips a water pistol. The piety of historical and moral necessity whispers, "May they never actually be used, whatever they are!" The ghosts of Hiroshima arise to say, "Amen!"

Again, this is not the whole story. The curse of scientific creativity has produced splendid side effects. With the help of science man is learning how to live longer between the paroxysms of world destruction. This reminds us ever so little of the consecrated efforts of the doctors to save a condemned murderer from pneumonia so he can be hanged on schedule.

Prolonging life, and making it ever more comfortable, are slender blessings when the essence of man's being has been warped out of recognition. His knowledge and love of being corrupted at the source, is it likely that his creativity will escape the icy clutch of death's black kingdom?

4. *Anxiety.*

The kingdom of death has a natural ally in anxiety. Anxiety is the ontological misappropriation of time. If man had no sense of time, he would have no anxiety; but a humanity without the sense of time is something beyond our comprehension. This is why we have not hesitated to identify anxiety as one of the ontological fundamentals.

But we must not overload the affinity of anxiety with death. Even the most painfully inflamed awareness of futurity does not necessarily spread ruin upon every project and prospect. There are real threats to existence and value. Awareness of these threats is the beginning of wisdom. So far as anxiety is simply that perception, it is also a testimony to the wisdom of the Creator. "Teach us to number our days, that our hearts may be inclined to wisdom" is an expression of the piety of this wisdom.

Nevertheless anxiety surrenders to death. This happens when a person accepts the future as no longer indeterminate, that is, as a threat which might materialize. Thus the line between the present and the future disappears affectively; and anxiety is transformed into despair. So again man's ability to create (actually to conjure) impossible possibilities is disclosed. Viewed metaphysically as well as commonsensically, it is impossible to erase the boundary between the present and the future. Viewed ontologically, anxiety accomplishes this very impossibility. Thanks to the power of imagination, the time sense is captured by despair, one of death's chief lieutenants.

5. *Guilt.*

"To be human is to be guilty." The truth of this ought not to be seen as a theological-dogmatic pronouncement but as an authentic reading of man's essential being. Guilt is accountability, and as such it is the ontological element in which the moral phenomenon of responsibility is grounded. Like anxiety guilt is possible ontologically because man has a duality of consciousness, he is at least potentially spirit. Thus guilt rests upon man's being an agent who acts responsively. Man hears and answers; and part of the time he listens to and answers himself.

The radical corruption of guilt comes about through the union effected between guilt and time, a marriage not made in heaven. It is a marriage made by man and applauded in hell. The time sense of man is an awareness of the past as well as an awareness of the future. Indeed, one of the philosophical plausibilities of our time is that the sense of time in man is primarily awareness of the past, the awareness which makes history possible.

Man lives as a vassal in the kingdom of death so far as he suffers the corruption of his essence by the marriage of guilt and time. In this condition every project and every prospect seem merely to continue or repeat the past in which he is purely and simply guilty of evil, that is, concretely and ethically guilty. In this condition the boundary between present and past has been obliterated. Time is now shame rather than threat. Judgment is no longer the terror to be anticipated, it is the damnation to be endured forever. Forever, precisely because the past has brought time to a standstill.

The power of spirit by which this terrible triumph of the guilty past is rendered a "possible impossibility" is memory. Memory is the central "essence factory" of consciousness. Memory abstracts shapes and qualities from the passage of time and preserves them as presently experienceable in their felt pastness. Memory, that is, works with essences (in this sense) rather than with flux. Thus to lose oneself in memory does not mean that one recovers the past in its full concreteness, because passage is in principle omitted. (We might argue with some plausibility that memory reduces whatever it grasps of the past to propositions: one remembers that, not how or what.) Contrariwise the creative appropriation of memory goes beyond the mere recital of what happened into how it might have happened, because the present actuality of the past is drenched with the affectivity of the present agent. So the epic poet plays upon present emotion by appearing to summon the real past. He summons the past in order to cement the devotion of the living to a teleology which "o'ermasters Time."

The kingdom of death upends the order of creation. The guilty one is engulfed by the past. Every passing moment merely illustrates, in one way or another, his timeless essence: he *is* only and absolutely the evil he has done.

Thus life in the kingdom of death is unable to sustain the now of God's time; and the spirit is lured into the last and most dreadful counterfeit of being. In bondage to death, human life is locked into an alternation of lifeless immobility with grotesque spasmodic movements: the hellish parody of the created rhythms of action and repose, giving and receiving, speaking and listening.

When the spirit of man has gone over into the kingdom of death the halls of his castle now and then ring with humanlike voices, but there is no longer any real conversation because each inmate talks only to the dead. Now and then a cacophonous imitation of laughter can be heard but joy has fled the castle. Orgasm is available but there is no love. There is wailing and gnashing of teeth but there are no tears. Now and again no sound is heard but there is no silence.

This castle was designed to be the temple of the living God. But now the master is death. He never appears but he is everywhere in it.

IV

Jesus Christ is man. Therefore he has direct access to the kingdom of sin and death. Jesus Christ is God. Therefore from a position well inside the castle he has dealt the lords of darkness the blow from which they will never recover. The *coup de grâce* is Resurrection. The Risen Lord restores to man the power fully to be in the now of God's time.

Thereby additional meaning accrues to the text, "He who was without sin was made to be sin." To say that Christ is made to be sin is to say that he walked within the borders of death's kingdom, it is to say that "he was made to be like us in every respect." But it is not to say that his membership is properly confusable with simple mortality. To be able to die is not what it means by being made to be sin. Man has a propensity for endowing mortality with a stubbornly antidivine meaning. He leaps to embrace the satanic formula, "If death, then there is no God, there is no mercy, justice and all-power to realize the good, at the heart of things." So the metaphysical-religious answer to death, the immortality of the soul, is in its own sure way also antidivine, simply because God can be dispensed with in a cosmos where the soul necessarily participates in eternity.

To be made sin is to be seized by this propensity of man to endow mortality with antidivine meaning. Jesus Christ, by his own utterance of the project and prospect of the Cross, becomes a violent offense, first to the disciple Peter (Matt. 16), and thereafter to everybody and everything which conspire to put Jesus on the Cross. Once there, he is the ultimate offense: it is too late to change the project and the prospect. So two more satanic formulas flash into view. "And they began to say, 'Others he saved, he cannot save himself!' ": as though the Savior of mankind could have had any thought for saving himself. "If thou art the Christ, come down from the Cross!": as though the essence of his life and work was obviously invalidated by the present facts of awful suffering and the imminence of death. These taunts are more than simple human malice recoiling from the one who would not play malice's game. These taunts, these outrageous expressions of antidivine outrage, are diabolical inversions of the first law of God's Kingdom. They are also expressions of a satanic antidivine impatience: better a live and discredited wonderworker than a dead Christ. Christ will indeed come down: dead.

In this steadfastness in "being made sin," in this obedience to the thing impossible for a savior of mankind, death upon the Cross, we have the beginning of the end of death's kingdom. The power that nailed Jesus Christ to the unspeakable offense is a power more elemental than Rome or Caiaphas, and more human than Satan. It is the human spirit. More specifically it is the human imagination violently self-alienated from the Source and the Perfecter of human life. A concentrated fury of revulsion against mortality comes down upon Jesus Christ, not just the disappointment of historical expectation. The Son of God is the unbelievably choice object upon which to vent the propensity to make mortality antidivine. Jesus Christ dies. Say, rather, that he is killed. But even this is not quite right. Say, then, that he is offered up by man to the princes of the kingdom of darkness. Say, finally, that the whole terrible routine of the trial and crucifixion of Jesus Christ is a satanic parody, a diabolic counterfeit, of man's proper offering of himself in love, peace, and joy in the service of God. It is the first and only authentic Black Mass. "He who was without sin was made to be sin."

But Jesus Christ is not a mere victim of this human propensity for being mortally offended by death, a propensity vulnerable to diabolic stimulation and direction. Romantic piety has the virtue of being able to apply a kind of counter to the representation of Jesus as victim. Piety of this sort represents Jesus Christ as allowing things to happen rather than as a victim succumbing to forces beyond his control. So Jesus Christ stands before Pilate and the whole obscene chorus of lying accusation; and because of his devotion to the purpose and the Father of the Kingdom, he holds his own immense power in check. But the power is there, all the while. So his tormentors may be likened to lunatic moths darting at a flame potent enough to liquefy a city of steel. Who then was really the victim? We know now that Pilate is no match for the man whom he presumes to sentence to death; and if all of the might of Rome could have been focused upon that man, the outcome would not have been altered. From that moment Pilate steps into history as a venal bureaucrat whose end is less interesting than that of Judas Iscariot. He is a pawn in a game which he could not have hoped to win even if he had known the stakes.

These romantic representations are of value in the preaching of the Gospel only so far as they help to balance the representation of Jesus

Christ reduced to victim, reduced, indeed, to another pawn in the game between God and Satan. In all of this we must insist that Jesus Christ is sacrifice but not victim. He enters the kingdom of death as sacrifice. Humanly regarded, this is the essence of his work, it is this that defines and caps his teleology, it is in this that he is perfectly obedient.

Sacrifice has inspired great feats of speculation and provoked great storms of polemics. We have declined to attempt the one and have steered a course around the other. There is a place for both, but the place for neither is on the groundfloor of theological reflection. The fundamental theological task is to discern the ontological notes struck by the sacrifice of Jesus Christ for the "sins of the whole world."

The first of these ontological notes is openness to the demands of God in His Kingdom.

The second of these notes is courage in the full face of every human antidivine propensity.

These two ontological notes are so firmly united in Jesus Christ that because of him self-sacrifice is everlastingly symbolized by the Cross, even in the secular world, self-sacrifice, that is, in the grandest conceivable cause. Moreover, the perfection of this unity reflects the unity of God and Man in Jesus Christ.

His courage in the face of every human antidivine propensity is redeemed from self-appointed martyrdom by his openness to the will of God the Father. He does not intend to be merely the victim of man's antidivine propensities. He does intend to participate in the Father's project of redeeming man from the devastations wreaked by the expression of these propensities. This intention requires that he meet the full brunt of these powers. But he accepts this assault in his own way, the same being the perfect unity of courage before man and of openness to God. Receiving the full assault in his own person he therefore places unalterable limits upon the powers attacking him. Jesus Christ has been on the offensive from the beginning. The human and demonic powers assaulting him have no great threat left but to waggle the finger of death under his nose.

Now this is not an empty gesture. Let us be sure about that. The enemy can do that much. He can threaten to kill and he can kill. That is why we say that this gesture, this waggling the finger of death at Jesus Christ, is not an empty gesture. But it is a futile gesture. The powers of darkness can kill him but they cannot prevent him from dying unto God the Father. So he does not defy the threat. He meets it in order to envelop it. Thereby he takes the powers of darkness into his essence, into that teleology in which he and the Father are one.

This is human shrewdness and courage at their best. It is shrewdness because a man must die sometime anyway, so if a man can use his own death to offend, and perhaps even to cripple, the prowling enemies of human life, there's a bargain! But it is courage also, because how can a man be sure that his death will accomplish what his shrewdness perceives as a real and wonderful possibility? So prudence whispers: It might be better to wait for the next opportunity, perhaps the next cup of suffering might be even more meaningful. Thus shrewdness declines into expediency, and courage becomes a self-lie.

But Jesus Christ knows that his time has come. This is the hour adumbrated in the beginning, it is for this that he has come forth. He prays: Father, if it be thy will, let this cup pass from me! This is the last breath of life for man's antidivine propensities in the person of Jesus Christ himself. Tonight they stab for his heart, for the vital center of his being; and they fail; so on the morrow they must be content to buffet him in the face and about the head and otherwise to torment the flesh. He has finished with the body, for the time being.

Any man of resolute adherence to principle will make enemies, unless he has a genius for not making himself understood. But he cannot ever be absolutely certain that this enmity is a response to his principles rather than to his character. There is the further possibility that his principles are wrong. Courageous adherence to wrong principles is not to be confused with courageous adherence to the right even though it is a lost cause for the present and foreseeable future.

The righteous and courageous man is not yet the proper similitude in which to express the readiness with which Jesus Christ accepts the demands of sacrifice. He has provoked enmity where it counted, he has produced resistance and conspiracy against his essence (his intention), his project and purpose, rather than against his character or his principles. From the beginning he has been probing the chief complication, corruption, and confusion of human existence, he has taken as his target the capital offenders against the plan of creation. He is therefore to be sacrificed under a capital charge rather than hung for a chicken thief. "He said that he was king of the Jews." He did not say this, and his accusers know that he did not say this; but it is a sound practical way of cutting through the religious chatter about messiahs, true and false.

The import of Jesus Christ as sacrifice goes beyond this. The full brunt of the most potent and concerted antidivine propensities of man is received by God Himself. In the imagery of the parable, the prince of the realm rather than a hired hand is seized, violently maltreated, and killed. This is a similitude. God cannot be killed. But the body in which He reveals His purpose can be destroyed. This will not defeat the purpose; but the enemy has no other recourse. From the outset Jesus Christ makes it very clear to the enemy what he is after and that he means to have it. So death seizes him. And death is seized by resurrection.

Thus the sacrifice is accepted. Even from the Cross Jesus Christ dies unto God the Father, and in that his work in the body is completed. From here on it will be Christ the Spirit who will work everlastingly in the body of mankind to bring man to that perfection of communion for which he was created.

Resurrection is God's unequivocal and absolute indication that the sacrifice has been accepted, as well as His accreditation of the authority Jesus Christ claimed for his work in the body. It is an accreditation that can be published only after the death of Jesus Christ because his death is an integral part of the teleology in which the Father and the Son are one.

Resurrection is also the *coup de grâce* administered to the kingdom of death. But since man dies quite as obviously now as in 500 B.C. and on Good Friday, we must certainly ask about this victory. We must as certainly answer in terms of the essential elements of man's being.

V

1. *Death.*

Through the power of the Resurrection death is reduced to mortality. The sting of death is pulled, its power to spread infection, like a fire out of control, is broken. The Risen Lord does not accomplish this merely by assuring all and sundry that now they shall live forever. The time is coming when death shall be no more; but in the meantime we die. Thanks to the power of God unto resurrection we need not die like flies. As in Christ we all die so in Christ we shall all live. To bad faith the first "as" is the great stone of stumbling. To good faith it is the door opened wide for us to participate in the teleology of God's Kingdom. Death may now be accepted as an element in that teleology. "The Lord gives and the Lord takes away." He does not take away what He has revealed in Jesus Christ as the grace and truth of the Kingdom. Neither does He give to us something withheld from Jesus Christ the first-born son, i.e., immunity to death. In Jesus Christ we are called to participate in the life of the Kingdom; and we are called to participate altogether and just as we are. We cannot therefore leave out of the essence in which we are called to participate either the fear of death or the moment of dying. Both are included in the plan of creation. Because of the seal of approval God has put upon the death of Jesus Christ, the Resurrection, we may also hope to offer up our fear of death and the moment of dying as testimony to the glory of the Kingdom. "We may also hope. . . ." This is a hope for us, it is not a certainty, and it is not a certainty precisely because our participation in bringing it to pass is essential. So long as Christ is only my companion this will not come to pass. It may come to pass when I say of him, "My Lord and my God."

2. *Love.*

Love may now look forward in the highest confidence to the death of the last propensity to make something and to love something antidivine. In his person and work Jesus Christ has already begun this in and for us. He offered himself up in the face of all antidivine powers, to the end that man's life might be delivered from their curse. If he had been conformed to the enemy in opposing him, if he had met hate with hate, the enemy would have won; and we should all be yet in bondage. He was not conformed to the enemy; and thereby the enemy is confounded. We are therefore of no necessity still in bondage to the spirit of enmity. We may participate in the Resurrection, we may find that the love of being rises irresistibly from the depths of our own being, until "love ye one another" has become both the first law of being and the source of unalloyed delight.

3. *Creativity.*

Creativity participates in the power of resurrection, it is delivered from the spurious necessity of making gods unto itself and out of itself.

Every false god is the product of human creativity gone to seed. Man cannot climb to heaven by piling up these creations and stepping from the top of such a magic mountain straight into the arms of the one true God. He cannot do this because the false gods will not cooperate with one another. Why should we expect lying spirits to trust one another? But the decisive reason is that God has come to man, with grace and truth for the healing of the mortal wounds inflicted by the self-lie. So now we know in the depths that a false god is but human creativity infatuated with itself and thus turned aside from its proper good, the celebration of the inexhaustible richness of being.

This is to say that in the Resurrection a great hope is planted in the depths of man's being: the time is coming when creativity will be neither unwitting curse or recoil of imprecation, because man's spirit will be at peace with the creative purpose and power of God.

In the meantime creativity is freed from bondage to the negativities. Death no longer calls the tune to which life must dance. Delivered from the spurious necessity of aiming at immortality for the works of our hands if not for our souls, we can in good faith speak a true word to the age. If God can use it for the edification, instruction, or delight of some age as yet unborn, that is His business. Thanks to Jesus Christ the Risen Lord we do not struggle any longer with the spurious necessity of building for eternity. We can expend the last ounce of creativity in saying a timely word, in adding richness of meaning to the now.

4. *Anxiety.*

In the Resurrection the future is restored to its proper place. "Be not anxious for tomorrow" is a counsel of perfection and thus a source of despair, unless we hear it faithfully from Jesus Christ. We know in him that the now is cherished by God because He has taken it as the time in which to speak. Therefore we are at liberty to train every power of concentration upon it. "Sufficient unto the day"—is the everlasting Lord. God is the participative power entirely adequate to every moment. He is the master of the future who is fully present now, and He does not cheat by exhaustively enjoying the future as though it were present. We need no longer be under a spurious necessity to be anxious about the future because we know now who is Lord. Therefore we can do better than acknowledge faithfully the boundary between now and future, the boundary dissolved in imagination by anxiety. We can also be content to live wholly unto God in this present moment.

5. *Guilt.*

The Lord of Resurrection restores the boundary between the present and the past which guilt dissolves. In Jesus Christ we now have a past that once had us. The folly of trying to escape the past, and the wickedness of letting it engulf the present, are alike broken open by the Risen Lord. He does not erase the past, he does not wave a metaphysical wand over it to make it disappear. But he puts the past where it belongs, just as he puts the future where it belongs. He does not stand between me and the guilt my sin earns. But thanks to him even the foulest sin, the black essence of all sin—betrayal—does not drive me from grace and truth. I can still attach to my sin that further element of antidivine longing; but I cannot have what thus I long for, not even cold comfort from a quiet grave. I can still seek death as relief from guilt too great to be born. But death has no power to absolve me, it cannot answer when I speak to it; and that mountain of guilt which I feel as mine, is a monstrous inflation of frustrated ego. I have done terrible things, but guilt for these does not make me kinsman of Satan, except in my diseased imagination. With a proud gesture of obeisance to the kingdom of evil I can say, "Henceforth, evil be thou my Good/ and good be thou my evil." The gesture is rhetorical, because evil no longer has a kingdom. Whether we live or whether we die, we are the Lord's. Whether we sin or whether we do not sin, we are the Lord's. Satan never really owned us. He lied, as always; and for a season—a crazy eternity—we believed him. That season has past.

Nonetheless I can still die of thirst in the very spot in the desert from which the living water flows. If I do so, if I persist in trying to do so, is this a rebuke to Providence? Has Christ lived and died in vain because I can still love the darkness rather than the light? According to the plan of creation man is free. Jesus Christ renews and reforms this freedom by disclosing the shape of the Kingdom. But I can still say No! The difference is that I know now what this negation means: it is a proud salute to nothing.

VI

The things we have said concerning the work of Jesus Christ as the efficacious sacrifice accepted and sealed by resurrection are obviously the thinnest possible sketch of an interpretation. In drawing the sketch we have had in mind the primary responsibility of the church to preach Jesus Christ as the power of God unto the transformation of the world. We have deliberately couched this in terms of a reconstitution of human existence rather than in terms of social revolution and cultural upheaval. The interpretational choice has not been dictated by any commitment whatever to the false philosophy of individualism. There is a context in which to say something about revolutions and upheavals; but first we must see how history is grounded in man's being. So from the beginning we have said that Jesus Christ came into history. He did come into history, to be sure, he is acknowledged in the church as the Lord of history. The interpretation of this acknowledgment follows upon the interpretation of his becoming a man and having lived perfectly unto God in the body.

CHAPTER XI

Man's Being as History

I

There are three reasons why we must put history next on the theological agenda.

1. The Gospel makes heavy demands upon history.
2. The present age finds it very difficult to understand some of these demands, to say nothing of accepting them as valid.
3. If it is to preach faithfully the Gospel of Jesus Christ, the church must resolve the conflict in its own heart between (1) and (2). Both laity and clergy belong to the present age as well as to the church. So the conflict between (1) and (2) is not a conflict between laity and clergy. Rather, the possibility of this conflict hovers above the church as a whole and over the world as a whole.

II

The heavy demands the Gospel makes upon history are felt as soon as the church begins to interpret the person and work of Jesus Christ, which is to say as soon as the church begins to preach the Gospel of the Kingdom of God. The Holy Spirit, the divine "Interpreter," does not permit any aspect of the "old man," here any element of a non-Gospel view of man's being in history, to elude Christ's renewing and reforming power. Christ in the Gospel demands a novel rerepresentation of man in history. To meet this demand Christian reflection has to endure the pain and confusion of a categorial revolution, or prove faithless to the Holy Interpreter by using the old categories in the old way. God requires the church to communicate the Gospel rather than to mutter to itself. Thus the church must use a language already in existence; but it must conform this language to the world revealed in Jesus Christ rather than to the old world. This is the categorial revolution which the church must endure as an unavoidable inference of the Gospel.

Four categories are forthcoming in this situation. We shall certainly not suppose that this list is exhaustive; but it contains more than enough to keep the church productively occupied for the foreseeable future in its engagement with the "mind of this present age."

A. *Destiny.*

Fate, rather than destiny, is the notion with which the natural man is likely to begin and conclude his account of history. As an interpretation of history fate has six essential elements that we must sketch with care. This view of history is the first one the church encounters in faithful preaching of the Gospel; and it is the last to let go.

1. Fate expresses the sense of the "brute givenness" of events. Historical events in their immediacy defy appropriation by rational schemes of interpretation; and by humane and cheerful expectation. "Things simply happen" is the mundane way in which fate is expressed. So far fate is history's quarrel with time, because time lulls consciousness into supposing that successiveness and continuity as such guarantee the persistence, if not the enhancement, of value. Then things happen that destroy this suppositional rapport with time. These events may be so brutal in the destruction of life and value that every teleological interpretation of time is embraced by the general ruin, rather than only the vaguely conceived rapport with time as the producer of values. The doctrine of fate is the strongest possible reinforcement for the feeling that "one increasing purpose" is not visible, as the golden immortal thread upon which all our mortal years are strung.

2. Fate is the sense (and this sense readily achieves doctrinal dignity) of an iron-fisted cosmic governance of human affairs totally indifferent to individuality of being and value. If the plane is "fated" to crash the presence in it of sixty-five bishops and thirteen nuns will make no difference. The plane goes down because it is "supposed" to.

Under our very eyes, in other words, fate has become something more than the sheer maddening randomness of events. It has passed over into some kind of law, indeed a kind of law that does not allow any exceptions and leaves nothing to chance. The fated world is one in which everything is accidental but it is also the world in which there are no accidents.

3. Fate is the name for momentous events which make the difference between life and death. Fated occurrences are the doom-sealers and death-dealers in the lives of men and worlds. In the "decrees of fate" man dimly sees but powerfully feels immense and implacable powers from whose determinations there is neither escape nor appeal. No matter how cunning his ruses he has an unbreakable "appointment in Samarra" with his fate.

4. A very large part of the power of fate springs from its perfect nonarguability. It participates in the absoluteness of accomplished fact. "What will be will be" is logically indistinguishable from "what has been has been." This does not deter the natural man from making fate the foundation of his account of history. Turned philosopher the natural man (the Old Adam) might very well argue that none of the categories of history is rich in predictive value. Their value, he might add, is their elucidation of the past.

This is a point well taken. The categories of history are valid only for the interpretation of historical being; and the past is assuredly one dimension of historical being. Moreover it is precisely the dimension which cannot instruct the living as to the course they ought to pursue. Even if the doctrine of fate is linked with the doctrine of time as circular, the elucidation of the past cannot possibly instruct man as to where he is now in the cycle.

Historical-cultural pessimists seem often to overlook the possibility that history is more than time past; and especially in those moments when they are sternly chiding Americans for not having a sense of history. The sense of history, in such tutelage, is barely distinguishable from fate. It amounts very nearly, if not altogether, to saying that "there is nothing new under the sun" and innovators had better know this. This sentiment has indubitable validity in lyric poetry and up to a point in epics. As a political sentiment it is the proud father of great mischief, since it means, "anything new is bad, everything old is good, and the oldest is the best." In politics, to put the matter axiomatically, the appeal to the sense of history is made to justify either inaction or reaction, as the circumstances indicate.

5. Fate cannot escape all teleological coloration of history and the cosmos. The fate of a nation is its place in an all-inclusive scheme, its fate is its finally appropriate grave. Kingdoms rise and fall in

response to an awful insistency at the heart of reality. This insistency is obviously a nonmoral rhythm. The grave of time accommodates iniquitous Babylon as well as Judah, the lovely innocent; but the mysterious tides of the world sweep all such distinctions away. In the finality of fate, and in its indifference to human preferences, the wise find much food for contemplation. On the upswing of empire this finality is fortune. On the downswing this finality is doom. Fortune and doom are the two faces of fate.

The fate of the individual is the point at which he is caught, it is the point at which his personal power of self-determination breaks down completely and he becomes an effect, and perhaps a by-product, of forces beyond his control. These forces defy moralization, they are beyond good and evil. Who has not felt that he deserved far better from the powers of the world than he has gotten? But one must bow the neck to the execution of fate. What must be must be. Perhaps in the long run things work together for good. In the short run they seem to work together to obliterate the last trace of individuality of being and value. (In our time people are prone to make society rather than the cosmos the realm of fate. They see institutions functioning amorally, once they see beyond the illusions and hypocrisies of the conventional world. The decrees of the massive institutions of society can be hated but they must be obeyed, e.g., war simply happens, it is not the result of free choices made by individuals. Even the mysterious power elite is caught in the interaction of historical forces that arbitrarily make and break even the mightiest and most splendidly endowed persons.)

6. The emotional reality of fate is not pure despair, for the reason just cited. The cosmos enforces a law upon history, reality is not pure randomness. Moreover to be overcome by powers one could not have withstood in any case is no disgrace. To have defied them even for but a moment, however brutal and final their rebuttal, is admirable. Few there be who strive for such perfection of heroism, but the few number some giants in their company. For the rest, there is some comfort in knowing that things could not have turned out otherwise. The heroes have the great lines; but the audience is only man.

So there's an end on it. When man says fate, he confesses that he is a meaningless moment in a cosmos perfectly unfeeling in all its members except for the human heart. Worlds and men arise and pass away in response to cosmic rhythms we cannot call either good or evil. In all of the great events wherein souls are lost or gained, we are but pawns of mighty forces so dark, silent, and unheeding we cannot call them purpose.

The Gospel of Jesus Christ has a fundamental quarrel with this account of history, an account that cuts history off from essential humanity and absorbs it into cosmic function. God's demand in Christ is that the fallen creature, this natural man, must learn to say everything in the language of destiny that he has said to himself in the language of fate. Therefore:

a. History is indeed a rebuke to sheer time. What man is cannot be learned from continuity and successiveness. He learns who he is in the concrete moment and not from the (mythical and abstract) order of time as such. He is neither made nor undone by time itself.

So it is true that historical events do have an element of randomness. "This did not need to happen, even though it did," is but one way of saying that the historical event cannot be discovered in embryo in the past; and the present moment does not contain the future. Therefore if history has any law, it is a law which cannot be deduced from the cosmos. Cosmic law will be a grossly improper similitude in which to express a law of history. As a creature of flesh man cannot make flesh do what is impossible for it, he cannot extract his formed flesh, his body, from the rhythms of nature. On the other hand he cannot learn from these rhythms whether a society of free men will survive the competition with "closed" societies in which the regnant and tyrannous theology erases the distinction between cosmos and history. Freedom is built into the cosmos only to the extent that God rules the cosmos. But God will not do for man what he can and must do for himself, and that is to commit himself resolutely to the realization of a good open to him only because he is spirit.

b. Man is the historical creature who participates *by choice* in a teleological order which embraces the cosmos but cannot be learned from the cosmos. Spirit, not the cosmos, governs the rise and fall of empire, because empire is a human project and not a biological determination. As a human project empire may be undone by the sheerest contingency—"my kingdom for a horse!"—but this hardly proves that the universe is indifferent. Human schemes must be projected over possibilities and powers which may or may not accept them. Some of these powers are the wills of other human beings.

Some of them are biological forces under the loose control of the human spirit. Some of them are physical forces over which man has no predictable control.

Any one of these diverse factors drawn into the equations of empire may rebel and bring the most powerful and presumptuous down in final ruin. Whether from dismay or gratification men say then, "It had to happen"; or, "Whom the gods would destroy they first make madly proud"; or, "What bad luck!" They may even say, "Look! the universe is opposed to empire!"

Nonetheless the doctrine of fate has part of the truth. The universe seems to have no favorites. Babylon, the proud oppressor, fell; and cruel Assyria is now a plague only to students obliged to memorize the names of her emperors. But hapless Belgium fell also in 1914. Nero was assassinated, and we say, "Well done!". But Lincoln was also assassinated, and this is a great tragedy. Kennedy was assassinated, and the nation weeps in a deserved paroxysm of grief and shame. So the "law" of history is strangely inclusive and nondiscriminating. We can forgive a natural law for being this. How can we forgive a law of history for violating our deepest and truest moral sensibilities?

The Gospel makes it very difficult for us to talk seriously about a law of history as though history were an order of being functioning independently of its constituents. History emerges from the encounter of man with God. History does not claim man as a subject claims a predicate, because the things and powers about which man must make a decision are always present and accounted for in the kind of ontological integrity which demands ontological integrity from him. As a historical being he must contend with destiny. He ceases to be historical when he resigns himself to fate.

c. Therefore it is fitting that real history, time in the teleology of destiny, is seen in life-and-death events. History is the momentous and memorable rather than the trivial and commonplace. Destiny embraces all kinds of trivialities, but its true shape comes to light only in the momentous. Trivialities heaped up or strung together do not acquire momentousness. "Lives of great men all remind us"—that they could distinguish the important from the trivial.

Here the romanticizing imagination sometimes simply bogs down in the swamp of contingency. What, for example, was Lincoln doing on April 14, 1865? What did he have for breakfast? Suppose that a severe headache had kept him home from the theater, etc. etc.

The romantic imagination strings together contingent details, real or imagined, as if those were the preparation for what happened in the evening at Ford's Theater. Really to learn what Lincoln was doing on that fatal day, we need to know what he had said so recently in his Second Inaugural. The essence, the teleology, is there. There the shape of the man is visible. There the shape of things to come can be seen. In a nonlogical way John Wilkes Booth follows from the Second Inaugural. The spirit Lincoln there invoked and expressed is bound to be contradicted by the spirit of men who believe that the sacred rightness of their cause vindicates, if it does not inspire, their hatred of those who oppose it. And here a law threatens to formulate itself. History breeds this kind of diabolical insanity. Men come to find a cause eternally right in the moment of its historical and final failure; and conclude from this that the right has been cheated by villainy most foul.

d. So necessity must somewhere and somehow be discovered in history. Fate errs in finding the model of necessary connection in the finality of accomplished fact, as we have seen in the axiom, "what will be, will be," the confusedly futuristic reading of "what has been, has been." The future is not "what will be." The future is "what may be." If the future is in the grip of necessity, it is a case of mistaken identity, it is not the future. Where then is the real factor or quality of necessity?

The Gospel answers: *in the call of God to life in the community of His creation. Man can be only what God calls him to become.*

The strangeness of this necessity becomes apparent immediately when we make the proper distinction between destiny as the objective of human action and the energy for the determination of that action. The call of the Kingdom is the revealed teleology, the essence, of God Himself. There is a sense in which this destiny can be said to energize man; and there is a sense in which it cannot be said to do so. In one sense it is conceivable that Peter in response to the call of Jesus Christ might have said that he preferred to fish. One man in the Gospel narratives (to say nothing of his numerous spiritual descendants) preferred his business investments to the call of discipleship. What we learn from this is that there are many ways to lose the Kingdom and only one way to have it. We learn this from the very shape of the Kingdom. The call in Jesus Christ discloses the shape of the Kingdom in and to the powers of human life. In this sense the call activates these powers. This is the sense in which a teleological order activates the powers it incorporates. Whatever their energies men cannot pursue a nonexistent good with any hope of success. Conversely the proper disclosure of the good does not guarantee that men will have either the energy or the will to pursue it. It does guarantee that they will be inadequately human unless they do so.

Through the Gospel of Jesus Christ God demands fundamental revisions of this account. There it is made plain that man has no other calling than the call of God. People may claim to have business elsewhere but they have no business elsewhere that is a negotiable substitute for this call. This call reaches into the roots of human existence. This is its necessity.

(We are accustomed to wondering whether a person is called to be a mechanic, a surgeon, or a minister of the Gospel. Where it is a matter of livelihood no one has a call. One hopes for a salutary combination of inclination with capability. Relative to his society a person's only call is to seek a salutary combination of public usefulness and personal satisfaction.)

The call of God in Christ summons man to round all of the details of concrete existence into the shape of the Kingdom, so that our time and substance, moment to moment and element to element, may sing the praise of the Kingdom. In terms of the Pauline injunction, this is a matter of making "the body the temple of God." Our response to this absolute ontological demand is at best partial—it is part of the riddle of man's being that he can divide himself; but some of the finest achievements of civilization result from the effort not only to hear the call but to obey. On the other hand it is also the case that the noblest resolve of spirit in us to obey, to give God the glory, may be undone, confused, and confounded by the most trivial of contingencies. Such a thing can happen only where the spirit is free. There are days when this condition seems anything but providential.

e. The call of the Kingdom embraces the rise and fall of all of the kingdoms of the earth. Perhaps the cadence of this inclusive process is imperceptible to all but the mystic seers of history, but the effects are plain for all to read, mark, and inwardly digest. Let us note, however, that this process in itself is not a clear mark of man's historical being. It is such a mark when he perceives in the rising and falling of kingdoms a reflection of the personal struggle to reconcile the necessity inherent in teleological order with the fierce independence of contingent events.

In the heat of this struggle actually to be historical the doctrines of cosmic necessity are potent temptations, simply because they rule out any such real contingency. How comforting it is to know that the virus which ruins my health does not do this on purpose but is simply hurrying along on its own business in its own ordaining causal nexus, which happens to include my body. So what appears to be an accident, my having this virus at this time, is not at all an accident if we mean by that an exception to a law of nature or an event only contingently related to other events.

The success of such doctrines in surveying the vast spread of the cosmos is the promise of their failure in grappling with history. *The essential and particular meaning of the historical is that of a project which might have succeeded, beyond its actual success, in mastering merely cosmic events.* The cosmos decrees that men must eat to live. It does not decree that men must pay Chicago meat packers for any part of this necessity, although in fact they do. But they might decide to stop eating anything with the mark of Chicago on it. Then night would fall on several economic empires.

Let us look beyond the mundane instance to the generalization: What we take to be iron necessity in the life and death of kingdoms is in reality the free play of spirit. The spirit may be cramped by temperature variations, annual rainfall, nitrogen deficiencies in the soil, malarial swamps, etc. Those are or may be serious limitations upon the scope of spirit's action, but they are not determinations of its actions. Rome was a mighty empire, a going concern, through and across many cosmic events and in spite of adverse natural conditions. Rome's fall has suffered many causal explanations. As a rule these are more edifying than valid. Whatever the explanations we must say that Rome is dead, her project and prospect have expired the moment the spirit acknowledges that to be human it is not necessary to be Roman. As a historical habit Rome persisted for many generations after that moment had been reached, but the creative power was gone; and for centuries her genius (the same being political) was expressed in fighting the most protracted rear-guard action in Western civilization to date. From this astonishing demonstration some have gathered the lesson, *sic semper imperium!* There is another lesson to be learned from this, a lesson properly ontological. The very element of man's being which makes history humanly possible, also makes possible the long roll of rising and dying empire. The ax of the executioner is freedom, not cosmic accident, not necessity in any form which quarrels with spirit.

f. Thus despair is a confession that one has gambled on chance and has been defeated by freedom. Whoever bets that Rome will live forever, and today worships her as everlasting, is taking a chance against impossibly heavy odds. Nothing of human achievement lives forever, sometimes it merely seems forever. If the bet is heavy enough, freedom to face an alternative and make something good of it is nipped in the bud. Rome's habit becomes the individual's will; and the human project and prospect are surrendered to historical accident.

Despair as a response to history has a single virtue. It has hold of a real feature of historical being, namely, that a kind of finality invades every moment of the temporal process. But despair as an ontological acknowledgment is radically faulty. Someday Rome will fall, someday I shall die. From these certainties despair concludes that all is lost now because the lethal processes are already at work—they *must* be at work, because my end is on the same time line as my beginning. This feeling of lostness is allowed to submerge every element of contingency in events and of freedom in the person. Thus fate detaches the value of the process from the certainty of its end. Thereafter the certainty of the end infects the value of the process of time as well as the value of the present moment.

Destiny, the shape of the Kingdom revealed in Jesus Christ, includes the end in the value of the whole process and in the value of the moment, the now. The Cross of Jesus Christ is our assurance that there is nothing either appropriate or inappropriate, timely or untimely, in the time or the manner in which one dies. Our cultural sensibilities may be outraged by the moment and the mode of death but not our ontological certitudes. Ontologically the only thing that matters is what we apprehend as the value of that death in relation to everlastingness. I know that I shall not live forever, but I know also what will. Thereafter the question is not, to be or not to be, but, whether I can commend my spirit to Him who alone is everlasting, with all of my energy as well as with the last breath of life.

The destiny revealed in the Gospel empowers me to go forward from this moment in which the shape of the Kingdom is revealed to embrace everything which the future may have in store for me and for the world. I need not be anxious about meeting my fate because I have already met my destiny in Jesus Christ. Having seen in him the shape of the Kingdom of God, I have learned everything needful about the shape of the future.

III

B. *The Demonic.*

Contemporary civilization evinces a great deal of self-confidence about the devil. He does not exist because he is an affront to our refined moral sensibilities. Our ethical view of man and the world has ushered him out of the cosmos and out of history. He is the only deposed monarch of modern times to whom no one is willing to offer asylum. This seems hardly fair since so many modern empires were built with his help and could not have been built without it.

This rude dismissal of the devil has two striking aspects. (1) It is a verdict made necessary by the enormous successes of the doctrine of fate. (2) Liberated from the devil the demonic goes forward on its own to achieve two kinds of success. The first of these is (a) categorial. The second (b) is a reinfection of moral sensibility. We must briefly attend to these developments, in order more properly to comprehend the severity of the demand upon history made by the Gospel.

1. Worldly wisdom is committed to the separation of fate from the devil and thereafter to the extirpation of any lingering piety toward the devil. Sanity and the unimpeded progress of the race are involved in the achievement of this double aspiration, because so long as people believe that cosmic powers, either malevolent or benign, determine history, they are ethical cripples. Chance, not purpose whether benign or cruel, is King. So chance and fate are wedded to each other—and give birth to freedom! Enlightenment shatters the chains of superstition. Rational man, clear-eyed, cold, steady, and sober, having repudiated the empty husks of traditional religion, proudly bestrides history. He is alienated from the masses only until he can redeem them by universal education, and thus bring them to share his spiritual home in a homeless cosmos.

In such a view the devil is obviously a witless anachronism. The devil depends upon a providential teleology. Without that he becomes an archaic figure of speech. Eventually we shall have to decide whether a providential teleology entails the devil. For the moment we can hope that the dependency is asymmetrical.

2. Temporarily exiled from a spirit ruthlessly cleansed of all teleological credulity, the devil bides his time. When he comes home, he rolls in immensely enriched and increased by the exile forced upon him by the imperial powers of the Enlightenment. Freed (miraculously, as it were) from vile imprisonment in Satan the demonic achieves the two successes noted above. Having no longer a home in the cosmos of scientific reason, the demonic proceeds to reinfect history, as follows.

a. The demonic becomes a theological-metaphysical category. How could it fail to achieve at least this much success? There is something destructive within the creative spirit, there is a love of destruction in man's heart, there is a vast power for evil in man's institutions. These are phenomena with which the category of the demonic grapples.

b. The second kind of success is far more concrete. It is an infection of moral sensibility. The devil comes back as diabolism. Diabolism is the belief (the sentiment, really, because powerful emotions are attached to the idea) that men, nations, and civilizations are alike undone by brilliantly conceived and furiously concentrated human villainy, villainy concentrated by hellish intensity into distillations of pure evil. In this purity of distilled evil men see cruel bastardy of beast and angel: of impulse beastly, of intellect angelic.

Having banished the devil we are free to diabolize every adversary in mortal conflict with us. In the exercise of this freedom a law of history appears: The greater the stakes involved in conflict, the purer the diabolic character of the adversary. So it is one thing to strip from the peeping tom every amiable human aspect, leaving him nothing but an obscene eye. It is quite another to view a formidable enemy locked in mortal contest with us as though he were malice incarnate. Actually we are double-minded about the voyeur. We loathe him but we know that he is ill. On the grand stage of history we are much more single-minded. The enemy there is simply wicked, and in his wickedness he is a a paragon of health, intelligence, and power.

Diabolism goes from strength to strength in contemporary civilization. The unrelenting depersonalization of society and of the individual lends mounting power to the spirit of alienation. The victims of depersonalization, the beings in whom the spirit of alienation dwells bodily, desperately need an adequate living hate object, a someone rather than a something to blame for their misery, and, ideally, a villain weak enough to be vulnerable at least to hatred if not to ruination. Here a kind of inverse rule appears: The greater the ravages of depersonalization, the greater the necessity for a personal hate object, on the condition that the personal concrete object and focus of diabolizing hatred is, so far as he is merely bodily, but the symbol, the creature himself, of an immense, inexhaustible and infinitely cunning evil behind him. The personal object of hatred created by the spirit of alienation is hardly more than the "front" of an evil power as boundless and monochromatic as the hatred the victim feels for the cause of his wretched condition. Therefore every weapon must be turned upon that hideous strength, cunning must be met with greater cunning, violence with greater violence, lies with greater lies. Evil must be overcome with its own instruments, or one has failed to keep faith—with the good!

As the spirit of alienation attacks realm after realm of contemporary life, the objects of diabolizing hatred are randomly multiplied. As people come increasingly to feel that evil powers have isolated them from an Eden they once enjoyed or which they believe is their inheritance and just desert in any case, they look about for a hate object that will meet the specifications we have just sketched; but above all else it must be available for the expression of this hatred. So the enemy may be Jew, Negro, Communist, Radical, Catholic, Liberal, etc. It is someone who is visibly as weak as the victims are, if not more so; but who is invisibly in intimate contact with vast powers of evil.

The victim of alienation has no program as such beyond destroying the evil creatures standing between him and Eden. Therefore he is himself highly available to people who are quite ready to inflame his hatred for the sake of his vote.

(A peculiarly poignant expression of the built-in evil of institutions is found in the relation of Southern political leadership to the fears and hates of its constituency. Certainly at the national level this leadership knows well enough that the revolution is an accomplished fact. The leadership cannot afford to admit this at the local level. The result is one of the most remarkable parades of obstructionism in American history not only for its time span but also for its self-righteousness. It is certainly true that the South suffered cruelly after the Civil War from vicious reprisal and exploitation, though probably not so desperately and systematically as the legend of the South represents. It is also true that the South has persisted in living beyond the law of this country for a hundred years; and to this day upholds the shocking pretense that the illusion called State rights takes precedence over the moral demands of political democracy.)

"Revolution" is the comprehensive name for the alienating powers at work in contemporary society. The real and the imagined creators of revolution are therefore the most precious objects of hate and fear. To the victims of revolution it does not greatly matter that much of the revolution has been unplanned, because someone ought to be made to pay for the devastation. So another "law" of history emerges: The less dramatic and less well-planned the revolution, the more random the choice of object upon which to vent hatred.

The most important revolutions in contemporary civilization are of this sort. They are revolutions that are not designed by any single person or even any particular group of persons. They are unplanned upheavals in the common life. A fundamental condition of the good life in a society is altered, but so slowly or so undramatically as to escape attention until the damage is irreparable. So no one has willed that the common life should be diminished but it is diminished. No one has intended that his own aggrandizement, or his group's, should decrease the life and the value of others, but they have been decreased. No one wanted the progressive instrumentalizing of human existence to unleash the spirit of alienation, but it has been unleased, and who is mighty enough to throttle it without destroying the victim in the process? The moral foundations of Western society have been loosened and weakened, but not as the result of a policy aimed at producing these terrible effects.

These effects of a revolution as comprehensive as it is unplanned raise diabolism to fever pitch, precisely because no villains of sufficiently heroic stature are visible in the scene. So it is necessary to invent them. Behind the mask of ordinariness, what perfection of perfidy may lurk, what genius of diabolical inventiveness may hide! Behind the bungling but well-intentioned efforts to right the foundering ship, what fiendish calculation may have charted a course straight for the rocks!

Diabolism is a severely disorienting and debilitating sickness of spirit. Permitted to run its course it destroys its host and pollutes the moral climate with the carrion. Sturdy souls may be able to resist the disease in their own bodies, but they may also find themselves ill-equipped to combat it in the body politic. Certainly the infection does not yield to mere preachments or to revisions of educational philosophy and curriculum. The problem is demon possession. The solution must be exorcism. But exorcism under what rite and by the power of what name?

While the church stares weakly, and the intelligentsia incredulously, at such questions, the revolution gains momentum. The moral foundations of Western civilization, long ago weakened at the vital points, have crumbled; and we are the children of judgment sitting passively (except for the inner turmoil) in the rubble, or playing frantic games to while away the time. In a time crying for reconstruction what have we to build with? Irrational value preferences, fleeting spasms of fellow-feeling, intelligence (that cunning product of witless evolution), and a random selection of residual beliefs about the goodness of man picked up on the silent shores of the Judaeo-Christian tradition.

In this situation diabolism threatens where it has not already triumphed. The myth breakers (the demythologizers) are very weak troops to throw against the cavalry of diabolism. They are so many Cub Scouts sent out to stop the Comanches. Inside the walls the medical corpsmen (the psychiatrists) hurry through their mumbo jumbo of exorcism, and train their peashooters on Magna Mater. And where are the priests and prophets of Jesus Christ? They are busy preaching that all things and all manner of things will yet be well. They prophesy that a return to the Ten Commandments will cure all the evils of the body politic. They promise that the demons will all go away if we will practice positive thinking.

IV

The Gospel does not argue the advantages of having a personal devil, real as these may be. On the other hand the Gospel obliges us to take the demonic seriously, not only because it reminds us that there are nonaccidental concentrations of evil but also because Jesus Christ is there proclaimed as the victor in the conflict with the powers of evil. To this we add that Jesus Christ is victorious over diabolism as well as over the devil. We need now to supply some of the principal elements of this account of history.

1. For the time being God shares the world with the powers of evil but He does not divide His sovereignty with them. As we have

seen, they have an appointed rather than a primordial grip upon time. No explanation is offered for the fact that they have any kind of grip upon time and spirit, because any explanation of this must be either mythological or speculative or a hybrid with features of both and no integrity of its own. Wherever they came from man struggles with powers which delight to harass and, if possible, to undo him. These are the powers of nonbeing. Thus a riddle and its solution are given together. The riddle is, How can nonbeing have any power? The answer is, By delegation of power from being.

2. The power of nonbeing is the power with which every expression of creativity must struggle. Expressed in mythological images this negativity is a drag in the nature of things. Psychologically and culturally this negativity is a love of nullity and a propensity for the nullifying stroke.

Such powers presuppose the creativity of being. Expressed in romantic terms, the powers of nonbeing are the recoil of creativity against the finiteness of every concrete realization of itself (one thinks of people who are enamored with the mystery of procreation but hate their own real children). Apprehended Biblically (the Bible admits nothing of this romantic dialectic) the powers of darkness are given determinate shape by the very act of creation. By creation the darkness is overcome but not destroyed. Mythologically the legions of hell were once with God in heaven, whence they fell from excess of ambition. Ontologically that by which anything exists is also that by which what does not exist, does not exist. Thus negation makes possible, but not actual, the spirit of negativity, because negation means merely the positing of one thing to the (necessary) exclusion of something else. The spirit of negativity begins as a great fondness for what has been excluded by creation and thereafter becomes a potent recoil against what has been created. This is the very essence of anti-creativity. It is potent because it is gathered in from the vast spread of things excluded by the creative act. It is, indeed, a kind of infinity directed malefically against the finite, the actual, the created. Thus the madness of Lucifer. It is not simple ambition which drives him to hopeless war against God. Lucifer is also the self-appointed advocate for everything that might-have-been but never has or will be. He is the first and greatest among those who love lost causes because they *are* lost causes.

3. Therefore the delegation of the power of negativity or nonbeing must not be interpreted with the model of a grant of charter or license.

What God grants to any living creature is life. He grants freedom to those created to be spirits. The life of the creature is always allotted and appointed. The creature of spirit may abuse his freedom, but not forever and not with impunity.

4. The abuse of freedom is an illustration *in fine* of the powers of nonbeing springing to life from the creative act. Consciousness in man is self-doubling, as we have seen. In this potentially creative condition illusion also finds its origin. Here the devil comes into his own as the counterfeiter. He cannot create the raw materials; but he encourages a native propensity for using the raw materials, spirit itself in its latency, to shape a world in the likeness of the ego. The devil himself is always behind the mirror, never in it. This has led many enlightened people to suppose that they could prove the nonreality of the devil by showing that the back of the mirror is really quicksilver.

5. So the powers of darkness gain entrance into the body of human life by guile rather than by the sheer overwhelming weight of being. The massy weight of being lies with God. The devil is a host of accidents without substance. He is antiessence rather than essence. He has no program except mischief. He can only raid, he cannot risk another pitched battle. (Like Iago, he has nothing to gain from his deviltry.) He has no home of his own, there is no kingdom pledged to his lordship. He can play a lord but he cannot buy a kingdom.

Ontologically, then, the devil is in a very exposed position—when there is light enough for men to see the adversary. A word will drive out demons, a weapon as light and ready-to-hand as that! But this word is futile if it is uttered by a darkened and lying spirit. The word must be spoken by someone open to the power of God's Kingdom, and therefore by one who uses the word for the sake of the Kingdom rather than for his own glory.

6. Men are men and devils are devils. Men are not devils, they are not incarnations of diabolic wickedness. Ontologically this means that the devil has no power to participate in essence, he has power only to imitate essence. Ethically (as well as ontologically) it means that mankind is a community which only God has the power to divide. Diabolism is a thing of the devil because it creates and nourishes the illusion that there is one community of the righteous and another one of the unrighteous. It is thereafter diabolic business when the righteous launch holy war against the unrighteous; and it is no less

so when failing to bring on such violence, the devil persuades the righteous to disengage and withdraw from the world rather than to share its power and pleasures with the unrighteous.

But we have tarried too long over the devil who might after all turn out to be a figure of speech. Even so if in departing this scene he could persuade us that we have nothing to fear from the powers of nonbeing, he would have served himself to the end rather than God or us. We can therefore afford to say again how these powers take shape.

The particular will to affirm what does not exist and will never exist so long as God reigns, and to deny what does exist, is the supreme achievement of the powers of nonbeing. Rightly to apprehend this it may indeed be possible to eschew satanist terminology. If that language threatens to blur the apprehension of the unitary community in which all men live and must live, we should firmly put it aside.

In the Gospel men are not devils even when they are alienated from the community for which they have been created, and oppose it violently. Do we not sometimes rightly suspect that this animosity against their own good has been inspired either by the arrogation of that community to the righteous alone or by the cheap sentimentalities in which its goodness is extolled?

7. Human projects and prospects are frequently blocked by accidents that no one could have foreseen and that no one can effectively cope with when they occur. From this grim experience men learn to elevate vicissitude to categorial status in the interpretation of history. The historical event is the momentous event. The momentous event may be a terrible testing of wisdom, courage, loyalty, love, and hope; and any or all may break and run. On such occasions the powers of darkness embattled and circumscribed though they are themselves, have ample opportunity to wreak mischief. But so soon as we begin to lose sight of the fact that these powers *are* embattled and circumscribed by power and goodness not our own, we are ready to conceive of history as the story of man's singlehanded engagement with the powers of darkness; and to feel that man has been callously thrown into the pit of time to work out his own salvation in mortal conflict with the forces of evil. This is a radical misconception, a false philosophy, and a corrupt religion. It is compounded of delusions of grandeur and persecution; and it is seasoned with self-pity, a mortal sin. History is indeed an encounter, but the encounter is first and last with God. History abounds in vicissitude not merely because man's

flesh is subject to a thousand natural shocks but also, and far more decisively, because any expression of creativity *may* produce the recoil of negativity. So the primordial prospect of answering creatively the call of God the Almighty Father—the prospect of saying a simple Yes to the absolute Yes of God—is complicated and beclouded by the freedom of spirit in man. Man therefore encounters God in His power of unswerving righteousness. So history is also the story of divine judgment. Over and over again men devise grand schemes for the amelioration of human misery, as a response to the demands of the righteous God, only to see these schemes inhumanly applied, as though the schemes were incomparably more important than the living human beings for whom they were devised. In addition to this, men learn to expect that every proposal for change will be bitterly resisted by the haters of change. Short of hell itself, every actual arrangement of human affairs, no matter how grossly inequitable, pleases some people, namely, those who enjoy a disproportionate amount of its power, comforts, and dignity. But the haters of change can always appeal to history and specifically in history to the sad fact that grand designs for human betterment often fall into the hands of ruthless idealists and of venal self-servers. Thus the great possibilities for significant dialogue of man with man on the proper destiny of man are often ruined by squabbles over the division of the spoils. The design is lost and only the fact remains.

In these ways, and in others too numerous or too appalling to mention, men manage to fall into "nonhistory," they put their own being into brackets. So great is the scope of human freedom that the self-bracketed spirit is able to lose the sense of the momentous and let time shrivel to tedium.

Nevertheless history marches on, to coin a cliché. In America now we worry about this. We wonder whether what merely looks like a recoil against the creativity of Western civilization may in fact be a creative thrust against which we are recoiling. We seem to spend much more time and substance defending what we have than affirming new possibilities either for us or for others. We are commonly so busy reacting to threats that we fail to respond to possibilities.

"Man" is the name of a community. History is the name of its life in time. Destiny is the name of God's righteous determination that we shall be that community in concrete fact rather than in prophetic envisagement only. And there is no or else. There might have been an or else, had it not been for Jesus Christ.

V

C. *The End.*

Man's being is stretched between the envisagement of an end and the realization of the end envisaged. Envisagement brings together the present and the future. Realization brings together the present and the past. Earlier I stated this duality as the difference-in-unity of essence and participative act. Here I use the language of envisagement and realization to emphasize how man's being must be thought as historical.

The Gospel of Jesus Christ makes a very great demand upon history by showing once and for all that the end is both (1) the culmination of time, and (2) the consummation of man's destiny.

1. Everywhere in the New Testament Jesus Christ is represented as teaching and as being in himself the end of time. He did not expect time to stop when his bodily life had been terminated. Rather, he made many provisions for the sustenance and guidance of the life of faith throughout all time to come. Then and now the demands he makes upon the life of faith are severe; but hardly any is greater than the demand that the faithful must see the shape of the end in his life, suffering, death, and Resurrection. This demand is met only by the continuing ministry of Jesus Christ in the Holy Spirit. God the Interpreter gives a knowledge of time's end to the life of faith.

The life of faith is thereafter immediately thrown into conflict with the natural man, both in his realization as Everyman and as the man steeped in "all the vain deceits of philosophy." Everyman knows that time must have an end. His natural piety assures him that the time out of which he dies will run on indefinitely, an assurance which both saddens and cheers him. But he knows that his time must and will have an end. Instinctively he would be happy to forget this; and there are aids and accessories in our civilization to sustain and augment this instinctive recoil against the end of his time. Indeed sometimes he must think that civilization is a providential conspiracy to postpone the end of his time, or, that failing, to distract him from taking the end too seriously. Even funerals have become so bland and handsome that a person who does not long somehow to be able to enjoy his own must be a little lacking in sensitivity.

But the end is even more offensive than the assurance of the end of my time. The whole human story will end one day; and none of the paradoxes spun by philosophers on this theme will postpone the hour thereof. Here again comfort, scientific as well as philosophical, is at hand. That day will be a long time coming, if science can read the cosmic clock correctly. Philosophers assure Everyman that his anxiety about the inclusive end of time is essentially a linguistic confusion. But Everyman has command of a knowledge more fundamental than this science and this philosophy. He knows in his bones that death comes to all men as it comes to him. As there was a first man there shall be a last man too. Through the mixed blessing of imagination Everyman is able to project himself affectively into the situation of Last Man. There he discovers that his situation and Last Man's are not essentially different. Last Man, poor devil! will not be able to have a nice funeral; but on the other hand no one will have to pay a king's ransom for it either; so perhaps things balance out fairly and squarely —in the end. Turned philosopher on his own account, Everyman reaches an impeccable conclusion: It makes no practical difference how the end is envisaged now. What difference does it make whether Last Man is frozen to death or is burned to a cinder? Or whether he is the last one to die from radioactive fallout after the last big bang? When it is over it is over. Period.

We have already seen how men reach for the comfort of fate at this and at similar points as they travel a one-way street leading to the end. So we must point out that the impeccable conclusion is wrong. The end envisaged and the mode of expectation do make a great deal of difference now.

Thus the end envisaged in the Gospel clearly includes the termination of the time of the whole world, but it includes much else, too. The abstraction of the temporal end from the rest is the source of bad doctrine as well as of other sorts of religious confusion. Time ends with the coming of the Kingdom in glory. What this means and how it is to be appropriated have already been published in Jesus Christ; but not a "when." The now in which the righteousness of the Kingdom is preached, the now of repentance, the now of this ministry of love unto all men, the now in which God the Interpreter, the Holy Spirit, lives in our midst and we live in the peace and joy of His life: this now is the authentic forecast and the faithful adumbration of the glory of the Kingdom. When the glory is revealed the tension between envisagement and realization will be resolved; and the full energy of being will go out into participation, which is the perfection of communion with God. In the meantime, in this moment of anxiety and guilt, the end is envisaged in the mode of hope, itself the gift of the Holy Spirit. This hope is a participation in the life of the Kingdom. Hope in the Spirit is not a denial of the world. It is not a wish for an earlier rather than a later termination of time. It is a holding fast to the futurity of the Kingdom. This hope is made possible by the love of Christ and obedience to his commands.

All kinds of people are affronted by the Gospel representation of such an end. The modern world has invested heavily in time as in itself everlasting and creative. Modern man is as fully exposed to death as Neanderthal man, he moves as inevitably to an end (although most of us hope that one by one all of the killing and wasting diseases will be curable). Nonetheless modern man invests a great deal in the endless future—for somebody, as though the universe had made a firm commitment to allowing the human enterprise time unlimited. If he takes seriously his own ontological intuitions he knows that these suppositions are false and that the hopes founded on them are illusory; but, again, the everyday world of modern man is largely a creation of such suppositious hopes.

The Gospel speaks to these ontological intuitions. They do not escape its reforming and reorienting power. The Gospel is particularly insistent upon the reformation and reorientation of the way in which the end is envisaged. An end internally related to the essential process of man's being will elicit a response different from that elicited by an end externally related to man's essential being. Death represented and accepted as simple annihilation can in the nature of the case have only an external and negative relation to man's essential being unless his being has been crippled by the poison of self-hatred. People can reconcile themselves, sometimes at a deeply reflective level, to the fate of simple annihilation, and yet go on to envisage and realize splendid things. Moreover the end proclaimed in the Gospel *can* be accepted in the form of belief only externally related to the central business of one's existence. In this case there is no real reconciliation to the overmastering love of God.

In the light of these things it is necessary to say again that how the end is envisaged is of the greatest importance. Jesus Christ is the revelation of man's destiny, in him God tells man what to expect as the consummation of the human story. But Jesus Christ is also God's instruction how this end is to be envisaged. The Kingdom as man's true end causes now the utmost consternation to the devil and to every counterfeit formation of being and value. If (as though there were any doubt about it!) we have disported ourselves in masks and expended our small grants of energy in being mere reflections, we have good reason to be terrified now by a command that one day will shatter even the peace of the grave: Drop all masks and break every mirror! If this is the first business following upon the general resurrection of the dead, we can begin now to tremble, with the devil.

But there is a trembling of joy as well as of fear. Jesus Christ discloses the end appointed by God in such a way that we can receive it in the hope and joy of children whom the Father loves now and forever. This is in part the joy of anticipating a fullness of life for which we have always longed in the depths of our being. It is also in part the joy of knowing that for the rest of our days we can afford to be a little reckless in giving ourselves away. To give oneself away means two quite different things. Now we can let it be known what we really are, we can afford to let the truth out, we can let the story be told, we can begin to let go of the concealments and disguises behind which we have fearfully lurked. But we can now afford to give ourselves away in the second sense. We can spend ourselves freely and wholly, we do not need to keep something in reserve in order to meet the heavy demands of other times and circumstances, we can begin to love others as God's Christ loves all. These things we may do now because the shape and the certainty of the Kingdom have been revealed. Therefore the joys and sorrows, the tremblings and agitations of fear and joy we now experience, are not worthy of comparison with the things that are to come; for nothing shall ever be able to separate us from the love of God in Jesus Christ, now or ever.

2. Jesus Christ is the revealed consummation of history. In him God discloses the ultimate import of the human story. From him, therefore, we know what our essential and ultimate striving must be. From him we learn how to be historical without being the creatures of history.

But what is the problem about being historical? It is the problem of having one's whole being (so much of being as is susceptible to the administration of spirit) stretched between envisagement and realization. It is the problem of not having (or being) a secret self of ineffable reality and inestimable value to love, cherish, and obey above all other being and value. So, finally, the problem of being historical is the problem of having to acquire an essence rather than of having the ontological privilege of investing a preexistent essence wheresoever one pleases, to the infinite enrichment of the lucky object of our choice.

This is not to say that man is without secret places. The secret places of his being are made possible by the self-involuting potencies of spirit. Nevertheless the manifest powers of spirit are not emanations from the secret places. So to look upon these powers reverses the actual situation. There is a power rather than a place for thinking of oneself. This is a deliberative, meditative, cogitative power that is in no sense a reflex. Moreover some of the operations of this power are self-validating without being self-referential. For instance, the pleasures of meditation do not require any external explanation or justification; and they are never so keen as when one meditates upon something other than the value of meditation. (It is wrong to pity a god but how can one help but pity Aristotle's? This god expends his whole being in an eternal thinking upon thought. Certainly Aristotle reached this result from a painstaking examination of what being other than God requires. But he had already assumed that "requiring" is a one-way relationship.)

So there is ample warrant for saying that man has an inside and an outside. The real distinction has been greatly abused both by commonsense and by philosophers who alternately abuse and laud commonsense. Some human acts are self-referential, e.g., I say that I know what I "intended" when I struck the policeman. The "what I know" does not modify the predicate—the pain of his injury is not diminished nor transmuted by it. Neither does this "what I know" modify the act—hitting a policeman is what it is whatever explanation is forthcoming. So the "what I know" must modify the subject whether or not it tempered his action. Let us suppose then that this is the way it ought to go: "I struck the policeman because he was savagely bullying a sweet old woman who reminded me of my mother." I appear to be saying that the policeman was the cause of my action: "I wouldn't have struck him if he hadn't been a scoundrel." But perhaps I am really saying that the cause of my action was a sentiment of my own, or, more likely, a compound of sentiments: "She looked like my mother," and, "Policemen who are bullies ought to be punished," or, more simply, "I hate bullies, uniformed and otherwise." Actually my reference to "what I know" about my action is not necessarily a reference to anything *I* have done in the past. It is much more likely to refer to an initiating cause operating on me now; and to a teleological pattern which includes my past as well as my explanation of the present. This pattern includes my actions and my explanations. Whatever is secret about it simply does not exist. Whatever is nonpersonal about it simply is not real.

At this point our attention is called to a striking feature of this teleology. *It is essentially projective.* The self acknowledges the pattern but the self does not possess it. The ontological explanation of this strange situation is that man's being is essentially expressive. This quality of his being by no means rules out real self-identity. It does mean that the self-identity of the human subject is manifest only in his expressions, not in his potentialities. No doubt there are unique potentialities in each person "from the beginning." Neither the subject nor any other creature can know what these are or whether they exist until something is made overt, until something is expressed. The essence is the manifested project, that in which the person participates as his characteristic expression. This project is stretched over time rather than merely pursued in time. The self learns its identity from this time-binding power of the project. Even if the project is self-aggrandizement—"self above all"—it works only so far as time and the world lend themselves to it or can be taken in by it. The world is actually more than a mirror reflection of the self, and time is more than the pulse of the self. Human expression is a proposal to time and the world; and any proposal may be thrown back in the teeth of the proposer. The self achieves actual identity only in the proposals (the projects) which are taken on by time and the world.

(Thus we see why "selfishness" is necessarily a mistake as a policy. If it is possible to be unreflectively selfish, as a child is, well and good for the theory. The instant the theory is converted into a policy, or into a justification for the mere fact of selfishness, selfishness as a principle is scotched. I may want nothing but my own value from the world. This is exactly what I cannot have until the world lets me in on the secret of who I am. But by that time the self knows itself as process rather than as substance, and as one value among many. The instant that selfishness becomes policy—becomes not only a generalization but a norm—it is no better for my purposes than for yours.)

The world into which the self tosses a proposal is itself highly plastic. The world is a give-and-take affair. I become in a very complex situation in which becoming is going on all around me. Some persons with whom I must deal have already acquired identity; and of them I can say that my changing will not change them, they are (relatively) fixed points of reference. (Until now this has been the function of the aged in Western civilization. "The old people are the wise people," theirs is the wisdom of the unchanging moral order. They have a rich acquaintance with suffering and death and with the other high gods. Therefore they can be trusted, they know what endures. Now this is radically changed. A man is now as wise as his earning capacity. It follows that when he can no longer work his counsel has zero value. At the same time people feel obliged to make the aged physically comfortable—in institutions. It is supposed to be axiomatic that this rich institutional life is the best thing for everybody. Politics is the only remaining exception. True, maturity of counsel is identified with ability to stay in office; but in politics survival is the elementary rather than the ultimate value. So we can be thankful that the political order is still an exception to the otherwise general practice and policy of putting the aged into retirement at the earliest possible moment.) Those who have achieved identity do not provide me a material definition of the good but they do allow a formal definition of it: I need not be what they are but I must come to be as they are, that is, determinate realized individuals. To be such is to have incorporated time in the project, not absolutely (needless to say) but so effectively that time is no longer that prime instrument of movement and value. The realized person does not need to travel because "he is already there." He no longer needs the "time of experience" (novelty) to teach him who he is. He has acquired the time of reflection. The time of reflection may become diseased and degenerate into nostalgia; but the time of experience may never arrive at significant form (self-identity) until life is over. This is the disease of Romanticism. Wisdom, however, is more than the absence of disease. Wisdom is that condition in which destiny is a present enjoyment as well as a future consummation. It is that condition in which the object of enjoyment is a power and form already manifest in the subject.

So the end is prefigured in the beginning; but this is known only when the end has taken effective command of the whole process. Therefore we say again that the glory of the Kingdom of God is already felt in the powers of the Holy Spirit: faith, hope, and love, of which the greatest is love. Endowed with these powers, what man has need to importune God to hurry the glory of the Kingdom along? All of that man's time has been drawn into the project and the prospect.

So let external forces carry him where they will. He knows that all things work together for good, for them who love God.

VI

D. *Providence.*

The Gospel presents a providential account of history. This account is a complex affront to the prevailing winds of doctrine, commonsensical and sophisticated. The complexity of the affront is so great that even at the outset we are tempted to say that the cultural assimilation of this aspect of the Gospel is the principal root of the complexity. "Providence" has been crossbred with fate, fortune, sheer luck, self-righteousness, and a certain native optimism of outlook characteristic of American civilization. On the sophisticated metaphysical side, Providence has been made to stand or fall with philosophical theism. There in fact Providence has been subsumed under the category of Theodicy.

We are not quite so ambitious or foolhardy as to suppose that these assimilations and confusions can be dissolved by waving the wand of the Gospel. Nonetheless the theologian who has accepted a primary responsibility for speaking to the preaching church has, as the church itself has, an obligation to set forth the Gospel account of Providence as starkly as possible. We shall now attempt to do this.

1. History and the cosmos are under one administration: He who is Lord of the one is Lord of the other. Therefore no event or power in history or the cosmos can throw off or escape God's overarching purpose. Everything that is and everything that happens anywhere has its place in God's project.

Hardly any other element of the Gospel is at once so offensive and so precious to the natural piety of contemporary culture.

2. Yet history and cosmos are two realms.

Speculative theologians, ancient, medieval, and modern, have been remarkably persistent in trying to persuade the two realms to become one. Those ancient speculators, the Gnostics, enveloped the cosmos in the drama of Fall and Redemption; and left nothing of the cosmos to stand on its own feet—nothing is left with an ontological integrity able to defy, if necessary, man's feverish pursuit of salvation. At its speculative-religious worst, Gnosticism writes off the cosmos as the work of a very dubious deity who cannot be cured of his bad habits.

Modern speculators have embraced elements of metaphysical idealism that endorse the view of man as being entirely historical. Unlike Gnosticism this view does not necessarily bring the cosmos into the drama of salvation. Indeed it aspires to divest the cosmos of any religious (existential) significance.

Idealism of this sort can do interesting things in the line of Biblical interpretation. Creation, for example, becomes essentially the act of God by which the covenant with Israel is established. For reasons fairly hard to divine or credit, Israel proceeded to spin (or borrow) cosmological yarns the import of which is that the entire cosmos, and not just the People of God, springs to existence when God speaks the creative word. But again, given the appropriate idealistic reading of man, these cosmological effusions can be set down as lyrical adornments of Israel's faith in the Lord of history. Here, and throughout, idealistic theologians probe for meaning and urge us not to linger over the fleshpots of fact.

How are we to understand this theological withdrawal from the cosmos? Our bafflement is diminished when we remember that theologians were made to feel ill at ease in the cosmos by the triumphs of the Kantian philosophy. Latterly the brilliant successes of the natural cosmological sciences, philosophically ambiguous though they are, have made the discomfiture acute. Kantian philosophy deprived the theological idealists of any motive for cosmological speculation. Scientific cosmology has deprived them of any intelligible content. Hence if the myths of Scripture are to be preserved they must be philosophically pasteurized: they have nothing to do with mere fact. Surely it would be even more hygienic to screen out all of the myths, lay an interdiction against the mythological consciousness as such, and treat Scripture as a poetic illustration of philosophical doctrine independently discovered and rationally warranted. The fact that modern man (that illustrious norm and objective of contemporary idealistic theology) has his own mythology, would count neither for nor against such a theological program. An independent deterioration of the idealism would be a serious problem. A theology which pins its validity to a philosophical outlook may be driven to plead existential (rather than religious or historical) authenticity as a substitute for validity.

Withdrawal from the cosmos is a serious mistake even for speculative theology. For practical theology it is a disaster. This fundamental theological discipline recognizes no higher authority than the

Gospel. The Gospel speaks directly to the constitutive ontological question man puts to the cosmos: What are the prospects of the human good and of the good as such? This is not a scientific question even though scientific theories may be adduced in support of an answer. The question is not whether human life can learn to endure the physical conditions of Mars. It is not a question about the minute biochemical range congenial to human life. Rather, the question is: How far is the good applicable to whatever exists? Man already knows that the good is a fundamental category for the interpretation of his own being. If he overlooks it he can only give a thin and cheating account of his being. But is he a cosmic freak in this respect? Man knows that he is a teleologically ordered being. Is he the dunce of the cosmos because he hungers to know how his teleology is related to the universe?

Science gives very slender help on these ultimate questions beyond the assurance that the universe is ordered to man's appetite for knowledge in the scientific mode. But if man's own being is in any way a model with which he can think reality, he has no more warrant for isolating the true and the good from each other than he does for collapsing their differences.

Thus the question of the relation of teleology in man to the cosmos will not be silenced either by scientific and philosophical revolutions or by theological embarrassment. Man is compelled to live in two realms. One of these, history, is his own. The other, the cosmos, is not his, even though he is familiar with it as the flesh of his own body. Only up to a point, and that not precisely predictable, can I impose my purposes upon the molecular structure of the flesh of my body. Conversely, molecular structure cannot point out the path in which my feet should walk. Molecular structure makes possible all manner of things above it in the great chain of being. Yet the molecule in its elegant patterns does not potentialize any being above it; and it does not judge any of them as to their fitness to survive. Molecules cast no vote in the grand assizes of history.

But if cosmic order is more faithfully and clearly divulged in molecular patterns than in the actions of men, we should have an answer to the question about the engagement of powers above man in his own pursuit of the good. The answer would be that there *are* no powers above man, relative to the good. The cosmos is molecular pattern and biochemical tropism in varying degrees of complexity. Man is either one of these complexities; or, if it should turn out that he really is a teleological being, he is a stranger in the cosmos and the veritable clown of the universe.

To deny that the cosmos is a real unity of teleological operations is to deny that the cosmos exists at all. The word would be a concession to the conventions of everyday commonsense discourse. If this view is supported with materialistic arguments, man ceases in principle to be a question. The cosmos near at hand, his own being and life, is dissolved into molecular pattern, or into the next fictive state of affairs science devises. If the view is supported with agnostical rhetoric about the great mystery of the world beyond our doorstep, it becomes a plea to accept truth as one of the disguises of the good.

Christian theologians have not been severely tempted to take up the option of subsuming history under nature (cosmos), for fairly obvious reasons. But the reverse route of idealistic subsumption is committed to the same logic, and is burdened with the counterpart difficulties. The advantages of the idealistic option are not sufficiently great to offset the embarrassments of the logic and the counterpart difficulties. However, there is a more telling reason for contending for theology's freedom from the logic of subsumption. In his address to man's essential being, God in Christ speaks to a creature who lives both in the cosmos and in history. Man is made from the dust of the earth: molecules, carbon compounds, amino acids, and whatever else science can discover or posit. Man is also a living spirit: he can hear God speak and he can answer appropriately. He can make his body a tabernacle of the everlasting God.

3. Thus man has a commitment of being in both realms.

There are ranges of order below and above us. We have inside access to some orders and outside access to others. Our purposes make a perceptible difference in some orders but not in others; and this works both ways. As will man is not determined, or even influenced, by any order which is itself not will. He need not (and Christianly ought not) be concerned with the bearing of the physical orders upon his destiny. Thus the Bible is severely antiastrological, as today we must be severely antiastrophysical, in respect to the question of the good. Astrology was originally rejected because it was trafficking with heathen gods. It was rejected finally because the astrological order is no god. To say that it is also no order is a weak anticlimax. Man answers only to the Lord God, there is no other god to hear him; and he must not believe that any power less than God has a right to command his absolute devotion. He draws energy from orders that do not accept his vote in their governance, but he is not their creature. Eventually dust to dust; but not then, or ever, at the command of the dust. The Lord gives; the Lord takes away; and in His giving and His taking He is absolutely free to be Himself, God the Father Almighty, maker of heaven and earth, and the Father of our Lord, Jesus Christ.

4. The nonhuman orders are not man's creatures.

This is as true for the orders over which he has a partial command as it is for the galaxies. The cosmos belongs to God, not to man. Man has absolute command over no part of it, not even over his own body. His command over what he does command is "lease authority": he may use it for a time, and he must learn to use it for the purposes for which it was designed and loaned to him. If he does not rightly use it, that part of the cosmos that has been put under his temporary command will rebel, and his life will end in the tumult and terror of civil war.

The revealed unity of the divine administration of the cosmos and history does not allow the collapse of either into the other. The stars do not dance to man's tune, but their dance is not alien to God's inclusive purpose. The nearer forces of nature testify that the Lord is present. They do not do this by drastic irregularities in their order but by perfect responsiveness to the demands the Lord makes of them. They are there when history is enacted but they do not participate in it. The history made then and there did not change them. "When Christ was crucified, the angels looking down wept." But the stars and the stones and the broken bones did not weep.

VII

Jesus Christ is the revelation of God's providence. He is the end of history. He is also the revealed purpose of all creation. By faith in Him man apprehends the end of history, he is able to see the hand of God in the whole of history, from beginning to end. He is also able to see the hand of God in the appointments of the creaturely powers of the cosmos. As the consummation of historical existence Jesus Christ is the same word by which everything has been created. Therefore Jesus Christ is not a wonder-worker. Wonder-workers are counterfeiters, whether they are represented mythologically or otherwise. They pretend to have mastered some secret of the powers of beings. In this sense Jesus Christ has no secrets. His being is so completely expressed in his act that his life is an open secret. He knows why God has created the world and why He has called man to be in the world. This knowledge and truth is a perfect unity with Christ's own projects. He is therefore the one through whom everything was done that was done.

The hard core of the problem posed by these traditional affirmations is to relate the principle of creativity to a historical person. This can be done easily enough by making the historical person an illustration of the cosmological principle. A solution of this sort is not acceptable for fundamental theology. The inverse solution probably is not acceptable for the purposes of speculative metaphysics, namely, that the historical person, Jesus Christ, is "in charge" of the cosmological spread of creativity. Yet something like this appears to be implied, if not expressed, in the Christian claim that Jesus Christ is the Providence of God. For on the one hand the cosmos as such everywhere exemplifies the principle of creativity both in the fact that it exists and also in how it exists as a cosmos. On the other hand a historical person, no matter how great his power as measured by human norms, lives and operates within a very limited time and space. The human being acts directly upon some orders of being and not at all (perceptibly) upon others.

The Gospel proclamation of Jesus Christ makes the principle of creativity a fundamental expression of his person. Man learns from Jesus Christ why the cosmos has come to be what it is, and whither it is bound. As man Jesus Christ is quintessentially historical, he is more historical than anyone else. As God he is the teleology, the essence, of all that exists whether its being is historical or not.

The proper inferences of these affirmations may be detailed as follows:

1. The end of history revealed in Jesus Christ is the life with God "prepared before the foundation of the world." What is manifested in Jesus Christ is the same power that has called the whole cosmos into being.

Obviously the macrocosm cannot be summoned to testify to the glory of this one lordship over all that exists. The microcosm can and does so testify. The microcosm is the cosmos ordered to a concentration, a point of intensity, in which the whole issue of the powers of being and the good is exposed in the clearest possible light; and no matter how many light-years Andromeda is from Hackensack. In this concentration of being both the reason of history and the answer to the question, Why something rather than nothing? are laid bare.

Only in the knowledge and love of such a realization of being are we able meaningfully and wholeheartedly to say that the providence of God is all-governing.

The Gospel proclaims Jesus Christ as the all-governing providence of God. He is this concentration. He is therefore both the center of history and that being and that good, upon which the whole creation converges. In him "all creatures are fitly framed and joined together."

2. This convergence (this gathering) of the creatures and the powers of creativity into Jesus Christ is expressed as the "fullness of time." All time before the Incarnation is preparation for his coming. All time since is preparation for his coming again.

The very word "preparation" outrages certain tender sentiments of contemporary civilization. It activates lightly sleeping hostilities against the mechanical models with which theological orthodoxy has frequently interpreted history. For our part we can hardly fail to be sympathetic to a recoil against any interpretation which moves human beings about singly and in vast imperial systems on the board of history like so many soulless things; and makes the inward stirrings of intuition, presentiment, and decision, as well as the rising and falling of empire, to be so many events plotted on the master time map of divine prescience. Contemporary civilization has already seen quite enough of depersonalization to warrant great sympathy with this recoil. Contemporary civilization has lent itself also to the elevation of mechanical models with such foolhardiness that we can well afford to aid and abet resistance to any religious consecration of such interpretations of history.

Other sentiments are outraged by the Gospel identification of providence with preparation. On the face of it, preparation reduces man before Incarnation to being a mere phase of an eschatological-historical process. So pre-Incarnational man is a poor creature living toward and for a good and a glory he can possess only as shadow and not as substance. He is comforted but not fulfilled by the solemn assurance that his existence is a moment in a process which embraces the whole cosmos. Stripped of its façade of piety (whether orthodox Christian or orthodox Marxist or orthodox evolutionist) this eschatological annihilation of man in any moment or phase short of the end, for the greater glory of Holy History, is an offense to every humane sentiment.

The contemporary world has paid a bitter price to learn how these eschatological reductions work, whether they are proposed in the interests of the Classless Society, Superman, the "loftier race than e'er the world hath known"; or of a child generation that must have every advantage that the parent generation can mortgage its future to provide. Back of all these reductions running the gamut from the sublime to the stupid lies the common conviction that the real fulfillment of human history is available only at the end of history. Thereby the tension between envisagement and realization, the constitutive duality of man's essential being, becomes intolerable. Contemporary civilization is the sad story of the variety of ways in which eschatological man has tried to break down this tension.

In revealing the end in Jesus Christ God has passed judgment upon all such dehumanizing eschatologies, whatever their religious hue. If earlier times are preparation for the Gospel this does not mean that God loves those generations less than He loved the generation to which the Gospel is revealed. It means rather that the fulfillment of the forerunners is forthcoming when they with all the faithful of all generations are gathered into the eternal Kingdom. God did not call them to live toward us as to their goal and good. God the everliving was their Lord also and He called them to live unto him, and He gave them a word sufficient for this purpose, though He did not give them that plain revealing of His purpose which is the Incarnation. Moreover it is not the process of history as such which contains their fulfillment, or ours. Their life, and ours, is hid with Christ in God, this Christ who is God incarnate, the Lord forever with His people, until the end of time.

3. We have no sooner overcome the fright and hostility produced in all of us by preparation, when we are attacked by the Second Coming. Suspicions and hostilities swarm all around again, and the fear of being confused with the Pentecostal brethren joins their ranks. This fear is as unrealistic as it is uncharitable; and it is as uncharitable as it is lacking in good faith. Christian existence is an appointment made with the Christ of God: "Do this in remembrance of me until I do come." Thus the past is hallowed, the present is redeemed, and the future is enjoyed.

"Until I do come" is both a promise and a command. Pentecost is the fulfilling of the promise. The command is to receive the Gospel of the Kingdom with faith, hope, and love until the glory of the Kingdom is fully manifest.

The coming of the glory of the Kingdom brings the cosmos again into the picture, because it springs from Resurrection, but also because the universe is made to participate much more dramatically in the consummatory event. The skies shall erupt into beauty terrible to behold. The blare of the trumpet of Judgment shall echo to the remotest galaxy. Graves, marked or long forgotten or never known, shall give up their human dust. And all of the particles thus liberated shall dance toward one place of divine assignation. And all carbon molecules once engrossed in human flesh but long since otherwise employed, shall be drawn irresistibly to Zion's holy hill, to keep an appointment made in the dawn of creation with the Lord God.

Such visions of supernatural distress and splendor bring the cosmos into the picture with a vengeance. God's actions for and upon man become the absolute center of the cosmos, as truly as though all of the planets of all of the galaxies sent their respective heads of state for the occasion. In fact the Second Coming makes far heavier demands upon the cosmos than the first coming.

We sense great instruction in these representations of the Gospel, if we could but understand them. They seem to tell us that the immensity of the cosmos (both the extent and the complex interrelationships of its forms and orders) can be made intelligible only by relating it to the good. Abstracted from the good, the cosmos as an object of understanding becomes a mass of equations signifying nothing; and as an object of perception it is merely the indeterminately infinite "possibility of sensation." But seen under the aspect of the good, the immensity of the cosmos is the ramification (imaginatively and speculatively) of order to infinity. Apart from the attribute of immensity the cosmos is the order of actual orders (rather than the sum of all particulars). But even the cosmos in its immensity does not permit the deduction of order from order; or of actual existents from order. The actually existent participates directly in the primordial energy of being; and this is the explanation of its factuality. Yet the existent cannot create its own order, it must accept membership. History occurs in its own right when an order of consent appears on the scene, an order actually grounded in and contingent upon the consent of its constituents. Thus the historical order is grounded in creaturely freedom. As such it is nearer the heart of the Creator than any other order, because the teleological principle, the good, is now internally related to the particular, i.e., to the concrete historical person.

Jesus Christ is God at hand to redeem the order of consent from the grip of powers which bend the spirit out of shape and thereby alienate man from his freedom. These negative powers are themselves historical rather than cosmic. They are not constituents of a positive order somehow made unhappy and hostile by the proximity and charm of the historical human order. The negative powers are parasitic, they are antiorder: in any society they are rebellious, destructive, and antiteleological.

It is not the import of the Second Coming that these powers have gotten out of hand since the first coming, and must therefore be attacked and reduced again. What is done in the Incarnation is neither undone nor redone. History is not a repetitious tale told and retold pointlessly. It leads on until it is finished. In this history the Gospel is never preached twice in just the same way, because the people to whom it is preached and they who preach it are more than mere continuants of once-before-existing persons. God continues to speak, history continues to happen. Thus the Second Coming is represented in the Gospel as the culmination of the story rather than as a reprise or a second and command performance. It is the end projected in the beginning and as such never realized until its appointed moment arrives. Therefore it means more than the confirmation of something already reported. It is the completion, now unimaginable even to the sturdiest faith, of the whole historical reality.

In this representation of the Second Coming God's control of time is absolute. The determination of the appointed time is purely and entirely God's rather than something inherent in the process of time as such. In the determination of the Second Coming the freedom of God is again demonstrated; and so again the proclamation of the Gospel runs into a constitutive philosophy of contemporary culture. This is the view that time itself determines the maturation of human purposes because time is somehow in command of the good. In this way time has become a great god in the pantheon of contemporary culture. The Gospel is the judgment of God upon this deification (and demonization) of time, because it reveals man's calling. In the power of the Holy Spirit he is to grow into the likeness of Christ, the "first-born of many"; but it is God rather than time who carries man thitherward. "Carries" is the wrong expression if it suggests that Jesus Christ sweeps an inert and complacent humanity into the Kingdom of God. St. Paul's testimony on this matter is very clear: "we ourselves, who have the first fruits of the Spirit, groan inwardly as we wait for adoption as sons, the redemption of our bodies" (Rom. 8:22, RSV).

Creativity is part of the ground plan of man's being; but the fulfillment of this purpose requires the most painful and wonderful energizing of his own freedom. Such is the providence of God.

So we say again that the Second Coming is not to be charged off to the nature of time. Neither time nor any other aspect or element of the creaturely world betrays a predisposition to come to a halt at the Second Coming. This is our reason for saying that even the sturdiest and most devout apocalypticism is an exercise in futility. Any attempt to correlate the Second Coming with stupendous cosmological events is beside the point, unless the point is merely to give a bizarre tonality to the confidence of good faith that all things work for the good because God works in all. Even then we must ask what are the lineaments of astronomical structure that we should see the glory of Christ prefigured there? What are the features of atomic behavior that whisper, "The end is near"? A time is coming when all creation shall joyfully manifest God's glory. But in the now this glory is more faithfully and authentically prefigured in the joyful readiness of man to obey Christ's commandment than in any dream of cosmic catastrophes. God has not published the schedule of events leading up to the coming in glory. He has published a command: "Do this until I come." Therefore so much of the world as we command is to be kept in readiness for the life and work of God the Spirit. Clearly His ways are not our ways. Out of His abundance God provides all things needful for life in the Spirit. Our way is to waste our substance wondering whether God knows how mightily we long to see His glory and how richly deserving we are to partake thereof in eternity; and how much we shall enjoy seeing the enemies of righteousness getting their just deserts, all of whom bear striking resemblance to the people who make life difficult for us.

4. Unless providence is interpreted in terms of what God has provided in Jesus Christ for life in the Spirit, it is a peculiarly appropriate target for the hostile reaction of the world. For example, what is now harder to believe than the cheery sentiment that history is the steady overcoming of evil by good and is thus the progressive realization of divine ethical purpose? Even when this sentiment is purged of the egregious elements of self-congratulation in it it is still hard to take seriously. The modern world has been inundated too frequently by catastrophes kicked up by man himself to make that kind of optimism anything but a sedative. Whatever must be said about the harshness and brevity of life in primitive societies, or in Western society in

more barbaric (!) ages, the scientific mastery of the technics of destruction of things, minds, and souls cannot be called moral progress except under the rubric of black humor. We ought of course to compliment ourselves for not throwing useless people to the crocodiles. The fact is that there are not enough crocodiles for the purpose; so Hitler and company turned to advanced technics for this purpose. This is progress of a sort, and the Western world will carry to its grave the shame and the guilt thereof; and the conviction grows that more progress along this line will bring us to that grave betimes, and deservedly too. Progress, again? Throughout countless ages countless millions of people in the Eastern world have starved to death and supposed all the while that this was ordained by the cosmos. Now we know that they were not done in by the cosmos. This of course is progress. But people are still dying there from starvation. We persist in saying, in fact, that they die like flies, even though we are afflicted by the terrible question whether "like flies" means only their uncountable number or their inability to move us to efficacious compassion—after all India simply has too many people to start with. Progress, still? Today in prodigiously wealthy America people are dying because they are too poor to buy the food they need and they cannot afford a doctor; and the kind of places they live in would make an Iowa hog blush in embarrassment if he had to call it home. This is a fate difficult to charge off to the blind ordinations of the cosmos. Once millions of human beings accepted slavery as the determination of providence. Now in the land of freedom Negroes are excluded from the voting booth with a piety which for blindness and ferocity far surpasses that which turned the Gentile from the Holy of Holies in ancient Jerusalem.

These things ought not to inspire a denial that real improvements in the human lot have been made by the application of intelligence and high moral passion. But they are undeniable warrant for refusing to identify Christian faith in Providence with such improvements. There is a Biblically grounded optimism, but it has nothing to do with the natural propensity of modern man to believe that at last he has put his feet on the escalator of progress.

There are people still who are so exercised by the natural suffering of the lower animals that they pick a philosophic-religious fight with providence. Do they really hold it against God that the gentleman's code of conduct cannot be read downward into nature? Nature red in tooth and claw is no lady. Perhaps in the great by-and-by God will explain all of this—to ladies. In the meantime there is a much more momentous contention with the hand of providence in history, that is, with the governance of human forces making for good and for evil. Man is capable of magnificent creative achievements and he is also capable of swift unheeding descent into foul blackness. Where in this mixed history are we to discern the overarching beneficence which guides with unerring wisdom the course of human events to glorious consummation?

5. The question directs attention to a general characteristic of historical outlook and of historicity as a way of qualifying man's essential being. The "eye of the beholder" and the "angle of vision" have a peculiarly decisive significance. What one looks for in history very largely affects what one finds, unless the past has been isolated and alienated from the present. It is possible to so isolate and alienate the past, as scientific history has demonstrated. Presently we shall have to discuss this achievement, but here we must be sure to emphasize adequately the significance of the "eye" of the participant in the interpretation of history. Thus some claim to see that history is on the side of increase of happiness. Others see that the forces of history are wholly indifferent to man's happiness. Some see freedom as the goal of history. Others see that history is moving inexorably towards the destruction of freedom.

For our part we cannot fail to see that there is something very remarkable in this great contention over what is to be "seen" in history. Man is here talking about what he sees of his own being in relation to powers beyond himself. Whatever men take to be the supreme good for human existence is likely to be posited as the goal of history; or, conversely, what they take to be the supreme evil for human existence. This positing of the goal of history is more than a perception of an actuality or of a possibility. This positing of the goal of history is also a concrete decision. It is not a mere reporting of the state of affairs called history or the historical situation. Seeing is certainly involved; but decision is just as intimately and significantly involved. Expectation and commitment permeate the very stuff of history and render it immune to any but the most ephemeral and contingent defeats. One may be momentarily disconsolate over the ruin of private happiness; but it is bad faith to despair of the vindication of a greater good in the consummation of history. The faith is bad both because it is a breach of trust and a defect of vision.

On this matter the Christian and the Marxist seem to be similarly if not identically constituted. Each is committed to a belief in an ultimate goal of history toward which the whole creation strives. Each believes that the process of history is both irreversible and all-conquering. Each tries to relate himself most appropriately to this process, and thus to seek and to serve the destiny of man. Each confesses his own sins of bad faith, that is of having been seduced here into betrayal by the persuasive arguments of nonbelievers, and there by the apparent misfirings of the siege guns of history.

But there is also such a thing as bad faith in the treatment of the historical past. Refusal to be downed by what seem to be harsh reverses in the grand unfolding of the drama of salvation is one thing, and in its own way an admirable one. Denial that there are such reverses is quite a different matter, and one not at all admirable. Expectation crushed to earth may live to rise again; but it takes either sheer blindness—self-inflicted at that—or the most appalling dimness of moral sensibility to deny the tragic fate of great expectations. Catastrophe lies in wait for every conceivable human project for history, even for nihilism; and of course we mean catastrophe of human invention and prosecution. Faith, hope, courage, and compassion may prove equal to the terrible occasion of fiery trial. But they may not. And this is why every faith in history, every positing in hope and love of a great good as the goal of history, seems to be a gamble posted against incalculable factual odds. Man here bets on himself, not merely, not really, on the blind forces of history abstracted from his own being. We are strongly tempted to conclude from this that the touts of history are all frauds.

6. In the eyes of the Christian the Cross of Christ is the judgment of God upon every form of bad faith with history. The Passion Story is compact of betrayal, irresolution, failure of nerve, and unrealism induced by the rigid preconceptions and precommitments that blind the eyes of the spirit and drive it to dreadful outrage. A human being can be more outrageously abused than Jesus Christ was, no doubt. But he is Messiah sent from God to establish the Holy Kingdom in the earth. He comes to his own people, to those whose faith in the Covenant of God struck a mighty blow against bondage to fate. But his own received him not. This is infinitely more than the old sad tale of love rejected and of true prophecy spurned. It is the unique story of holy compassion crucified by the hostility of human righteousness. And the suffering it discloses is too great for heaven and earth to endure.

In heaven angels wept and on earth black silence reigned when the Christ of God died upon the riven tree.

Put it paradoxically. The agony of good faith with providence begins precisely when the ultimate realities of human faithlessness are confronted by the ultimate faithfulness of God.

The Crucifixion is more than God's judgment upon bad faith. It is also the gateway through which all must pass who would enter the glorious kingdom. "Except ye be crucified—": each man by grace must keep an appointment made by God with so much of the suffering of the world as he can freely take upon himself. In this God is glorified. In this Christ is obeyed. In this man keeps good faith with history.

This does not mean that Crucifixion must be converted, for the particular benefit of the unbeliever, into a demonstration of how all of the suffering produced by historical calamities is absorbed into the suffering of Christ. To do that is to crucify Crucifixion. God in Christ commands us to forswear every effort to make a good thing out of evil by producing a sufficient reason for its occurrence. (It is no part of Christian calling to join the friends of Job.) Jesus Christ does not provide instruction in the reasons for mischance, misfortune, death, and damnation. These being the lot of man, the ultimate problem is how to be related to them most appropriately, which is to say most humanly. Not to lose the human, say, rather, the personal essence, though one is called to endure the worst that history offers, this is the test of Providence. Such is the teleology of the Christian life. It does not explain all things by referring them to antecedent causes. Rather, it opens the eyes of faith and the heart of love to the Spirit who in all things works the higher righteousness.

It can be said, then, that to believe in Providence is to believe unreservedly in the human project and prospect. But it is first to believe in Jesus Christ, the God-man.

VIII

A goal toward which history moves but which it never reaches is an instrument of damnation. The romantic spirit will not concede this, of course, since it prizes struggle over achievement. Where this sentiment still prevails consummation has a horrid ring. It smacks of death, or at least of dying. Consummation has the sound of finality:

an arrival beyond which there is no departure. It has very strong overtones of a situation in which ego is carried beyond itself. This is surely a death, and it is a death which terrifies the ego not yet fully alive to the life of the spirit.

The terrors quickened by consummation must be acknowledged and endured because history is a story with an end and with an ending. In the end there is death. This death is generous and all-inclusive—to die is in itself hardly an indication of selective and special treatment. But in the end there is also resurrection. As death embraces all of mankind, so resurrection embraces death and all of the dying there is in the body of man. In the end there is the everlasting beauty of the Kingdom of God. The end of history is therefore a consummation beyond the wildest soarings of expectation. Ego still infatuated with itself cannot even begin to dream of the richness of being yet to be disclosed in this end of history. Good faith in the revelation of God in Jesus Christ is able to see that this consummation embraces, constitutes, and permeates the whole of history. God, He who is before time and beyond time, and with whom alone is life eternal and abundant, is with us in time. In Him we have access to the unbreakable unity of Crucifixion and Resurrection. That unity is the destiny we discern and accept in Jesus Christ.

Fear of consummation and despair for a consummation too grand to be attained are the two faces of the sovereign anxiety which presides at the heart of contemporary civilization. No calling could be itself more sovereign or more demanding than to preach the Gospel of the Kingdom of God to such an age. The sovereignty and the demands of this calling are discerned by good faith only in Jesus Christ, they are not read off the face of the world. To preach the righteousness of the Kingdom and the hope of the glory of the Kingdom, to pray for the coming of the Kingdom, and to live both patiently and creatively in the present: these can be done in the spirit of truth only from within the Kingdom already manifest. The works of love for which the Holy Spirit energizes us are kingdom projects rather than so many gestures in which the Kingdom is merely anticipated. The works of love are not presentiments of God, they are the work, deed, and act of God. In doing them, and in proposing to do them, to ransom the time, we look to the author and perfecter of faith, Jesus Christ. The world has no coin with which rightly to recompense the servant of the Gospel; but this is because the works of love are a free-will offering and not because the coin of the world is evil. The price for preaching and for hearing the Gospel has already been paid by Jesus Christ. Therefore the only way to do either is to do it freely. Nothing costs as much as this freedom. That is as it should be because nothing of creaturely attainment is worth so much.

No description of the consummation of history is made available to the church, so far as that consummation is understood as a state of being. So far as it is understood as an act and as a quality of relationship, there is a world to say, and, even better, a world to show forth concretely. That appointed and ordained act of consummation is and will be love. That quality of relationship is and will be freedom. The love and the freedom yet to be, will dwarf the present realities, when the glory is revealed.

The full glory of the Kingdom is now apprehended and enjoyed in hope. But what a hope! It is an expectation beyond all destruction by frustration and despair; and yet it is a hope perfectly relevant to frustration and despair. It is the hope which is the gift of God's love in Christ, from whom nothing is able to separate us.

There are many forces which come forward in history to break us off from this hope of the Kingdom grounded in the actuality of the love of Christ. Sickness, loneliness, guilt, hostility, terror of death—who will attempt to catalogue the proposals forced upon faith by the actualities of history? Fully exposed to the time-bound wrath of all such powers—and sometimes they gather in frightful alliance—we are given the hope of Christ as armor and weaponry against them. This is the providence of God: not that in our puny strength and flickering resolution we should prevail, but that His purpose might be fulfilled even in our weaknesses and afflictions. In the end even the demons shall praise Him. Granted, in the meantime they have something else in mind. So far as we live now in Christ and he in us, we have nothing else in mind.

CHAPTER XII

The Quarrel over History

I

The church cannot afford to flatter or placate contemporary civilization where it most grievously errs. To let fundamental errors go unchallenged would be in effect to renounce the authority in which the church preaches the Gospel. For how shall the church be believed when it preaches Jesus Christ the God-Man if it has not made a serious effort to correct profound misunderstandings about man? The vigor of the current anthropological controversy in theology is an indication of some such awareness. It is hardly an unambiguous indication, to be sure, since again theologians are willing, if not anxious, to abandon God as a theological topic and cling only to man. I do not believe that it is in any way accidental when thereafter historicity is discovered to be man's essential being. Such an account of man comports well with a theological posture oriented upon contemporary culture—i.e., with a theology accountable to contemporary culture both for its content and its norms.

So what begins as an academic theological controversy shortly emerges as a quarrel with contemporary culture. To make this a significant quarrel it is not enough to show that its theological errors have very deep roots; or that these roots have produced strange fruit within the life of the church. It is also necessary to show that the error *is* an error. This is a theological demand. The situation calls for a dialectical attack and defense and to mount this is not the duty of the preaching church. The Gospel which defines the duty of the preaching church is not a dialectic, except in the sense which earlier we called the "dialectic of the Kingdom of God." The Gospel is faithfully proclaimed only in the indicative and imperative moods. Theology employs other moods as well; and so again we see why theology cannot take the place of the Gospel as the word God has given the church, in His own indicative and imperative, to preach until the world passes away.

This is not to say that the preacher in the pulpit has no right to make a case of Christianity. It means only that the case properly made from the pulpit does not consist of theories, of theories proposed or theories refuted. In the pulpit the preacher is not ordained to be one of "the debaters of this world." Unfortunately the "vain deceits of philosophy" can be illustrated quite as handsomely from the philosophical excursions of preachers as from the religious pretensions of philosophers.

II

Theological contention with contemporary culture over the historicity of man's being dictates an attack upon a dominant conception of the past. This is the conception of the past as a scientific object, in which the past becomes an abstraction and an isolate.

We do not doubt that this conceptualizing of the past, apparently indispensable for the creation of a scientific history, has been productive. It has produced generalizations that seem to be analogous to the laws of nature. It has placed (in axiom rather than in consequence) ancient, modern, and contemporary man in an intelligible continuum. It has fostered the hope for a system of explanation in which the ostensible uniqueness of historical existence disappears; and the end of historical man becomes a meaningful, though not overwhelmingly amiable, possibility.

Our first question about this remarkable achievement and hope of contemporary culture is whether it really offers knowledge of man's historicity. In certain obvious ways the answer is affirmative. For one, we can certainly hope to learn how the men of the past lived—not why but how. For another, the creature who wants to know this is quite a study in his own right and in his own habitat. I do not mean to cast aspersions at the historians as a special class of *Homo sapiens*. I mean that the ontological (for that is what it is) proposal to learn about man, and not just about man in the past, by isolating the past, is a very striking proposal. (I suspect that it would not have occurred to anybody but modern man.) For the historian advertises his wares as beneficial for the user; and the benefits are not limited to possession of some odds and ends of information about, say, the Hittites. There is something beneficial about the knowledge of historical depth as such. Presumably the benefit goes beyond the solemn reminder that as the Hittite is so shall we all be one day, a reminder that is much more the business of the preacher than of the scientist, except perhaps on Layman's Sunday. To have the historical sense is to have something more than the curiosity and patience to find out a great deal about the Hittites. To have the historical sense is to be aware of the continuing reality of the past, not as something claiming attention from its resting place in the British Museum, but as something claiming attention from the present structure and movement of man's being. The past that is really historical is still with us. It requires interpretation because it is still with us. Interpretation itself cannot establish the connection of the past with the present. It can do no more than elucidate a connection already there, that is, bring it up into clarity of meaning.

The past as a scientific isolate has been lifted out of that continuity in which alone historical events are real. Once this continuity is severed, by memory blackout or by the objectifying mind, it cannot be knit up again by any power of the finite spirit. Thereafter the past can be reconstructed speculatively, or by the aesthetic imagination; but the connections posited between the past and the past (that is between one moment and another moment of the past), and between the past and the present, are creations of scientific speculation or of the poetic consciousness.

Here we begin to feel threatened by a paradox. Surely knowledge of the past, the historical past, is knowledge of man's own being, so far as "man" is the name (and the proper name at that) not only for a historical construct but also for an ontological situation: that situation in which I am one with all things human wherever they occur in time and space. Yet if the historical subject (the historian, broadly understood) posits the connection with the historical object (man in the past) then it follows, apparently, that man is the singular creature who posits his own being. But the beginning of the historical sense is memory. And the beginning of history as something told about the past is something told to quicken and deepen memory. Yet memory does not posit the connection with the past, it *is* the connection with the past. In the beginning memory is not something thought about, it is the past enjoyed in present feeling. Hence if man posits the connection with the past the past so established must be something devised by man rather than lived by man.

The knowledge of the past as something posited by the historical subject (man in the present) is therefore knowledge of an isolate, not merely because time and other men have played dirty tricks on us by covering the tracks of our predecessors, but because it is a kind of knowledge calculated to be an end in itself.

Moreover the past of scientific curiosity is an abstract object or isolate so far as the question "What really happened?" is already prejudged to be answerable in terms of a causal nexus embracing the present, in which the investigator operates, and the past event or entity. The thing that "really happened" is something subsumable under categories of explanation taken for granted in the present. Thus the real event is something conceivable in a nexus intelligible to the present state of consciousness. The present state of consciousness is teleologically related to its own system of causal explanation, which, so far as it is scientific, is nonteleological.

It is both commonsensically and axiomatically true that the interpretation of history always proceeds from a present to a past. The intent to isolate the past, to render it primarily an object of investigation, is a distinctively different enterprise. Part of the difference lies in the explicitly nonmetaphysical (if not antimetaphysical) bias of scientific history. I do not mean that Thucydides, for example, is explicitly metaphysical. His problem is to assess the meaning of what happened in history rather than to isolate factuality in the welter of mere plausibility. To prosecute his program, to do that kind of history, he acknowledges a living continuity. Indeed the present in which he works historically is invaded by the past, it is under very powerful pressure from the past; so much so that the work of the historian might be said to be a bulwark raised against the excessive demands of the past, lest it engulf the meaning of the present. Thus the timelessness required for any serious and sustained work of reflection is hollowed out of a timeful tradition—in his case that marvelously organic human creation we call Hellenic Civilization.

This abatement of time (at once the presupposition and the product of any powerful reflective spirit) is a very different phenomenon from the feat of abstraction by which the past is transformed into a scientific object. In the latter, the past event is assimilated to a system of causation in which the distinction of the past from the present has no meaning essentially different from the distinction between earlier and later. "Earlier" refers to one phase of a system of energy, "later" to another phase. But lived history is a value system in motion, it is not a causal nexus or system of energy. (One may offer reasons for supposing that the causal nexus is more real, but these are so many metaphysical ventures, and science has no stake in their success.) In actual (lived) history the past is the event, or agent, which preforms the decisions and enjoyments of the present. Preforms rather than predetermines: it is not a matter of propensities but of the shape of the given world upon which propensity operates. The near past is the shape thinly distinguishable from the present agent and the present world. It is that part of the shape (form) over which present agency has lost all control except imaginal enjoyment. In this enjoyment the subject and the object are still affectively identical. By the same token the "remote past" (so far as it is the real past) is much more clearly and cleanly distinguishable from present agents in the present world. It is remote because its reality is communicated by more and more intermediaries. These intermediaries are not just "witnesses." In fact these intermediaries are not primarily witnesses. because the mediation of witnesses can only be counted once: it is good for the second generation but witness value has no unique mediating validity thereafter. The first generation can tell the second generation "what we have seen with our own eyes." Not having seen these things, the second generation can only bear witness to the integrity of the first generation, it cannot bear witness to the authenticity of the testimony made possible by the perceptual powers and favorable circumstances of the first generation. The second generation, and thereafter the generations to infinity, can tell the same story but it must have different grounds for believing the story, different, that is, from the experiences of the generation which reports what it has seen for itself. If subsequent generations accept the story (the history) it must be because they find the story itself credible even though they have no sound way of testing the original witnesses—other than by the credibility of the story!

The intermediaries of the remote past are poets, philosophers, and historians, most of whom are not eyewitnesses. They mediate the remote past by invoking the "shape" that overarches that past and this present. This is a shape that seizes the aesthetic and volitional powers rather than the powers of external perception, in the abstract. So who is most nearly right about the historical reality of Julius

Caesar? The scientific historian? Or Shakespeare? Or Thornton Wilder?

The easiest answer to this question is, each may be right but in different ways. How different are the ways? Surely the historian will not settle simply for the facts. Surely the poet will not settle for spiritual validity. Scientist and poet alike reach for something each calls truth. The truth of the former is the function of an explanatory system. The truth of the latter is an imaginative penetration of the being who did what was done. To both of them we say that the "what really happened" of history demands an ontological penetration.

In the case of the remote past this penetration cannot be achieved existentially. It must be done formally. (So there is good reason for saying that history is an art.) But the form can only be evoked from the past (actually from the affective-volitional continuity of the present with the past), it cannot be assembled from the plausibilities. The evoked form may incorporate factual inaccuracies and factual blanks, and yet be "historically truthful." Schiller tells us what Wallenstein may have felt; but the evocation has such power that we say, "Here is the real Wallenstein"; and mean, properly, here is the form which controls the factual details, it is not assembled from them.

Scientific history has cut itself off from the forms of representation, except for incidental purposes, by reaching for processes assimilable to a causal nexus, rather than for unique agents. So understood a process has properties but it has no formal features: it is abstracted both from essence and from existence. Thus scientific history purports to tell us what caused the Civil War. We already know: men did it. The people who started that war did not mean to start *that*; but their inability to envisage the terrible ramifications of what they did mean to do, is only human. In April 1861 they did not know that what they were about to do was to test "whether this nation, or any nation so conceived and so dedicated, can long endure." They unsheathed the "terrible swift sword"; and the nation is still bleeding from the wounds. But it endured.

Nevertheless curiosity about historical particulars can, when rightly directed, uncover and correlate data in astonishing ways. Such achievements may not change the big picture, but they may relieve it of one or more mere superstitions. An enterprising historical scholar may learn that the enemy melted away from in front of the hosts of the Lord because they were devastated by dysentery. It is axiomatic that an army tied *en masse* to the jakes is a poor bet to scale the heights of martial valor—a brute contingency Tolstoy seems to have overlooked in his magnificent account of the freakish ways in which martial greatness is achieved and undone. But whether dysentery, plague, or a massive tidal wave of homesickness sweeping all discipline before it, the psalmist (the rhapsodist of Israel's history) knows the big picture: it was the Arm of the Lord which scattered the fearsome might of the heathen host, like so many dead leaves before a hurricane. The poet has command of the "shape" of that history, the design of it is perfectly clear to him. His explanations, if he proposes any, are certain to be very different from the explanations proposed by scientific history; but they will be of one piece with the design, the shape, of history. The scientific historian is in a very different situation.

Scientific history has been determined very largely in its choice of explanatory modes by criteria of empirical plausibility. These criteria come directly out of the philosophical prepossessions of contemporary civilization. Thus the question, "What really happened?" very quickly becomes, "What can *we* believe really happened?" The historical question becomes, "What is the intellectually credible thing to believe?"

III

Contemporary theologians have a particular interest in the fate of this question. This interest is now widely advertised as "the quest for the historical Jesus." The argument with contemporary culture over history is also a quarrel about Jesus Christ. From our point of view the quarrel over the historicity of man's being, and the quarrel over Jesus Christ, are one and the same.

At the outset the quest for the historical Jesus is the same question that modern historian is always asking, that is, "What *really* happened?" As we have already seen, this question is effectively the question, "What is the truth in the welter of plausibilities and implausibilities?" This appears to be a very sophisticated question because it is launched by a consciousness which already knows that every age has seen, if not created, its own Jesus. Every age, every epoch of civilization, has its particular and peculiar spectacles, its own filter, through which the claims and testimony of other ages are seen. In the terms employed in Chapter IV, each stage of civilization (to say nothing of different civilizations) draws upon its distinctive and decisive intuitions of ideality in order to represent Jesus Christ to itself.

This situation is exploited to the full by historical relativism. Consequently good faith struggles to find and to hold on to something objective, something there once and for all presiding over the fascinating historical parade of images and conceptualizations. This objective something must be the Lord Himself. But here the agony of good faith becomes most acute as it becomes most sophisticated philosophically-historically. This objective something, the Lord Himself, may be posited by the unconscious desires of the historical subject, the man of good faith trying to discover "the real Jesus Christ." Thus the question arises whether "the Lord Himself," Jesus Christ in full ontological integrity, is demonstrably more than a mysterious X-point upon which all representations converge at infinity.

The quarrel over history here moves to its decisive phase. The church is committed unreservedly to the Gospel; and now this means that for the life and mission of the church the representation of Jesus Christ in the Gospel is decisive. In the Gospel Jesus Christ is vastly more than a mysterious X upon which religious aspirations, and the representations produced by them, converge, as anyone can plainly see whether or not he accepts those representations as true and binding.

But the church must draw the issue more sharply than that. The Gospel itself is the criterion of plausibility to which every philosophical prepossession in the church must yield. Jesus Christ contains the definition of historical plausibility; and therefore the church is guilty of a very great error in elevating a commonsense or scientific or metaphysical outlook above that definition. This issue must be drawn as sharply as possible because even systematic theologians in our time seem often to struggle helplessly to reconcile the methods and outlook of scientific history with the demands of the Gospel. The standard distinction between the "Jesus of history" and the "Christ of faith" is a nearly perfect expression of this helplessness. This is the situation made inevitable by a philosophical alienation of factuality from value and meaning. Given this alienation the historian does what he can to square up the figure and agency of Jesus of Nazareth according to the criteria of scientific plausibility. Thereby the principal forms of representation in which Jesus Christ appears in the Gospel are jettisoned: for what does science know of

Lordship, of Sonship, of Messiahship? Science can only report that people seem once to have believed certain things subsumable under these terms. To which we say that the terms, the categories, are attributions which appear in acts of acknowledgment. They cannot be made to function in explanations, or even in descriptions. Explanations and descriptions of the people who made these acknowledgments are neither here nor there with the question about the being thus acknowledged. So also for explanations and descriptions of their outlook and state of mind—assuming that we have access to them. From the directives for experience given in the Gospel we may safely assume that the apostolic intermediaries of these directives believed and practiced what they preached. But they went to some pains to deny that they were preaching themselves. In fact they spend very little time talking about experience and a great deal of time talking about the being whose lordship over all things is to be acknowledged throughout all time to come. Clearly they work everywhere from the conviction that God has broken through the network of interpretation that consciousness is forever erecting and in which it is forever enacting itself. The apostolic intermediaries of the word of God also just as clearly assume that God has transformed the interpreting consciousness with His own forms of representation: in the world and in the consciousness of man God has enacted Himself.

The distinction between factuality and meaning is not thereby erased. It too is transformed. In the history of Jesus Christ the question about factuality becomes the question about the identity of an agent. The question about meaning becomes the question about the teleological pattern which incorporates every agent without threat to the identity of that agent.

"What really happened?", this standard contemporary historical question, is a very weak and inadequate way of putting the question about the identity of the agent, because it assumes that this has already been established. The standard contemporary question may also assume that historical agents are all so many nodes in the causal nexus; and this assumption reduces agent identity to a secondary level of importance at best. Conversely the question about the identity of the agents assumes a knowledge of certain events, a fact clearly indicated by the question, "Who did it?"

The "it" may also require a good bit of clarification. For instance, how much is included in the "it" whose perpetrator we are seeking by questioning history? Nonetheless the shape of the "it," the commandingly interesting and important event, is already known even if there is some uncertainty about its boundaries.

Moreover the question about the identity of the agent does not start from scratch, it does not come out of the blue, there are already some plausibilities in the air. If there are not, history has not yet been made, the thing has not yet occurred; or it is too soon for its momentousness to have registered. So in one sense, everybody knows who did it. The agency has, in other words, been commonly imputed to one source rather than to another. So the question, "But who *is* he, really?" has some real point. Sometimes in fact the import of the question is dubiety, or even skepticism. "Could *he* have been the one?" Example: "But we know him, he is Joseph's son. Could he have done this marvelous thing?" In this latter mood people sometimes stare so hard at the putative or *prima facie* agent that the marvelous thing done is obscured by a spreading dubiety. Or, even worse, the character of the thing done is transformed because people deem it unlikely, if not impossible, that it could have been the work of the *prima facie* agent. This does not necessarily mean that the incredulous have another candidate to take the leading role, to function as the real agent. It may very well mean that the *prima facie* agent has already been "placed," that is, identified, in a way that prevents the people who have placed him from acknowledging him as the real agent. The shock of recognition has been cushioned by layers of preconception and preinterpretation. Lacking other candidates one would have to say one of two things.

1. It was really done by X, an unknown party.
2. It could not have happened because the only candidate, the *prima facie* agent, could not have done it.

Logically there is another option.

3. The *prima facie* agent is the real agent; so we must have been mistaken in our first identification of him.

The (3) option is taken up repeatedly in the Gospel history itself. What Jesus Christ has done, and done right out in the public world, compels a reappraisal of who he is. The reappraisal takes the form of an acknowledgment or confession: "Thou are the Christ, the Son of the living God!"

Scientific history takes the (2) option, in the case of Jesus Christ. If there are no demons, for example, Jesus Christ did not cast them out. So the imputation of such agency to him is a historical error, and his claiming to have done so is a metaphysical error. By dint of great devotion and great ingenuity theologians have been able to redeem Jesus Christ from having committed also a religious error. The demons were really psychosomatic illnesses over which Jesus had a "spiritual" command.

Some of the contemporaries of Jesus Christ took the (1) option. They said that he was the ostensible agent in the casting out of demons but the real agent was Satan himself. Jesus has two things to say to this remarkably human acknowledgment. (a) Satan is not so infernally stupid as to make war deliberately upon himself. (b) He, Jesus Christ, shares the purpose as well as the power of God the Father; and this so perfectly that the distinction between ostensible and real agency is no longer significant in relation to himself.

Scientific history is thus self-exposed as a philosophical contention. It is the substitution of model systems of causal explanation congenial to the contemporary mind for the forms of scriptural witness. Humanly speaking we should say that there is only one reason why this substitution has not created with it a religion different from Christianity in everything but name: people persist in positing an X mysteriously and providentially managing the variety of representational forms in history. This pious positing applies a brake to the complete assimilation of Jesus Christ to contemporary civilization. At the same time it is a process which leaves hardly a trace of factuality discernible on the sands of time.

IV

The question about meaning must be transformed into the question of teleological pattern. But transformed from what? From the enterprise of discovering a mental content to which the linguistic forms refer, e.g., Lord. Meaning now becomes the reference to the intentional mode, that is, to an essential order that embraces all possible participants. Thus the meaning of the acts of Jesus Christ is an order of being in which every (human) creature realizes the whole order in coming to full power of expression of his own being. This is why the commandments of Jesus Christ have such supernatural limpidity and simplicity. "Follow me"; "sell your holdings"; "forgive your erring brother seventy times seven"—if you are in the dreary business of keeping a perfect record of Times Offended and Times Forgiven. "Don't put on airs when you say your prayers." Everywhere and always Jesus Christ opens up an order in which *who you are* is determined by your power of love rather than by any antecedent reference to social status, lineage, piety, character, or earthly power. In the Kingdom of God identity is acquired in the love and service of God.

Accordingly the meaning of Lordship is the place in the Kingdom enjoyed by Jesus Christ by virtue of his obedience to the will of the Father. His supremacy appears in what he is able to will for the salvation of man, rather than in an antecedently acquired dignity of essence. God the Father establishes him in the highest place of honor because of his ministry.

In this way identity and meaning draw together. In their convergence factuality is the signification of the time and place in which the Lordship of Jesus Christ is revealed.

This is indeed a transformation. Now we need no longer ask whether three Oriental potentates actually hove into view on the 6th of January. It seems unlikely that the coming of Christ was prefigured astrologically. But on the other hand the coming of Christ threw the teleology of God's love visibly around mankind as a whole. For the rest, the cadence of the Three Kings is liturgical, not factual recitative. The liturgy is true only in principle, it is true only because the teleological order has already been established by what Jesus Christ did in fact.

V

The heart of the argument over history understood as the past is the Resurrection. Here is the real bind for those who seek to make the Gospel demands upon history congruent with the regnant science and philosophy of history in contemporary culture.

To begin with, we can have very little doubt that the Resurrection is a greater offense to modernity than the Cross is. The Resurrection calls for more explaining away, for a greater effort of assimilation, for greater sophistication of philosophical attack. Even the plain citizen in the pew is part of this. He has long since become accustomed to biting his tongue when he comes to "the resurrection of the body" in the Creed. The Virgin Birth is not really so offensive because at least part of the birth of Jesus was normal, after all; whereas the Resurrection is in no respect the common sequel to human death, so far as the eye can see. Moreover the Resurrection undiluted makes more of the body than contemporary spirituality finds comfortable.

On all counts therefore the Resurrection sends contemporary spirits scampering after the real facts of the Resurrection already convinced that what the New Testament spirits believed about Resurrection is the most slender of all plausibilities, if indeed it can enter the realm of plausibility at all. Yet nothing can be clearer than that the Gospel history all flows from the Resurrection. Without the Resurrection there would have been no Christ to talk about. There would have been only a dead forerunner, or a dead pretender; and take your choice.

Elementary fairness requires us to add: without belief in the Resurrection. The necessary condition upon which the action of the apostles rests is not necessarily the indispensable psychological condition for all Christian obedience.

We must make short work of this reservation because if we become preoccupied with it we shall have lost both the battle and the campaign. We may make short work of it by remembering that the mode of representation in which Jesus Christ appears in the New Testament is everywhere and essentially acknowledgment; and by adding to this the ever-dangerous all-or-none stipulation. This perilous addition means that the New Testament itself provides no logical or ontological principle by which the acknowledgment of Jesus' lordship can be reduced; and certainly none which permits the excision of the only—absolutely the only—ontological principle determining his lordship, the Resurrection itself. It is only in his Resurrection that Jesus is accredited and certified as the Lord. Remove this accreditation and Jesus descends to the ranks of the prophets of Israel. Or he becomes an existential hero. In either case the New Testament loses its preeminence in the determination of the mode of acknowledgment. Thereafter Jesus Christ is acknowledged to be only what is congenial to the reigning representations of ideality in civilization.

Such is the fate of the quest for the historical Jesus, old or new. Early and late this historical quest has been governed by the assumption that the New Testament mode in which Jesus is acknowledged as Lord is itself bound to a peculiar historical mentality, perhaps admirable in its simplicity, sincerity, and earnestness, but long since overcome or left behind by the dialectic of history.

The only sound instinct at work in this process is an implicit fear of the Resurrection as a most formidable threat to the integrity of the dialectic of history. For the Resurrection is particularity indeed, it is particularity in its most offensive form: here and here only the ascendancy of spirit is guaranteed! The Resurrection is not thereby a vindication of a metaphysics. Neither is it the rejection of a metaphysics. It is the absolute vindication of the promise of God to renew His creation by fashioning His Kingdom in time and space. Therefore the Resurrection is the foundation and the capstone of New Testament history. In it the last enemy is subdued: death loses its vaunted power to alienate spirit from the inclusive purpose of Almighty God.

Within limits, the question, "What really happened?" is still legitimate in and for the life of faith. Its legitimacy and its fruitfulness also are within the boundaries of acknowledgment; which is to say that the question, "What really happened?" is now understood as a variant of the question, "What has the Lord done?" The question, "What really happened?" is not Christianity manageable in any other sense. In any other sense the pursuit of circumstantial details becomes an exercise of the romantic imagination. Or it becomes a fond and futile hope of building details into the shape of the Kingdom; or of finding a selection of details that can be assimilated into some other system of meaning; or of proving one New Testament witness against the others.

Within the boundaries of acknowledgment, the "What really happened?" is much more concerned with the manifestation of power and authority than with the perceptual filling. The New Testament presents a uniform front on the matter of power and authority. In it there is not the slightest question as to who speaks in the Resurrection. It is the same Jesus who commands, comforts, and empowers the faithful, Jesus now appearing in his triumphant Lordship. Furthermore their life with him is forever secure because the power in which he is risen is committed also to them to the end of time and the world.

Therefore the perceptual filling of the Resurrection is no more important for us than for Paul, no more important relative to our resurrection than to the Resurrection of Jesus Christ. The where and when in our case, relative to the perceptual order, are unavailable temporarily, to be sure; but they are also nondecisive in principle. We already have in Jesus Christ the hope of the glory of the Kingdom. The glory itself lies beyond our span of years, beyond the span of time itself. We may enter into that glory only through the portal which God in Jesus Christ opened at the expense of the kingdom of death and damnation.

VI

The past is but part of the quarrel of the Gospel with contemporary culture for the command of history. The present must also be disputed. Here the dispute is centered upon the fearfully exaggerated confidence civilization displays in the present as cause of the future. This is the second aspect of the preoccupation with the present; and it is a preoccupation that alienates man from his real historicity, and converts the present into illusion.

One of the most striking aspects of this preoccupation with the present is its one-dimensional projection of continuity. Time runs from present to future; but not from present to past. We have already seen how scientific history alienates the past as an object from real continuity. But the future is treated as though it were held in an unbroken nexus with the present. In this nexus present is the only real time. Thus the greater the expenditure of intelligence in comprehending this nexus, the more the future is brought under control; as though the future were a finite field of possibilities over which a sufficiently powerful mind could range with perfect knowledge. If therefore the human mind were a mental power approaching that perfection asymptotically, the hope for subduing the terror of the future would be a profoundly realistic hope, a lodestar indeed by which to inspire, if not to administer, civilization.

This speculation is unpardonably excessive on the ontological side. The future is not a finite field of possibles awaiting the act of selection. The future is the next stage—and the next and the next to infinity—of a power of action in a field of powers in which agents act responsively in relation to other powers. If any of these powers acts freely the future is illimitable—for so long as it lasts. Its illimitability is qualitative rather than temporal. The display of qualitative richness obviously requires time, but time is not the agency of its unfolding.

The threat of the future is therefore resident in the potentialities of existent agents and of agents yet to be. This does not make it less formidable. If anything, it makes the future more formidable because the future may belong to agents now living under terrible handicaps piled on them by human stupidity and wickedness. Accordingly we can understand very easily the dementia of King Herod in the Gospel story. Somewhere in his kingdom the seed of his destruction may already have taken root, an unlikely growth in an inconspicuous corner, but with the future already in the grip of his baby fingers! And it is a certainty: in that One was the power to bring the spirit of man up out of darkness into light, up out of bondage into freedom, up out of terror into joy. Against such a power what can Herod or Caesar or any other worldly domination do, except furiously rage?

When God Himself enters the field of human powers, panoplied in His free power of love, the illimitability of the future becomes absolute. This does not mean that time is then licensed to run forever. It means that throughout time unbrookable divine power is at work drawing inconceivable beauty out of finite materials. The future is realized precisely in this drawing forth of spirit, in this empowering of spirit to conjure form upon form in which to express the richness of being.

In Jesus Christ the future is restored to peace with the present. We have enough of the Old Adam still to tremble at the thought of the future. Have we adequately provided for it? How much of it shall we live to enjoy? Each man has his own wrestling match with Old Adam. The Old Adam is that stale habit of spirit in which we seek to capture the future in those images in which ego is lord forever. But the Old Adam has met his match in Jesus Christ. In Jesus Christ we are caught up into God's purposes as "children of the promise." We are His to whom the future belongs.

VII

Contemporary culture has a divided mind about the future. On one side there is the attitude that the present is somehow in command of the future. On the other side there is the hope that the future is interminable, after the model of a series which has no last member, or after the model of a field of possibles without boundaries.

The two sides of this divided mind cannot be made congruent. If the future is interminable in either way, it is out from under the control of the present, since the present is not interminable.

Of the two sides, the fondness for the boundless future is dominant. The boundless future is perhaps the most highly prized rationalization of the actual state of contemporary civilization, because the boundless future allows time for the redemption of every exclusion, the rectification of every mistake, and the fulfillment of every good cut off by man-made disasters. The boundless future is in fact so precious that it is the operating part of the conventional belief in the immortality

contest at all. But before that we might lose something more precious than the tattered flag of life: faith. Faith not understood as belief but as fidelity and as fidelity to the good whose authority over our life neither death nor any other creature can effectively challenge. Yet because we are spirit that authority *can* be challenged. We tremble at the prospect for ourselves if we were to be tempted beyond our frail native powers of fidelity.

The Gospel is a very great comfort to men in these fears and agitations. In the hour of maximum danger the Spirit will give us words in which to make that same pledge made first by the Pioneer of our faith. First: Thy will be done on earth as it is in heaven. And at the last: Father, into thy hands I commend my spirit.

In the light and power of this assurance we can afford to be more nonchalant about the agonies of the body that flog the spirit, but not necessarily to its destruction.

VIII

So the church preaches. What God has given to man, man must not seek to alienate from his own being. Man is historical because God has given him spirit. He can hear God speak and respond. History is what God and man have had to say to each other. There is sound and fury in it, because man too has a will; but it signifies everything rather than nothing.

CHAPTER XIII

The Life of the Church in Christian Civilization

I

Whenever we reflect upon the life of the church we cannot but marvel at its strangeness—surely it is fearfully and wonderfully made! When our reflection is ordered to the requirements of practical theology astonishment and chagrin threaten to run away with us; for there we have from the outset to acknowledge that God calls upon this strange creature to humble itself in "Christian" culture for the glory of His Kingdom. So in our reflection a formidable thesis takes shape. What the church really is, is disclosed in preaching the Gospel in a civilization that contains an immensely varied response to it. To call this civilization Christian is to say that the church cannot escape having to confront and live with the effects of its own life and preaching in history. Such is the judgment of God.

The proper development of this thesis requires that we begin with the being of the church considered in itself.

II

1. The essential life of the church is spiritual. It is the Holy Spirit through which the church has its own unique being. How then shall we speak properly of the church as holy?

The presence of God in the church renders the church holy. God continuously present to purify and to nourish the historical community of Christ is the spiritual presence. The church received its mission from Jesus Christ; and it carries out its appointed tasks through the power of his spiritual presence. Through this power the people of faith are united one to another in a holy community.

It is an axiom of Christian history that the loftiest truths contain the germs of the worst heresies. So here we must be as well forearmed as possible against the religious conversion of the church into a holy thing, a thing holy in itself. That is holy which is purely God's doing, because God alone is holy. Things become holy in man's sight by a natural course of derivation: a thing, either natural or man-made, is associated with a demonstration of divine power; and it comes eventually to be reverenced as the container of that power. In this way divine action is humanly routinized when He appears, when He comes, God will not fail to visit the sacred thing or the sacred place. The next step is inevitable. By stroking the thing, or by various and sundry incantations on the sacred ground, men can make God appear and bless them.

The holy power of God is His creative and redemptive love. He is to be worshiped in and for this, and not because He can destroy what He has created. Through Jesus Christ God communicates this holy power to the community of the faithful. By the work of this power in its midst the life of the church becomes holy. So far then as the church is the community of the faithful, it is holy; but not as a container of God the Spirit.

Yet this, the commonest understanding of the holiness of the church, is much harder to control in the concrete than in the abstract. Abstractly considered, nothing is easier as well as more desirable than distinguishing between what we cherish and what we ought to adore as alone holy. We love and cherish the church because we have enjoyed lovely moments there and we remember having heard there the voice of the living God. Something spurs us on to say that therefore the church is holy in itself. For this extravagance we pay very dearly. We are called upon to apologize for a great deal in the actual behavior of the church, in fact for so much that theologians are hard pressed to contrive barely plausible rationalizations. In turn the preaching church is called upon to defend these theological speculative rationalizations of the church's real history. These interpretations, compounded of special pleading about history, of loot got from raids on metaphysics, of poetry, and of rhetorical devices concealed as dialectics, have themselves to be defended thereafter as the direct contributions of the Holy Spirit.

Such religious-theological involutions are intensely interesting and in their own way instructive. They are all irrevocably self-defeating so far as they are governed by the desire to establish the church as holy and divine.

2. Thus defeated by the empirical realities, we are comforted by believing that the church in heaven is holy in any case. How can we doubt that the company of the faithful in heaven has an unobstructed vision of the Glory of God and knows nothing but the purest joy throughout the endless day in His presence? Let the congregation here below arise and say Amen!—and pray to join that company. In the meantime there is the stern necessity of acknowledging the reality of the church on earth. We rejoice that the church on earth has a beautiful mother in heaven and we wish that the family resemblance were more commonly visible on earth. Here too God is continuously present, but the brotherhood is not always joyful. It is not always obedient, either. So it finds comfort in the fact that the night follows the day.

3. Accordingly we return to the beginning. "The holiness of the church" is purely and simply a way of speaking of the presence of God the Spirit come to infuse the community with the powers of the spiritual life of Christ.

We can have no interest in trying to catalogue these graces, these powers of the living Lord in His church. But we do have an interest in recognizing that these communicated powers fall into two broad divisions:

a. The transitive world-affecting powers, such as prophecy, interpretation, healing, exorcism of demons, works of mercy, and the arts of administration.

b. The intransitive powers, such as endurance, patience, long-suffering, gentleness, forbearance, hope, steadfastness, forgiveness; and the spirit of prayer; and faith.

This fundamental distinction is seriously abused when it is used to divide Christians into those more suited for service in the outer world and into those marked, again by reason of particular spiritual endowments, for intramural service in the church. The abuse of the distinction quite overlooks the fact that wherever the Christian serves the Lord he must follow Him in the outer world. How could we ever imagine that a church obedient to Him would represent itself as an asylum existing apart from the world into whose quiet peace the storm-toss'd soul can retire for the rest of his life? Perhaps the church so represents itself from time to time because it knows that it certainly does have a secret life in God. When the abusive hurly-burly of the world becomes too much for us we have at hand this truth to corrupt into the illusion of a retreat from the brutal dangers and subtle temptations of the world.

So one who prophesies has as much need of the intransitive graces as one who spends his days in meditation. One who spends his days in meditation has as much need of the transitive graces as one who preaches in the market place or disputes with the learned doctors in the groves of Academe.

4. The holiness of the church is to be understood and interpreted in relation to its *organic being*.

The organismic character of the church's being has two principal aspects:

a. The church exists bodily.

b. The church has a unitive being.

a. God's gift of Himself as Spirit (the same being the ratification of the gift of Jesus Christ) is the engracing of a bodily life. Apart from that bodily life there is no spirituality after the manner of Christ open to man's participation.

We have already taken note of the fact that nothing in the faith of the Christian is more susceptible to corruption than spirituality. Let us therefore be content here with the grand principle derived from the Incarnation: the divine perfection of grace and truth is visited upon flesh; and so it shall be until the end of time. From the beginning, spiritual power is ordained to the organization of physical energy for the sake of the higher righteousness. It follows that alienation of the spirit from the body is a work of sin.

This is not to say that spirit cannot exist without a body. The Christian faith includes a belief in the existence of spiritual beings higher than man. These are acknowledged to be higher because of their greater power and range of expression rather than because of greater freedom from bodily form. God Himself is pure spirit. His purely spiritual being signalizes His perfect plenitude of expressive power rather than (primarily) His freedom from bodily form. The revelation of God the Spirit is in fact the absolute sign of God's good pleasure in bodily form: for the community of the Spirit, the church of God's creation, is a body.

To say that the church is a body means both that the church is made up of human beings and that it has an institutional form like other institutional forms. The church is a body among other social bodies.

As to the first: since the church is made up of human beings, their bodies are under the authority of the Holy Spirit. In the language of the New Testament, the person called to faith in Jesus Christ must consider his body a temple of the Lord. His body is to be viewed as an instrument tuned to the highest degree of responsiveness to the bidding of the Spirit rather than as a being bent upon its own teleology.

The church is also body in the sense that it is an organization in a world of organizations. So just as the body of the Christian is under the general laws of the cosmos, so the institutional body of the church is under the general laws of the human social world. The body of the Christian is exposed to everything that afflicts flesh; and his spirit is exposed to every affliction body can visit upon the spirit. So also the body of the church is exposed to all of the ills that afflict human organizations and harass the spirit which that body was designed to serve. The body of the church can suffer hardening of the arteries, like any other institution. It can suffer the consequences of living a soft fat life. It can become paralytic. We need not seriously attempt to compile a textbook on the pathology of institutional life. It is enough to know that the providence of God does not contain an immunizer against any known social disease or malfunction.

Can we seriously believe and teach that a diseased body is still the church? Is there not something repugnant in such an obligation?

A diseased body is still body, no matter how repugnant the sight, sound, and smell thereof. A paralytic human being is not less human because of his affliction. (Some marvelous triumphs of the creative spirit have been wrought by people who got only grudging assistance at best from the body.)

We are entitled to say at least this much about the church. Diseased, it is still the church. But we must say something more than this, too. It is still the church because God has given a pledge in Jesus Christ, He has forged a relationship, He has given His word; and He is everlastingly faithful to this word. Therefore the people of faith are not only obliged to live in this body, the church, in its sickness and its health; but they are also to thank God for its preservation.

Faith in this providence of God is greatly strained at the moment. In fact it is experiencing agony. Many earnestly thoughtful and vigorously prophetic Christians have given up on the massive body of the church. Its sickness is a great offense to them; and they are convinced that it is a great offense to God, too. So they are recasting the theology of the church, their preaching, and their practice. They demand a reformation of the church that makes heavy drafts upon ideality. A tightly disciplined, spiritually charged cell is to take the place of a church that has become the museum of middle-class culture-religion. The army of Christ (often indistinguishable from a shapeless mass movement headed one direction rather than another by leaders more interested in aggrandizement on earth than crowns in heaven) is to be dissolved; and highly trained, wholly dedicated partisan units are to replace it. It seems that in the post-Christian era the church must break up and re-form as guerrilla teams for the duration.

Surely the massive body of the church cries out for radical medicine. This is doubted only where body fat is confused with spiritual prosperity. But the demand for a pure body, for a transparently spiritual company, is a rejection of the church of Jesus Christ. Let it be granted that the church in Suburbia, whatever its denominational stamp, is often much more of a religious country club than it is the obedient servant of the Gospel. But who among us is authorized by the Gospel and the Spirit to say that this disobedience has canceled the mission and the authority of the church, no matter how outrageous its captivity? Only God can do that. Though He sends prophets with whips of scorpions to chastise His disobedient church, He does not change His mind, He does not withdraw His word, He does not withhold the power of the Spirit.

So the massive body of the church is no more of a lost cause than the small self-reflecting cell in which readiness to lay bare the inmost detail of private life is confused with the power of grace and truth in preaching the Gospel. With all the corruptions of wasting disease in the massive body in full sight, we have no Christian reason for giving up on that church in the interests of a cadre of prophets appointed by private conscience alone.

b. The church has an organic life in its unitariness.

Whoever is of the church of Jesus Christ participates in the common life in Christ without respect to worldly eminence or the lack thereof. Each is a member in the organic sense: a member is one through whom the central power of life courses, rendering him as valuable and estimable as any other, no matter how lowly his office in the spiritual community. In this common life the Holy Spirit produces that internal relationship to the Kingdom of God, the absolute teleology, by virtue of which we call God, Father, and our neighbor, brother.

Thus the gift of the Holy Spirit is unity, a unity that reinforces the distinctiveness of each member. This gift enhances the participational power of each member by giving to each a new essence, a distinctive place in the teleology of the Kingdom. This place ought not to be confused with the job assigned to an individual in the institution, whether or not that assignment is the result of cunning psychological tests. His distinctive place in the teleology of the Kingdom is a singular power to express love for God's creatures, a capacity of spirit (of imagination, heart, and will) to envisage and to launch a project for doing good to all men. Nothing forbids a happy coincidence of this singularity of destiny in the work of the Kingdom and an assignment in the institutional structure. Nevertheless the institutional assignment does not presuppose that singularity of destiny. No man is born of the Spirit to become a bishop. Nonetheless a bishop may become a saint, no matter what the odds-makers say. In fact it is one of the sillier prejudices of the intellectual elite in the contemporary church that possession of institutional power is strictly incompatible with spiritual grace. The prejudice is a rank confusion of humility with impotency. It is not uncommon for men to seek high office in the church because they are ambitious (though they are not supposed to admit this). It is not axiomatic that ambition rules out either high competence or high integrity.

No living institution is merely the sum of its members. If the members are not imbued with a common spirit that institution is not really in the land of the living. But the common spirit requisite for institutional life is a reflex and involution of particular loyalties; as though each act and agent of loyalty picked up momentum from compresence and concurrence with other such acts and agents. The authority of the institution emerges from this compresence and concurrence. Each member can see for himself that the institution has a power at once larger than his own power and yet proportioned to it. If it were not for the authority of the institution its force would be inhuman. Given a deep and widespread disaffection in the heart of its members, even its force would evaporate.

Such observations may tempt us to conclude that institutions have fictive being only, that is, that they exist only in the minds of the members, a member by definition being a person who subscribes to the fiction. This is not a valid inference because in fact the members have a common mind in the sense suggested above. A member has not only a private mind, he is a participant in and agent of a common mind as well. Without the latter he has not yet come fully into man's estate.

Now the organic being of the church has a significantly different footing from anything sketched here of the foundation of institutional life in general. In the church the life and power of the community is not a reflex or involution of the act and agent of loyalty. The act of loyalty, the pledge of the agent, is a response to the pledge of God Himself. Thus the authority of the divine-human community is not at all incremental: it is not pulled in from the constituents but is centered, singular and autonomous from the beginning. This is why we say that the church is not a voluntary association. The church comes to be by the word, the given pledge, of God, not by the consent of the members. God has first chosen us. If He had not, we would not be able to choose Him.

At this very point we stumble upon something very strange indeed in the life of the church. The authority of the life of the church is not displayed decisively in its structural administrative arrangements. Such arrangements pertain to housekeeping. This does not mean that they are contemptible or unreal for the life in the Spirit. It does mean that these arrangements are not the essential life. The essential life is expressed in the preaching of the Gospel, in prophecy, in sacrament, and in the works of mercy. The real authority of the church comes into play only in the execution of these assignments.

But let us repeat that the housekeeping of the church is nonetheless important. The secular affairs of a congregation can be administered in ways that desperately embarrass the preaching of the Gospel. Congregations which live handsomely on the income from slum rentals may have a hard time convincing the world that this is what Jesus Christ meant when he said, "Blessed are ye poor"! You make it possible for Reverend Doctor Doakes to drive an Imperial and to take trips to the Holy Land—have you seen his color slides of Golgotha?—and in general to live well enough that the fattest cows of Bashan in his parish are not ashamed to be entertained at his board if not in his bed.

Presently we shall argue that the housekeeping assignments of the church do not include the general superintendence of the morals of civilization. At the moment we must be content to note that while the internal administration of the affairs of the church certainly *does* include a profound concern for moral health, this concern is very closely related to the fitness of a church to carry on the work of the Kingdom of God. Comparison with the life of an army is inevitable, as the very early use of such metaphors in the history of the church indicates. Every member ought to keep in shape, which means being fit, and remembering what he has been trained to do under combat conditions. Every member ought to be alert and keep his heaviest armor and weapons at hand at all times. Obviously the metaphor is designed not so much to convey the sense of the infinite value of each person as to express the vast importance of the objectives of the campaign. Accordingly we may have mixed feelings about the metaphor, a mixture dictated by the extraordinary degree to which the value of the individual in contemporary civilization has been suppressed by institutions in which the objectives and behavior seem impersonal in the highest degree, if not simply inhuman.

When everything has been said that needs to be said about the distinctiveness of the life of the church a postscript must always be added: this distinction must not be a wellspring of self-righteousness and vainglory on the part of the people of the church. The actual history of the church displays enough vanity, irresponsibility, waywardness, malfeasance, and betrayal to have sunk any other institution without a trace. Yet the church endures. It endures because God, its Creator, Judge, and Sustainer, has not canceled His pledge. So even when the "spirit of enmity" prowls in the church and lays waste all around, the Spirit of unity does not abdicate His throne for a season of security and peace at some Avignon. The voice of the Spirit is hard to hear in the offensive uproar produced when each part says, "I am the real church, I alone have been obedient." But the Life given for the freedom and joy of perfect union in God is not dismembered. He who alone is holy and without blemish of discord so lives in our discordant and disjointed life that together we may become like Him. That we cannot do apart from one another. In this fact alone we are given ample warrant for the theological subsumption of unity under holiness whenever we reflect on the being of the church.

5. The fifth cardinal feature of the church's life is its rhythm of going-out and return. Inevitably the diastolic and systolic rhythm of the human heart comes to mind as the ordained metaphor with which to express this feature of the being of the church. If we yield to this inevitability let us do so remembering that the whole life of the

church is expressed in what the metaphor stands for. That is to say, when the rhythm is broken up the church falls at once into severe illness; and if the rhythm were not restored the church would die. So an important truth about the very being of the church is conveyed in the erstwhile popular hymn, "If Your Heart Keeps Right."

Now we have to see what it means to say that the whole being of the church is expressed in this rhythm of going-out and return.

a. Under the impetus and illumination of the Holy Spirit the church goes out into the world with the ministry of prophecy, interpretation, exorcism, and healing. It goes out armed with the graces of the Spirit to make the Word of God fruitful in the world. Nothing of the world is to be spared this invasion, because the world is the Lord's and He will have all of it delivered from slavery.

b. Under the insistence of God the Spirit the church withdraws into the secret life of sacramental grace. Every Christian sacrament is a disclosure of the Kingdom of God. But there is a time when man's spirit must adore God in all of the beauty of His holiness; then the stress of campaigning is abated, the love of conflict is stilled, and the ministering company is ministered to.

Did not the Lord Jesus say to his disciples when they had just returned from the evangelical mission, "Come away by yourselves to a lonely place, and rest a while"? (Mark 6:31). It would be easy and natural to interpret this as a quasi-medical prescription of a rest cure after a season of grueling work; or perhaps as the inauguration of ministerial retreats in which boredom vies with irrelevancy for top honors. We must pray for strength to overcome such tempting interpretations; and to see, rather, the sovereign wisdom of the same Lord who sends his disciples out into the world to preach the Good News of the Kingdom. Neither going-out nor return is a mere means to the other. In each phase of the essential rhythm the Spirit glories; and in their unity the Spirit triumphs.

In this rhythmical life of the church something of the design of the Creator of all things is revealed, for whatever lives shares the rhythmical pattern with the life of the church. It is not man alone who lives in the alternation of work and rest, though it may well be only man who endows his sleep with the mysterious power "that knits up the ravell'd sleave of care." Yet the rhythms of our life surely encompass more than this. Human life is an effective, and now and again beautiful, unity of action and repose, expression and silence, giving and receiving. This rhythm of ebb-and-flow may be geared to the immense cycles of the cosmos in ways we are just beginning to discover scientifically but have known otherwise since the beginning of the human story. This is a speculative possibility of rare attraction. "Deep calls unto deep." Mystic intuition has often inspired speculative minds to probe the depths and heights of the cosmos and of the human spirit to find the ultimate rhythm uniting all. In days when theologians participated with zest and good faith in the speculative enterprise, they talked of Creative Spirit as that ultimate rhythm. The day may come again. In the meantime we are intimidated by the hardihood of theologians for whom the cosmos does not exist except when scientists are talking about it.

There is a somewhat more serious reason for eschewing the speculative venture. That is the immediate commitment made here to practical theology. For this purpose the creativities of spirit in the fashioning of civilization are much more to the point; and especially in a civilization still widely acknowledged to be Christian.

III

We ought to have no difficulty in sensing the promise of great complications for a church which lives in Christian civilization. This promise has long since been fulfilled. Many of the paradoxes and much of the confusion evinced in the concrete existence of the church have their origin in the shifting content of the claims Christian culture presses unrelentingly upon the church.

1. We begin with the persistence of a common expectation: the church ought to accept responsibility for a civilization still advertised as Christian. Much of the vagueness of this expectation can be traced to an antecedent vagueness about Christian civilization itself.

What then is the idea of a Christian civilization? Currently it is the idea of a social order built upon the practically effective acknowledgment of Christian values. That society is Christian in which each person is treated in principle as the equal of every other person; and in which the arts of peaceful arbitrament and persuasion have replaced coercion and violence. A Christian civilization honors the pursuit of justice, peace, and equality as the proper worship of God.

2. Further specifications of Christian civilization are not hard to find. A state, if not a civilization, is Christian in which the leaders are examples of sound piety; and the larger number of citizens are members of the church; and public education fosters Christian char-

acter whether or not there is public instruction in the offices of religion.

The most striking aspect of these general notions cannot have escaped our notice, namely, the very slight degree to which they are imbued with the knowledge and love of God as revealed in Jesus Christ. In these widely current views even Jesus Christ is an exemplar of the normative virtues of friendly helpfulness, respect for personality, cooperativeness, team spirit, etc. Jesus is for the underdog and against the bully. God becomes the chief value, or at least the sustainer of the chief value. "Christian civilization" is thus a name for the achievement at which the universe has been aiming from the beginning. God has wisely (indeed with marvelous shrewdness) guided the whole course of human history to this grand climactic moment, our day of destiny. God fights with us against all our enemies. Though a thousand fall on our right hand, the pestilence shall not come near us.

The church has suffered sea change at the hands of Christian civilization so understood. It has been absorbed into the life of the Christian social order without apparent remainder. Even its harshest judgmental voice has an assigned place and function in the order: it is good for us to be given hell from time to time—the blood circulates better after such treatment. Indeed, it is not a bad thing to be warned about Judgment, especially when the preacher tells us how simple it is to get to heaven, or at least to avoid hell; and how much of wordly power and eminence can be combined with sure hope of heavenly bliss. In a Christian civilization neither God nor Uncle Sam is too harsh with Dives, if he establishes a foundation for the cultivation of spiritual values.

3. There is another conception of Christian civilization incomparably richer than these popular notions. "Christian civilization" denotes ages of great creativity in art; and a range of noble moral aspirations; and a spirit of humble openness to the living will of Him who only is God and visits His wrath upon all mortal pretensions to holiness. Christian civilization emerges in history because people of faith necessarily give inclusive social expression to their faith. Christian life cannot be confined to the private inward man. The Spirit will not forever abide a sectarian aloofness from and contempt for the world. So where Christians are not merely a numerical majority but are also found consistently in positions of great importance in public affairs and in the transactions of the market

place, it is likely that a society will appear which is permeated by Christian ideals as well as nurtured by the Christian story. In such a society artists find unique symbols imperiously interesting for aesthetic expression. Finally, when the faith has become an essential part of civilization, indeed its informing spirit, Christianity is then part of the mind with which the world is perceived and interpreted. It becomes the dominant world view. It also becomes the angle of vision from which the world is perceived.

These conditions prevailed for a very long time in the Western world. Now that the West is supposed to have entered the "post-Christian" era, we are not sure that any of these conditions can be taken for granted any longer. This puts the church in a peculiarly difficult situation. It is urged to come swiftly, surely, and powerfully to the defense of human destiny against the brutal corruptions of godless communism. But the church is filled with doubt whether thereby it pledges itself to defend a system of values no longer normative, or perhaps even relevant, by appeals no longer persuasive, or perhaps even cogent.

Atavistic behavior in the church is a predictable response to such inhuman pressures. "Corporate memory" goes to seed as mere nostalgia. Hope is reduced to daydreaming of a miraculous restoration of power and glory. How could it be otherwise when from one side the church hears that it is responsible only for the preservation of the private virtues of mid-nineteenth-century small-town life; and from another side it hears that it ought to formulate ethical principles pertinent to contemporary society? When confusion so profound is pressed home in the heart of the church, we may well wonder whether it will find courage to choose the harder part: to spurn the soft security of the kept life for the rigors of free ministry of the Gospel to a world in conflict.

4. The time is opportune for the discovery of another meaning of Christian civilization: civilization is Christian only in its spirit, not in its concrete realizations.

The spirit of a civilization includes both its moral climate and the directions taken by its creative thrust. The spirit of civilization is not to be understood mystically as though it were a metaphysical reality apprehendable only by superpatriots. The moral atmosphere of a civilization is not isolatable in a pure form, but neither is it a mere abstraction from the sum total of mores. It is that which the responsible and intelligent person understands and seeks to do because of its rightness, that is, because of a particular relationship to the good. Thus the moral climate is more than the sense of what will be condoned as distinguished from what will be applauded. "What is compatible with our fundamental traditions" would be nearer the mark. In its negative form this is a reference to "the things that simply are not done." Everybody knows that such things *are* in fact done. To say, nevertheless, "they are just not done" is to say that responsible and intelligent people will not do them under the illusion that doing them is right. Immoral things may be done by moral persons; but so far as they are moral persons they think ill of themselves for having done them. (Without any intent to cast personal aspersions I think that we must lament the rise of a Kinsey mentality in the moral climate of the age. This is the mentality in which the revision of moral outlook and legal statute alike is dictated by what people say about their actual behavior. If an impressively large number of people are fornicating with mathematically impressive regularity, society ought to lift both the legal penalties and the moral opprobrium from fornication. I do not know whether the apostles of this sweet reasonableness would extend their gospel to shoplifting, income-tax evasion, and classroom cheating. Perhaps they feel that none of these things has the cosmic importance of Sex. Certainly none is so interesting.)

Concern for the moral climate goes beyond solicitude for the preservation of tradition for its own sake. Tradition itself must be judged by the good. In the perspective of Christian faith this good is imbedded in a human reality that transcends all of the divisions and exclusions created by civilization. This human reality is an ethical commonwealth embracing mankind as such. Relative to this commonwealth some traditions are good and some are bad. Because of its reality we revere persons above laws and traditions, and the concrete good of living persons above customs. Reverence for custom and law is certainly desirable, indeed it is necessary for the existence of society; but it needs to be controlled by a larger and deeper reverence.

So far then as the moral climate is concerned, the church contributes more significantly to it by preaching and practicing openness to the concrete good of living persons, than by demanding backward-looking veneration for the moral achievements and ethical principles of earlier ages. The church ought to be concerned for the spirit of civilization. That spirit is a respect for tradition. It is also an aspiration for a better life for more people in a better world.

In its mores and positive law society indicates what behavior it requires and what it will permit. Beyond the socially necessitous and permissible stretch the far horizons of aspiration. Here and there something in this vast expanse is tinged with social inducement: for this particular achievement one may expect a premium, perhaps prestige, prosperity, and praise while one lives, and an honored grave when dead. These things are only occasional and random spots on the map of aspiration. By a decree of deep ontological wisdom they are only infrequently represented as the greatest of all good things to be aspired for. Better than all of the cash-value premiums society can hold out as bait to arouse the highest powers of aspiration there is the inner satisfaction that such aspiration alone yields. Even though circumstances throw it back to earth, broken and frustrated, the soundest worldly verdict about aspiration is: Better to have aspired and failed than never to have aspired at all. This verdict is a reading of the ontological situation. God the creative Good is at work in the tug and lure of creaturely aspiration. Ideality in the abstract has no such power. This is the power of God the creative Spirit.

Society imposes various restrictions upon the aspirations of its constituents. Somehow or other people must be induced to aspire for what is best for that society, because the next stage of that society is implicit in the present aspirations of the people (and in their fears and guilts). In a Christian civilization people are enjoined to aspire for life in the essential community of spirit revealed in Jesus Christ. This community transcends every actual civilization. It is therefore a matter of great importance for a society to discover whether Christian symbols are everywhere visible in its cultural expressions. But this means that the church occupies an exposed position. As the preacher of the Gospel the church must nourish and protect the flame of aspiration for the Kingdom of God. But of every cultural realization of this aspiration the church must say that it is not an absolute norm for subsequent aspiration, even though it expresses a great love for the Kingdom. Every realization of the good open to man's aspiration is itself good for a time; and none of them ought to be interpreted as everlastingly normative.

The church does not find life very easy in this situation. Things would be much simpler for the church if it could faithfully hold up the civilization of some earlier epoch as the epitomization of the divine Kingdom in time; or if it could say, in good faith, there the human kingdom reached the golden apex of human aspiration. In fact, however, the great Christian ages of Western civilization are moments in which powerful symbolic realizations took on a life of their own. In the Middle Ages, for example, narrational painting reached splendid heights. The masters synthesized command of naturalistic detail with thematic faithfulness. Such realizations inevitably induce a mood of reverence in the pious, as though here the Gospel story and the Lord appear absolutely in their own right. This is illusion; and we know that it is illusion just as soon as we attend to the thematic development. The Virgin, for example, in endless celebrations of her eminence, is no longer the simple child-bride of Nazareth, bewildered, dazzled, terrified, and overjoyed by the birth of a son, as women have been since Eve. She is a high-born elegant lady, sweetly unperturbed by the transaction, comporting herself as though every honor bestowed upon her were already contained in the contract. The theme may well do credit to the ideals of (high-born) motherhood in the Middle Ages. But there is not even the slightest trace of it in the Gospel. The aesthetic development of a devotional theme reaches the heights, unquestionably, but like the devotional theme itself, the aesthetic realization achieves a life of its own that at best is thinly related to the Gospel. Undoubtedly the Gospel is the remote cause of these great realizations; but the Gospel has long since lost command of them.

When the break comes, a break with the aesthetic if not with the devotional norms, we can hardly say that the reform or the new birth is a return to the lordship of the Gospel over the aesthetic and the devotional. The *Pietà* of Michelangelo in the Duomo is a very good illustration of this. Not bound by the sovereignty of Mary-worship, he has made Mary a recessive figure, a woman blurred by immense grief. She is obscured both by the body of the Christus dreadfully distorted in death, and by Nicodemus whose godlike power and compassion envelop the dead Christ. But we cannot say that this is pure Gospel either. It too is a realization of form that stands on its own. Narrative lingers; but it is encompassed and subdued by the formal achievement. Even the narrative is idiosyncratically imaginative: why *Nicodemus?*

As the new spirit deepened its hold upon Michelangelo and upon the great multitude of creative spirits of that epoch we call the Renaissance, the historical-narrational mode all but disappears. The mythological on the one side, and the celebration of nature on the other, achieve ascendancy. Elegantly clothed human figures no longer gracefully symbolize the eternal spiritual world in their gestures. The nude female form comes front and center, but not primarily to tell a story, Biblical or mythological. Beauty is here and now, it is this body; and the rest of the world exists to show this beauty to best advantage. Yet the background is also executed with loving mastery, its relationship to the nude is in no sense symbolic, it has a rich life of its own. The world open to the senses is now open to enjoyment for what it is in itself. The way in which light is handled by Renaissance masters illustrates this. Light no longer streams from heaven but is diffused, it has become an earthly glory. It no longer renders the flesh the diaphanous veil of eternity, it makes the body desirable in its own beauty.

But even in the Christian Middle Ages, formal achievement is an object of creative aspiration. The Gothic cathedral is the great case in point. No one questions the piety of its creators, that is, their manifest intent to praise God in stone as well as with psaltery and horn. Nevertheless the Gothic is a superlatively beautiful formal achievement that does not in itself advertise which God is to be praised, except through the particularities of cultic ornamentation. As architecture Gothic does not plainly tell the story of Jesus Christ. It may express the permeability of the physical by the spiritual, as so many lovers of the Gothic feel that it does; but this metaphysical instruction is a secondary achievement, if in fact it occurs at all. True, the greater interior spaces make one feel very small and insignificant; but so does a towering mountain. The difference is that the mountain does not need to explain why it does not talk about Jesus Christ. The Christ of the Gospel speaks not to make man feel submerged and overpowered into nullity, but, rather, to quicken the power given by God to say Yes to the Kingdom of God. If therefore the Gothic reduces human life to something infinitely small, it may score a cosmic victory but just so far it departs from the Gospel. Obviously this is not the whole and essential story of the Gothic. Along with all other Christian art the Gothic cathedral enacts the drama of salvation, into which it weaves a great deal of nonbiblical history; and with such artistry and spiritual fidelity that apostles and demons are as real as the kings and dukes of France.

Nonetheless the Gothic, as well as Michelangelo's *Pietà,* is a formal achievement able to stand on its own feet. The piety of Christians may appropriate it and in doing so come finally to think of it as holy. Art *per se* knows nothing of holiness.

Something very much like this must be said of every aspect of civilization that is a formal achievement claiming attention for itself. Let us say again that the forms of creative expression may be absorbed into the particular behavior of a religious community, with remarkable subtlety and power. This does not convert these forms into so many authentic representations of the Gospel.

The same point can be made about another realm. The church must have a political form, a stable pattern, a body, for its daily life in the world. This order must have rulers and subjects, captains and foot soldiers, etc. The figures of speech are numerous but they ought all to make the same point. So political piety (rather than aesthetic) finds one such form a strict implication, if not explicit provision, of the New Testament, which after all does mention presbyters, deacons, etc. Certainly we can have no objection to the most detailed structural pattern for church life, even when it is accompanied by theological rationalizations for the janitor and the choirmaster. Mischief begins with the supposition that one is obeying God when one obeys a bishop. Mischief goes from strength to strength when people are ready to die for the preservation of the political form of the church, or are ready to surrender to it the right and obligation of personal judgment. Here the lessons of history are written in blood: ecclesiastical autocracy and tyranny are worse than their secular counterparts because they claim divine sanction for the same tactics.

It may nonetheless be the case that some political forms are better than others as instruments for ordering the life of the church called to preach the Gospel. The church does not become disobedient to the Lord simply because it tries to learn a few political lessons from the world. But we must also apply the converse. The world is not Christian, it has not come into real obedience to Jesus Christ, simply because its affairs are administered by godly men.

5. What does the label "post-Christian" pinned to contemporary civilization signify? Perhaps that the creativities of our time are not preoccupied with the representation of the Christian story. It can hardly mean that Christian moral aspirations and ethical principles have ceased to function. Whether these are really Christian is not our present concern. Our present concern is to ask whether the restriction of Christianity to the spirit of civilization does not do

the very thing we argued earlier was disastrous, viz., that it confuses the spirituality of the Gospel with the ideality of culture. This confusion does occur, as we have admitted. Now we say that this occurs when the essential rhythm of the church's life has been broken. When this happens the church is left to the mercy of powers some of which will reduce the Gospel of the church to a culture piety, and some of which will alienate the church from the world and leave the church panting and sweating for its own safety. The collapse of the essential rhythm of the church's life has created the appearance of a civilization that is now out from under any real guidance from the church. The pace, the momentum, and the aspirations of contemporary civilization are all too much for a church that has lost both the power of authentic prophecy and the grace of its secret life in Christ. Rather than prophesying the church now is largely content to scold the world for this or that sin; but its wrath is quickly softened by fruits of repentance for which tax deductions can be claimed. The church administers the sacraments; but these are rationalized by a metaphysics that ought long ago have been mounted in a museum and in any case has nothing to do with the revealed Kingdom of God. The church summons the hurrying hysterical world to prayer; but it assures the few who remain awake and attentive that prayer is good for business, domestic relations, international problems, and high blood pressure.

Thus a conclusion is forced home: the church is the reason why contemporary civilization can no longer be called "Christian," if to call it Christian were any considerable gain for the church or the world. The church was not planted in the world to govern it as a regal presence clearly born to rule. It is here to preach the Kingdom of God. Imaginative and devoted people have sometimes believed that they had learned from the Gospel how to form governments, depose kings, provide for the aged and infirm, organize agriculture, build universities and hospitals, wage wars, punish malfeasance in public office, etc. etc. As an expression of gratitude to God for the marvelous creative powers of human life, a readiness to credit the Gospel with the full compass of creativity is indeed touching. In any other modality, to do so is nonsense. This is why the problem of the church's relation to the creativities of the human spirit is insoluble in principle. It is not simple waywardness which carries an age beyond the understanding and the spiritual guidance of the church. The church itself seems forever to be using the achievements of past epochs, in art, politics, or morals (to say nothing of theology, hymnody, and architecture), as the reins with which to control aspiring creativity. Such a performance is a corruption of the conservative impulse, a betrayal of memory, and bad faith toward the living God.

IV

The church cannot faithfully discharge its mission as a critic of civilization unless the organic health of the essential rhythm of its life is restored. When its life enjoys that health the church is able to endure existence in tension with contemporary civilization, looking upon the world neither as an enemy ripe for destruction nor as its patron and keeper.

We return therefore to the rhythm of prophetic mission and priestly offering of sacramental grace. Earlier we identified this rhythm as the going-out in the power of the Holy Spirit to proclaim the righteousness of God; and the return to the secret life in Christ in which the hope of glory burns more brightly than all of the suns of the firmament.

1. Prophecy is that mode of preaching in which the revealed righteousness of God is the platform and criterion of the criticism of culture. It is that mode in which judgment is pronounced upon iniquity in high places and upon complacency in low places. Prophecy is also that mode of preaching in which the delineation of the shortcomings of contemporary life is derived from the prophet's knowledge of God's righteousness and his own knowledge of how aspiration functions in persons and societies.

Consequently prophecy creates great tensions between the church and the present age; but not simply because the ways of the transgressor, both of high and low degree, are plainly labeled and requital unsparingly demanded. Prophecy is likely to create personal hostilities toward the preacher and toward the church that sustains him in the prophetic office; but these hostilities are not the essential tension—even though personal hostility may rise high enough to drive the prophetic preacher from his assigned congregation. This may well happen where ownership of the local church appears to go along with great affluence as a spiritual dividend. So let it be said that an owned and kept church has no berth for the prophet. And then let it be asked what such a church can do that has *any* Gospel validity? The liturgy seems to offer a blessed haven from such a question; but this is an illusion. The sacraments of Biblical authority are themselves proclamations and celebrations of the Kingdom of God. Surely unless the revealed righteousness of God is celebrated in the liturgy, the sacraments fall under the dominical denunciation of vain repetitions in which unfaith places such great store.

In all such strictures upon the actual behavior of the church we are contending with a fundamental Biblical truth. The Gospel of Jesus Christ and the interpretive life of the Holy Spirit cannot be divided and alienated from each other. So a church which believes in preaching and ignores the sacraments is certain to become the ventriloquist's dummy mouthing the piety of civilization. A church which believes in the sacraments and ignores prophetic preaching is a miming actor who has forgotten the book. (Personal hostility directed against the preacher is a tricky thing. It can prompt the preacher to scale the heights of self-exalted martyrdom. It can be confused with hostility provoked by things very different from the spirit of prophecy. Autocratic behavior, bad breath, boorish manners, butchered grammar, indolence, and a fondness for choir boys have also been known to arouse a certain degree of antipathy in congregations.)

The tension of most decisive import between the church and contemporary civilization is created by that prophecy which interprets the shortcomings of aspiration geared to the normal and native capacity for self-transcendence. This is a capacity for forming a just estimate of one's conduct and character in the light of aims and standards presumptively binding upon all moral agents in a given society. A person who exercises this power might be said to be acting in adverse interest, since in all likelihood his cool, knowledgeable, and candid scrutiny of himself will produce things injurious to his erstwhile good opinion of himself. Disagreeable and perhaps shocking things now squarely held in his perception of himself, he may have nothing left upon which to compliment himself except his relentless truthfulness with himself. "Whatever else I am," he may feel compelled to say, "I am not a liar to myself."

Self-transcendence falls into further complications in contemporary civilization, such as the extremely precarious condition of aims and norms once presumed to be binding upon all agents. All of these are objects of unsparing and often unsympathetic criticism; and the self-examination of the moral man is deemed incomplete, if not dishonest, unless he participates in this unsparing criticism of all aims and norms. As a result, the erstwhile fixed points in the moral firmament are loosened and swim about like desiccated cells in the retinal fluid of the eye. They are elements of moral judgment but they are not its decisive elements. One is therefore bound to ask, How is one to judge the validity of prevailing aims and norms?

The question is a veritable demon of discomfiture. Many people are afraid now to trust their powers of self-judgment because they have heard and believed so much about the unconscious self, that mighty power in the murky depths armed with demonic deceit and propelled by uncontrollable lust for self-aggrandizement. If every conscious aspiration is only a disguised thrust of the real subterranean self, the end result can only be the annihilation of the moral agent unless he is spared this fate by some happy accident. So we are exposed to the shocking novelty of persons wishing to be something less than persons—to be nonpersons in order freely and spontaneously to express the subterranean self. Part of the harrowing of personhood in contemporary culture is the lure of such fantastic corruptions of freedom.

Self-transcendence has a further complication. It requires an assessment of the aims of corporate life as well as of individual aims. But what does it mean to say that a society, such as the nation, ought to exercise self-criticism in its dealings with comparable societies? It might mean that in their representative utterances and actions the leaders of the nations ought to acknowledge the finiteness and partiality of every human creation. We are not entitled to see much more in this than an attitude or outlook uniquely fostered by historical religion in Western civilization. This nation's greatest leaders have had this attitude, in tragic depth; but it has been far easier to praise it in the honored dead—especially if they were martyrs—than in the strong-willed living. Moreover it is difficult to show that such an attitude is the specific mother of astute policy in a leader or the potent discipline of fanaticism and recklessness in the people. To be sure, the leaders of the nation act for a people whose life is colored by a common history. This common history is not so much the sum of what has happened as it is a consensus on the value of what has happened. How then shall the people assay the rightness of their cause in the inevitable conflicts with other nations? That is dearest to them that most nearly matches the corporate image of what they are and what they have a right to become as a people. To impose upon this image the standard of universal good smacks either of irrelevancy or of disloyalty.

Culture Christianity is powerless either to illuminate or reconstruct this situation. This radical and irredeemable failure of culture Christianity is fully known to be that only in the light of the prophetic preaching of God's righteousness. Apart from that word the blood-guiltiness of the people is only the consciousness of having been false to their own history and expectations.

The prophetic ministry of the church discloses further dimensions of falsity and betrayal. The nation, as the self, lives in the human commonwealth. The good of that commonwealth can be violated. For violation of that good God exacts requital. Such is the prophecy of the Kingdom.

The church also prophesies, "All flesh is grass"; and only the everlasting God is God and is worthy to be adored. This prophetic proclamation of mortality is more than preaching the certainty of death. That certainty is to be acknowledged rather than prophesied. The prophetic message deals with life and the conditions in which life is blessed. "Seek ye me and ye shall yet live," thus saith the Lord. God has not promised to back man's self-determined aims and standards. Ideals are not God's dwelling place. God has so revealed His righteousness that men may see the good and evil in their conduct and in their aspirations, and thus learn to do good and eschew evil.

The church inevitably illustrates the judgment of God's righteousness in its own life. The blatantly meretricious, fraudulent, and filthy in society are not likely to appear there. Its sins are likely to be much more agreeable to good taste, discretion, and high-mindedness. The contemporary church is rarely guilty of disturbing the peace with loudly offensive behavior. (Occasionally a minister of the Gospel is caught out in a gaudy sin and is enthusiastically pilloried by the tabloids and by the delighted gossipmongers generally. People frequently suppose that the church is thereby discredited. A military man can commit the same sin without prompting people to call for the dismantling of the army; and no one argued that the Constitution of the United States was discredited by the behavior of Warren G. Harding. But the church is often presumed to stand or fall with the morals of the clergy.) It is more likely to confuse complacency, security, and a good reputation with the peace of God.

Nevertheless the church also consciously preaches the righteousness of God in judgment. In prophetic utterance it proclaims the truth of the living God in which man may correct his perception of the good and order his existence accordingly. The good is more than the claim of an abstract ideality. The good is the righteousness of him who says, "Seek me and ye shall live!"

The demands of God's righteousness are bound into concrete historical existence as the determinate charter and covenant thereof. To exist as a concrete being is already to have a particular destiny; and this applies both to persons and to communities. Thus concrete existence expresses "the law in the inward parts." This is a particular relation to the righteousness of God.

Prophecy is the divinely appointed instrument for the disclosure of God's determinate will. The prophet is not appointed to offer lofty praise of the moral universe as such. God's particular demands cannot be met by a salute to justice in general and a high regard for moral value in the abstract. He demands righteousness in the inward parts, His commandment is laid upon man's vital center, the wellspring of man's most decisive and creative acts. There God demands faithfulness in the fulfillment of a distinctive destiny. Upon those who reject that and thus leave the world the poorer for that failure to realize a unique good—upon all such God shows a face of wrath. In such a failure one violates a particular reason for existence; and the human community is by that much diminished.

When we say, then, that God comes to the defense of the moral order, we mean to say that He will not permit specific rebellion against the good to spread out to embrace the whole essential human community. God loves this community. He has pledged Himself to redeem and perfect it. To this He has pledged himself, not to order in the abstract, and not to the idea of the good. ("God is no respecter of persons" does not imply "God loves abstractions.")

Thus prophecy is a much richer and more hazardous mission than the office of leading civilization to repeat the Ten Commandments. The prophets of the Old Testament preached the Law as a personal-communal faithfulness to the perfectly righteous God. The Law, in their representation, is an instrument of the divine-human communion, the Covenant. So it has been ever since, in authentic prophecy. God has a specific "contract" with each person and each people. Prophecy is ordained to illuminate that contract and to remind all parties of the second part that the contract is still valid and binding.

Prophecy when it is efficacious throws the party of the second part upon corporate memory, in penitence and in gratitude. "God spoke to our fathers." God speaks now; and the prophet is licensed to use the most vivid and potent contemporary language in which to convey the thrust and scope of God's everlasting and particular will for the good. Thus the past lives, or comes again to life, in the prophetic word laid upon memory. In the living Word of God the present age understands what God has done and what men are up to. The prophetic church preaches the law in the inward parts: the essence which makes the distinctive life of person and society possible.

Prophecy is also ordained to sharpen perception of the signs of the times. In this prophecy is diagnostic rather than predictive. The prophet is not licensed to make solemn or hysterical prognostications. He has not been sent to hurl that fearsome threat: "Because you have been stingy in supporting the church your banks, crops, cattle, and seminal fluid shall fail!" (The threat is merely the inverse of the faithless promise: "Because you have been generous in support of the church you shall wax rich, beautiful, and mighty!") Prophetic diagnosis is very different from all such faithless incantational predictions. Old Testament prophecy is very easily and commonly misunderstood on this point. The Old Testament prophets, those mighty men of God, certainly preached that faithfulness will have its reward, but the reward is what God has promised from the beginning: He will dwell in their midst. Therefore they will inherit the land, and the land will become marvelously productive, and the desert will become a beauteous carpet of roses, and the lion will savage no more, and men will live in peace. It is from these mighty old Testament preacher-poets that Western civilization has received its most beautiful eschatological images, rather than from the apocalyptic patchwork of the book of Revelation. Rather better than Mark Twain, Isaiah would have understood that a street paved with gold is worthless for human traffic; but a desert transformed into a prodigy of fertility and a paragon of beauty is an image that rejoices the heart of the tenement prisoner as well as the hard-pan farmer.

The church prophesies when it reads the contemporary situation correctly, laying bare the shape and movement of the "principalities and powers" contending in proud hopelessness against the righteousness of God. Men are forever looking backward to see whether in some former glory they can find the simplifying tool with which to master the present. When this fails, as fail it must, they consume precious time and energy in bootless anxiety about the future. How great, then, is the need for the prophetic word rightly disclosing the shape of the present and calling men to that particular obedience in which their particular destiny is to be found!

But let us say again that the prophet does not offer a blueprint version of God's demands. Comprehensive social programs are not for that reason to be rejected as perversions of the divine order. Intelligence, wisdom, ingenuity, and courage must of course be organized for the improvement of society, and surely the need for such organization was never greater than it is now. But we ought not to claim a direct specific divine authorization for specific organization of human resources. Each society makes specific response to God's demand for justice from all men. The response to this essential demand must be specific because every corporate life is afflicted with specific injustices. These responses are not always dictated by an acute awareness of the magnitude or quality of these injustices; or by a marked readiness to confess corporate and personal guilt for them. Indeed the response is often the product of a vague but relentless uneasiness which swiftly runs toward palliatives devised to relieve this uneasiness in the possessors of inequitable privilege rather than toward atonement which at once offers restitution to the dispossessed and digs out the roots of the evil in the body of the common life. Atonement so concrete, inclusive, and fundamental certainly demands social planning of a high order. We add, hardly as an afterthought, that the planning itself is vulnerable to corruption; and the corruption can spring from idealism as surely as from crude or cynical power drives.

2. The prophetic mission of the church in the world can be faithfully pursued only when the church remembers that it has a life apart from the world, a secret life hidden with Christ in God. The life of priestly service is not a mere preparation for the prophetic mission, a briefing session for a campaign to conquer the world for Christ. God reveals Himself in the secret life as utterly adorable in His own life. He is the Lord who ministers both to the greatness and the meanness of human life.

In the secret life of the church the glory of God is even more effectively concealed than on the stage of history or in the vast spread of the cosmos. Where is His dazzling glory in the Bread and Wine and mechanical incantations of the priest? Where is this glory in the ceremonies of marriage and of baptism? Yet in all of this the Kingdom of God is disclosed to the mind and heart of faith. It is disclosed in such commonplace routines that the faithful alternately doze and shiver politely with aesthetic thrills. Ought we to conclude from this that nothing is really going on? Or that the secret life hidden in Christ consists of an esoteric essence available only to mystic perception? By no means! The power of the Kingdom, God the Spirit, is at work in these commonplace routines; and one day, very likely without warning and certainly without fanfare, the heart of good faith catches fire with the love of God in the perfection of His holiness. So it is not very astonishing that speculative theologians read metaphysical wonders into these humble observances; and people are restless under these humdrum ministrations of the Holy Spirit; and priests bedeck themselves in the accouterments of dramaturgical sovereigns. For here, even less than in the world, is the church able to put the glory of God on display for the humiliation of the world. Indeed here the humiliation of the church is intensified. It comes into the secret life that is prepared and administered by the Spirit, hoping to find an all-conquering answer to the world's taunt, "Where now is your God? Show Him plainly to us that we too may serve Him!"

Over and over the church replies to this taunt (though it is more than a taunt) by pointing with an air of feverish triumph to the grand side effects of its secret life in God: hospitals, prison reforms, abolition of slavery, peace of mind, neighborliness, etc. etc. These are fruits of repentance and thank offerings of obedience. They are not the signs of God's presence, they are not proofs of His existence or testimony to His purpose. If the world gains a good impression of the Christian company from such services to humanity, well and good. But people are not transformed into the likeness of Christ by doing and admiring good works. This ought not to diminish the value of good works. If it does, they have been loaded down with more meaning than they can sustain.

God calls the church to a secret communion with Himself. The whole of the authentic life of the church in the world derives from the secret life it has in God. This secret communion includes prayer (itself more richly varied than we can pause now to indicate), and the celebration of the Lord's Supper. The authority given to the church to preach the Gospel of the Kingdom in Jesus Christ is given in the secrecy of prayer. In the secrecy of the Lord's Supper what was thus given is renewed and reconfirmed. God is known as the Lord only in the life of prayer. God is known as God the all-loving Father only in the remembrance of the sacrifice of Jesus Christ the Son in the Lord's Supper.

What transpires in this communion cannot be expressed in words and gestures essentially dissimilar to it. Prayer in the church of Jesus Christ is not a kind of metaphysical meditation. The Lord's Supper is not an illustration of the Sacramental Universe.

But what is so secret about prayer and the Lord's Supper? The secrecy does not lie in the fact that the church does these things out of sight and sound of the world; or in the fact that the church sometimes posts Keep Out! signs; or in the fact that the church conceals its innermost transactions behind a bewildering variety of ingenious mummery-flummery, such as saying the Mass in Latin. Secrecy is not subjective privacy nor cozy intimacy. Neither is it the result of practicing the arts of obfuscation and religious sleight of hand. Prayer and Eucharist are secret because the world cannot follow the church into the depths of God's life without surrendering its own essential and illusory self-sovereignty.

Nevertheless the world is always represented in the church's communion with God, because Jesus Christ has gathered the world into his love, and he has commanded the church to pray for the world without ceasing. He has also commanded the church to die for the world after the manner of his own death. In this we have another reason why the world cannot follow the church into the secret life with Christ in God. The worldly mind is bent upon fleeing from death, it passionately denies the reality and the necessity of death, it looks upon its own death as an insuperable obstacle to believing that God is sovereign in the cosmos. Over against this the church is summoned to go to meet its death; and to go readily, and to go joyfully and not merely readily.

The secrecy of the life of the church goes beyond anything so far suggested. The heart of the secret is the sustaining and renewing of the church in ways that the eye cannot follow and the mind can but dimly understand. The church dies in the secrecy of prayer and Eucharist. The church is secretly resurrected in prayer and Eucharist. The manner of its dying and rising and living again are the secrets, the "open mysteries," of God.

Because of this secret life in God the church is invincible in preaching the Gospel in and to the world. No worldly power can prevent the church from preaching the Gospel once it has put on the full armament of God. How could ordinary death, or the ordinary threats of death, terrify the church into silence when it is already carried by the Lord Jesus Christ into a death the mere prospect of which inevitably terrifies every worldly power? How could seduction avail against a church risen from death into the fullness of God's life? What could the powers of the world offer to the church dead to all such blandishments, to lure it from love of the Holy Kingdom and to corrupt or quench the burning passion to preach the Kingdom until the world itself is no more?

But by the same token a church indifferent to its secret life in God is hardly a foe worthy of the subtlety and the might of the worldly powers. Such a church will do almost anything to feel loved by the powers of the world. It will not even dream of holding away from the world any secrets or any loyalty whatever. In any serious emergency in the life of the world, the powers of the world have nothing to fear and nothing to learn from a church that has forgotten the secret life in God. Indeed the powers of the world can count upon such a church to provide an eloquent spiritual defense for the reigning way of life, if the faithless church can first be led to believe that this way of life is Christian. Naturally it would not do to invite the church to a lynching. After the lynching the thing to do is to persuade the church to preach patience, forgiveness, and forbearance—to the next of kin of the victim. On our knees before God we weep in great shame and wretchedness for a church carried away into such whoredom by the spirit of disobedience. But so far as we are obedient to the ministry of the Holy Spirit we dare also to intercede for such a church, for with God all things are possible.

In the secret life in God the church rightly apprehends God's purpose in setting the church in the world; and rightly takes unto itself for comfort and for joy the life of God and the power of God's love. He will raise up the church from the grave of disobedience, anxiety, and pride; and send it again out into the main thoroughfares and the byways, alleys and dead-end streets, to preach the Gospel, without fear or favor.

V

The hour is always later than we think: the power of God's Christ is always richer and mightier than we dream. The night draws on: God reigns in the darkness as in noonday. Rightly to relate these two truths to each other, the one so bright, the other so dark, and to preach their unity as the Gospel to a world absolutely pledged now to the defeat of the one and then the other, seems an utter impossibility. This is the impossibility the church is created, chastened, and sustained to perform. With God all things are possible. God, Father, Son and Holy Spirit, is with the church yesterday, today, and until history reaches its end. He only is holy. Let the church find unity, peace, joy, and power in loving Him above all else.

CHAPTER XIV

The Criterion of Preachability

I

We have proposed preachability as the principal criterion of adequacy to be employed in assaying the results of the theological criticism of culture. The task before us now is to examine the criterion itself. In every particular endeavor for the acquisition of knowledge, examination of appropriate and decisive criteria is obviously important. It can hardly be less important where the endeavor is religious.

1. The first thing to be noted in the criterion of preachability is that its valid employment presupposes a faithful church. The church is commissioned to preach the Gospel of the Kingdom of God revealed in Jesus Christ. The church lives in the power of the Holy Spirit when to do this is the joy of all its desiring. Faithfulness in the first instance therefore is obedience to this commission. Only in the second instance is faithfulness to be understood as the resolute promulgation of sound doctrine. Eventually we shall have occasion to consider how far and in what ways preaching the Gospel involves preaching doctrine. At the moment our concern is to emphasize the faithfulness of the church as the will to preach only the Gospel of Jesus Christ.

When this will falters the church is confronted with a dazzling variety of other things to preach: psychological self-help chitchat, moralistic exercises in self-righteousness, little essays in religious history, metaphysical disquisitions, fulminations against the godless enemies of Christian civilization, idealistic crusades against war and injustice, etc. Once the church is free of the Gospel it finds the world full of all manner of things to preach.

We have no interest in enumerating scientifically the possibilities for the corruption of preaching. Suffice it to say that they are numerous indeed, given some imagination in their combination and rotation. We have a much greater interest in taking note of the fact that corruption reaches the modality as well as the content of preaching. I mean by modality the kind of rhetoric employed and the resources of language exploited. For example, moralistic preaching characteristically appeals to what the regnant consensus of the fellowship already is ethically, or at least what it proposes to be. The preacher rhetorically becomes one with this regnant consensus. The preacher and the high-minded consensus together stand over against the unrighteous and unworthy. No doubt the publicans and sinners are exhorted to renounce their evil ways; but they are not to infer from this that they will be received into the fellowship of the righteous with open arms. Increasingly in middle-class culture-Christianity the publicans and sinners are not given this golden privilege. They serve much more commonly as the providential background against which the virtue of the righteous stands out in bold relief. So the human community having already been divided into the two communities of the good and the bad, the function of moralistic preaching is to warn men against joining together what self-righteousness has taken apart.

Those who participate in the high-minded consensus probably have imposing budgets of guilt and anxiety about their worthiness. But the rhetoric of moralism assures them that they could be much worse off—at least they are worrying about their souls. Moreover—thank God!—they can do something about their worries: self-help is at hand.

So a supplementary rhetorical mode is exploited: the sermon that proclaims the Gospel of psychological self-help. When the church assumes this posture it encourages people to believe that there is no real evil in human life greater than mental depression, self-doubt, and kindred psychological negativities. The preacher appeals to his hearers to have done with these works of darkness. He assures them that they can do this if they want to: the secret is to be positive and confident in outlook no matter how formidable the actualities appear to be; for nothing can hold out against the cheerily positive attitude.

Something in us responds gratefully to flattery of this sort, especially if it comes with religious wrappings. Nor can we have much doubt as to what in us is flattered: the image of ourselves as good and sufficient to solve all of life's problems. The ability actually to cope masterfully with life is rather unevenly distributed in the human species. The image of mastery often burns brightly where the ability is dim; but even if this were not the case we should have to say that the Gospel of Jesus Christ does not recommend the fond caressing of that image in any case.

The rhetoric of psychological self-help flatters the people who conceive themselves already as being in masterly control of life's problems. But it exacerbates the problems of people who do not so conceive themselves; and adds the further dimension of guilt for not being able to manage. Thus this gospel is very similar to moralistic exhortations to an alcoholic: buck up, be a man, give up your vice for the sake of your family, your job, your pride, your good standing in the community, your credit at the loan company, and your liver. Some alcoholics may need to hear this; but the rhetoric in which it is pronounced may drive them over the brink. At the moment we are considering the rhetoric; and so we say that rhetorically the preacher of this gospel stands on the holy, healthy, high, and safe ground of self-righteousness to which he bids the sinner ascend. Both existentially and rhetorically this posture wilts under the fierce light of the Gospel of Jesus Christ.

2. The faithful church has in the Gospel of Jesus Christ both a content (a message) and a rhetoric. Here our attention will be given to the rhetoric, on the understanding that the content and the mode of expression can be separated from each other only abstractly and analytically.

a. The church accepts the Gospel as the disclosure of the actuality and the destiny of man in the Kingdom of God. The original and absolute disclosure is in the life of Jesus Christ. From this disclosure the church receives a language. Thus from the very beginning of the church's life the Gospel is a power of speech. This ministry of speech precedes all of the apostolic gifts.

b. The reason for the priority of the power of speech is clear in the Gospel itself. By virtue of this gift of language, this power of speech, the church shows its colors, it identifies the one for whom it works and under whose authority all things are done by the church in the world. In the preached word of the Gospel the church exposes the reason for its own existence. The preached word lays bare its own essence, the teleology in and for which the church lives. The preached word of the Gospel is therefore God's introduction of the church to mankind. Even as He introduced His only-begotten Son to mankind (cf. Mark's account of the baptism of Jesus in the Jordan), so God also presents the church to the world, so also He lays bare the credentials of the church's preaching in the language He gives to the church.

c. Thus the preached Gospel always begins with the recital of what God has done and therefore with the disclosure of the identity of the one who has done these mighty things. Necessarily, then, the first word of the preaching of the faithful church is the word that identifies God in the power and beauty of His actions and in the unapproachable holiness of His righteousness.

d. Thereby the rhetorical stance of the church and the preacher is already defined and determined. The preacher does not call attention to himself (unless it is to say that he is the least of the apostles). If he can help it he does not advertise himself or the regnant consensus of the fellowship or any realization of Christian holiness in history as having already attained the righteousness of the Kingdom. If he can help it, if the church can help it, no salvos of self-congratulation are fired in the preaching of the Gospel. Faithful preaching does not dramatize the distance between the righteous man and the unconfessed and unshriven sinner. Faithful preaching expresses the overcoming of all alienation in Jesus Christ. Here rhetoric gets its clue from the ontological situation. From the wisdom of the Creator and in the grace of the Redeemer mankind is one community. Rhetorically therefore the preacher discloses his identity with the humanity of his hearers rather than with their achievements and failures. He has not been licensed to berate his hearers for their failures nor to praise them for their virtues, as the first order of business. In their common humanity they are an offense to the righteousness of God; but God Himself has taken the steps to reconcile mankind to His righteousness. In their common humanity, and not as Jews or Barbarians or Romans, and not as Communists or chiselers or arsonists or adulterers, they have worshiped the no-gods. They have made Man the criterion, indeed the essence and the good of all creation. In their common humanity they are illusionists, the creators and the worshipers of untruth.

e. The rhetorical obligation of the preacher (and of the church as a whole) is therefore to express to his hearers what they already know about themselves. But the rhetorical mode ought not to be accusative. Forensically the preacher is neither the judge nor the prosecuting counsel nor the jury.

The preaching represented in the Acts of the Apostles is a fascinating rhetorical model for the contemplation and emulation of the faithful church (cf. 2:14-36; 3:12-26). There the hearers are reminded of what they already know. Jesus Christ walked the same earth on which they stand; and did mighty deeds the meaning of which they doubt or dispute but the factuality of which is beyond doubt or cavil; and was crucified in their presence and by their consent (extracted either in a mock plebiscite or by their retreat to the quiet suburbs—to which the faithless church is still retreating); and was buried in the same earth which one day will receive us all; and was raised from the dead. In all of which the Lordship of this same Jesus was made as full and plain as the sun overhead. Then comes the magnificent and transparent culminating rhetorical thrust: What further are you expecting? Consider rather what God now expects of you!

f. From this model we ought to learn that the preaching of the Gospel is to begin with nonargumentative and nonanalytical (in the logical sense). The preacher is not called upon to prove a theorem, e.g., that Jesus Christ was the God-Man. He is not empowered by the Holy Spirit to prove that God exists. The first and all-commanding objective in the preaching of the Gospel is to disclose the pathway into the knowledge of God and communion with Him. This is the pathway of obedience to the Kingdom. This is the pathway of obedience to the commandment of the Lord of the Kingdom. This is the pathway opened by Jesus Christ. What God has opened no other power can close.

g. As in the beginning so now the preaching of the Gospel is incomplete without that culminating rhetorical thrust: What further are you expecting? Consider rather what God expects from you!

This element of the rhetoric of the Gospel is converted by a faithless church into a great emotional pressure to make an immediate decision for Christ; as though salvation were a product which could be sold by finding the most vulnerable spot in the buyer's resistance or indifference. This is a perversion both of the message and the rhetoric of the Gospel. It creates the illusion that the fellowship of the righteous, there to receive the sinner with open arms and hearts bursting with holy joy, can be entered by crossing the magic distance between the pew in which he is sitting and the altar rail, a distance symbolizing the distance between a disordered and immoral existence and life among the high-minded consensus. It fosters the illusion that once he has crossed the line he is safe in the arms of Jesus; and from that holy haven he can look out with satisfaction faintly tinctured with compassion upon the vast mass of humanity, still rooted in sin.

From the rhetorical viewpoint alone this is terribly wrong. The sinner has been moved, when the devices fire as they are supposed to, before he has been personally addressed. He has been reduced to a movable object, he has become a target, he has been downgraded into plastic stuff. He has been neither personally addressed nor represented in this kind of preaching. The intent has been to subjugate him to irresistible psychological pressure.

Faithful declaration of the Gospel is essentially different at every level from these aberrational expressions of evangelistic zeal. When the church preaches faithfully the rhetoric itself becomes representational: there is a place and a moment in it in which every hearer can begin to recognize himself. This is what we mean by the personal address of the Gospel. The Gospel brings all mankind into the teleology of the Kingdom of God, but not as a nonpersonal undistributed abstract mass. The concrete person is addressed where he is and as he is. If in that moment and in that condition he is moved to acknowledge that he too is a sinner before the beauty of God's righteousness, the Holy Spirit is at work. But the Holy Spirit is not sheer psychological pressure. The Holy Spirit is God with man in the world to carry on the work of Jesus Christ. He is marvelously rich beyond all the powers of earth and heaven. He is most clearly known in the perfecting He brings to our awareness and acknowledgment of ourselves. When the Holy Spirit is at hand human life is exalted rather than downgraded and debased. The person experiences a miraculous access of freedom, as he is called into personal subjecthood from diffusion and abstractness. By the power of the Holy Spirit he becomes a participant rather than a target, he becomes an essence rather than a program.

Therefore in the church we can never weary of pondering and preaching the gift of the Holy Spirit in Pentecost. Whatever we may want eventually to make speculatively of supernatural infusions of one sort or another, God the Spirit communicates to the faithful a power of communication. This is a language rather than a tongue. It is a rhetoric perfectly proportioned to the truth which it is given to express. "Every man understood what was being said." God help us but there are days when we are tempted to believe that this was the last time this has happened in any church anywhere. But such despair, or cynicism, as the case may be, is itself a sign of bad faith.

h. The representation of preacher and hearer alike in the preaching of the Gospel is concrete rather than general, theoretical, or abstract. Two things are thereby illuminated:

The remarkable variety and power of aesthetic expressions of Christianity.

The fundamental role of practical theology for the preaching church.

i. This is noteworthy on several counts, not all of which are immediately pertinent. For example, the Gospel story was the preeminent narrative content of painting for centuries. Certainly a painter (at least an old-fashioned one) must have a subject. This obvious necessity is as nothing compared to the matchless power of the Gospel (indeed the Biblical) story in the imagination of Western man. It will not do to say, "What else should one expect in a Christian civilization?" So far as Western man ever felt the compulsion to be Christian in his creative expression, it was surely the power of the Story that supplied that motivation and objective. Even when the spirituality of the Middle Ages was shattered, the power of the Gospel did not wane or go underground. Renaissance masters performed their marvels with beautiful and lascivious harlots as models, thinly disguising delight in the texture and form of the flesh in mythological trappings which could not mislead any knowledgeable schoolboy. So there is Titian. But there is also Rubens, and there is Rembrandt. Each developed in his own way the most agonizing element of the Passion Story: the descent from the Cross. This is the most agonizing because now man is without Christ. He is the dismal creature who has nothing to show for his own tenderness of hope and cruelty of frustration except the dead broken Christ. This is a moment in the Gospel in which every man can find himself. Both Rubens and Rembrandt caught the terror and the sublimity of this self-discovery. Their rhetoric is no longer simply narrational. The representational (in the sense in which we are using it) now takes precedence over the storytelling art as such.

This is only a random illustration of the power of the Gospel in the creative imagination. It is drawn with but one objective in mind: to suggest that art, committed as it is to the achievement of the concrete universal, is a natural though not always a comfortable ally in the Gospel-inspired quest for self-representation. Theologically there is a reason for this endlessly creative affinity: the Incarnation. Because Jesus Christ is God and Man, every man may expect to meet his authentic representation in the Gospel; and to meet it as seized—not raped or blurred—by the judgment and redemption of God's righteousness.

I do not mean to suggest that every man is in the Gospel merely as an aesthetic (or aesthetic-ethical) type or as an abstract possibility. The faithful preaching of the Gospel draws upon a power of decision and participation built into the hearer. By the exercise of this power a mere type becomes a personal representation.

In drama we have an obvious though weak analogy. The action of the drama elicits a participative response. The beholder is not summoned to relive his private past, his idiosyncratic memory is not deliberately stirred by the dramatist and the actor. Rather, the beholder is summoned to be now, imaginatively and emotionally, something and someone being acted out on the stage. He is not encouraged to ask, "Is that the way it was?" If the dramatist and the actor have done their respective tasks well, the beholder participates in the present reality of what is being acted.

But the analogy is weak and may prove misleading. The action of the drama ought to elicit a partial response only; and precisely the response of emotion to an imaginative representation. The beholder is not supposed to be stirred to the point where he leaps across the footlights to take personal charge of Julius Caesar's revenge; or assure Romeo that Juliet is really quite all right; or warn Oedipus that he is making a dreadful mistake; or plead with Don Juan to find a nice little woman, marry her, and look forward to the presidency of the PTA as the crown of his rehabilitation. The drama is an imitation of an action. The participation of the viewer is properly aesthetic only. He is not supposed to leap into action or come to some weighty decision (unless it were to write a better play than the one he has just paid fifteen dollars to see). If the play is a good one and well performed, the emotions aroused find an adequate and proportionate expression then and there.

How different is the Gospel representation of every man! Here imitation is canceled, not that imagination might be crippled or bracketed but that it may be released to carry the hearer into the heart and power of the world revealed in the Gospel. Here the participational power embraces and masters the distance so essential to the work of art. The hearer becomes this sinner or that sinner caught up in the Gospel narrative. Now he knows who Peter is, and Judas, and Mary, and Magdalene, and Pilate, and Nicodemus, and Pilate. Here there is no problem of casting. Each of us has a singular talent for betrayal, mendacity, furtiveness, self-advocacy, and self-excuse. Thanks to the grace and truth of the Gospel each of us can come to see this singular talent exercised upon the Lamb of God. We can see its true color only when it is brought up out of the comforting shadows by the Crucified Lord. Each of us can come to see how he appears when seen from the Cross. From that perspective, from the angle of vision (the natural man would rather die than have it) which the Cross affords, no innocent bystander is anywhere in sight; and let the Mariolaters make what they will of this. Humanity altogether (rather than some noxious fraction) put Christ there. This is what men do with their freedom, it is not what God has done through an impersonal cosmic decree. Christ died for us all. God be thanked for that, because we all killed him.

This is but one dimension of the Gospel's power of concrete and universal representation. Every man is also represented there as having a singular talent for creative love. Creative love goes far beyond doing good to those who do good to us. Creative love goes beyond this mere reciprocity—nowhere more plainly displayed in contemporary culture than at Christmas—into the incredible enterprise of making good to appear out of evil. This involves doing good to those who have done evil to us—even if the evil thing they have done is no worse than their having ignored us.

Here we must say again that Jesus Christ is God's business with mankind. In Jesus Christ God tips His hand: He is everlastingly at work to maximize the good. But there is something even more precisely in the mode of personal address in this Gospel. God discloses a place for every man in this enterprise. God is infinitely more than a being favorably disposed to the presence of good in the universe. We cannot liken Him to the discreet unexceptionable private citizen who is sure that justice and mercy are of good repute. God never gives evil a minute's respite, he is never satisfied with a favorable balance. (He must be eternal because every moment of time is so precious in His sight.) He is everlastingly at work to maximize the good. For us, because for Him, this is a corporate enterprise. The Incarnation is the published articles of incorporation.

Such being the Gospel the church cannot rest until it finds the appropriate rhetorical form of representation. To be sure, the church must always preach for decision. But the decision to join something must come after the moment of truth in which the hearer has become also the seer and the feeler. This is the moment of truth in which a person knows who he is because he is being personally represented and personally addressed in the preaching of the Gospel.

II

Hopefully, the primacy of practical theology for the preaching church is evident in the foregoing. Further amplification of this thesis may be in order.

1. The concrete personal representation of the person to himself is a disclosure both of his ontological and his cultural situation. The Gospel is faithfully and authentically preached only when the preaching church knows in detail the actual situation of human beings in contemporary civilization; and sets forth what it knows in the most compelling idiom available. This does not mean that the president of the United States, the chairman of the board of General Motors, and the president of Chase Manhattan ought to replace the Three Kings in the Christmas pageant. Pageantry aside (though we should all welcome some interesting innovations here too), the church needs to give its best and most prayerful thought to the expression of the definitive ethical imperatives of the Gospel. We do not suppose that turning the other cheek, for example, can mean in our situation what it might well have meant to a Christian community in Rome or Corinth in the first century. But the differences must be interpreted in such a way that Christ's commandment, Love ye one another (an imperative rather more fundamental than the illustration of turning the other cheek), is not canceled or obscured by the particularities of our situation in history.

Preaching the commandment of Christ must, in any case, come before preaching the righteousness of the law of the Old Testament. The church falls into profound error when it invokes history, theology, or the moral structure of the cosmos as warrant for doing what the moralistic church in our civilization has done: subsume the righteousness of the Gospel under the law of Moses. The moralistic stance of the church is false to the Gospel of Christ, both rhetorically and religiously. The moralistic church preaches what it fancies to be the righteousness of Moses quite as though it had never heard Jesus Christ say, "The law and the prophets were until John . . ." (Luke 16:16). Having forgotten this the moralistic church cannot properly remember what the same Lord meant when he said, "Think not that I have come to abolish the law and the prophets" (Matt. 5:17, RSV). A large part of the tension between the faithful church and contemporary civilization, and of the inner tension of the church itself, can be attributed to the duality expressed in these two teachings of Jesus Christ. For the faithful church must interpret both things, and do so in an organic connection rather than as a riddle or paradox to be mouthed ritualistically from time to time. Contemporary civilization has a moral texture distantly related to the righteousness of the Old Testament law. The church must not set the law of Christ in a simple dialectical relationship to this moral fabric, no matter how remote its connection with the Old Testament law. Everyone knows (which of course does not make it true) that corporations cheat, lie, and steal. (These things are done on a grander scale than the private citizen can ordinarily dream of equaling.) Some corporate immoralities are legal and some are not. When they are illegal particular persons in the corporation may be punished. When this happens a great outcry will be heard in the land if the men punished are exemplary private citizens. But of course the court cannot send the whole corporation to jail—after all the stockholders are the corporation, as management ritualistically swears at the proper times. So the corporation goes to jail vicariously. This harsh treatment does not always have an adverse effect upon its business.

As corporate existence becomes more and more complex in contemporary civilization more and more people are asking, "But what then *is* stealing?" and, "Who then *is* responsible?" The complexities of organizational structure and administration seem to imply a corresponding complexity of moral judgment. The latter complexity is actually a burgeoning confusion.

In this situation many people say (and it is a reasonable guess that many more feel) that the church ought to give elementary moral instruction. And what would this be if it were not teaching the time less validity of the Ten Commandments? So what will people think when the church faithful to the Lord Jesus Christ replies that it has been sent into the world to preach the higher righteousness as its particular work in the world? Obviously the moralistic church is afraid that people will say the church has let the world down. But if the church does *not* put the claims of the higher righteousness first in its preaching, it is faithless to Jesus Christ. Faithless to him, the church would do well to petition for membership in Reform Judaism, where

Moses is properly honored as the greatest of the prophets and not as the recording secretary for the eternal moral order.

Unquestionably the church must take for granted the validity of an extant lower morality. It ought never to advertise the liquidation of that morality by the higher righteousness of the Gospel. On the other hand it ought to insist that the value of that lower morality consists entirely of the health it imparts to the social order. Here health includes peace within the borders; provisions for redressing inequities; limitations placed against the freedom and power of malefactors; access to the basic requisites of life and dignity for all of the people; and strength to resist encroachment from enemies beyond the borders.

The meaning of the distinction between the lower and the higher morality can be expressed as follows. Obviously a healthy society requires of its members a common respect for the rights of others. Society does not and cannot require the creative love so central in the higher righteousness. That does not cancel the validity of the lower morality. It does not even supplement the lower morality in order to make it impregnable to decay or perversion. Unfortunately the absence of such a relationship linking the two moralities has often lured the unwary into alienating them from each other; or into postulating a total indifference of the higher to the lower. Practical theology is intended to illuminate and if possible to overcome such errors, because in it we undertake to relate the Gospel to the actual situation of contemporary man. The Gospel includes the ethical imperatives of the higher righteousness. One does not need to accept them to have sufficient warrant for judging that cheating is wrong. One does need to be a faithful Christian to see why honesty is not a ticket to heaven. There are good men outside the church and there are dishonest men in it. Neither the good men outside nor the liars inside are safe from the judgment of the righteous God. For the good man outside may use his honesty as a wall of alienation between himself and the generality of mankind; and the liar inside may use his piety as a wall of alienation between himself and God's demands for common decency. The New Testament gives no support to the supposition that Jesus Christ found harlots and crooks more amiable companions than men of honor were; though it is equally clear that the real immorality of the former did not protect them from him; and the real virtue of the latter did not predispose them to accept his proclamation of the higher righteousness. Men of honor may be more in love with honor than with God or man; and more in love with themselves as honorable than with anything else. If so, they are in worse shape vis-à-vis the higher righteousness than harlots and crooks. It does not follow that harlotry and crookedness are prerequisites for the vision of the highest good.

2. The condition of the prevailing moral code is itself a very important concern for practical theology. In contemporary civilization the prevailing code does not offer much by way of definition of the objectives and principles of the moral life. The prevailing code is very largely concerned with things the doing of which will bring disapprobation in a peer group. The worst of such things may alienate the perpetrator from the company of good men.

Conceived in such broad terms this situation is hardly unique. What is more nearly unique is the dimming out of any sense of a code which overarches—or stands beneath—this society as a whole. There is a business code and a bourgeois outlook and a far-out set, etc. etc. Apparently one is to aim at being accepted by the group that attracts him most; and be prepared to accept the conditions of membership therein.

Surely this is an exaggeration. So far as a national life persists as such, an elemental—if not over-all—code persists in it.

The preaching church has an obligation to understand how this elementary moral code works. This obligation is easily misunderstood. We have seen that the first and preeminent of these misunderstandings comes into view in moralistic preaching. Often enough the moralistic preacher has a woefully insufficient comprehension of the plurality of operating moral codes. Perhaps this accounts for his ardor in assailing the sins of worldliness, especially irregularities of sexual behavior, the immoralities of politicians, and the evils of alcohol internally applied. He may assume that his outlook is actually shared by the people who matter most, beginning of course with Moses and Jesus and concluding with his own peer group.

In itself there is nothing disgraceful, dubious, or comic in a person railing at behavior and principle which he conceives to be wrong. It is a graceless performance when the church launches the kind of moralistic attack that can spring only from an assumption that God's demands reach no further than the prevailing code. Clear-headed people who live under that code know its limitations. It is not necessary to guess what they think of a church which recommends the prevailing code as the full requirement of God. They know that such a church makes God very small in the minds and hearts of men. It makes their hunger for a life of creativity, peace, and joy a snare and a delusion. But the moralistic preacher is not likely to hear this story from the people who live it. What can you say to a man (when you are cold sober) who is more concerned with the evils of the cocktail hour than with explosive racial tensions within spitting distance of the church—and there are people ready with the spit? What can you do for a man who recommends that megalopolis return to the moral code of a mid-nineteenth-century Ohio village, except to try to protect him from the actual world? It is probably not a groundless fear that a heavy shot of actuality would unhinge him.

The obligation of the faithful church to penetrate the existing moral codes is not an obligation also to shore up weakened and sagging institutions, as marriage and the home are widely presumed to be. Yet how often do we hear the church preaching something like this: "God wants you to be better family men and women! Mothers, give up that bridge club and make your home and family your all-in-all. Fathers, spend more time at home, spend less time at the office, the golf course, and the poker club, etc. etc." But what is the family, thus recentralized under the (mortgaged) home roof, supposed to do with this wonderful increment of together time? Go back to playing Rook, caroms, dominoes, and Authors? Replace the martini with V-8 juice, and the bourbon nightcap with Ovaltine? Is this how health is recaptured for the family unit? The potable substitutions might indeed be a healthy thing, especially for the adolescents in the family. But the objective, even in moralistic preaching, is a healthy institution. An institution is healthy when its teleology (its essence) embraces and elicits the best and strongest creative energy. If this seems excessively idealistic, we might settle for saying that an institution is healthy when it provides the foundation, if not the context, for the expression of such creativity. To revert to the case in point, the clubby family does not necessarily do this. The praying family does not necessarily do this. In American civilization at the moment the clubby family is organized around the (assumed) pleasures and needs (in that order) of the child generation. The praying family is organized by and around the parental generation. Neither pattern guarantees the health of the institution or of its constituents. Moreover the church's advocacy of either pattern as expressing the will of God may very easily overlook entirely the network of society of which the family is but a small part; and especially the economic network. Economically every member of the family, except the babe in arms, is exposed around the clock and calendar to the pressures of spiraling wants and needs. It is part of playing the American game to yield measurably to these pressures. To do so has become part of the moral code or at least part of the moral climate. So now it is almost immoral not to want a better house, a bigger car, better clothes, more labor-saving household machines, better colleges, better vacations, all for one's family. If we were to name the goods and services which have escaped the spiraling pressure we should discover that the church cannot be put on that list. The church has a standing committee on development, if it is not already committed to building bigger and better educational plants, sanctuaries, and church camps. The reason generally given is that people do not want to tie up with a cheap operation. People want the best for the service of the Lord; which of course means air conditioning, first for the church parlors, then for the sanctuary, and finally for the parsonage. And before long the churches will also need the best in electronically produced singing because congregations are rapidly losing every capacity and desire for making a joyful noise unto the Lord. Imagine how spiritual it will be to have "In the Garden" piped into the sanctuary and adjustable in volume both to fill that holy place with holy sound and to provide a sweetly solemn background for the eloquence of the pastoral prayer. It may then be necessary to turn the volume up again when the Lord's Prayer reaches "give us this day our daily bread." Bread is not really the problem.

Moralistic preaching has done nothing either to illuminate or to transform any failing or changing institution in contemporary civilization, not even the church itself. Such preaching, as we have already said, is a perversion of the Gospel; and is therefore a vain and infertile thing. In this preaching the church does not tell the Story properly. It does not preach the commandment of Jesus Christ properly. It does not adorn itself with the beauty of sound and sight which is praise of God's glory. The church which takes this posture in the world has no grounding in practical theology. Therefore its doctrine is metaphysical attitudinizing which hits a responsive chord only when it offers spiritual justification for a way of life credited as the good life by the right-thinking consensus. The consensus is the people who are already committed to that way of life. For them the church's justification of it is at best an amiable superfluity.

III

Rightly to employ the criterion of preachability requires a clear understanding of the rhetorical elements of the Gospel. Our final task in this chapter is to give a sketch of these elements.

1. *The Gospel is a story.*

The prevailing theological style calls this rhetorical element history. We have no serious objection to this semantic habit so long as it is understood what kind of history is intended. It is history in which circumstantial detail is missing now and forever. Speculative-historical theology is now and forever unhappy about this situation. Thus the heroic attempts to determine scientifically where Jesus Christ was born, upon what roads he walked, whether the Via Dolorosa was a one-way street, what became of the Cross, the location of the tomb, which fig tree was cursed, etc. to infinity.

The story, on the other hand, does very well without such circumstantial details. In the story Jesus Christ says that he has no place he can call home. This does not mean that he never slept under a roof. What roof does not matter. In the story he is thirsty and so he stops at a well to have a drink of water. What well? One with water. And he talks with people there at the well. What people? People who think they would be blessed forever and inexpressibly happy if they could have all the water they wanted; and happiest of all if they could have all the water in the world; and very religious, even unto holiness, if their well had been used by Abraham and is now off limits to unbelievers and unseemly people in general.

Some details are of course firmly pegged down in the story, for example, the day Jesus Christ died. For that he picked a day already important. (It would have been a great help to memory if Lincoln had died on July 4. As the child said, "It is so easy to remember when Jesus was born because it was on Christmas Day.") These details are pegged down by the story itself because they are essential points of the story, they display the essence, the teleology, of the story.

The rhetoric of story is very different from the rhetoric of exhortation, on the one hand, and from the rhetoric of metaphysical speculation on the other hand. The story is told to illuminate the human condition under God. The story is an exercise in representation. It is a representation in which action and personal identity form a perfect union.

Faithful preaching always includes some element of the story, something Jesus Christ said or did in which the unity of his being and his work is represented; and therefore something in which the perfection of his participation in our being and our destiny is represented.

2. *The Gospel is commandment.*

Faithful preaching always contains some element of the story of Jesus Christ because in the story the Lord gives imperatives which for faith are everlastingly binding. The quality and the sanctions of these imperatives are essential elements of the Gospel's truth. Indeed it is the imperatives that hold the line against the possibility of evaporating the story into an edifying once-upon-a-time. Accordingly the rhetoric of imperatives is an indispensable part of faithful preaching.

Even in the abstract the rhetoric of imperatives is an interesting and complex affair. For example, what am I really saying when I tell another person that he *ought* to do something? The language does not seem to create the obligation, yet the language must have some value relative to the obligation or an intelligent person would not resort to it (except after the fact as a reminder of duty neglected). Moreover the rhetoric of imperatives may very well include the display of reasons why a person ought to acknowledge such-and-such as his duty. One would suppose that the display (and perhaps analysis) of such reasons was offered to build up the motivational strength adequate for initiating performance. But certainly some of these reasonings about duty are intended to clarify understanding, as well as to provide motivational reinforcement. Thus the question, "What ought I to do?" is sometimes a shorthand version of the request, "Give me some reasons for doing X rather than Y, reasons that have to do with the relative values of X and Y." (One of the more poignant little comedies in the current life of the parish minister is often enacted at and around this point. As a result of more or less systematic indoctrination, at its worst a pious and scientifical brainwashing, the more recent alumni of theological schools are very reluctant to be directive in the office of pastoral counselor. The good pastor in this office is not judgmental, he is not directive; and as we have ourselves insisted throughout, he is not to be moralistic. So when someone puts this kind of question to him, "What ought I to do?" he knows that he must not answer it, whatever else he does or does not do. He is permitted to ask, "Well, what do *you* think you ought to do?" But it may be the case that the party of the second part already knows what he *ought* to do, and is now trying to discover whether there are reasons for doing it or for not doing it. It is possible to say whether these are good reasons without becoming authoritarian; provided, of course, that the pastor knows something about reasoning as well as about counseling.)

Some of these abstract considerations about imperative language have a bearing upon the rhetoric of the Gospel, as we shall undertake now to indicate.

a. Jesus Christ assumes that his hearers already know that a real imperative admits no exceptions and only self-excuses rather than reasons can be given for not doing one's real duty. In other words, if men know the law they are without good excuse or justification if they fail to obey it.

b. But does this apply to the higher law of the Kingdom, to the commandment of love? It is one thing to say, "Don't steal!" or, "Don't lie!" It is a very different thing to say, "Don't hate!" or, "You ought to love your neighbor." The essential difference is not that the latter demands control of feelings and the former demands observance of rules whatever one feels. The love Jesus Christ commands is a mode of action, it is a way of relating oneself to other persons. It may be that this way of acting presupposes a loving disposition with which one may or may not be blessed. Such a disposition cannot be commanded, it does not appear in response to a command. It can only be enjoyed if present and lamented if absent. But to act so as to maximize the good is much more than a matter of disposition. So to act is the commandment of love. One need not be blessed with a loving disposition in order to return good for evil. One need not be an interior saint not to meet calumny with calumny, or to restrain violence with firmness rather than by destroying the violent person either from desire for revenge or from fear for one's own safety.

c. Thus the exhortation of the Gospel to look upon any other person as a brother is a divine reminder of the ontological situation. Whether I hate this brother or not, or whether or not he hates me, we are stuck with each other. Nothing can make me like him if I cannot strike a significant quarrel with my own feelings; but we are members of the same essential community. Therefore an affirmative response to this situation makes more sense than any negation of his existence I might desire. As for the feeling component, art, rather than morality or metaphysics, makes the most of the conformability of feeling to actuality. (I have attempted to explore this in Chapter XV, below.) Morally speaking, I can at most master my feelings to the point of not being carried away by them into immoral behavior. If I behave immorally I cannot offer my states of feelings as sufficient reasons for my behavior. So again we must note that the Gospel says not one word about having pleasant feelings about your brother. It is very clear indeed on the obligation to seek his good whatever one's feelings. Granted, if one's feelings have made the interior life a jungle out of which nothing but savagery can come, one has something to confess before Almighty God, whether or not the psychiatrist hears about it. Such a dreadful condition is of course a sickness. It needs confession as well as treatment because the spirit has been an accessory to its own descent into the noisome slime of the jungle.

d. The rhetoric of the Gospel includes several kinds of reasons and arguments. Perhaps the most frequently employed is this: "Jesus Christ has done this for you; so you must now do something of the same form of value for your brother." Reduced to an abstraction this is: If such-and-such a good has been done for you, you ought to do the same thing or its equivalent to others.

The validity of such an argument (though perhaps we ought to call it a rhetorical appeal) depends very largely upon the kind of good done in the first place. If, for example, a man has saved me from drowning, I suppose that I ought to save others from drowning, if I can swim and if the occasion ever arises. But the fact that I cannot swim, or the fact that the situation has never arisen in which I could do the same thing for someone else, does not in any way release me from the obligation to do something of comparable quality of value for someone else. Someone valued my life as much as his own, even if he were hired to do what he did (say as a professional lifeguard). He may have figured that he had a better than odds-on chance to pull it off; but he could have been mistaken and lost his life in the gamble. Therefore I ought to be willing to risk my life, or risk a very considerable part of its value, for the life of another.

In the Gospel this is made a very particular imperative. Jesus Christ has died for all men. Therefore one ought to recognize the obligation to sacrifice oneself when a comparable or congruent good is at stake. This means that the death of Jesus Christ and his resurrection have created a new ethical-ontological community which lives in the power of each person to love the common good above his own life. It also means that one will never lack opportunity to make a very great sacrifice for others. Man sees to that. He sees to it with such devotion that we wonder sometimes about the slackness of Providence.

e. There is another kind of imperative evident in the rhetoric of the Gospel: If you would live in the enjoyment of God's favor, there are things you must do.

This imperative presupposes that the righteousness of God has been disclosed. There can be no doubt whatever about the splendor of life within His approving love. If there is such a doubt it must be because the righteousness of God has not yet penetrated the consciousness of the hearer of the Gospel. For his benefit therefore the story must be told and retold. What God has done for him must be enacted and represented with as much power as the preaching church can summon. This does not mean that he is to be preached at as though he were a mere objective. When the story is faithfully told—and faithful preaching is never mere monotonous repetition—the hearer is drawn into the story. It is his story which is being told, it is his destiny which is being projected.

If, even then, the hearer doubts the goodness of life within the affirming righteousness of God, theologians are likely to conclude that Satan has corrupted his heart, probably with God's consent. The nontheological truth may be that this particular hearer has a very dim and weak heart. Or it may be that he has a very different theology; and perhaps even another religion.

If the hearer is already a subscriber to another faith, the Gospel has neither metaphysical arguments to effect a metaphysical conversion, nor a rhetoric of imperatives that will stand on its own feet in independence of the knowledge of God in Jesus Christ. Philosophical theologians may have some warrant for trying their hands at such arguments. The preacher of the Gospel has no such warrant. He has no comfort from the Gospel if he ventures to convert the infidel by metaphysical assault and battery.

This situation creates many puzzles and heartaches for the church sent to preach the Gospel to civilizations which know not Christ and have instead all kinds of other religious commitments. This was exactly the situation of the church at the outset of its career in history. Why then do we suppose that the rhetoric of the church must be radically altered because the church now confronts Islam instead of Mithras? The church still has the same Jesus Christ to preach. It has the same story to enact. It has the same love to share. We begin to suspect that the puzzles and heartaches are most acute where the church finds its preaching and its life already on hand from earlier expressions of its faith. Thus it is Christian civilization which is the great problem for the preaching church, not Islamic or Buddhist or Hindu civilization. Christian civilization conceals its worship of no-gods behind the mask of Christian conventionality.

f. So the faithful church has to persuade the people of its own cultural constituency that they are already the beneficiaries of God's perfect righteousness in Jesus Christ. Thence the preacher ought to proceed with maximum clarity and momentum to the great "therefore": the commandment of Christ is fully binding upon you.

Another therefore follows hard upon this: the preaching church is the confessing church because all men in the church fall short of the glory of Christ. Christ died for all men: this is the beginning of his glory. A new mankind, a new community, has been created in his name and by his Spirit: this is the consummation of his glory in the present vision of man. But often enough to make us weep bitterly the church acts as though God had done all of this in order to make some people feel that they are better than other people. This is why Christian self-righteousness is such a terrible offense against the glory of Christ.

But Christian morbidity is also an offense against the glory of Christ. In the church we are all guilty of grievous and manifold failures of charity; but these sins do not invalidate the commandment of Christ. His commandment remains everlastingly the frame of reference in which our lives have their meaning and their purpose. So even if confession is not a happy occasion it must always be an affirmative occasion. In it we are always to remember that Christ died for us all, that we should not be prisoners forever of our guilt.

g. From time to time the preacher of the Gospel finds it necessary to adopt the rhetoric of the subjunctive contrary to fact. The preacher has sometimes to say: "It is as though you have never heard the commandment of Christ!"

Why is this ever necessary? Because the resources of imagination under the command of the spirit of disobedience are astonishingly large and varied. Take as a sample the reduction of the story of the Gospel to an amiable romantic fairy story, a once-upon-a-time infused with sentimentalities dear to the righteousness of contemporary civilization. In this perverted story the hearer cannot recognize his real being in his actual situation. He can see only an agreeably distorted image which serves as an inducement for him to become what he would like to have; whereas what he needs is a summons to become what he ought to be.

The rhetoric of the subjunctive contrary to fact is designed for those who have ears but do not hear and eyes but do not see. It is the rhetoric of God speaking in wrath through the cloud of dark unknowing, that cloud which conceals and distorts the true lineaments of the spirit from itself, that obscuration generated by the spirit of disobedience which wages war within us. The rhetoric of the subjunctive contrary to fact is the rhetoric of judgment formulated as denunciation. The Lord thunders His wrath not at the raging heathen but at the people of the Covenant in Christ who say, "God will not be really angry or for long if we appease Him with graceful little tokens of repentance."

Unquestionably the people of the church find this rhetoric very unattractive. The preacher is likely to find it correspondingly unremunerative. To omit it from the preaching of the Gospel for either reason is faithlessness. To advance theological reasons for its omission simply compounds the felony.

The trouble here is partly the fault of the church. People are used to being scolded by the preacher. They have learned that it is very easy to appease him; and it is easiest of all to appease him with sincerity. (So it is permissible, though of course not very edifying, to be a racist, if one is sincere.) How then will the people be able to understand and believe and repent when they hear that God cannot be appeased? And when they hear that they have nothing but filthiness in which to stand before His righteousnes? And when they hear that there is no saint on earth or in heaven but who trembles at the very thought of God appearing in the terrible brightness of His glory? And when they hear the word of Jesus Christ: "Woe to you who say Lord, Lord, and ignore the plain demands of the Kingdom!"?

The rhetoric of the subjunctive contrary to fact is not the rhetoric of prophecy. Nor is it the summons to prayer. It is the rhetoric of accusation; and it is valid and necessary when the Word of God accuses. Then the preacher is the spokesman for the whole church driven to its knees and crying from the depths: "Mea culpa, miserere"; O Lamb of God who takest away the sins of the whole world, have mercy upon us!

When the Holy Spirit works in this cry (a cry both of great despair and of the greatest hope) it is transformed into praise of God most high and holy. Then we remember in profoundest gratitude that part of the Gospel story in which Jesus Christ appears to the disciples at the side of the sea, unmistakably himself, unmistakably the Lord. Then Peter cries out, "Depart from me, thou holy one of God, depart from me because I am a sinful man!" There is not the least likelihood now that the Lord will let him go, there is not even the slenderest possibility that the Lord will leave him, or any who make that good confession, beached on the shores of hell. In that moment, from that encounter, Peter will learn how to live for and with the righteousness of God; and finally he will learn from it how to die for the glory of Christ's Kingdom. So in this Peter is surely the church. By grace he is —ourselves.

IV

Practical theology is the first theological step to be taken by the faithful church. The church can learn only from the Gospel of Jesus Christ what to preach. The church can learn only from the most diligent scrutiny of contemporary life how this word is to be mounted, in what idiom it will be intelligible. The living church preaches to living persons, not to the people of the past or the people of the future. In the Gospel the church has something infinitely precious to communicate. It must therefore exercise the utmost sagacity and shrewdness in determining the idiom in which to cradle this Gospel of Jesus Christ: God for man and man for God.

Concern for the right idiom is itself a part of (or a consequence of) the acknowledgment of preachability as the first criterion of theological adequacy. We have already noted that this concern is far more than the desire to be understood; but it is not less than that. In the program of practical theology the church aims at being understood as the preacher of the Gospel rather than as the spiritual exponent of cultural values. This assumes a readiness in the church to take the Gospel at its face value as the decisive criterion to be applied to its whole life and therefore to its preaching. As criterion the Gospel cannot be reduced to the simple bare question, "What did Jesus himself preach? The Gospel is a representation of the Kingdom of God. The Kingdom of God points both to a state of affairs and to a norm by which all other conditions and powers are to be assessed. To preach Jesus Christ is to preach this Kingdom; and the warrant for this identification is the New Testament itself.

To discover the preachability of a propositional rendition of the Kingdom is therefore something quite different from discovering what the congregation and the wider constituency are prepared to accept as meaningful and true. If the "strange new world" of the Kingdom is put before them as an absolute novelty they will have no handle with which to grasp it. Theologians may say, "Leave all of that to the Holy Spirit." That is a fair illustration of counsel and doctrine so bootless that it deserves to be called impractical theology. In a bit more serious vein we should say that it is a good illustration of how doctrine can be used to rationalize a human error rather than to elucidate the human situation. The earnest desire to set forth the promise and demand of the Holy Kingdom in clear tones is itself to be understood Christianly as the work of the Holy Spirit. Failure so to preach the Kingdom is profoundly humbling; but it is not necessarily the case that God is proportionately glorified.

We may conclude that preachability is a dual criterion. It is a measure of the church's faithfulness to the Gospel of the Kingdom in Jesus Christ; and it is a measure of the church's readiness to ask the world, "Are you getting the message?" Since the church is human that question may quickly and anxiously be supplemented with another: "Do you *like* the message?" And this with yet another: "Will you go on loving me even if you don't like my message?"

This deterioration of the question about being understood is the effect of anxiety. The process is familiar to us in the realm of interpersonal relationships where wanting to be understood is a form adopted by wanting to be loved. Most of us would prefer to be loved than to be understood in any situation where we could not be both, and these situations are not confined to fiction. Indeed the Gospel quite miraculously anticipates this situation. We learn from it that one cannot afford to be fully understood except when one is fully loved.

So also, at least analogically, for the church of Jesus Christ. It wants its message to be preachable because it too wants to be loved. In good faith it knows that this is an inversion of its own being for the Kingdom of God: it is already loved where being loved matters most and there it is loved absolutely—by God, Father, Son, and Holy Spirit; and therefore her message is eminently preachable. For this God, having left witnesses everywhere and in all times, now reveals the absolute inclusiveness of His love. He has come into the body of this world to claim mankind for communion with Him forever.

V

So we conclude on the thin note of a theological abstraction: what is true is alone preachable. On the basis of its faith the church proclaims a very great and very beautiful hope. Its faith is grounded on nothing more nor less than the actual love of Jesus Christ. That is the truth. "In a word, there are three things that last for ever: faith, hope, and love; but the greatest of them all is love" (I Cor. 13:13, NEB). Whoever acts and can act from the love thus envisaged and celebrated is truly of God and from God; and is therefore properly named Lord; and the same Jesus Christ is he.

PART III

APPLICATIONS

Introduction

In the following chapters I have made some trial applications of critical theological principles to the realms of art, politics, and mass culture. It would be gratifying if I could come forward here with a clearly rational justification for the selection of these areas. This I cannot do, except to say that in these areas the Christian critic often makes serious mistakes, some of which are unnecessary. Unnecessary because they proceed from confusion of principles rather than from clearly perceived inferences from principles.

So this is perhaps as good an occasion as any for observing the levels on which Christian criticism moves, where level properly signifies the quality of self-consciousness and of conceptual clarity with which the Christian responds and reacts to the cultural environment. A protest against smut in the movies is sometimes quickly and surely identifiable as a social reflex released to protect a conventional attitude toward the regnant sexual conventions. But the same protest is sometimes to be understood as an expression of loyalty to an ecclesiastical ruling. What the church says is smut *is* smut; and let us assail it *pro Christi*. Then again a movie may be indicted for smuttiness by someone who is not motivated primarily either by the social reflex or by ecclesiastical loyalty—though he might feel friendly toward both—but rather is concerned to expose a meretricious aesthetic performance for what it really is. The critic in the last instance holds a watching brief for something which I am afraid we shall have to call truth.

Christian critics of course operate on all such levels. I have no objection to that, needless to say; but I hope it will be reasonably clear in these applications that the critical obligation to truth cannot safely be scanted. Actually it is, I believe, the first, the fundamental, obligation of the Christian critic.

CHAPTER XV

Christian Criticism of Art

I

Every major realm of culture presents its peculiar problems to the Christian critic; and though nothing is to be gained by an attempt to establish a comparative rating of the problems as we go from realm to realm, we have also to confess that the faces art turns toward the Christian critic are formidable and seductive in the highest degree. The formidable aspect is the judgment of art upon the efforts of religious people to make art the footstool of religion; a judgment sometimes rendered in the interests of the integrity and freedom of art, and sometimes in the interest of art gathered into a cultic community competing with the church. But art has a seductive face as well, luring unseasoned and ecstasy-hungry spirits into belief that art and religion are ultimately one; or, even better, that the really rich and viable heart of religion is the aesthetic component. Naturally the seductions do not end here. Art is forever tempting the Christian critic into easy identification of its meanings, and especially into meanings compatible with Christian attitudes and teachings. Yielding to these temptations rarely if ever produces insight richly significant for either art or religion.

On the other hand so large, powerful, and rich a realm as art cannot be spared invasion. The spirit is one, finally; and all it produces and effects bears the stamp of this unity; and whatever it produces and effects has vital interconnection with all else in its domain. Hence apprehension of reality and expression of truth in art (and as art) cannot be ignored by people seeking to know and to serve God. However straight, direct, and pure the Gospel is, as received immediately from the hand of God, artistry, if not art, appears in its communication between mortal persons. Moreover the servants of the Word of God have every need to cognize the world in all its essential lineaments and to ask of it, *Quo vadis?* in all sympathy and patience. Yes, in *all* sympathy, as one who inquires after his own health and his own prospects, for this is in fact how the case stands. We have seen how thoroughly even the nonparticipating Christian is enmeshed in the world, and how some of its ventures and its treasure are dear to his heart for reasons only remotely and fantastically religious. Even if every trace of self-love had been miraculously expunged from our hearts, we would yet be constrained to love the world and thus to glory in its beauty and to celebrate its goodness in creation. Even if we had become creatures so diminished in power of love as to be able now merely to emulate God's love from afar—simulate, rather—that, even so, were our duty, hard and bitter as it would truly be then, since to simulate a love not felt must be the harshest fate we can endure while yet in this world.

But now I may have suggested that the Christian has need for art as though his faith in every important feature and detail were already made up and he lacked but an adequate and appropriate instrumentality to put it across, an instrumentality related externally and extrinsically, at best, to the Gospel itself. The truth is, the Gospel is not apprehended until it is expressed. Thus greatly appropriateness and adequacy of expression matter. The Word of God is not known for what it is until it is spoken again and responsively. It begins its life in us when it is heard, but it comes to majesty, beauty, and power only when it is given forth in the world and is thus readied to return to God burdened with fruit. Too, the responsive expression of the Word of God, since the Word is from God and is God, cannot be a sterile repetition, a lifeless and mechanical playback, as though God the All-Wise had ordered, "Repeat after me, please," out of distrust either for the fidelity of reproduction or for the ability of his own Word to endure distortion *ad infinitum.* In other, perhaps more positive, terms, the Word of God is a command to create through significant speech, it is an order to form a world rather than to inherit one in simple filial piety.

The artist is, of course, a true child of God because he is a world former, a world creator. Around and within is a world antecedently formed; but that world is not his end product, it is his point of origin, a point from which he moves outward at the velocity of light. He may love it dearly as a child his parent; but he loves the world of his formation more and better, as a parent his child, as a man the woman of all women.

So the truth which the artist is under divine commission to show forth is a truth strangely applicable to two worlds. His showing forth reveals the given world in a singular way: he turns it inside out. Thus some aspects of the extant world come into vision for the first time in their proper quality. This may well be an appalling experience, so much and so keenly that we accuse the truthteller of malice and cruelty. But he has another world truthfully to represent, a creature of his free imagination, penetrable only by imagination. If he has great powers and if he brings these powers into fulfillment through great discipline, the extant world is interfused with the world of his free creation; so that the old world, with many protests and with much looking back, is transformed. Thus our world is not at all well understood as a world through which Michelangelo, Shakespeare, and Mozart have come and gone; it is the world created by them and by our response to their arts. To be sure, men can get by without knowing or caring a thing, even the least thing, about such mighty spirits, but they are not living wholly in the real world, they are living somewhere in the dense thicket of the world, where the horny feet of many beasts of burden have made roads that allow their lords and masters to travel in the best of circles under the illusion of getting somewhere.

The proper interest of the Christian in the arts, then, is hardly to be thought of as finding a way to preach the Gospel. It is an interest in coming really to know the Gospel that God has delivered for the salvation of the world. Christ is for us merely extant, rather than existent, until we give him out to the world in Michelangelo's *Pietà* or in "Jesu, Joy of Man's Desiring," and in every other significant form which the spirit sees fit to release into the world. It is not enough that he should be the eternally extant word: he must also be the living idiom.

II

What is art? A great deal of high-order reflection has gone into answering this question over the centuries, to the net effect, it must surely seem to the dabbler, of infrangible puzzlement and confusion. It were presumption to claim (or perhaps even secretly to hope) to show a way through the puzzlements; but I may be allowed to make a modest contribution to the confusion. "One step enough for me, O Lord."

I believe that the larger number of things needful to our present purpose can be served by focusing attention upon the artistic employment of symbols, as a way of burying under some show of reasonable management the immensely imposing question, What is art? The reason for this concentration upon symbol is very simple. *The mental substance of art is symbol.* An artist has a medium—words, metal, movements, etc.—but he has also a material of the mind, the symbol. What is a symbol? I take the question to mean: what are we saying of the Cross, e.g., when we say it is *the* Christian symbol? The Cross "represents" or "stands for" something beyond itself; it expresses a reality greater than itself. That reality is condensed, contracted, and concreted in the Cross. Moreover other ways of expressing that reality are weaker and poorer and thinner than the symbol. Say, i.e., that the Cross symbolizes self-sacrifice, or the perfection of God's love; or say that the Cross stands for the whole earthly career of Jesus Christ and the solicitude of heaven for human wretchedness and wickedness. The translations of the symbol are weaker, they are less vivid, more abstract, general, lifeless, for anybody who is able to grasp a living reality through it and beyond it. The translations, in other words, are further from that reality than the symbol is. A living symbol participates in the reality it expresses or reveals. To say it participates is to say that it is of a piece with that reality, it arises out of that reality in a singular spontaneity, force, and naturalness.

These general descriptions of symbol are reasonably correct, I believe, for symbol everywhere, i.e., in all of the major realms of discourse and expression, science, religion, politics, etc. Each of the realms imposes its own peculiar restrictions upon symbol, to be sure, but these do not change its essence. In general the life of the symbol becomes harder the more severely it is circumscribed, that is, the more tightly it is hauled to highly conventionalized sign language, as in science; but even there purely conventional signs may be seized upon by the symbolizing spirit for its own richer purposes, e.g., $E = mc^2$. But symbols in art is our principal theme, to which we now turn.

III

The artist uses symbols to show forth reality not otherwise discoverable. Through symbol he makes reality in the mode and order of feeling. He instructs us, as no one else can, how we are to feel about things, i.e., how these things can be more fully and more rightly grasped in proportional feeling, than otherwise.

For this purpose, then, it is not a matter of any great importance whether the artist creates new symbols, since the novelty he would elicit is a matter of power and nuance of feeling. If symbol, old or new, can be infused with novel feeling, the artist has so far attained his purpose.

We cannot infer from this, however, that the high calling of the artist is merely to stimulate feeling. Proportional feeling is the objective of aesthetic creativity. The phrase suggests an astonishing notion: there are wrong ways to feel things! Ordinarily we suppose that a feeling is a kind of natural occurrence insusceptible of rational direction and immune to questions of rightness and wrongness. Who has not said of himself, "I can't help feeling the way I do"? The implication is clear: I *can* (or ought to) control my actions but my feelings obey some law other than conscience and intelligence. But these commonsense convictions are called into profound question by art. To feel rightly about something is at least as important as acting correctly in relation to it. Moreover one can learn to feel about something as one ought. For this, the first step is learning to grasp what that thing really is, since the concern of art is with proportional feeling. Thus the artist undertakes to purify and strengthen the power of perception. How does he do this, characteristically? By the discipline of symbols, which I take to be the following:

A symbol requires to be grasped by a mental (spiritual) act able to ride over and get behind the immediacies of existence; and, in fact, nothing can serve as symbol which does not require so to be grasped. (A life completely bound, if any human life is, to the immediacies has no capacity for symbols.)

Given the symbol the mental act which grasps it also grasps (perceives) the reality it expresses. In this activity the mind is not struggling to master the object according to a plan inspired by subjective desires and preferences. The intent is to know; and for this purpose the mind is prepared—is eager, actually—to let the object speak for itself and for reality beyond itself as symbol mysteriously gathered into itself as symbol.

The distinctive aspect of the aesthetic use of symbol is the concentration upon feeling as the key to adequate perception of reality. The mental act of perception is a seeing through feeling. A seeing, we must insist, in order to distinguish aesthetic sensibility from the merely reactive order of experience. Thus the artist presents a symbol; and he presents it in a setting and atmosphere most appropriate to the right apprehension of the meaning of the symbol.

The symbols of art are therefore to be understood as of one piece with reality and not as surrogates for reality appointed to their task by human need and ingenuity.

Granted this, we have to determine whether the artist is best understood as being a channel through which reality symbolizes or expresses itself; or is the real creator of symbol, a maker thus (as it were) of reality.

The phrase "reality symbolizing and expressing itself" seems hopelessly rhetorical and sententious. Nevertheless it expresses a recognizable viewpoint held by a rich variety of thinkers throughout the history of reflection on art and religion. The word mysteriously and invincibly given the prophet in ancient Israel is one form of the view. Another form is the notion that symbols arise spontaneously and irresistibly from the depths of the unconscious (individual or collective), and are responsive only to rearrangement, enjoyment, and neglect, none of which is creative in the strongest sense of that word.

On the other hand new symbols do appear, in the arts and elsewhere, coming forth from the fertile minds of particular persons who knowingly fashioned them. No single mind can generate all the meaning that will accrue to a symbol, but he can nevertheless produce the symbol. The poet takes hold of something lying close to hand in the natural world, and fashions it into a symbol—"Ode to a Nightingale"; or he contemplates an artifact resurrected from the tomb of classical antiquity, and contracts and condenses a whole world of meaning into a luminous symbol—"Ode on a Grecian Urn." Is this not creation? Not in the weightiest theological sense but nonetheless in a significant sense?

Seeing things from this viewpoint we should say that even the symbolic attainments of the past ordinarily supposed to be inalterable by any potency of present or future time, retain an essential plasticity.

Having lain fallow for generations (or perhaps not so much fallow as unregarded by any but conventional usage), a symbol may then be seized by a powerful imagination and given new life; not just revivified, but taken up into new patterns and thus given new meaning.

Such minds may be the chosen instruments of a purpose and power not their own, they may be so many channels and vessels of God's grace. If so, then God attunes Himself altogether marvelously to the humble state of His children, for these greatly fecund spirits stride the earth and sound the depths and penetrate the airy sky as lords and masters; and their freedom and potency are not mere posturings.

So, then, if we wish to take comfort in the resonance of the phrase "reality expresses itself in symbol," or otherwise say that the artist (the real artist) is also (along with prophet and saint) subject of divine inspiration, we may do so justifiably only if we say also that the reality which expresses itself includes human spirits, and that the inspiring God finds no embarrassment in habituating Himself to the human spirit as to the manner born.

I am more than half-minded to take up with such a view, partly because it has important bearing on the thorny question of the truth of art. On this question the people of the church have a distressing habit of coming down on the wrong side. Their predisposition is to treat art as decoration and entertainment and thus to deny it particular and unique access to reality. So understood art can be used, and is, to illustrate truths already received and expressed. I do not mean to say seriously that people of the church are wholeheartedly committed to using art for purely didactic and propagandistic purposes. The actual situation is rather worse than that. Conventional feelings rather than conventional beliefs are the churchly truth to which art in the church must answer. Conventional feelings are sentimentalities; and the church life in our world is richly endowed with them. So we should little wonder, when one senses and understands the terror aroused in the men of this age by the novelties of the age of science, that even a little of the tried-and-true, of the safely familiar, of the clichéd tradition, is so much balm of Gilead, and tender lullaby, when the devil rides outside.

Whatever the cause, the restriction and reduction of art to the merely expressive augurs ill for church and world. Somehow the spirit must win through again to the substance of reality, or die of malnutrition, if not suicide. What prospects are there, then, of our being again guided by the shadows of art into the substance of reality?

Before attempting to answer this question, I want briefly to examine the phrase used above, "merely expressive." Expression is commonly distinguished from description and explanation: and is presumed to be a response (at best) or a reaction (at least) to something already existing either in the inner or the outer world. As to description, if we use science as a model, we see that it is delineation of something in terms of its structure, its relations, and its behavior. As such description presupposes as *fait accompli*: an anatomizing of that something, a scrutiny of it governed by the need to isolate the essential features of that thing from the nonessential features, not necessarily with a view to describing it in terms of the essential features only, but in any case with a view to placing essential and nonessential in the right relation to each other. So the description of an entity proceeds on the basis of an externality of relationship between the object of the description and the describing mind. Only an object can be described, only something which can be lifted out of, or arrested in, the flux of experience, by the act of attention. The flux itself cannot be described, it can only be expressed.

Explanation relates an existent (present) entity to antecedent entities; or (and this is a different mode of explanation) it subsumes the existent entity under principles which are independent of flux, even though flux is their concern. Thus, to say that y is an effect of x may mean that from x, y is derived, and that y is subsequent to x; so that no x, no y; but also, given y, now no x (at least not x-as-cause-of-y; x may survive but has gone on to other things, or has become y). On the other hand we sometimes mean, in speaking of causal explanation, to call attention to the order of the cosmos (or to the orderliness of reason); so that "x causes y" is simply an epitome (epitomization) of reality; and hence it is not the case that no x, no y; but it is the case that "no x causes y" (or, for any y, an x), then no cosmos, no reason. This seems very like saying, "We will play the game our way, or not at all"; and this would be a sound program if we did not know any other rules, or had not heard of any other game.

Explanation in the second mode moves dangerously near expression, because it appears to be a matter of reading things one way rather than another, depending, in the choice, upon one sort of human interest rather than upon another.

But should we be at all happy with the view of expression as an interest-controlled response to something already existing in either the inner or the outer world? Hardly. Expression is the participative life of spirit, it is that life of spirit in which the person is one with the creativities of reality.

In the participative life the subject-object relation is transformed; and, specifically, the externality of that relation is overcome. Objects become objectives; and interests become intentions.

Objects of course remain. The poet speaks of familiar things. These familiar things have a life of their own; but they are no longer free to be themselves in an unknown external world; they become objectives, i.e., they are suffused with potentiality, they are not but are everlastingly committed (for the moment) to becoming. The nightingale will not become a turkey buzzard, in the poetic envisagement, but he will become what the authentic enjoyment of the poem makes him. The nightingale is, thus, a potentiality never to be exhausted in fact or as fact. He is all the occasions in which the poem is read with imaginative understanding—when, that is, the poem expresses our grasp upon reality, and not just Keats's.

That is why we say that in the participative life interest becomes intention. The poem is created by a particular person and thus arises out of his interests, his desires, his needs, his experience, etc. Through the alchemy of the creative imagination (more properly expressed as the work of the Holy Spirit) idiosyncrasy of inner life becomes singularity of meaning. The poet is in the poem. How true! But we can recover the poet from the poem, not the poem from the poet. The poem is a projectile: it started from one point (the densely matted undergrowth, the psychic matrix, of a man); and wings its flight into the heart of things; and we can chart its course only by traveling with it, each starting in turn from his own psychic matrix, and rising thence, on the power of the poet's winged words and forged spearhead of symbol, into the light of actuality; from which vantage point alone the realm of potentiality can be seen adequately.

So we have said that only expression is able to cope with flux, with the actual movement and quality of that reality. Coping with flux is participation in it. It is of course human participation that we are speaking of; and human in the most potent and luminous mode, i.e., creativity. In the other modes of human life flux is seen as an enemy of unspeakable malignance, worse than death, or a power in league with death. We know other modes, too, in which flux is hailed and embraced as alone lovable because it brings all things to naught. Nihilism can be understood quite as well as love of flux as love of nullity—better understood, actually, as the former once we see clearly that love of nullity is mere rhetoric. The phrase is an improper way of designating a love which esteems and covets nothing so much as it esteems itself. Thus we commonly speak of being in love with love (ascribing this roseate condition to adolescence or other less amiable forms of immaturity) and mean by it a state of feeling desired for its own sake and only accidentally relating the subject to any object other than himself.

But love is also (and preeminently) an activity. Hence love of flux (the highest or purest form of nihilism) is activity which is self-sustaining and self-rewarding only so long as it does not have to be fixed upon some perduring being. Related in depth to such being, by being in love therewith, one must be patient as well as agent, one must suffer the other being because one cannot be the other and remain oneself. Thus the wonderful thing about flux: it attacks substantial being so vehemently that release from being patient is promised, and one is left with prospect of endless self-action; and after that (or in addition to that), nothing.

Creativity is the most humanly significant response to flux; and what we have called nihilism is a corruption of it. The creative response to flux is at once a participation in it and a rebuke (though a loving rebuke) to it. First, participation: creativity is a spontaneous uprush of feeling, appetite, and image, a moment and mood in which self-activity seems aboriginal, fecund, and irresistible. But creativity is also a rebuke to flux: by its power something is made or done which has (actually or putatively) perdurability. The artist is not at all satisfied to entertain novel feelings. The novelty of the feeling is so far entertained only by the introspective review of his private experience. As artist he wants to express his feelings by making something itself novel in some measure, which will forever stand as the work of his hands. Thus the "mortal puts on immortality, the corruptible puts on incorruptibility." Not that the artist shall live forever (his piety may or may not embrace such a dogma) in his own right; but the work participates in immortality. "A thing of beauty is a joy for ever."

How can we miss or minimize the pathos of truth in this faith, this hope, this love, of the artist? The work of his hands is very fragile, whether it is the Parthenon or a Sèvres porcelain, the Ninth Symphony or *Hamlet*. Yet he has made it, in the depths of love, to endure forever! Is he not therefore a fool, a fool tenderly to be loved but a fool withal? He is not a fool, unless to be truly wise is but a mode of folly; in which case folly is beggared by wisdom rather than contrariwise. Better than we he knows how fragile are the flowers he has created. Paint fades, metal rusts, stone erodes; but, even worse, men forget or misconstrue or prostitute; and the thing of beauty, into whose creating a man poured the blood of his heart, wastes away and is no more; and a blind, witless, and brutal world is immeasurably the poorer. Where is immortality in this performance? At the heart of it, of course. The process, not the product, participates in immortality because the process is creativity and creativity is the inner life (the mind, the heart, the soul) of flux. Thus we must have courage of truth to say that the artist walks in the footprints of the Almighty Creator. Flux is his life, the unremitting ceaseless tide that sweeps old worlds away and casts up new ones. Nothing that God makes itself remains forever, and He makes things of quality somewhat stouter than we can ever dream of making: galaxies, and electrons, and crystals, and snowflakes, and gray geese flying into the golden dawn. But none is licensed to remain itself forever. Each one dies, giving place to others. Interminably inexhaustibly flows the life of God.

And God loves everything that takes form and place in His life. ("Almighty God, who hatest nothing Thou hast made"). So also the artist, whose power to make something good is his love, or, at any rate, whose power would be weak and futile without love. Indeed, the volatile energy of creation *is* love, rather than biological exuberance.

Thus the pathos of art is one with its greatness. Of all human achievement it is the most insubstantial; and of all it is the most substantial. A thing of mutable light-and-shadow, it gives body to the truth of being. A thing of illusion, howbeit ever so disciplined by cunning design, it reflects reality with a faithfulness calculated to terrify all other illusions but none so wholly as that illusion called self-deceit.

Being the stuff of illusion art can hardly master (or even seriously covet) that kind of truth the philosophers call correspondence and others call imitation or representation. Likeness may be found in a work of art but it is disciplined by a larger intention, i.e., faithfulness to the demands of creativity. Creativity, we have argued, is the reality to which a work of art must be faithful beyond any other aspect, agent, or mode of being. All else in the work of art is illusion, is proposed, achieved, and gathered in as illusion, where art speaks in its own voice for itself. Under the spell of a rich performance in the theater one is nearly persuaded that the enacted person and the actor are one and the same; nearly, but not actually, because we knew all along that Miss Judith Anderson is not Lady Macbeth; but we knew all along that under the command of genius we are the subjects of authentic emotions in which the reality of Lady Macbeth is apprehended. The actress is not like Lady Macbeth, so far as we know. The illusion is proposed and accepted as such. The reality revealed in the theatrical illusion is a moral structure in which moral agents come to tragic end. If no such moral structure exists, the drama is interesting merely as an expression of a bygone day's error in supposing it did exist; but such art is invested with real life only when such errors are shown to be momentous, whatever the state of moral philosophy.

The illusions of art are able, as hardly anything else is, to expose the illusory character of the normal, the conventional world. I believe that the suspicions of art and artist so deeply engrained in plain, sensible people in our age express clearly an anxiety for the conventional world. They might well be suspicious. That world has little chance of survival when it is compelled to see itself in the mirror of authentic art. Unconventional behavior on the artist's part is certainly not the real threat—at that point he may be an unconscionable poseur and is therefore not to be taken more seriously than the Babbitts he so loudly scorns (and to whose Foundation he is likely to appeal for a traveling fellowship). The real threat is authentic art itself because in it we see what love of truth can lead to as transformation and transvaluation of the given world. Such consequences are not necessarily self-consciously striven for by the artist. He may want only to say what he sees for himself and to say it without the slightest touch of prophetic fury. But since he already sees through the mists and false fronts of the conventional world into possibilities and portents of a far richer world, and this at the tip of his tongue or almost within the grasp of his fingers, he is not likely to be taken in by the normal world; so, no matter how amiable his personal relationships to those who are taken in, he in his freedom, his freshness, his boldness, and his courage is a threat to them. In return they (the gulls of the normal world) try to buy him and to ignore him and to throttle him—whichever course seems most likely to succeed; and from time to time they enjoy some modest little triumphs of this order; but all to no avail since none of these triumphs is anything more than an accident, a pure freak of luck, and since every such mean success lashes some other artist into a tearing prophetic fury, ready (if, in fact, not already dedicated) to pull the whole temple of Mammon down upon the Philistines.

Self-deceit (the master and model lie) is the illusion that suffers most cruelly in the mirror or art. The lies a person tells himself are the deadliest enemy of truth in the inward parts: they keep a man from knowing who he is and what he may do and ought to do. Self-lies bottle up a person's creative powers. Bottled up, choked back, dampered down, those powers smolder darkly until they go out altogether or erupt in lurid and seemingly pointless violence—many a murder has been a work of art.

A work of art requires, both for its making and its gathering-in, a release of creativity from its unnatural inner oppressors. The antecedent formation of the person is therefore called into judgment by the work of art. He brings (necessarily) to the work a particular bundle of interests, feelings, ideas, and convictions; and the key to the whole formation is his image of himself. If this image is blurred or distorted, he may be able to render an accurate account of the objects which interest him but he will tell the truth about nothing; or, as spectator, he may be able to match up the art object with what he takes to be the corresponding object in nature, but here again this process does not have anything to do with the truth in the work of art. In both cases the meaning of the work is absorbed into an antecedent reality: the psychic constitution of artist or spectator. (This absorption is what we mean, ordinarily, when we speak of making sense of a work of art.) Something like this must occur if the work is to speak to us. But we must ask how it is possible for the work to speak in its full and proper voice if we are ordained to hear it only in our own? If it but remind us of ourselves, conscious and unconscious, how can the work of art ever (would to God it were oftener!) strike us as being an incursion of truth from the great world beyond? Not to have been so struck is simply never to have breathed the air of art's realm; and I am unable to believe (even if I wanted to) that anyone is naturally that dim, dull, and rudely incomplete.

The answer to the above questions is that art is achieved only when transformation of antecedent psychic patterns does occur. Pattern, yes, not feeling alone: the world, as a consequence of the artistic achievement, not only feels different (richer, more alive, more luminous), it has a different shape, it is a different world. Therefore art is a potent threat to persons who have a very heavy commitment to the received world, the world of convention and conventionality. For such victims of illusion art can be loved only in one of its prostitute forms, e.g., entertainment. The prostitute does not intend to change things; she wants only to live off their present shape and quality. So entertainment proposes no fundamental changes in the received and standard world.

Of course the prostitute may become high-minded, putting on not only the air of virtue but (incomparably more ruinous) the reality as well. She may take to handing out religious tracts, she may exhort to the pursuit of sound morals, where lately she solicited a rather different response. In other words, entertainment may be converted to propaganda. When the conversion is accomplished all sorts of untoward consequences may be expected, of which perhaps the most distressing is a selling out of one package of doctrine and restocking with a very different line. Writers who in one age use their art to promulgate the gospel of socialism may, in another age, drop that gospel as though it were of Satan's invention, and take up with the gospel of N.A.M. Of course, a man has a right to a change of mind and heart. He has also a right, of a kind, to sell his skills to the highest (not to be confused with the loudest) bidder.

Thus only when the prostitute has become a pious exhorter is she in any considerable danger of becoming subversive. Before that she is immoral but not in a way likely to gull any but the purest clods. I mean that impure entertainment is a source of corruption at most for a weak and silly private citizen here and there; while false doctrine can destroy the body politic and never stoop to vile language or lewd image in the process.

Our argument has been that the truth of art is entirely bound up with the grounding of creativity in the real world rather than in the unreality of the subjective world. That is why we have railed at entertainment and decoration as synonyms and substitutes for art. The artist does not embellish a reality already extant. He creates the world anew, afresh; not, of course, in its entirety (where does it exist, in entirety, save in the past?), but in the novelty of form given to its inner life.

If the argument is sound, we may expect to encounter difficulties from religion, to which we now turn.

IV

Is art itself religious?

Is art the most significant barometer of the spirit of a cultural epoch?

Is it possible for the church to use art for its own purposes without destroying (prostituting) art (artist)?

What does the man of faith look for in art (works of art)?

Many other questions could be asked under the heading of the Religious Aspects of Art, but the four specified are a fair sample, and we shall settle for them.

1. Is art itself religious?

Art is religious only if any effort to deal with reality is religious. (Artists and their followers may develop cults around art objects, or around the artistic life, but that is another matter.) So generous a view of religion is not likely to provide a differential interpretation of any aspect of experience or to validate (or invalidate) any hope of glory; and, moreover, it fails notably to say anything about art.

Art is most intimately engaged with the deep emotions. (I suppose that it is from this fact people sometimes leap to a view of art itself as religious.) But the artist characteristically touches the emotional depths in a way, and with an implement, peculiar to his vocation.

How, then, does the artist touch the "deep springs of the soul"? I mean, with what intent, to what purpose? as well as, in what attitude of his own? He moves into the deep places in the interest of exposing them to perception as pure objects. It is his intention that we should not only feel certain things but also perceive the feeling, have it, scrutinize it (as it were), in all its intensity, and in all its uniqueness. He fails if his performance prompts us to say, "Ah, how like a woman!"—for there we are in a mood to make abstractions and abstract comparisons. It is the feeling in its pure state, not in its densely matted relationships, that he is after.

This means that the artist (and thereafter art) has, when he is about his real business, a curious independence from the normal anxieties to convert the world into something consummable, i.e., to something that can be used for something else. He celebrates the world, he does not redeem it for some ulterior purpose.

The implement with which the artist touches the emotions is the image. He bestows upon the image a kind of attention not easily to be confused with a religious interest: it has an intrinsic value for the artist. Whether or not he is able to make an image march to some metaphysical tune, he is well content to make of it what he can, i.e., to draw out of it what it contains by placing it in an arbitrary frame of reference.

I am saying that the artist as such sits loose to any external purpose, to any aim or value that does not grow out of the images which command his attention. Art (so far as it is an affair of artists) is therefore not identical with religious interests; and may, in fact, collide with some religious interests.

2. This view may well be put out of countenance by a widely current conviction: art is the most significant barometer of the spirit of a culture. In other words, if you really want to know the inside story of a people at any given time, go to their artists. I believe this view is a significant (i.e., interesting and influential) error.

The merit of the view is the underscoring it provides for the truth-telling aspect of art. Art is a serious enterprise; and it is serious about the truth. But this does not mean that the truth is either described or controlled by the spirit of the culture. For what is that spirit? Do we suppose that an all-comprehensive mental process expresses itself in the culture and otherwise in the life of a society? I do not believe that such an absolute exists, either as a mind or as a "collective unconscious." A cultural epoch has dominant styles, and a prevailing climate of opinion, and a consensus of sensibility, and, perhaps, a standard ideology or normative theology; but the epoch has also important recessive characteristics, centers of dissidence, and prophetic nuclei (both atavistic and futuristic). Artists seem to find living space in either case, in either camp. But, if this is so, what artists reveal the real spirit of the epoch? Those who win, the ones who create a style, who impose reform (or change, at least) upon sensibility, who infuse, thus, novelty into the web of the common life. The victors do not show what the culture contained implicitly. They show forth what creative persons can do.

I do not at all mean to minimize the power of the artist to plumb the depths of the human spirit. If he is endowed with sensitivity far beyond the ordinary he is certain to feel acutely the afflictions men must endure; and these afflictions include those common to men in all ages and peculiar to a particular epoch. Thereafter he may express with terrible and beautiful vividness what is going on in his age, so far as it has a registration in feeling. But his mode of action goes beyond expressing something already existent or actual. He touches the point of weightiest traffic between the spirit and realities beyond the spirit.

I conclude that the art of an age is indeed a profoundly important barometer of the condition of the spirit; but little is to be gained either by setting up a rating chart of significance in order to ascertain what is the most important expression of an age, or by supposing that art is only such a barometer.

3. It is possible for the church to use art for churchly purposes without prostituting or subverting art only if churchly purposes are not already a corruption of the spirit. Where the spirit is already cheated out of freedom and spontaneity, and where it has surrendered truth and now feeds on the husks of illusion, art can be used to seal the tomb by prostituting itself to the purposes of propaganda, decoration, and entertainment. But contrariwise, the essential churchly purpose (to preach the Gospel to slaves, the halt, and the blind) demands rather than merely allows the artistic modes of action. Hence, where the creating love of God in Christ is apprehended, art will shortly appear. Extant art will be appropriated, and the appropriation will transform the material thus taken up; but new art will also be forthcoming. The new creation, in turn, will eventually become ossified (it will become a tradition). In time creative spirits, miraculously open to the power of the living God, will throw off bondage to the tradition, and forge a new word. This new word may become the wellspring of a new world.

When the church comes round to serving men rather than God, it undertakes to superintend the course of history. Then art (as well as everything else) comes under ecclesiastical control. Ecclesiastical imperialism is no better for art (and for the entirety of human value) than any other tyranny. Since this fact is understood by artists at least as well as by any other breed, we are entitled to a solid optimism for the future greatness of art.

4. The man of faith looks for the things in art which are properly there; or, if they are wanting, he has just cause for labeling that work bad. If he is properly rooted and grounded in faith, he does not look

to art either for sound doctrine or for confirmation of merely conventional attitudes toward anything of importance. The man of good faith looks to see in a work of art beauty first and foremost and then truth. If he is of good faith he will be edified by his discovery of both. He will be depressed, and upon occasion outraged, by the absence of either from the artistic performance. Art which fails thus to enrich him, however grievously painful the discipline required in order to grasp it rightly, is not worthy of the name.

Correlatively, when the man of faith is induced to look for other things in the work of art, he is guilty, from his side, of a failure as ruinous for the spirit as the failure of the artist.

The present age is marked by failure on both sides. Which has sinned more, or earlier, does not really matter. Repentance matters; and a desire to amend our ways and walk henceforth in godly rectitude and joy.

CHAPTER XVI

Christian Criticism of Politics

I

No area in our culture is more formidable for Christian interpretation than politics. People in the churches commonly approach the criticism of politics with a truly remarkable body of folklore images and illusions. Politicians have heard so much nonsense about their world, solemnly and piously uttered in the church, that they are strongly predisposed to believe that the churches are incapable of anything better. The result? The churchman examines the politician to see how he fits into the folklore scheme. The politician examines the churchman to see what moralistic clichés are the best pitch for the religious audience.

Our first task is to examine some of the elements of folklore about politics. For this purpose I introduce you to Jonathan Wesley Sunday III. He is a figment of the imagination, with both feet firmly planted in the real world.

JWS is a walking and reasonably animated bundle of illusions concerning politics. As best we can we must sort these out and place them in some kind of intelligible order. So here is a Syllabus of Illusions, compiled from JWS's observations on politics:

1. A person is more likely to be morally compromised, if not ruined, in politics than anywhere else. This is because:
2. Politics is more susceptible to serious and even fatal corruption than any other realm of human life.
3. Accordingly, good men will not run for political office or otherwise become embroiled in politics except under extraordinary circumstances. From this it follows that:

4. Politicians are people who probably would not be able to hold down an honest and/or difficult job—because of either mental or moral defects. So:

5. The people never have a really good choice at the polls—they can choose only the lesser of two evils, whether of policies or persons. Accordingly:

6. The people deserve far better than they get; but they cannot do anything about it, because:

7. Political parties, machines, and politicians are all fundamentally alike. Hence it is pretty clear that:

8. The church ought never to get mixed up with politics. Anyway:

9. Religion should occupy itself with spiritual things, and let practical realistic men take care of a pretty messy world (politics), for which, if they are practical enough, they will get paid far more than they are worth anyway. Still:

10. It is a Christian duty to vote. But the thing to remember is:

11. Always vote for the best man, that is, the most moral candidate. The chances are he will be a Republican who has been persuaded to run for office to clean up the mess.

JWS seems never to remember whether he was an Independent or a registered Republican. When told that he was on the Republican registration lists, he came clean and gave these reasons for his having identified himself with that party:

a. His family has always been Republican. When pressed on this point he admitted that an uncle on his mother's side had gone West around the turn of the century and had gotten mixed up with La Follette in Wisconsin.

b. Almost all Protestants are Republican. So far as he knows the only exceptions are seminary professors and misfits who are still rebelling against their fathers. When pressed he admitted that these two categories were not necessarily mutually exclusive.

c. The Republican Party is somehow less political than the Democratic Party. Republicans seem to put ethics first and power last.

d. Republicans seem to have a stronger conviction about keeping religion out of politics.

It is not necessary to indicate whether JWS is a clergyman or a layman. He could be either. He manages without great difficulty to be both.

The power producing and controlling these illusions is self-righteousness. Self-ignorance is here, too, but the most powerful determining force is self-righteousness. Consider (1), (2), and (3). JWS believes that he is not as other men are—he is purer than politicians. Moreover he is self-justified in tending to private affairs and private virtues. It is hard to be righteous in politics, perhaps impossible. But God demands righteousness. So JWS avoids involvement in politics. What could be simpler and more conclusive? And what could be more unreal, as an attitude toward the world and toward oneself? How has JWS managed to talk himself around into believing that politics is more susceptible to moral corruption than business, for instance? Does he really believe that Boss Tweed is a deeper-dyed rascal than Jay Gould or Dan Drew? Frank Hague than Charley Insull? Tom Pendergast than Harry Sinclair?

JWS does so believe; but he did not have to talk himself into believing that politics has the highest immorality factor of all realms of human existence. This was the air he first breathed; and now his spiritual lungs would find a draught of other air very painful indeed. He has always believed, without examination or patient scrutiny, that the business world is a realm of transhuman law, where forces are perfectly counterbalanced, until and unless they are upset by human tinkering; and the politicians along with reformers and dreamers are the prime tinkerers. On the other hand politics is the chaotic world of human impulse and power drive, a world in which law is man-made, adventitious, and partisan. The politician covets power and he resists violently every effort to curb this power, once he has it. The businessman seeks a just profit. If left to itself and its benevolent Providence, the market will automatically check such incidental abuse as may occur from time to time.

JWS claims the sanction of heaven itself for his irresponsibility and for the illusions which feed it. He is not willing to say that he cannot live on the salary a public servant gets. He will not admit that he is afraid to expose himself to public criticism—which will be his meat and drink day and night if he ventures into politics. He has got to claim the immunity and the privilege of the higher, the private, righteousness.

Somehow a way must be made through the defenses protecting JWS's unrealities. Perhaps simple, practical questions will be better for this purpose than the ponderous ethical-theological heavy artillery so long in use both by JWS and his critics. Suppose we ask whether the political world is not far more sensitive to moral judgment than JWS's business world? The county treasurer is legally and morally censured and punished for embezzling public funds. His political future is not too bright, even if he has connections. But investment officers in banks, insurance companies, etc., with vastly greater economic power in their hands than all the county treasurers in America, are not so exposed to public view and censure. Who is the villain if the dubious investment policies of an insurance company force penury upon aged and infirm? The economic order as a whole, JWS will say. Who can say where poor judgment leaves off and dishonesty sets in, in so complex a world? Are policies proposed in the interests of employees? directors? stockholders? policyholders? the public at large? No matter what the questions, there are ready-made answers in JWS's arsenal: You are hired to further the company's interests, and so you do your job and you look for moral justification if and when it seems to be necessary. Furthermore, when moral justification does seem necessary, it is easy to find: things just did not work out as we thought they would. In general the system works very well, but now and then somebody does get hurt—and that is life for you. Still and all, it is the best system, and to call too much attention to its occasional and incidental misfires, would seriously damage morale. Thus, the fault is not in our judgment or in our integrity but in our finiteness.

Is JWS capable of seeing that the machinery of politics is more sensitive to moral judgment than the social mechanisms with which he is more familiar? What does he make of the severe difficulties experienced by many business leaders in making the shift from their world to public life? They complain of the inefficiency in policy-making—in politics you have to argue with people in order to get things done. And, of all things, you have to clear yourself of having a special interest in the welfare of the company in which you own a great deal of stock! In business self-interest is the vaunted law. In politics you look out for public interest, or go through every motion of doing so.

In the political world the zone of accountability is more sharply defined than in many other areas of social existence; and swift settlement of claims is the rule, not the exception. Moreover the devices of self-justification are much more transparent and much less encumbered with theological trappings. Thus, our sinful friend, the defalcating county treasurer, does not and cannot fall back upon a theological justification for his didos. Charged with his offense he may say that his enemies are out to get him, that he has been framed, etc., but he does not argue that the public good is really best served by every man energetically pursuing the course for which he is indicted. He does not justify himself by saying that outside forces are illicitly interfering with the smooth and otherwise benign operations of the laws of his world. The law found him with his hand in the till, and that is that. He may curse his fate in being caught, but he does not accuse the system of having put more temptation in his way than finiteness can endure.

JWS reacts very strongly to the assertion that the machinery of politics is moral. So would you, if you had his ideas about morality. Look at items (3) and (6) in the Syllabus of Errors. Who is his good man? Somebody not previously involved in politics, certainly, thus a person all fresh and pure from business or one of the professions. (Not from the academic world, since those people are either radical or visionary or both.) The good man is a highly respectable private citizen, a family man, church member, sturdy participant in nonpolitical civic organizations, etc. Ideally, the good man should have no great need for the money which public office will bring him, since he will then be above corruption and can prove that duty alone has precipitated him into the public arena, at considerable sacrifice of personal interests, etc.

In the good man, then, we have a person of integrity, efficiency, honesty, and honor, so well-stocked with all the domestic virtues that he can be wholly trusted to love, honor, and obey the public good.

How shall we prepare JWS for the painful shock of reality? Domestic virtue, however fine and estimable in its own backyard, does not automatically equip a person with courage and wisdom requisite for effective public service. Domestic vice, for that matter, does not automatically destroy high qualifications for public service. The political world can not afford to put a premium upon libertinage. Neither can it afford to overcapitalize chastity and sobriety at the expense of courage and wisdom in public life.

JWS's good man is fatally weak at the decisive points: he is confused as to what the public good is, and he does not know how consideration of the public good takes shape as public policy. Public good is larger and more complex than anything his middle-class Protestant domestic instincts would prepare him to suppose. Public policy cannot be made on the assumption that government is a cross between family and a business enterprise. As a politician he cannot arrive at important decisions as he does as an (ideal) head of a family, by consulting each of his constituents. Neither can he sell his decisions as he sold his product in the market. The enjoyment of his product was presented as a desirable end-state, but his public policies are not end-states to be enjoyed in themselves. Policy decisions lead to further policy decisions, some of which will be radically different from their direct antecedents in the time-line. This is a fundamental difference. Peace cannot be merchandised as a Cadillac can. You do not expect a man, once he has bought his Cad, to say "Now what?" The thing is to be enjoyed in itself, until you have a new model to sell him. But with peace? Peace is not an end-state, achievable by persuading people to act on certain impulses and whims in abstraction from everything else. Peace is a temporary condition of a dynamic international society. No matter how powerful the nation which loves and seeks peace, other powers at any given time also have some high trumps, and they can be counted on to play them as they, not we, see fit. Therefore, to try to persuade people that peace can be had by simply pulling the right party lever, and by adopting a simple policy once and for all, is enormously dangerous and profoundly immoral nonsense. Sooner or later the salesmen of peace will have to tell the public why peace policies have brought the world to the brink of war. Public policy, let us say it again and again, cannot be sold. It can only be proposed to the judgment of the persons affected by it. To the judgment, not to the impulses.

It is clear that JWS believes that he should vote for persons rather than for policies and parties. If he is right public office is a bonus, a moral achievement award, to be handed to upright citizens, almost all of whom are in one party, the less political one.

It is something to marvel at, this ability of JWS to be so wrong on such important things. Public office, particularly where policy is made and interpreted, belongs to those who give public indication that they know what the issues are in the administration of that office and how policy is made and effectuated through that office. Policy and party thereby come strongly and clearly into the very middle of the picture. A candidate who is unwilling or unable to give public indication of such fitness is not a man to be trusted with that office, no matter how high his rating on the Boy Scout achievement scale, no matter how eloquent the endorsements given him by churchmen. If he is really as nonpolitical as JWS hopes he is, then he is radically incapable of coping with the realities of the world in which he seeks a position of influence. He is a boyish St. George sent out with a quiver of moralistic clichés and pious illusions to slay a nonexistent dragon. This encounter is strictly no contest, but the only thing he will save out of it will be his cast-iron virginity.

II

What are the realities of the political world so sadly distorted in the folklore of JWS? Power, Justice, Compromise, Involvement, and Transcendence.

Power is the lifeblood of politics, the very substance of politics. Political power is the consent of the people to the exercise of authority in the interests of justice and peace. Every government rests upon consent. Some governments forcibly extract consent from some subjects, but no government has ever tried to extract consent from all its subjects in this way. Even a rigidly monolithic satrapy endures only so long as it has the consent of the governed, and the more rigid and arbitrary its controls, the more violent and inclusive the violence of the eruption which destroys it. So long as the masses are convinced that they are cattle, their consent may be taken for granted. But dark the day for the Lords and Masters when the cattle rise on their hind legs and scream for the blood of the oppressors!

Consent is the essence of political power. What the people consent to is the direction of the affairs of state by persons self-declared as ready and willing so to serve. Thus power is invested in the politician. Anyone is a politician who accepts responsibility for certain affairs of the state, whether he is a member of a Democratic town committee, an alderman, ward heeler, or president of the United States.

A politician has only such power as is granted by formal and informal arrangement. This is true as well for parties and for government in general. Without power, they are nothing. Power is their life. And what is this but to confess that all politics is power politics? To be a human being is to seek power. But better to say, all men seek the proper occasions in which to release or expend power for specific ends and aims. Power in the abstract is a mere concept, a puff of dreamstuff. Power can be enjoyed only so far as it is expended for a specific goal. The choice of one goal rather than another is a moral decision because, in making it, a person asks himself which is better, which is more truly good.

To seek power as an end in itself would be a profoundly meaningless endeavor. No evidence exists that politicians are any more prone to this folly than other people. But folklore cares little for evidence. A politician, to JWS, is a man who wants power, not a job, not fame, prestige, money, etc., but only power. A politician in JWS's book, would rather pull the strings behind the scenes than be president. Well, if you had to be McKinley to be president, it would be better to be Mark Hanna instead, or if you had to be Warren G. Harding to be president, it would be better to be Henry Cabot Lodge instead.

We note in passing that Machiavelli ought not to be confused with this folklore image of the power politician. Machiavelli was a man with an incorruptible dream, the unification of all Italy. To this end he was prepared to subordinate all policies and to devote all power. Power for power's sake has very little to do with his program or his political philosophy.

In politics, as elsewhere in the human world, power is real only so far as it is found in relation to goals and norms which serve to discipline, since they are what the power is for. If the end is peace or prosperity, certain policies have to be worked out and adhered to, through thick and thin. Intelligence must be employed to discover and design the instrumentalities proper to the realization of the end. The arts of persuasion must be diligently exploited to convince the people that the policies and instrumentalities proposed will really accomplish the desired end.

There are other disciplines for power. One of these is interestedness. Interestedness is a fundamental reality of human social existence. A person is his interests; and his interests are what he pursues at the behest of his desires under the ordering of his will. His interests are his stake in society. Society is a dynamic synthesis of human interests.

The persons under the authority of a government obviously have an interest in the behavior of that government. Not all of these people take an interest in this, if taking an interest means directly and carefully inspecting it. Infants and idiots have their interests in the state, but they do not examine its operations. They have appetites for which provision must be made by society because these individuals are incapable of successfully ordering their own appetites toward fulfillment. Society assumes responsibility for them even though they are not able to engage in reciprocating responsibility. In advanced, and particularly in Christian, civilizations, the proper care for such individuals is an important obligation of the state. In these societies people take an interest in what happens to infants and idiots.

It should be clear how interestedness functions as a discipline upon political power. The politician's business is everybody's business is one way of putting it. The politician is a deputy of society is another way.

Interestedness is socially effective and productive as a discipline for power only when it is properly organized and directed. How is this done? The special interest brethren have one approach. They try to persuade people that one interest is the key to health, security, prosperity, and godliness. Their objective is a passionate and arbitrary fixation upon certain desires and/or fears, so that people will come to respond automatically whenever the proper cue is given them. Some people obligingly cooperate with these programs, but not all the people; and not even the same people all of the time. Quite a lot of people do not like to be treated as if they were jukeboxes. They do not like to be had by every slick dealer who comes down the pike. The smart operators sooner or later find out that these prejudices in people are important. Then the high-pressure gospel-ranter salesman loses his contract, and the sincere, folksy, reasonable salesman takes over his job. The change in selling styles does not necessarily argue a change of heart in the men who call the turns. It means only that they are capable of learning, perhaps very slowly and painfully, what kind of creature the human being is. Certainly they dream of changing him; but for the time being they have to reckon with the given facts.

Are there other ways of organizing interestedness in order to make it effective and productive as a discipline for power? Certainly, though they lack the muzzle velocity of the contemporary campaign to mold public opinion. The announcement and elucidation of a public policy is one such effort to organize interestedness. This is where the political party comes into the picture, for these are important functions of the party.

It is a commonplace that the political party is an accident, so far as the founding fathers are concerned. Yet in a deeper sense the party is not an accident, it is a highly appropriate development of American political wisdom. It is, one might say, an entirely legitimate and natural implication of the rudimentary principles of the American political system. The government of a democratic people cannot cope adequately and justly with all of the group interests and private interests of its people when these are presented directly and nakedly. The heat is too great, and the conflicts too deep and many. A prior reconciliation and synthesis of these interests is greatly to be desired. Such is the function of the party in the American system. The party seeks power on the grounds that its pattern and program of interest synthesis are most appropriate and just for the people as a whole. Accordingly, the most effective criticism of a party at any given time is the charge that it is dominated by the interests of the few, and that these few are already overprivileged and overpowerful. The sense of the charge is clear: that party is no longer a synthesis of conflicting interests, it is a weapon used against the interests of the people as a whole, against the public good, and against the health of the body politic. It means that the internal life of that party is no longer democratic but autocratic or oligarchic and therefore that it is not a fit administrator of a democratic society. We are not concerned, perhaps fortunately, with the question whether in American history so weighty a charge has ever been wholly justified. Our point is that it is in principle the severest stricture of all. It is therefore not to be used wantonly, for when so ultimate a judgment is demanded, who may hope to escape unscathed?

The responsibility of a party, whether in power or out, is to the people, not to itself. In power the party must justify its use of same; out of power, the party must justify its resistance to the policies of the administration. Even when not in the saddle a party has a grant of power—the consent of its members and supporters; and in a national party this is a considerable matter. Moreover the party out of power is still a partner in the government. A regime or administration is effective just so long as it is able to make some working arrangements with the other party; it has to engage continuously in give-and-take, at least at the national level. And this situation is an important discipline in the use of power. Where the misuse of power is likely to meet with instant reproof, no matter how partisan and self-serving the spirit of that check, men do well to exercise power with discretion and with every show of judiciousness, not because they ride a blind and violently unpredictable monster, but precisely because other men are always at hand to prove that they can govern human beings more wisely and justly.

The goal of the party is consensus. Structurally the party is a synthesis of diverse interests. Dynamically it is a consensus-creating activity.

Consensus is not to be confused with consent. Consensus is assent or agreement to policy as right and just, where consent is investiture of authority to act for and in the place of those granting this authority. A party seeks consensus in order to exercise the power of the state. Consensus is necessary for consent in a double way. The party cannot achieve power without consensus, and it cannot exercise power without consensus. Within the party consensus functions as agreement on primary aims. Beyond the party consensus functions as acceptance of the policies presented by the party as the program for which power is to be exercised. This does not mean that a concretely clear line can be drawn between these two functions covered by the term consensus. It means that party discipline and unity are involved in the one instance; and in the other, effectuation of policy for the people at large.

Consensus is intimately involved with moral judgment. So much so that consensus might well be thought of as being fundamentally moral, that is, occupied with the determination of the public good. Thus consensus is not to be identified with public opinion solicited and organized for the accomplishing of the private aims of power-seeking individuals. For consensus it is not so important to find out what people feel about things as it is to elicit their active support of certain policies. They will want to feel right about those policies but more than right feeling is necessary: they must decide for them, they must do whatever is necessary to grant authority to see that those policies are realized. Thus consensus requires of each person solicited by and for it that he make a moral judgment, that he consult interests other than his own, that he envisage and weigh consequences, and that he publicly register his decision by choosing the party whose policies seem to him more largely right and just.

Since consensus draws so heavily upon moral judgment we must ask, What is the prime aim of such judgment? The answer is justice. Policies and performance alike are examined to see whether and how far they are just. The substance of politics is power. The prime objective and aim of the administration of this power is justice. Let us carefully note that the power and inclusiveness of this aim are in nothing diminished by even the most painfully rigorous and realistic depiction of the selfishness and meanness of persons delegated to administer it. In the public domain of politics performance is everything and private motivation and character are nothing. Structures and forces are available in that world to discipline power and the drive for power. These structures are man-made and are made for man; and whatever the religious thinness and theological naïveté of this person or that person among the founding fathers, these structures are quite as able to withstand today's egomaniacs as yesterday's. Neither has the primordial force, the indestructible power of the people, abated a measurable degree. Convince the people that the claims of justice are being violated in high or low place, and somebody will be made to pay.

What then is justice? Justice is a social order's most comprehensive policy whereby every constituent member of that society is to get, without fear or favor, what is owing him purely and simply as a constituent member of that society. Justice is thus the absolute minimum requirement of a social order and of society as such. That is why every society is and must be sensitive to attacks upon this absolute minimum. When this sensitivity atrophies that society is the party of the first part to its own dissolution and destruction. It has failed to honor the contract and thus ceases to exist as a living order.

Political structures have no other reason for existence save the administration of this policy we call justice. These structures are determined by specific decisions as to what justice requires. Since the requirements of justice are not uniform and static, the operations of these structures cannot be uniform and mechanical.

The requirements of justice are neither uniform nor static because the human world is a dynamic affair. The truth of this is well illustrated in our national economy. At what point shall we seek to stabilize national income and national production? No persuasive or cogent answer is forthcoming; and there are far more important questions, such as, What ought we to do to assure just distribution of economic power in an expanding economy? No one supposes that "just" means "equal." Justice is a matter of the absolute minimum: every member of this society ought to have so much economic power as simply and purely being a member of this society entails. No one, for instance, needs to starve. Where food abounds everybody has the right to eat enough to stay alive and healthy; and let us have no wretched cant such as, "Let him only eat who rightly works." Our society at any given moment does not need and cannot use everybody's work, and unless we can find nonproductive work for more and more people, nonproductive work which is also meaningful and fulfilling, we will be the wealthiest and the most abysmally neurotic company of unemployed the world has ever seen.

Again, no one in our country needs to face major illness or old age without adequate financial security. The problem is political:

What administrative structures can be worked out, and how can an effective consensus be elicited, in the party and in the country, to put these structures into effective operation? Relative to such problems the character of the individual candidate falls into proper balance. An individual's idealistic inclinations are politically worthless unless he can make clear how his moral earnestness can be translated into effective policy, that is, how he thinks party machinery can be consecrated to this end. Your good man who preaches on Layman's Sunday his fiery sermon about people huddled like cattle in the slums of Big City, and who yet runs with a political party which tries to hamstring every venture called public housing, is no longer innocently stupid. He is immorally stupid.

The business of the state is justice, relative to all internal affairs, as its business in all external affairs is the integrity and the security of the commonwealth in the family of nations. The business of the party is policy for which it seeks consensus and power. The business of the party worker is to perfect the discipline of the party as it reaches into the local situation. The business of the candidate is to interpret the policies, and therewith the fundamental principles of his party, relative to the peculiar problems of the local situation.

Policies are judged by the standards of possibility and honesty. These norms have to do with policy and public performance, not with private character and motivation.

The possibility of a policy is frequently called its practicality. A policy is practical if it meets the needs for which it is projected, and if there is a reasonable and calculable chance of its working. A policy is practical so far as resources are available to match the needs for which the policy is designed, and so far as they can be so exploited without serious dislocation in society. A policy is workable so far as an effective consensus can be elicited and organized in its support.

It can be seen that practicality, as a norm of political behavior, calls for the absorbed attention to the real potentialities and needs of real human beings confronted by singular circumstances. As such practicality runs far beyond consideration of mere utility or of mere ideals. The practical politician is a man doing his best to figure out ways and means for making the structures of his realm do what they are supposed to do. His ideal is a party producing policies and leadership which will evoke popular support and thus attain power. Therefore he is naturally interested in getting out the vote. Without votes a party, or a candidate for that matter, is mere talk, sociability, and ambition.

With votes a party (and this holds for a candidate) has power and responsibility; it has, that is, the life which is intended for it.

Honesty is the other norm. An honest party is one which tries to carry out the policies upon which it campaigned for power. An honest party is one which is willing to expose to public inspection its true policies and principles. An honest party is one which lets the world in on its calculation of internal strength—this is important, too, since elegant and just programs may be presented in a fundamentally dishonest way, that is, as things which other people are more deeply interested in having done than the effective leadership of the party making these proposals. A dishonest party, accordingly, says to the people: "We have not reached a real and productive consensus, we are retrogressive, vindictive, and immature; but we believe that enjoyment of power will make us united, alert to changing times, and amicable toward opposition. Give us then the opportunity to learn responsibility at public expense." It is true: a small man may learn greatness from being thrust into great occasions. But a party is not a man. If it cannot govern itself it cannot plead for a chance to govern the nation. Its plea is devoid of honesty. A party weak and ambiguous in policy and therefore in consensus is a party ripe for conquest by crass opportunists or by fanatical ideologies.

Honesty and practicality are norms that do not allow precise or exact measurements. This is true of all the norms of moral judgment. Yet we must make judgments using such norms and we must stand by such judgments until clear evidence of significant error in them is forthcoming. Such evidence must be concrete. It must be found in the actual performance, for policies cannot be adequately judged in advance as to their practicality and their honesty. Their goodness and badness can be seen only in what they succeed and fail in actually accomplishing. A policy is good if it realizes a measure of justice. It is bad so far as it fails in this and so perpetuates, perhaps consolidates and reinforces, an injustice. A policy that aggrandizes a few at the expense of the many is bad, whatever theological and ethical justification is submitted in its defense. A policy that pretends thus to serve the best interests of all is a horrid monument of duplicity and irresponsibility.

Decisions concerning policies are therefore moral decisions, since policies are proposals to serve the public good in one way rather than in another and are, accordingly, concrete programs for realizing justice. Without justice the social order dissolves into the constraints of unenlightened habit and the regimen of arbitrary force.

Policies are to be distinguished from ambitions. Ambition is a prime motivation in politics, as elsewhere. Motivation, though indispensable to any human action, is but part of the richly complex story of human action, whether the motivation is dishonorable or sublime. An equally important factor is intention, the aim-in-sight, the envisaged objective, of a course of action. Politicians seek power, but this is a truism about motivation. We need to know something more, namely, what do they mean to do with this power, to what ends will it be exercised, what aims will control its operations? The norms of moral judgment pertain to intention, as these are crystallized into policies and statable principles, rather than to motivation. A politician says that he will do thus and so if he is elected. Certainly he says these things because he wants people to vote for him. He may also believe that these things ought to be done whether he is elected or not. In any case we do not and cannot *know* what his motivations are, and we ought therefore to stay within the limits of what can be known. We can more profitably ask such questions as these: Ought those things be done? Can they be done? Can he do them? etc. Our problem is the quality of the intentions, not the (presumptive) quality of his inner life in proposing them. God alone can fairly know and judge the inner man. As mortal and finite we must remain with the practicalities and the honesties of public profession and public performance.

Now we come to the realities of the political world so crookedly apprehended in the folklore image of *compromise*. The folklore gives us the poignant picture of the purest and loftiest idealism having to come to terms with the sordid and brutal facts of political life: deals, unspeakable transactions in smoke-filled rooms, etc. Until, finally, our good man either prostitutes his idealism, in order to stay in office, or hurls his impassioned and unanswerable challenge into the teeth of the bosses, takes his licking in the next election, and rides his Rosinante back to his vice-presidency of the bank.

This gorgeously grotesque image is dear to the hearts of Christian (and other) idealists. Whatever the denominational stripe the idealist thinks of ideals as realizable goals, realizable but for the obduracy of man, of which, in his opinion, none is more obdurate than the politician. If only the politicians could be cleared away, we might have a good chance to realize a truly and perfectly just society.

But ideals are not objects for realization. Realizables are projects of imagination submitted to intellect for inspection and to will for enactment. Realizables are possibilities. Ideals are directives for action, not states or ends to be attained. Thus justice is not something to be realized, it is a commandment, an aim, a directive to be honored and obeyed. You cannot do justice, you can only do justly. A social order can be said to be just only in the sense that its structures and arrangements clearly reflect an effectively synthesized multiform intent to treat all its *bona fide* members alike, that is, without respect to individual and birthright differences. Being of unequal native powers and subject to the dispositions of chance, people will attain unequal place, name, and comfort in any society; but no person is to go without name, place, or creature comfort because of any accident of birth or vicissitude of external circumstance. Having said this we cannot go on to say that the degree of justice attained in a given society at a given time can be determined by measuring that society against an ideal standard, eternal and absolute, reposing in heaven. To look to heaven for a vision of justice would be absurd: the accomplishments of earth cannot be measured by the glory of heaven. Heaven is heaven and earth is earth. If God had designed that on earth we should merely imitate and reflect Heaven, He would have thought very poorly of earth. But this He did not, since He found it good. Wherefore our proper veneration of Heaven is to be sought in loving earth for what it is and may become, and not in hating it because it is not Heaven.

The way of justice is hard enough, in all conscience, without the gratuitous complications thereof presented by idealism. It is a hard, hard way because justice is for man and by man. No serene heavenly illumination banishes the shadows and exposes the pitfalls. No external power intervenes to make people just, or to make it easier for them to be just. Each must battle his own ignorance as well as the immense deposits of ignorance in the structures of society. Each must contend with his own will, as well as with the massive obduracy and hardness of heart of social structures. We know of course that institutions do not really have wills and minds over and beyond the wills and minds of living persons. The point in so speaking is but to remind ourselves that only a very small segment of our dealings with others is on a face-to-face basis and that the great bulk of all human interrelationships is impersonal. Society is in effect a complex system of conventionalized impersonal gestures.

Personal, impersonal: neither is to bear the full onus of guilt for injustice; and neither is to be cleared of fatal complicity. The corruptions of self-interest and of anxiety do not respect the difference.

To the question, Why is it so terribly easy for a person to slip into policies of self-aggrandizement? no answer can be given. The venerable theological answers are so many invocations of mystery and so many calls to piety and humility. They are not rational solutions to what must surely seem one of the most irrational of all facts: Why do people, knowing the good, yet do evil, of conscious design and set purpose?

We must say as much for the question, Why does normal anticipation of the future become anxiety? Surely in our rational and more serene moments we know that time and chance have each two faces, one of which is friendly. Yet we try to arrest time and to control the chance factor; and since inwardly we know that each of these programs is a losing game, we are also inwardly at war with ourselves; and we extend this warfare to include the whole world and Almighty God. If God is not on the side of our values and if He will not guarantee that our social order shall endure forever, then we will fight Him.

Thus all that is required to have a hard and often unprofitable time with the demands of justice is to be human. The demonic temptation to ignore the demands is no stranger in our hearts. The biggest weakness in Satan's policy here, however, is that it won't work. So Satan, like the idealist, is unable to cope with the realities.

The reality so dimly and crookedly seen in compromise is, then, this: in human encounters somebody loses and somebody gains. I mean, of course, in encounters where power is at stake. Put negatively, justice requires of a society that it cut its losses so far as possible. No one should lose what he really needs in order to be a human being. But this inevitably means that society will play take-away with somebody or other—with the people who have amassed more than they need. It isn't enough simply to produce new wealth to even things up a bit. Society has to take steps to prevent some people from getting control of a disproportionate amount of the new wealth. The steps taken are political.

Compromise has hold of another fact. Politics itself is essentially give-and-take. In politics no one, and no cause, always wins, however just the politics contended for. But the truth is yet grimmer. Clean-cut victory, reduction of the opposition to humble and penitent acquiescence in the policies of the winner, is hard to come by. Moreover you may win many a battle in politics and lose the war. You may win at such a cost that another such victory will ruin you altogether. I do not mean financial cost, but moral, moral cost and moral ruination. Specifically, honesty of the party and integrity of the person, for honesty (as discussed above) is to the party as integrity is to the person. A person has integrity when he is an effective and rational unity of loyalties. A person is without integrity when his loyalties slide and shift and waltz in time with external pressures and his own ambitions. To win therefore at the cost of honesty and integrity is to invite moral ruination and to prepare the ground for subsequent political disaster.

Honesty and integrity are never cheaply or easily acquired. In this they are like justice, as they should be because they are proper dimensions of justice. How, for instance, does a man know whether the order of his loyalties is healthy? How can he tell for sure that he is giving enough weight to a loyalty? A man can play sorry tricks with himself on these things, he can delude and bamboozle himself heroically. He can lie and lie and then begin to wonder whether his lies may not have some truth in them.

Another aspect of the political reality misunderstood as compromise requires attention here. A politician may find himself falling into a kind of double-standard morality in his relations with people. Men in political life have in general a fair notion of the realities of that life. The people at large do not have that knowledge and seem generally allergic to it. The people have accepted the folklore of American politics as gospel truth. They believe it and they want to believe it. So many politicians have compromised themselves, telling the people what they want to hear, but knowing how unrealistic and untrue the home-consumption version is. Even though they may not believe that their deals are immoral or wrongheaded, they know that the people do not believe in deals. People like to believe that you go in and fight for what is purely right; and if you win, there is another victory for righteousness; and if you lose, well, eventually right overcomes wrong, etc. But the politician wants to stay in business. He knows that you don't win all the time and that you never win a clean-cut and ultimate victory and that some of your wins were phony and that some of your losses were victories for justice. Whatever his theories his practice is proof that no man and no party has a monopoly on justice and truth. The parties need each other, the country needs them both. But how can he say these things to the people? Either way the decision is painful. It would be very good for the people to hear about the realities from the men most intimately involved with them, but as it is, the facts are largely left to the smartboys who write the syndicated columns, who are always happy to spread the inside story, the hot scoop, for good hard coin of the realm. Needless to say the inside story is frequently a small pinch of fact lost in a mass of rumor, innuendo, pontification, and old-fashioned trumpeting.

There is no easy resolution of this problem. It is the problem of the divided mind. One part of the mind seeks truth as the natural and life-sustaining element of the human spirit. The other part clings to illusions and fictions and lies, for the heart has made very heavy investments in these unrealities. Since the politician is not a heaven-sent savior, nor an impassioned prophet, he can hardly preach redemption to the divided mind, healing, reconciliation, and peace. But there is a better and more conclusive reason for his silence on this great problem: he has an inner knowledge of the pathos of the divided mind. This sickness has not spared him. But he is in a superior situation in one respect at least: he *knows* that he is sick; and he knows that the sickness does not excuse him, or anybody else, from the painful responsibilities of committed action in the political realm.

And so to the realities of *involvement* and *transcendence*.

Involvement is both a fact and a desirable possibility. Every member of society is involved with the political order, willy-nilly. Whether he votes or not he consents to the order and to the administration of its power. Even though he is a passive citizen other people are making decisions for him, and these decisions profoundly affect his everyday existence.

Involvement is also a desirable possibility, namely, conscious and committed action in the political world. Only thereby does a member of society come into his full rights as a citizen; and only thereby does a citizen assume his rightful and just responsibility.

The basic human fact thus exhibited in involvement is the interrelationship and interdependence of persons as persons. It is guaranteed in the plan of creation that we shall bear one another's burdens, whether we want to or not. We have the power, though not the right, to slough off much of this burden, to slough it off so far as deliberate inattention to responsibility avails for that purpose. We do not have the power to get rid of all of it, unless we wish to destroy ourselves as the way out from under. To be human is to live with others and for others, for meaningful personal existence is something shared, not something owned.

Relative to politics (to use terms discussed earlier) the individual must give his consent to a government, and he ought to take an interest in it, not a merely detached interest but a practical one. But we know what the realities are. The average citizen is a sleeping beauty; whether somnolent by nature or simply self-narcotized is a nice question. Aroused by powerful stimulants on state occasions—aroused but not awakened—he promptly retires to his hibernal snores, through which he continues to eat and to talk. All in all, a remarkable creature.

Somnolence and detachment are important sins against the health of the political order. They are sins producing false and dishonest satisfactions: self-righteousness for not being like the dirty machine politicians, for instance, pride for having had no part in the nominations of office-seekers and thus for being free only to choose on Election Day the lesser of two evils.

Involvement demands that we turn resolutely away from such gratifications and face the burdens to be borne for the common good. Involvement demands that we take firm hold of the existing political structures, not to reconstitute them in accordance with some idealistic pattern, but to extract from them a fuller and more just realization of their possibilities. We have no right to look for ideal working conditions, light, air, congenial companions, long vacations. prompt and liberal awards for meritorious service, as we try to face our responsibilities. The time is now, the place is where we are, our rendezvous is with the people at hand, no better than we are and no worse, and none of us better than we ought to be.

Transcendence is, of all the realities we have been examining, the most easily sold short in our age, both by practical and by spiritual people. This situation presents a grave and troubling question: How, without transcendence, can serious and true moral judgments be made.

The sense of the question lies in the meaning of transcendence, as do certain elements of an answer to the question.

Relative to B, A is transcendent if it enjoys some important independence of B, if, that is, some significant measure of A's power and meaning come either from A itself or from some other being than B. In the terms of moral judgment, a person transcends his social situation if the good he seeks in it has a wider, deeper, and higher meaning and power than anything he actually finds realized and complete in his social situation. Notice that we say a person transcends. It is not enough for the sought good to transcend a given embodiment, for the good as concept enjoys as much independence of any concrete situation as any other concept does.

In other words, moral judgment as such appeals to a world and reality much larger and richer than the present social situation. Men judge the good as human, not as Connecticut or American or white, etc. good. Such judgments are meaningful just so far as persons are members of a world, let us say a community, which embraces this society but is also infinitely richer, since it is all-inclusive. That community of all creation is the ultimate object of his loyalty, and the concrete norm of all moral judgment. Thus injustice is wrong, not because it goes against the grain of the American conscience, but because it goes against the grain of creation. American conscience is not an ultimate criterion, since in our more lucid moments we know that the American conscience at any given moment might be discoverably wrong.

Is the ultimate object of human loyalty merely ideal, or is it actuality? There's the question. If merely ideal, our transcendence is simply mental, indeed, imaginary. If actual, do we simply love ourselves in being loyal to the community of mankind, or are we loving the transcendently perfect God? The actual course and pattern of our moral judgments holds the key to this puzzle, for in those judgments we are working everywhere with the conviction that no human being or human order can rightly demand absolute obedience. The state places certain duties upon me, and it becomes a matter of conscience for me to carry these out. But the state cannot, and in fact does not seriously try, to determine my conscience as to *how* I shall discharge these duties. The same must be said for all finite duties and goods. Relative to all such we are always figuring things out, weighing the pros and cons, inquiring into consequences and implications, etc. before we make up our minds. It is not so with the ultimate loyalty and the supreme good. Toward these the whole being inclines, without calculation and, in a certain way, without decision. We cannot but seek fulfillment, though we may fail to find it. We cannot but share existence with others, though we may make the enterprise into a hell on earth.

Man often contrives shortcuts through and detours around the meaning of transcendence. Religion has a high availability for these purposes, because it makes the ultimate loyalty clear, definite, and manageable. Do this, repeat this, eat this, don't eat that, throw a dollar in the plate, and, brother, you have it made. But God sends the prophet, and the prophet speaks divine truth: "What does God require of you? Justice, mercy, and humility." Three little words, but how much careless, escapist, self-serving religion has been shattered by them! And how much remains yet so to be demolished!

The ultimate demands are of God. That is why they cannot be long evaded. That is also why they can never, on this earth and in this life, be accomplished facts. That is why they cannot be successfully violated. If they could be successfully violated, we should cease to be human. If they were accomplished facts, the forces of life would have ceased to flow, time would have stopped, and we should be either in a final grave or in heaven. If they could be evaded, God would be as uncertain of truth, and as irresolute in the love of good, as we are. These conditions are all contrary to fact; and we have no further traffic with them.

We are instructed by God to put first things first. Well, then, first with the truth, the truth concerning the human realities, and on to the truth of the political realm. Illusions must be treated for what they are, as self-deceptions perpetrated to escape responsibility, perils, tragedy, and guilt. No one is all the way out from under illusions; but the light is brighter where people have had the courage, as well as the disciplined ambition, to take active part in the dirty work. There moral judgment is no whit less painful or less agonized with guilt; but there people may know what the real problems are; and there they may reasonably hope to find a generous common life to work at them, and to endure with grace both defeat and success.

CHAPTER XVII

Christian Criticism of Mass Culture

I

Mass culture has become a topic very much like the weather—it elicits a great deal of talk but very little significant action. The human reality thus denoted is often attacked in prophetic fury. It is also an anxiety prone to despair. As a first step we must ask what mass culture is before proceeding to applaud or abuse it; or before despairing of the future because of its power and pervasiveness.

Since most civilizations have had masses (as well as *elites* and solitaries) it would seem that mass culture must denote some feature of the present age not prominent (or perhaps even actual) in other times and in other civilizations. The distinguishing feature we seek is the elevation of popular taste and conviction to an effectively unchallenged supremacy over all the principal modes of action and thought in our civilization. Accordingly we should err seriously if we were to make either the wide dissemination of knowledge (mass education) or the wide distribution of social power (democracy) the key to the present reality of mass culture. Either of these could have been accomplished without making popular consensus the supreme standard it seems to have become. Universal education and democracy have in fact been promoted in a logically accidental relationship to a theological and religious revolution that made the triumph of mass culture inevitable. The highest values of a society, as well as its minimal benefits of security and freedom, ought to be generally available to the members of that society. Yet the spiritual health of a society requires recognition of the great distance and tension between the minima of value and the maxima. Commonly we speak of the value system of a society as its culture; but the common values and the highest values together are not really a *system*. They do not lie in a continuum. Between them a real abyss opens.

The nature and moment of this abyss are of the utmost consequence for the understanding of the crisis of mass culture. The abyss appears first as the distinction between tradition and creativity, that is, between values transmitted from one generation to another, and the novelty-creating aspirations of free souls. That some values are minima has so far nothing to do with their place on a presumptively vertical scale. Rather, the minima are the common indispensable aims and norms of a society's existence. Whereas the maxima are the values that give human life a significance, and perhaps a power, transcending the time and place of the society in which they appear either as achievements or as serious aspirations and judgments. Thus the decisive questions about minima concern their persuasiveness, clarity, and durability; and the decisive questions about maxima concern their universality, luminosity, and fertility. Maxima are not distributable to all members of a civilization. Their universality consists in the realization of some essential possibility of being—whether human being or otherwise; and the survival business of a social order can be done without such achievement. In fact occasions arise in which the protection of minima makes maxima impossible; and there are other occasions when devotion to the realization of maxima makes survival business extremely difficult, it not simply impossible.

Mass culture could, then, be represented quite faithfully as that condition in a social order in which the aims and criteria pertinent to minima are forcibly enlarged to absorb the aims and criteria of maxima. Mass culture is committed to denying the reality of the abyss.

Therefore, of our own social order we must ask whether it seeks to efface the abyss between minima and maxima. More specifically still, as a people are we powerfully predisposed to judge all values in terms of their general consummability?

Even the bare mention of such an abyss arouses a great anxiety. Recognition of such an abyss must surely seem terribly undemocratic. America is the name of a remarkable success with political democracy. How then can we fail to be suspicious of the slightest suggestion of aristocracy in *any* realm? It pertains to the religion of mass culture to believe that "any man is as good as any other." Yet we have at the least a dim awareness that the best of this culture is the creation of extraordinary men—heroes, saints, martyrs, persons prodigally endowed with wisdom, vision, courage, and love. Between such spirits and the rest of us an abyss does indeed intervene. They are not always better than the rest of us in the everyday morality, but they are finally incomparably better than we are: they are creators of good. They enrich the world. They leave to others the tasks of pressing the good into preestablished molds.

Mass man is afflicted with a severe uneasiness about the creative spirits. He feels a kind of dependency on them; but he also feels an inner necessity to cut the creative spirits down to his own size. So he tries to levy against the creative spirits his own necessity for conformity to minima; and when this levy fails, he reaches for such accusatives as eccentric (or nut) or, as the last resort, subversive.

Deep and pervasive fear of nonconformity and of the nonconformist is one of the root conditions promising a triumph of the herd instinct. Another such condition is the loss of relation to value objectivities beyond the business of sheer survival. Given these conditions, not much more is required of, or left to, the masses of mankind in a social order but to become a herd with a law of its own. For then appetite, as invincible as it is capricious, becomes self-justifying, so long as its influence does not threaten the solidarity of the herd. The herd is threatened only by an attack upon its homogeneity, in which lies its immense power. For that purpose it matters much more that people should want to be alike than their actually being so.

The instrumentality in which the herd moves as one creature is unconscious consensus. Unconscious consensus is the appetitional concordance achieved by subrational forces, a concordance with all the power of legislation but with none of the encumbrances of ethical norms. Which is to say that in mass culture the consensus is right simply because it exists. No other vindication is either possible or necessary. Which is to say that the herd rises to domination of a social order only after any clear or potent sense of moral reality above and circumscribing human history has itself died.

II

Mass culture has become the supreme human phenomenon of the present age. Its triumph is absolute. What can we make, then, of another equally indisputable fact: this strange all-conquering phenomenon now enters the severest crisis in its history? In its triumph is its destruction. Does such a dictum make any sense? We cannot fairly say until we are sure what kind of triumph mass culture is enjoying.

Consider, then, the extent to which the public is something to be served rather than formed and led, and served without mention of the good in any form or context except flattery of the public's wisdom and power.

This attitude permeates our culture. It incorporates as its creedal core a belief that the public is an actual entity with insatiable appetites and absolute power.

Moreover a proposal to lead the public is generally very similar, in its motivations, to the public wanting to lead itself. It argues, that is, no significant reservations about the values of the public, but only a desire to get more of whatever is going around. Thus leading the public means roughly what sporting gentry mean when they speak of a horse leading the field.

Evidence supporting these modest generalizations is overwhelmingly abundant. We have discussed some of the evidence earlier in the chapters dealing with politics and the arts. Here I want to consider the religious situation. It is a rich lode of evidence supporting the thesis that mass culture is now achieving its greatest triumph.

Popular Christianity is rapidly approaching the state of perfect homogenization. It is religiousness rather than faith; it is geniality rather than love; it is sentimentality rather than passion; it is wish rather than hope; it is opinion rather than truth. Thus what Christianity is rapidly becoming indicates the success of the homogenizing process. Certainly opinion presents no difficulty. Let a man say, "That is my opinion," and he is prepared to allow that others have opinions to which they are as entitled as he is to his. They have their rights, and he means to support them—so long as they reciprocate. In any case he doesn't want the bonds of fellowship sundered, or even threatened, by *any* advocacy of a truth by which all opinion might be judged. Idiosyncrasy of religious behavior can be tolerated (though hardly encouraged) so long as the unity of society is not threatened. Actually the idiosyncrasies tend to lose color and vitality in American religion; and where they survive they are subjects for explanation and apology.

Contemporary Christianity, in other words, is a product of the demand to find a religion compatible with the instincts of a mass culture. So it is judged by its function: it exists to make men happy, or to keep them good in their own adequately motivated pursuit of happiness. To keep them *good?* This means to feed the need for self-respect by calling attention to moral conventions. The image of the good man purveyed by popular Christianity is the public's image of itself, with the workaday features highlighted, i.e., the need to keep the wheels turning, to do one's bit, the decent hard-working chap, etc.

The measure of the transformation of Christianity into a mass religiosity can be ascertained by scrutinizing carefully the dominant image of the minister exposed in the contemporary Protestant mind.

1. The minister is a defender of moral standards and moral values.

The people beyond the church appear to share this image with the people of the church. Indeed, this image is so widely and deeply held that many psychiatrists believe the minister is thereby disqualified as a counselor on really complex emotional problems.

What lies behind this image? The conviction that morality is grounded in the Christian religion, at least historically; and the conviction that the minister is an official protagonist of the Christian religion. Or we might put it this way. Since religion is concerned with morality (perhaps with more but not with less and not with anything more important) a professional religionist is professionally concerned with morality. The minister's vocation is to teach and to uphold sound morality.

This image is widely held by the ministry itself. Conservative and liberal share it. The conservative may think in terms of established moral customs and rules (particularly those applying to private life, to marriage and the home). The liberal may think in terms of moral values that run beyond the conventions and embrace the whole round of human existence. This does not mean that the liberal is less moralistic. The moral values of which he is interpreter and defender are presumed to be wider, deeper, and more rationally grounded than the conventions and attitudes regarded as normative by the conservative.

It is to be noted in this connection that the prophetic component in the vocation is undergoing significant alteration, here dropping out of sight altogether, there transformed. It is most vividly present today where the minister is most acutely aware of the problems of cultural pride, cultural relativity, etc. It has most clearly atrophied in those who adopt as decisive for themselves the role of Defender of Civilization. It is most remarkably transformed in those who believe that personal counseling is the best way to help people acknowledge the culture-transcending demands of the Gospel and appropriate spiritual resources for creative personal living.

2. The minister is the interpreter and defender, par excellence and essentially, of religious institutions.

Behind this image we find the assumption that a distinctively religious attitude toward the world and society obtains; and there is also the assumption that the religious attitude or spirit is institutionally concrete in the church. Accordingly the minister is expected to speak for church interests. He is expected to represent the religious viewpoint in those contexts in which its representation is deemed important.

People both within and beyond the church seem to agree on this. They are likely to disagree when the question is asked, Where specifically is the representation of the interests of religion important?

The representation and interpretation of the church is widely held to be a full-time, all-engrossing job. When the minister spends too much time in purely secular activities he is open to censure for neglecting his professional obligations. An important exception to this generalization can be seen in the minister's involvement with the affairs of fraternal organizations. But where this is an exception one also encounters the assumption that these organizations are at least semireligious.

This image is widely held in the ministry itself. One of the minister's favorite recitals is that one in which he recounts how many things he had to do in the course of any given day. These are all interpreted as professional activities in which the marks of his high calling are manifest. Taken together, they show that the minister is as busy as anybody else, and that religion is a full-time job.

Ministers are also strongly inclined to look upon themselves as the salesmen of religion. Their job is to get people to try God when everything else has gone sour on them. The minister proclaims that Christ can save the world after all. What is meant in both cases is that the church can do things for people that nothing else can do. People should therefore widen the patterns of their institutional loyalties in order to embrace the church. To persuade them that they should do this the church and its message should be packaged in an attractive and compelling way. In keeping with this we are told that visitation evangelism should make use of sound selling techniques and angles. Lay visitation teams are instructed to spend only twenty minutes on a given call, since studies show that product resistance builds up rapidly after that. Again, these teams should not accept stalling tactics; they should not leave pledge or commitment cards behind them. They should press for decision, then and there. Anyway, unsigned commitment cards kicking around the house are poor advertising.

In the same connection we notice the tendency on the part of many ministers to adopt executive-type attitudes toward their job as administrators of a large and socially significant institution. These ministers may wear clerical garb on Sunday. The rest of the week they dress and talk (with some qualifications) like executives.

3. The minister is a spiritual person and represents the interest of spirituality.

Spirituality is generally presumed to go beyond morality (or at any rate, everyday morality) and the religious institution. A spiritual person is one somehow effectively detached from gross mundane affairs. Even when he is obliged to traffic in such affairs, his heart is not in them. A kind of nobility is presumed to follow from this detachment. The essential components of this nobility are: extraordinary patience with the foibles of ordinary worldly men; extraordinary unselfishness with respect particularly to this world's goods; presumptive contact, intimate and continuous, with the higher realities, the things of eternity; willingness to acquire representative virtue—the kind that people heavily involved with gross mundane affairs and committed to the pursuit of temporal and fleshly enjoyments can somehow participate in vicariously.

This image is held by the ministry, but held in uneasiness. This is something to be without creating the impression of trying. It is a crown to wear modestly.

Even people outside the church are impressed by the nobility aspect of spirituality. They may not want to have it for themselves; but it is nice to have around.

The minister is very commonly willing to accept and to seek a kind of detachment from gross mundane affairs. These affairs dirty a man. They demand compromise with moral ideals. How could a minister make the spiritual life seem real and attractive if he were as dirty as everybody else? In order that compromise should not become utter capitulation to the forces of evil, the moral ideal must be concretely available. Thus extraordinary patience with the foibles of men must be coupled with purity of moral life. Otherwise the minister will be a blind leader of the blind.

A warrant is thereby provided for an effective detachment. This is not removal from the madding scene, however. The minister would like to have business men, politicians, perhaps even labor leaders, feel free to come to him and present their problems; upon which the pure light of the good would then fall; and worldly men would be absolved, as it were, and sent back into the fray. But in all these sordid and grimy battles which they must fight, and in which all are wounded, he is, miraculously, *sans peur, sans reproche, sans blessure.*

The new emphasis upon an intensive cultivation of the spiritual life has some significance here. In this area the minister can exhibit expertness. He can stand forth as the religious expert, a person able to manage an institution shrewdly, but above all, a person deeply conversant with spiritual realities not easily accessible. As such he has holy lore at his command: techniques and methods by which the spiritual realities can be efficaciously invoked for creative living.

Here is a role that enables the minister to hold up his head in a culture increasingly expertized. Moreover the religious expert is not necessarily a threat to other kinds of experts; and he is no threat to the secular social systems.

4. The minister is a defender of civilization.

People in the church and people outside the church are alike persuaded that our massive economic and political institutions, as well as many merely contingent aspects of these systems, are the direct and pure expression of the ultimate spiritual values. Our way of life is grounded in divine eternal moral law. Hence the minister has unique responsibilities when this civilization is under attack. It is up to him—even though he can count on considerable lay assistance—to point out that this attack is Godless Atheism, and that it aims at the systematic perversion of the moral-spiritual order. Defense of this order is incumbent upon the minister, since he is a professional defender of true morality and has access to weapons, as a spiritual person, which just might be the difference between success and failure. Therefore, to the barricades!

This is an image widely held by the ministry, even at the price of some heartburn. This uneasiness is aroused partly by the awareness of contradiction in the people's image of the ministry right at this point. They do not want him to be involved with gross mundane affairs. He is not to meddle in economic and political problems. If he does, he will be sullied. But lo! these very institutions are the purest possible concrete expression of the divine moral order! But uneasiness is produced also by the great shrinkage of the prophetic component in the people's image of the ministry and perhaps in the minister's image of himself. The Christian faith is radical criticism of our life and of every way of life. Should the minister maintain discreet silence concerning the Christian Faith, the better to employ religion in the all-out defense of civilization?

There seems to be a way out of this situation. It is a way out provided by the image of the ministry. The minister plays a kind of detached conciliatory role in relation to the vast complex problems in the internal life of our society. Here the minister stands for peace and harmony. Over against coercive and divisive policies the minister would show his people, and society in general, a more excellent way. This has to do with spirituality, a spirituality superbly practical, since its resources can be translated fully into cultural goals.

The minister sees himself as standing for peace and harmony in general. He is well-advised not to get caught out in the no man's land created by intense factional disputes; he should be above the battle. But if he is caught out there, he is generally expected to show that he is carrying water for the side that foots the bills, and preaching moderation to their enemies.

5. The minister is a real human being.

The image the people have, and particularly the people in the church, is of a real fellow. To fulfill this expectation the minister can join organizations that are ideologically neutral (organizations which are so ideologically safe that the point has to be made officially upon rare occasions only). Here he can mingle man to man. People outside the church can get the view of him, thereby, as a real fellow, a right guy. He can laugh as loudly as anybody else at the safe jokes; he can also show that he is struggling heroically not to laugh at the jokes a little on the ripe side. If he can tell very funny safe jokes, so much the better—provided that he does not show himself to be a mere buffoon. If his jokes are dubious, he had better save them for his own professional associations. In general, he ought to be relaxed so that people do not feel nervous about their conduct when he is around. When they are really open to judgment, he will give it to them straight from the shoulder.

Wholehearted response to this image is perhaps not a possibility continuously open to the minister, unless he can work out a meaning for his spiritual role which is compatible with this one. Certainly many ministers try to do this.

6. The minister is all too human, but only in respect to things which will not really debase him no matter how he manages them.

The minister has his personal problems, as the people of the church see him. Perhaps he struggles with ambition. People will understand a tension in him between a secular career in which his talents would earn him a place of enviable distinction, and a career of self-renunciation in the church. If he chooses the former, they will say that he had talents too great to be buried in the church. If the latter, they will admire his courage and unselfishness. Again, he may have a struggle trying to decide whether to seek power and fame in the church or to accept a position of great humbleness in the church, in which he pours out his life and love in inconspicuous heroism.

Home and family may be another area of legitimate temptation and testing of the minister. He can live in tension with a wife who wants him to seek the paths of glory, either in the church or in the world. He can become haggard and gaunt under the abuse of a neurotic wife; or through the disgrace of children who wander far afield from sound morality. But he should not be the source of his wife's sickness; or the inspiration of his children's folly.

On the other hand, the minister is not to be all too human in respect to things which can really debase and corrupt him. He may wrestle with ambition, and be thrown by it. He dare not wrestle with sex, not even in a friendly tussle. If a woman in the parish tries to seduce him, he is to be impregnable. If she is upper class, he is also to be understanding. It is proper for him to spend a great deal of time with her, helping her to understand herself and to see that she didn't want really to go to bed with him in the first place—she was simply defying her father, dead lo these thirty years.

Behind this image there is the assumption that the minister has access to extraordinary moral resources for his encounters with the world, the flesh, and the devil. Even though the minister may find this image sympathetic in real measure, he will probably not accept the assumption behind it.

Here we are in the area of most explosive tensions in the image the minister has of himself. That understanding which the minister is supposed to have for the foibles of others is now profoundly colored by non-Christian perspectives. He cannot claim exemption from their follies nor immunity from their sicknesses. If powerful impulses do not break out of his control and break up effective and acceptable patterns of his personal organization, this is not due to superior innate moral constitution. Upon occasion he will say it is grace; and upon others, luck.

As a consequence of these tensions another image comes powerfully to the fore in the contemporary ministry: the New Priesthood.

7. The minister has a new priestly office, namely, to teach a lore and transmit (or induce) a power for the resolution of life's worries and terrors.

This is a new priestly office because the lore is not the Gospel and the power is not grace. To the contrary, the lore reflects ideas and modes of thought very different from the Gospel, and most notably, of course, those stemming from Freudian ideology. The power is simply the person's own resources, now summoned to effect a satisfactory adjustment to his environment.

In this role the minister can be efficacious in spite of himself; what he says and does in it is *ex opere operato.* (Pressed, he too would have to cry, "Mea culpa, miserere!" This cry would be unproductive in the counseling situation.)

This is not crude authoritarianism. Ultimate authority is not represented as being conventional morality. But neither is it revelation of God Transcendent. The norm, the final authority, is the person's dearest image of himself or what he would like most to be. The lore is all methods by which the person can enthrone this image in the position of invincible sovereignty.

Through this role, the minister ministers also to himself. Here the ministry acknowledges that it has heard the taunt: Physician, heal thyself.

The new priesthood is a powerful role, particularly when yoked with that of spiritual person. Their union signifies to the people that the minister can show them that their dearest image of themselves is also God's image of them. Religion can be recommended to them as a support for their evaluation of themselves.

Thus the image of the minister expresses the successful assimilation of the professional leadership of the church into the spiritual atmosphere of mass culture. The church as a whole is not expected to do or say things which would threaten the security of the cultural realm in which persons must find their clues for a meaningful existence. It is possible to appeal to the ideal self against the sorry state of the actual self; and to appeal to the ideal America against the confusions of the present moment. But it is everywhere assumed that no legitimate criticism of the ideal itself is possible. This is the moment of triumph for mass culture, because the definition of the ideal can now be translated into the unconscious consensus.

III

Where the unconscious consensus triumphs, the power and authority of leadership appear to be invested in no elite whatever. In fact the very notion of an elite in any sense other than the economic becomes suspect. "Upper class" means economic advantage first and, as a poor second, the kind of sophistication money alone can provide; then, as a limping third, an exclusive social dynastic distinction originally grounded in great wealth.

Nevertheless even the man of the masses knows that the decisive administration of real power is in the hands of an elite, whether or not it is recognized as such. But what kind of an elite is this? How does it succeed in leading? It seems not to be the elite of intellect; and the effectiveness of its leadership seems not to be heavily dependent upon appeals to moral principle.

As for the elite of intellect, it falls (and falls apart) into two subgroups: scientists, and artists. The scientists, an elite of unquestioned intellectual superiority, have shown remarkably little interest in or capacity for moral leadership.

The artists have removed themselves so far as possible from the burdens of power. As a result of developments hardly susceptible of rational control, the artistic elite communicates largely with itself. The general public is felt by this in-group to be beyond redemption; and it is therefore turned over to the entertainers, who are creations and prostitutes of the unconscious consensus.

All the while science and art become increasingly available to the general public. Popularization is the form in which they are available. So the essence of real science and art is lost in translation; and what of each comes across to the masses is something very largely congruent with their existing expectations. Mass man looks to science for inventions to make his life safer and easier; and he looks to art for pleasure or at least for momentary release from pain. But he looks neither to science or art, any more than to religion, for reality, because he is sure that he has reality in his instincts, habits, and everyday images of the good life. He spurns a science which threatens this sense of reality, and grunts at art which reveals a world deeper, higher, and richer than his daily substance allows for.

But is there some other leadership group which fares better in proposing and enforcing moral correction of the unconscious consensus? If there is none then the very success of mass culture precipitates the most threatening crisis in its own life. For then momentum continues to augment as the sense of direction diminishes; so whatever appears to arrest momentum becomes evil *per se;* and if an obstacle actually succeeds in arresting momentum, the power thus backed up by the dam of frustration becomes a terrible threat to the structures of law and order.

Political leadership is still seriously in the business of providing moral direction to the unconscious consensus. In this respect, as in others, this leadership group is the most conservative of all elites. But even so these appeals to moral principles are very commonly discounted by the masses as so much pious rhetoric designed to advance the cause of the politician. This unconscious perversity comes to light in the exquisite anomaly of conservative political leadership representing itself as being most concerned to protect the sanctity of private property.

Left to itself, the unconscious consensus becomes arbitrary and capricious. It is constantly threatening to dissolve and reform around different goals. Thereby the individual is pressed toward becoming a shifting mass of conflicting reactions to a shifting mass of demands and solicitations. He is not expected really to think for himself. He is encouraged, by proddings both subtle and gross, to cast his lot for the group which promises him the largest package of ego satisfactions, including his being absorbed into a peer group which will do his thinking for him.

These things are occurring while the political order staggers from peril to peril. Danger, not security, has become the stable situation in the family of nations, and will be indefinitely. We sense, rather than see, that internal dangers are intimately related to the external ones. Moral lethargy, irresponsibility, hatred of austerity and sacrifice may not have created the external threats to our corporate future, but they certainly do not prepare us to cope with our enemies. We have become a people affluent beyond the wildest dreams of seers; and we are harrowed by the fear that enemies abroad and fools at home will conspire to take it all away.

How far then have our moral sensibilities eroded? Moral conventions were once understood by reflective minds to be the partly unreal outworks (or order of appearance) of a reality ethical to its core. Now it has become a dogma of popular culture that moral conventions are the wholly unreal screen discreetly (but futilely) cast over nonethical reality—even the schoolboy prattles cleverly about superego and id. But as mass man is progressively liberated from the power of moral conventions over his imagination, heart, and will, he is bound in ever-tighter servitude to group preferences. Can he be made over into nothing but mass man before he explodes and destroys his society with the shrapnel of his disintegrating self? There's a question; and a terror; and a hope.

IV

The Christian criticism of mass culture is differentiated from other critical operations both by its content and its posture. I want now to develop the distinctiveness of the Christian position by relating it to the propheticism of social science.

The propheticism of social science is a way of designating the attitudes and the principles of men whose first avowed duty is to present the facts in a pattern of explanation which can be credited by observational powers as differentiated (scientifically) from the powers of appreciation. Ordinarily the scientist is concerned to tell us what is so, and not what is good or bad; and when he essays the latter he does it on his own time as a person living in a society which cannot survive if too many people are pursuing evil rather than good, rather than on his scientific license, whatever it may be. Ordinarily this is the case. Relative to the problems of mass culture there are interesting exceptions: men, such as David Riesman and C. Wright Mills, Vance Packard and William Whyte, who apparently believe that the right presentation of the facts will (or ought) arouse and direct the moral passions. Thus the public is told what to think about a society which produces so many other-directed people; and about a society in which all of the important decisions concerning public policy are made by a small tightly organized group of unknown (to the great mass of people) men; and about a society in which more and more people are reduced to a computer code on an IBM card; and about a society in which status matters more to more people than anything else; etc. There can of course be no serious objection to a person, scientific or otherwise, telling the world how he thinks the world wags; but his opinion takes on more than biographical significance (an item in his personal inventory of interests, ideas, and passions) only when the principles informing his judgments are made evident to his hearers. Why should not informed and intelligent people make the important decisions in a society, rather than leaving controls in the hands of uninformed and stupid people? One sort of answer to this question would be: Because informed and intelligent people are not always wise and good. Another answer would be: Because the generality of mankind can profitably be relieved of ignorance and so rise to greater control over its destiny. But whatever the answer to this question (and to any question which seems to assume an automatic answer), the principles determining it, rather than the interests of the person asking it or of the person answering it, must be clearly exhibited before a rational decision about it can be made.

Another aspect of the propheticism visible in semipopular social science is eschatological threat. Unless something drastic is done about the galloping evil in our society, its fate will be one with Nineveh and Tyre, Sodom and Gomorrah. The scriptural allusions may be wanting, but the idea is there. Thus right-thinking people are rallied to a desperate cause, desperate simply and decisively because the masses will not heed and turn from evil to the good.

It seems to me that the mantle of the prophets has descended upon secular shoulders for several reasons. For one, churchly people in our time have failed to keep the appointment for that particular investiture. For another the new prophets suppose that their peculiar mode of access to the facts is a significant (if not the decisive) part of their prophetic license: they know, where others merely surmise, whither we drift and at what cost to the real good for man. But what inspection of fact yields expert knowledge of man's real good? What closeup acquaintance with Trend yields soundness of moral verdict upon the Whither?

Christian criticism of mass culture has no stake in minimizing the seriousness with which secular scientists raise ethical questions, or in denigrating the prophetic passion with which such men are assailing what man has done to man. The Christian critic ought to get on with his own constructive enterprise: to show how human creations succeed in corrupting and confusing human creativity; and to show that the evil in this consists precisely and altogether in the reduction of the visibility and the desirability of the divine-human community.

It is an integral part of such a program to show that the evils inherent in a mass culture, whatever they may be, are evil because they cheat human beings out of their heritage in creation, rather than because they are deprived of rights and privileges coming to them as members of a given social order. To do the latter is very wrong; to do, even inwardly to propose to do, or subconsciously dream of doing, the former, is to blaspheme against the Holy, because the place of the human spirit in creation is the work of God. God has created man to create. The human spirit is called into life not merely to enjoy a world already formed, but to add to the sum of value, in effect to be a unique value, to be something not otherwise possible anywhere else or in any surrogate form in the whole of the created universe. (This, I take it, is the kernel of truth in the awkward metaphysical apparatus historically identified as the creationist theory of the soul of the individual person.)

It will not do, therefore, to assail mass culture as the great enemy of freedom, however keenly we may feel that freedom *is* jeopardized by mass culture. This will not do because freedom itself requires criticism. People becomes slaves to things which are not evil until these things become chains; and what we have been calling mass culture in our time has made it very easy for people to enslave themselves to things not evil in themselves. Take status, for example. There is surely nothing unhealthy in wanting to be a member in good standing of the right social group, since no one can come into the richest exercise and enjoyment of his powers unless he participates freely and deeply in a community of persons. But when a person identifies the right group as the one which can do the most for him, can, that is, help him up the ladder of success most surely and expeditiously, he is learning how to sever the nerve of human community, he is taking steps to destroy his power to enjoy human friendship as a good in itself.

Or take conformity. Surely there is nothing unhealthy in people wanting to be in accord with one another, acting in concert, sharing values, etc. A man is not necessarily admirable because he stands out from the crowd. It depends upon what the crowd is up to, where it is going, and whether a person feels less than human for opposing it. A crowd can be a very poor thing to follow; and it can be a very good one. It is a very poor one when the people in it have confused sheer density of human association with that warmth and luminosity of spirit which are the highest attainment of love. Mass culture must be indicted for high crimes when such a confusion becomes endemic, for then people huddle together in a kind of biological necessity rather than from any recognizable demand of creative spirit; and are thus subject to all manner of impulses, some of them merely mean and silly, some of them hideously destructive, and all of them reinforced and compounded by density of association.

In its attack upon the evils of mass culture the church is faithful to the Lord only when its critical posture manifests the love of Christ and the hope for the Kingdom. It is terribly easy for the church to fall into the pitfalls of harshness of spirit and envy. Seized by the sin of harshness of spirit, churchly critics berate worldly men for their materialism, for their love of pleasure, for their indifference to the threat of eternal punishment; but taken together these rabid mouthings and rantings attest, in appalling clarity, to envy rather than love, and to despair rather than hope. The way of the Cross is mortally hard; and never is it more oppressive than when we are under divine injunction not to advertise the price it is exacting from us, an injunction only slightly more insufferable than the command to have joy in the hour of persecution. The fact of the matter is, or seems to be, that commonly the satisfactions gained from the life in Christ do not take the taste of the other life out of our mouths. Being deprived of the satisfactions of the life renounced for Christ and the Kingdom we come to imagine that they were more splendid than ever they were in truth. So we begin to swell with the noxious gases of self-righteousness; and our hearts begin to steam and sweat with self-pity; and we stand in the direst need of release from the cross of our own devising—a truly loathsome instrument of self-punishment and self-exaltation.

But how is it possible for the church's criticism or culture to show forth the hope of the Kingdom without falling into the sins of easy optimism on the one hand and despair on the other? To this question we have to say, to begin with, that with man this is impossible but with God all things are possible. Concretely this means that a properly penitent church exposes to the world the inner dynamism of God's mercy and God's judgment in its own life. The hope of the Kingdom does not allow the church to say to the men of this age that all is well or that all will be well. But often as not the church *is* heard saying such things. Just as often, in one way or another, it is given the lie direct. Yet the truth is not withdrawn from it. The Gospel is still committed to it and is still heard in it.

The degree to which the church in our age feels driven to preach an easy optimism is itself an indication of the anxiety felt in the bowels of the church for its own future, a future in which mass culture will have triumphed. How could we and why should we be spared the affliction of wanting to be liked and appreciated, we who are of the church? Customarily we have feared immorality far more than we have vulgarity; and this makes us one with the mass mind which is always at the ready to do penance (provided that it is reasonable) for the sins of the flesh, but sleeps peacefully through every sermon launched against the sins of the spirit.

On the other hand it must be said that God does not allow the church to fall unscathed into despair over the state of culture, now or in any other time. The church is not called to play the role of Cassandra. It is not even to think of itself as a weeping Jeremiah. The Gospel is to be preached, by word and example, under the relentless impulsion of the Holy Spirit, until the end of time. The final reckoning of all human accounts is unto God alone. The final disposition of all souls is in the hands of God alone. We are not therefore to encourage the men of this age to scratch frantically about to discover the signs of the End.

"The night is far spent; be sober and alert, therefore, and not as those who drunkenly sleep." The counsel is as appropriate today as ever. A church going soberly and quietly about its main business, and encouraging others to do so much as that with their several serious concerns, would indeed be an inspiration to a rattled world! For there is much to do. Consider, for example, how desperately the age needs to see the lineaments of the divine-human community, not in the misty heavens but here on the earth! How great is the need to see forgiveness as but one aspect of creative existence; and to see love overcoming everything fateful in the human situation; and to see the pursuit of justice as infinitely richer than the need to avert a well-deserved retribution! How poignant is the hunger, and insatiable with any mortal pap, to see people graciously received into communion simply and purely because they are the children of God! How incredibly beautiful it would be to see a company of people transcending the deadly competitive strife, living, as a company, in the supreme confidence that the earth is the Lord's and all time too and that He has ordained a place in each for quietness of mind and joy and peace in the love of one another!

All of these things God does provide to all who faithfully seek them in Him. Why therefore do we not seek them, for the blessing of the nations? Because we do not believe in God in the church. We believe in all sorts of good things: religion, morality, freedom, immortality, The American Way of Life, etc. So far as God is a mysterious power benignly pledged to all of our good things, we accept Him as a kind of silent senior partner in our human enterprise; but no further, except in verbal exercises.

It can be seen, therefore, how deeply mass culture has invaded even the inner life of the church, since the religion, the deepest and most powerful faith, of such a culture is something generated out of its own viscera to comfort its own mortal fears and to provide manageable objects for its aspirations.

Accordingly the Christian criticism of such a culture must begin within the life of the church itself. In the church itself opinion often enough parades as truth and expediency as wisdom; and status is as precious there as on the outside; and self-aggrandizement has legion forms and the virulence of plague. To confess so much to the world, provided, always, that they have been confessed first to God in good faith and good cheer, is an integral part of the life of obedience to God. But the great hope in so doing is not at all that the world might see how eagerly the church wants to join the great company of sinners, in which there is always room for more and more, but that the world might see, rather, how mighty is the grace of God over all the powers of earth and of hell. So even those who have sinned against the Spirit cannot be sure at all that they are lost to Him, who made us all for His communion.

CHAPTER XVIII

The Holy Spirit and Revolution

I

Contemporary social radicals can surely be forgiven some of their skepticism about any claim that Christianity is the permanent revolution. This claim has of course been made seriously by distinguished theologians, living and dead; and there is no reason for supposing that they were unaware of the social conservatism of the great mass of the church. Unlike the contemporary radical critic of the church, they did not therefore write the church off. One might speculate about ecclesiastical commitments or dispositional factors which prevented them from making the honest and clean break. There are excellent reasons for not getting into psychological guessing games, of which perhaps the best is itself the dispositional payoff in the game itself: self-congratulation. I should prefer another and rather different reason. That is a theological objective that is fourfold: (1) a delineation of some features of the traditional teachings concerning the Holy Spirit. (2) An argument that the Holy Spirit can be faithfully acknowledged as the fomentor of revolution in at least one sense. (3) A contention that contemporary Christian radicals are being driven to claim the Holy Spirit as warrant for postures and policies which set them against the actual church. (4) They thereby become the new self-righteous sectarians.

1. Historically the work of the Holy Spirit is understood to be the sustaining and fulfilling of the work of Christ as the Logos and Redeemer. God the Creator Father posits (calls into being) the structures of being. (This is excessively abstract. God posits the crea-

tures, which are structured beings.) The structures are essences[1] and the patterns of relations exhibited in the activities of concrete entities. From this it is apparent that ontological structures are to be distinguished from psychocultural structures, such as character, institutions, conceptual structures, etc. For our present purpose it does not matter whether the structures of being are literally the effects of the creative act or, on the other hand, whether they are features of God's being projected beyond Himself.[2]

God the Redeemer restores and regenerates structured beings. What happens to the structures thereby? The ontological schematisms of traditional Christian philosophy suggest one answer. I mean particularly the view of evil as an accidental feature of a substance or of a substantial individual. Redemption somehow relieves the created substance of this accident and thus releases the pristine powers of the creature for the realization of its proper end. But "accident" is hardly a satisfactory term for the ontological status of evil, since it suggests a positive quality or component, while all that the traditional view can assimilate is a defect or deficiency of the power of being of the creature. This means that evil, so regarded, is not essentially a structural affair at all; and therefore that redemption is not a structural affair either. The essence of the creature is not diminished by reason of sin, or otherwise fundamentally altered. If it were so the creature after the Fall would have only the most tenuous relation, if any at all, with the creature before the Fall.[3]

A structural view of redemption is a possibility, however. It may be argued, for instance, that redemption effectuates a total substitution of new structures for old. On such a view redemption becomes re-creation, the new creation. Such a view must give some account, thereafter, of the continuity of the old Adam with the new, the

[1] It makes little difference here whether essence is understood in the classical sense or in the sense used above in Chapter 6.

[2] Actually it does matter whether ontological structures inhere in being as such or only in created being by virtue of its being created; that is, whether we suppose seriously that God has or is an essence or is activity structured by essence. (Analogy of being seems meaningless unless we suppose something like this.) If we say God has no essence we then either place Him beyond being; or we eliminate the category of being as such and substitute for it two other categories, viz., divine being and structured being; and confess that we have no clear reason for applying "being" to both of them.

[3] So perhaps the preference for image talk in the tradition is not arbitrary. It is certainly much easier to picture the "effacement" or pollution or distorting of an image than it is to think of an essence (in the classical sense) being significantly altered or, for that matter, being altered at all.

sinner with the new creature; and this account cannot consistently be itself structural.

God the Holy Spirit brings to fulfillment the work of Christ the Redeemer. The Holy Spirit is the Sustainer of the new creature in Christ. The Holy Spirit is the Sanctifier of the new being. Relative to the structures of being what do these things mean?

There seems to be a prior question here, so far as the work of the Holy Spirit as Sustainer is concerned. What in general does it mean to sustain the structures of being? Is it not evident that a particular existing being sustains its own structures by virtue of its very act of existing? When this being ceases to exist, surely its structures perish at the same time and by the same stroke (that is, the ontological structures). So it would seem that such support as the Holy Spirit provides, it provides only to the new creature, not to the old. But this makes the Spirit subsequent to Incarnation, whereas the Christian Faith has confessed that in history Incarnation is first and the work of the Holy Spirit subsequent. Where, then, have we gotten off the track? When we supposed that the ontological structures were supported by the creature himself, that is, through his own powers alone. To the contrary, the structures of being are supported altogether and absolutely by the Holy Spirit, and not only the structures of the new creature. The structures have no inherent power of existence; and so far as they are incorporated into actuality they wholly depend upon God the Spirit. A generic ontological principle is exemplified in this assertion: structures are everywhere dependent upon the powers of actual agents. This perhaps amounts to saying that existence precedes essence, but only if precedes means ontological rather than chronological priority, that is, in the order of being as such.[4] The essence of the creature is sustained absolutely

[4] It is only and purely in God that existence precedes essence; but, since in God there is no actual precedence of the one over the other, the essence that follows upon existence must be that of the creature. Thus the essence of the creature is not an exemplification of an archetype in the mind of God. The theory of the divine archetypes has insurmountable difficulties in it, not the least of which is the implication that in eternity God contemplates alternative schemes of possibilities before He makes a definitive and (if you follow Leibniz) a properly inspired choice from among them. This notion entails a double eternity, one, the eternity before creation, the eternity of pure envisagement of possibilities; and, two, the eternity out of which creation is precipitated, the eternity that is not a correlative of time but is the concrete ground or *prius* of time. The second eternity is the absolute creativity of God; and the first eternity is really an abstraction from this. But if, in this scheme, the first eternity is denied (the eternity of pure envisagement), then the necessity of creation ineluctably follows.

not by his own existence, his own actual powers, but by the Holy Spirit. So also for the visible orders of nature and of history. These are sustained by the Holy Spirit, apart from which they have no power of actual continuity.

So far as traditional alternatives are concerned, this view appears to be purely pantheistic, since it would seem that all actual agency is the Holy Spirit. But this is not the case. What is given to the creature is a determinate power of being which may therefore very properly be regarded as his, though not his absolutely. Does it follow from this that the essence of that creature depends wholly upon his determinate powers of being? It neither follows nor is it so. So far as essence designates an actual structure and not merely a phenomenal isolate, it does not simply or purely ride the crest of existence as, let us say, a bit of effluvium rides a wave. When the determinate power of being of that creature dies away, its essence does not go all the way out with it; it takes on thereafter a pure propositional function and as such retains a timeless—and therefore existentially trivial—modality. This in the order of logical disclosure so far. In the order of piety we say that the soul has returned to God. In the theological-ontological order we say that the primordial power of the essence is nothing but the Holy Spirit. (Essence *qua* essence is grounded in God the Spirit: we speak only of the essence of the creature, of created essence.) For apart from existence essence is not properly understood as an abstract mode of divine envisagement. Essence, is rather, a possibility inherent in absolute concrete activity, which activity is alone the Holy Spirit. Wherefore to say that we have our being *qua* essence in God is to say that all creatures are grounded in God as the absolute continuant. We conclude that the existing creature exemplifies two powers of being: its own power of being, and the power of the Holy Spirit. Neither can be reduced to the other though neither can be separated from the other.

Let us note further concerning the visible orders of nature and history that these are possibilities in the Holy Spirit. They are not autonomous subsisting ontological orders through which the Holy Spirit flows to work the purposes of God. In themselves they have no power to bind the energies of even the creatures. In the minds of creatures these orders have to do with past and future. They are retrospective and projective and they cannot be adequately considered as simply normative and final. God the Father, God the Son, God the Spirit: this God expresses Himself in grand regularities, but there is no good reason for supposing that God is a being of unbreakable habit. The rhythms of God's activities are not best grasped as habit with its enforceable claims.

Through Christ the new creature is born. We have already indicated in a very general way the two possibilities of interpretation confronting us here so far as structure is concerned. We have now to interpret the work of the Holy Spirit as Sustainer in terms of these possibilities, the first of which is that the powers of being pertinent or proportional to a given essence are, in Christ, miraculously restored and revivified, but without substantial structural transformations. On these terms the Holy Spirit sustains these quickened powers. How? By revealing to the intellect the proper and ultimate end of human action; and by uniting Himself with the will of the person to pursue rightly this end; or, to take the extreme view, by actually becoming the effective cause within of the will's motions. But on any of these terms the newness of the creature is to be found in his restored powers, which the Holy Spirit continuously nourishes and reinforces.

The other general possibility merits some attention, namely, that redemption effectuates a total substitution of new structures for old. Now does this mean a total replacement of one individual by another? Or is there a determinate power of being which remains even when old structures are displaced, if not destroyed, and new ones are grafted in? If we answer in the affirmative, we imply that determinate powers of being do not depend upon the essence of the creature. Indeed, it would now seem that essence is consequent upon existence in some decisively important sense. Perhaps we should say that the creature aspires toward an essence and that an essence would be the crown of fulfillment of the creature. If so, we should then say that activity (operation) does not flow from essence but only from and together with envisagement of essence; and the essence so apprehended is not in fact a preexistent form or structure awaiting the vivifying kiss of its heaven-sent actual agent. The essence so apprehended is a pattern and policy for activity. Thus a realized essence is a relatively stable pattern and a relatively fixed policy. The essence, so conceived, has a time-binding power, in a certain sense; but the power is only secondarily in the essence, while it is primarily (so far as the creature is concerned) in his existence as such.

If then we say that redemption substitutes one essence for another, it means that something new and something more adequate is presented to the envisaging powers of the creature, something more adequate as pattern and policy for his activities. But surely the Christian view goes beyond this. The power of envisagement itself is transformed by God in Christ. In all of these operations the Holy Spirit is fully and intimately involved. First, because the new and more adequate essences are contained in the Holy Spirit. The specifics of redemption are left to the Holy Spirit by the Son![5] The Son establishes the New Order in absolute generality only. Specifications of the new order are left to the inspiration of the Holy Spirit.

In the second place the creature's power of envisagement are themselves transformed in redemption. This cannot be an external operation, an effect produced upon the creature by a foreign agent. It must be wrought within, by an agent perfectly participative in the life of the creature. This is the Holy Spirit, "nearer to us than breathing, closer than hands or feet." For what we are to be, we are in the Holy Spirit.

The Holy Spirit is God in us sanctifying us for the glory of His everlasting Kingdom and thus fulfilling the work of Christ. Relative to the structures of being, what is the work of sanctification?

It might seem on first glance that the work of sanctification is a matter of establishing firmly and finally within the creature the structures wholly adequate to his powers. So it may be, in the Kingdom beyond the measure and boundary of this life. So it is not, within this life. In this life the only truly permanent fixity in pattern and policy is that provided by death. Elsewhere relative fixity is the rule. Should we therefore conclude that sanctification practices a kind of deceit upon God—that something is called holy in God's presence which is anything but holy? Hardly. To be sanctified is not to be made holy in any ultimate and constitutive way. It is to be consecrated (poor and sinful though we be) to the life and work of the Kingdom of God. This is the doing of the Holy Spirit. To put the matter crudely: as in Jesus Christ God the Father testifies to His disposition to have us as His children, so the Holy Spirit is the specific program for carrying this out. The Holy Spirit is the power of God enabling us to grasp the relevant possibilities of creative action. It is in the Holy Spirit that we are able to know and to do the will of God.

[5] Relative to the inner life of the Triune God it would seem that the Father is the absolute power of being, pure existence as such, and the Son is the principle of pattern (Logos), and the Spirit is the Father's acceptance of the Son as the fulfillment of His own being—the only-begotten and wholly loved. Thus the structures of being are committed to the Spirit; it is through the Spirit that Jesus Christ renders his obedience to the Father.

What happens to the structures of being in this process called sanctification? Two things of paramount importance: the relationship of structure to agent is transformed; radically novel structures appear. Let us briefly consider each in turn.

The relationship of structure to agent is transformed, since it is the work of the Holy Spirit to reveal to us the beauties of Creation. The structures of being are grasped as expressions of the good God. Thereby the hope is implanted and nourished that personal and social structures might (may, rather) participate in something of this goodness of Creation, or more purely and justly reflect it.[6] But by this same token the structures of society do not now please God and cannot therefore be allowed to remain as they are. They must be changed, and they will be changed, and of that there is no doubt. The Holy Spirit works in us that we may see what change comports with the divine will and what does not. But above all the Holy Spirit instructs not to seek finality, absoluteness, and everlastingness where they cannot be found: in the works of our hands.

The work of sanctification is also that by which a radically new structure appears in the historical world. This structure is the church of Christ. The creation and enrichment of this structure are wholly and purely God's doing; and first and last it is an ontological structure; but it has also significant reflections or embodiments in the historical-social world.

To say that the church of Christ is an ontological structure is to say that it is a form of being welded indissolubly to powers of being. Hence the church is very much more than a form of social organization created by and for a company of agreeably like-minded people. The power of God has done particular things and is now doing them. These are done in and through a form taken not from the world but directly from eternity. God in the Spirit summons men to free participation in this community. The life thereof is the Spirit.

The pluriform churches are reflections, in all degree and hue, of the new order created in Jesus Christ and sustained by the Holy

[6] How rich with pathos is the dreamy wish of Rousseau: O for the sublime innocence of that misty past in which human life reflected purely the goodness of creation! Alas! for these dreary after-days where Nature's (rural) prospect pleases still and only civilized man is vile! Youthful, perhaps childish, as this vision is, it is still sweet and clean withal when it is compared with technological utopias. It fares even better when it is compared with the astounding conceit that the structures of our society and its economy are themselves created by the eternal fiat of God and shall never be moved!

Spirit. In most of them an antiquarian and imperialistic mentality appears. Who does not claim that the polity of *his* communion is not the nearest blood descendant of the primitive Christian community? And in many, perhaps in all, an absolutistic mentality appears. We are the true, real, and whole church, for the Holy Spirit tells us so. The dreary spectacle is thus abundantly endowed, the ageless spectacle of men claiming divine consecration for every accident of birth, whim of will, and necessity of instinct.

Apart from the outcroppings of pride in all such claim and counterclaim, there is one so far indestructible error: the assumption that an ontological structure can be, and has been, identified wholly with a historical-social pattern of human organization. Thus some can say with seriousness uncorrupted by irony that the church is clearly a presbyterial order, and others that it is an episcopal order, etc., etc. But the ontological order is a pattern of deep, indeed, of hidden powers. This order, this pattern, is the love of God in Christ Jesus, which constraineth us to love one another even as he hath loved us. Through Christ we are actually set in a relationship to one another, and to God, which hitherto did not exist. In this relationship we come, perforce, to be what we were not and could not be, before. "If anyone is in Christ, he is a new creature." The newness is structural; and in this life that is the heart of the matter. The Christian is not given additional length of days, neither is he endowed with supernormal powers which he can command simply by and in the exercise of his will. He remains entirely mortal. "The outer man wastes daily away," truly. Neither through the Incarnate Son nor the Spirit is the created determinate power of being quantitatively augmented or replenished. But through Christ this power comes to earthly fulfillment, the same being a foretaste of the heavenly, through acceptance of a new structure. Hence in the Spirit we are able to love another, not by an increment of natural power, but by being assimilated into a life which is God with us. The prospects of eternity have to do with a wholly mysterious, a wholly nonimaginable, an absolutely miraculous, union of the finite with the new structure. Then will the corruptible put on incorruptibility. Then will our spirits enjoy a condign, a most justly proportioned, and otherwise beauteous body; and spirit and body will rejoice together forever and ever.

In the meantime "the inner man is daily renewed," the man who for his faith, his hope, his love, depends wholly upon the Holy Spirit, the indwelling Life of the community in Christ. When therefore we ay that apart from him we can do nothing, we do not seriously mean that we cannot clean the barn or bake a cherry pie or write a pious book except first we fling ourselves upon God's grace. We mean that the ultimately fulfilling things can be done only in that community of which the Living Lord is the Life. Since no detail or circumstance of our life is beyond Him or beneath His free concern, we have no advance knowledge of what small thing, normally pursued or accepted by us as indifferent to our salvation, may become a means of grace.[7]

2. The Holy Spirit is the instrument of Revelation (so far as one may speak at all of a person of the Godhead as being an instrument relative to another person of the Godhead), as the Son is the content thereof. So far as the structures of being are concerned it is the Holy Spirit who makes manifest their created character. This created character is twofold. It is expressed as contingency. It is also expressed as relative perfection or goodness. Each aspect of created character will now be briefly considered.

In the dialectics of philosophical theology contingency is sometimes taken to mean a radical deficiency of power of being, whereby that particular being must depend wholly upon God for its existence. But something is left out of this account, or is inadequately expressed by it. To be sure, a contingent being is a being grounded in another, but contingent being is also being replete with intentionality. There is that in it which requires us to look beyond it into a different order of being; but this intentionality is not present in contingent being merely as defect pointing beyond the order of contingency to another order. Intentionality is a created richness of being, a richness of being by which finite is bound to and grounded in the infinite. But at the same time we must note that contingent structures are stamped with arbitrariness. Contingent structures, that is, disclose in themselves no rational relation to the forces or powers of being to which they are

[7] Those who make much of theophanies in nature, in the esctasies of aesthetic awareness, and in any startling or sublime arousement of feeling, seem to have misappropriated what on its own ground and under the discipline of the Spirit is a profound occasion of Revelation. The nature mystic, for instance, is deeply enthralled by the burning bush, so much so that he is, and would have been, deaf to the word of the Living Lord; for to this mystic the event is hardly event at all. He sees this thing as but part of that shimmering veil which is all of nature, a veil artfully and seductively placed over the face of ideal beauty. That artist who touches the bush with autumn's flame also streaks the western sky with beauty most prodigal, etc., etc. This view handsomely, indeed, lyrically, succeeds in converting all nature and all history into a transcendent game of hide-and-seek, where hider and seeker are the same.

bound by creation. We say of such structures, why *this* rather than *something* else? We do not thereby impudently question the wisdom of the Creator. We are only trying to discover whether there is an inner rational necessity uniting a given structure with determinate power of being. Contingency answers No. This does not mean that an essence and existence merely collide and become fortuitously glued together until death do them part. It does mean that the togetherness of an essence with a determinate power of being is a matter of fittingness, and this is an appropriateness essentially different from rational interconnectedness. The minimal structure (psychophysiological) given to the human at the outset is not a rational principle of being from which all his actions follow. This minimal structure is not a rigidly determinative ontological principle in any case. The same must be said for the normative essence toward which the will aspires. In both types of structure we apprehend contingency. The Holy Spirit teaches us aright as to the Being upon whom we wholly depend and to whom we, and all the creatures, are related through His absolute freedom, which is that perfection in God to which our contingency points. The minimal psychophysiological structure stands in a kind of continuum; but the given of bodily bias and of disposition is not that continuum mediating itself, *natura naturans*, to the human individual. The normative essence has also its important relations with cultural imperatives and social expectations. But the normative essence is not the continuum of the collective consciousness mediating itself to the individual. Behind the phenomenal structures and the deep structures alike (though these are not in the same mode of intentionality) there is a radical given. The Holy Spirit reveals that God the Father is the giver.

The second aspect of created structures revealed by the Holy Spirit is their goodness. It is only in the Holy Spirit that we can rightly rejoice in the goodness of the created order, because it is only in the Holy Spirit that we apprehend the intentionality of created structures as fulfilled beyond themselves. Apart from the Holy Spirit the goodness of creation is apprehended either as a kind of pleasure in being alive, a euphoristic sense of life, or it is a merely doctrinaire and parochial judgment upon the fitness of the world as a scene for the human venture. Through the Holy Spirit the created order offers up praise to its Creator who alone is the reason for its existence. Created structures point beyond themselves absolutely, and the being to which they point is their actual ground and their actual fulfillment.

Up to a point it is permissible to say that this universal judgment is a generalization, of indeterminable boundaries, from the particularities of Christian experience, for the Christian believes that the structures of his own being find their fulfillment of being beyond themselves. He understands his normative essence, for instance, as a lure for his will, leading him to participate ever more deeply in the life of the Community, until at last he has great difficulty perceiving where he leaves off and Christ begins ("I live, yet not I . . .").

Yet there is more here than this kind of generalization. There is an intuition concerning created being as such: the structures of created being are proportionally perfect thereunto—I mean of course the ontological structures. When seen as the signatures of God the Almighty Father, they provide the occasion for the right enjoyment of one's own being, an enjoyment very different from euphoria. It is by means of these structures that we apprehend the concrete richness of God's creation. Behold, how differently He has created us, yet to dwell together as one family!

From the proportional perfection of the ontological structures men find it mortally easy to derive a sense of being perfect in their characters and in the social structures they find about them. Thereby they lose sight and sound of the divine revolution, the sweeping away of even the most deeply entrenched institutions and the radical conversion of even the most settled character. Does this mean that the revolution of the Holy Spirit is visited exclusively upon psychocultural structures? Does it mean that the Holy Spirit falls upon such, or explodes within, as an altogether destructive force? Certainly human structures are destroyed never to rise again. Why should we say this is the Holy Spirit at work in us? It is easy and perhaps right for us to say this when these structures lie upon the human spirit as a dead weight, crushing freedom and creativity; but something in us in our better moments counsels patience and reflection in patience when we have to deal with such structures. It is not impious, though in a particular instance it may be an error, to say that this is the counsel of the Holy Spirit.

The root of this problem is not yet properly exposed in our treatment, and it is this. How are psychocultural structures related to ontological structures? We make out, roughly, the answer. Psychocultural structures have their efficacious being only in the human spirit. This does not mean, for instance, that a police force is the figment of a private mind lost in its privacy. But the value and the meaning of the police force are wholly within the human spirit, even when we say, "Obey the magistrates." When a people will no longer be bound by its own police arm, the latter has no other claim upon existence. So also for all the paraphernalia and appurtenances of law and order; and for all writs, constitutions, decrees, and statutes. When the spirit of man goes off and leaves them, they collapse into museum dust, and the breath of life honors them no more, save in the hush of reverence for the past.

Shall we say then that the Holy Spirit descends in fury upon psychocultural structures? The ontological structures are, rather, the focus of the Spirit's operations. The Holy Spirit leads the will of men beyond infatuation with the finite as wholly good in itself, for out of this infatuation, as an ideally boundless aspiration for power and glory, come the horrors of our history, the destructive rages, the cruel scrambles for gain and for safety, the insensate flights into annihilation. The Holy Spirit is not an accessory to the violence with which we cling to our idols and with which we demolish them when they do not save us. Neither is the Spirit to be identified with the ferocious storms of history, the demonic cataclysms that engulf nations without respect to size and devastate kings and charwomen without distinction. The revolution of the Holy Spirit is repentance. Repentance is the change in the depths wrought by the power of God. Repentance is a resurrection, a coming again into the light of the actual world of God's creation. The fruits of repentance may well include sweeping changes in the human world at large. But this is in the realm of contingency, and one cannot say that this change or that is the specific instruction of the Holy Spirit. In the realm of contingency we have to take courage in hand and work out such changes, reformations, and adaptations as seem to us compatible with the life of love to which we are called. In all of these activities we may rightly be sure of but one thing: whenever we attach transcendent meaning and dignity to a particular scheme of things, actual or ideal, the Holy Spirit is in our midst as absolute reproof and as unfailing promise of the renewal of our spirits in the service of the everlasting Kingdom.

3. Faced with unjust psychocultural structures which appear to defy reformation or removal by reasonable and humane methods, Christians sometimes resort to violence, of various sorts, and claim the inspiration and support of the Holy Spirit for these decisions. I do not know why they are not content to justify these harsh and costly

decisions simply by pointing to a good which will someday be seen to outweigh the evil. In fact as Christians we are often not content simply to do that. We want to be sure that God the Spirit is on our side. So we advertise our revolutions as divinely inspired. By implication we become instruments of the revolutionary power of the Kingdom of God.

The revolutionary spirit visible in the American scene is by no means primarily Christian or perhaps even significantly Christian in its leadership and announced objectives. I am concerned here only with the new liberal Christianity that is sympathetic with the revolutionary spirit. More specifically, I am concerned with an avowedly Christian attack upon psychocultural structures whose unworthiness longer to persist is signalized simply by their being the Establishment.

There is some empirical warrant for laying it down as a law of revolution that demonry must be imputed to the Establishment. Mere ignorance, sloth, complacency, or cowardice is not enough. Nor any combination of them. Only malice of the most formidable degree will suffice. Both revolutionaries and counterrevolutionaries seem to have no trouble finding this in abundance in the enemy.

Here the Christian revolutionary is up against an ally of the most formidable foremindedness, the dedicated communist. The true believer of that sect freely—zealously indeed—uses value-charged terms but he insists that he is using them "scientifically." That is, in a value-free way. "Parasites," "Imperialists," "Warmongers," "Decadence," etc., come quickly and briskly to mind. This is to say that the communist (or at least the communist theologian, the marxist) is free to use demonological language but (presumably) without demonological meaning. Here we are struck by a curious flavor of theological consistency, since the marxist does not believe that any spiritual power (good or evil) is causally efficacious in the movements of history.

Even a roughly comparable commitment to consistency as well as to revolution requires the Christian radical to make serious gestures toward ideality, if not to some kind of spirituality, as the true cause and objective of human reformations. Thus today the Christian radicals appeal to Jesus as to an ethical ideal and hero—even though historians have given up, altogether, on making out anything whatever of the social revolutionary in the Jesus of history. So the Christian revolutionary critic is—or ought to be—as short-tempered with historians as he is likely to be with any theologians except those who stand shoulder to shoulder with him in the Cause.

The revolutionary appeal to Jesus (only very rarely to Jesus Christ) leans in principle therefore upon the ministry of the Holy Spirit. Who else but the Holy Spirit can disclose to him the real (as opposed to the historical and the theological) Jesus? Who but the Holy Spirit has revealed the higher righteousness that stands over against (and not merely outside of) the psychocultural structures against which the true Christian is summoned to work? Who but the Holy Spirit can justify him against the sloth, stupidity, arrogance, and complacency of the consensus?

I certainly do not mean that the Christian revolutionaries are filling the air with a great clatter about the Holy Spirit. My contention is theological and not sociological; and it is therefore hardly worthy the notice of socializing revolutionaries.

The theological argument is hardly complex, and it has been sketched already in the preceding sections of this chapter. Here I restate it in these terms. The Holy Spirit cannot be summoned to justify either one's motives or one's policies as somehow springing from the real Jesus. Rather, the Spirit is the holy assessor of Christian performance in the Kingdom of Christ—in that community in which alone Jesus Christ is honored and obeyed as the Lord of History.

Ought one to say therefore that the Holy Spirit works only in the church? Long ago the church confessed in Scripture that the Holy Spirit works wherever He will to. But on the other hand to invoke the real Jesus on one's own in order to justify one's motives and/or one's policies is a naked draft upon ideality. Thereby one becomes highly vulnerable to the criticism of revolutionaries who categorically (though not always actually) deny ideality. The Christian idealistic revolutionary cannot claim to have Christian history on his side, either, unless he means to claim that true Christianity is always found on the side of sectarian protest against the massive corruptions of the actual church. This claim is hardly more than another appeal to ideality, this time to write the actual church off as a massive spiritual and ethical error.

Whatever we make of this reading of Christian history we cannot seriously deny that the actual church is a psychocultural structure that often enough has been on the wrong side of reform. But we ought not to conclude from this sad fact that the actual church has therefore been cut off from the Kingdom of Christ by the Holy Spirit. Repentance is not entirely unknown in the actual church. Moreover it is not crystal clear that it has more for which to ask forgiveness—even from God's angry men—than revolutionary sects, Christian and otherwise.

These comparisons are odious if their intent is to show that the actual church is the obedient and pliant instrument of the Holy Spirit in all seasons. There is no actual church, and there is no sect, to match this description. Yet in the church the Holy Spirit demands and creates repentance for this very disobedience. The holy work everlastingly renews and purifies the vision of a unity in which all are one and that one is Christ Jesus.

4. Traditionally the Holy Spirit is understood and worshiped as Deity present to sustain, purify, and enrich the unity of the church. Thus the Holy Spirit is not cited as the inspirer of division and of alienation between the "true" Christians and the "false" Christians. Wherever the Holy Spirit is, erring brethren are enjoined and invited to submit themselves anew to the law of Christ rather than to withdraw either in wrath or in guilt.

The Christian revolutionary now proceeds to embrace a violent contradiction. He wants the real Jesus on his side; but he invokes the sanction of the Holy Spirit to justify his own sectarian and antinomian propheticism. Before he announced the death of God he had already published the death of the church. Cheerfully (if not ecstatically) rather than fatalistically he writes his prophetic drafts upon ideality. With the credit thus acquired he establishes himself in dissent if not in revolution. What we need to learn now from him is whether his antinomianism is merely dialectical or, to the contrary, whether he seeks a country in which psychocultural structures will have all been dissolved and the spirit can play in perfect freedom over the unfettered ontological possibilities. Is the latter what he means by freedom, openness, and love? Or does he mean that the demand for justice will stand in the human constitution until man has become extinct? These are very different outlooks and very different hopes. The demand for justice presupposes psycho-cultural structures; but not only or primarily as law presupposes crime. Rather, as that in which amendment is to be made and redress of wrong provided. The demand for justice calls for a refinement of law, both in society and in the "inward parts." The dedicated and consistent antinomian has a merely dialectical interest in justice: it is the iniquity of structure rather than the inequity of the social order that is his prime target. The antinomian is not nauseated by evil. He is disenchanted with order.

II

I suspect that for the time being we ought to live without the venerable phrase, "Christianity the permanent revolution." The reason is tactical, not substantive. As the presence of the living God the Holy Spirit does not permit any psychocultural structure to preempt the world. He is the ferment and the end of all significant change. But only so far as we are willing to tarry in the church until the right reading of the law of Christ is forthcoming can we licitly claim to be living in the inspiration of the Holy Spirit.

The Julian Hartt Library

Series Editor: Jonathan R. Wilson

I. *Toward a Theology of Evangelism* (1955).
Introduction by Stanley Hauerwas.

A concise, seminal presentation of the theological vision that Hartt unfolds in his later work. The focus is witness to the gospel, but in Hartt's creative hands that focus illuminates the whole range of reality in compelling ways.

II. *Being Known and Being Revealed* (1957).
Introduction by Jonathan R. Wilson.

A brief, bold proposal for an ontology that reflects Hartt's work on the ontological argument in his doctoral dissertation and his commitment to Austin Farrer's notion of "rational theology" that parallels "revealed theology."

III. *The Lost Image of Man* (1963).
Introduction by John Sykes, Jr.

A theological illumination of significant 20th C. novels and, through them, an examination of the human condition and a proclamation of the gospel.

IV. *Theology and the Church in the University* (1967).
Introduction by L. Gregory Jones.

Hartt applies his theological powers to questions of commitment and criticism, the role of education in cultural formation and transmission, the formation of identity and morality through education and liturgy, and more. Throughout, Hartt's analysis and exposition takes surprising turns that continue to illuminate the task of theology and the life of the church in the world.

V. *A Christian Critique of American Culture: An Essay in Practical Theology* (1968).
Introduction by David Kelsey.

Hartt's major work defies labels. The subtitle identities it as "practical theology"; by that, Hartt means those doctrines that have immediately to do with the church's mission to proclaim the gospel. Those doctrines are presented in unprecedented ways as Hartt engages in cultural analysis, anticipates much that is found in "missional church" thinking, exposits a Christology and anthropology simultaneously, and sketches a theology of culture that equals any sociology of culture.

VI. *The Restless Quest* (1975).
Introduction by Jonathan R. Wilson.

A collection of essays and addresses that argue for Hartt's understanding of the task of theology of culture (Part I) and the practice of theology of culture as the illumination of our situation (Part II) and our politics (Part III) in the light of Jesus Christ.

VII. *Theological Method and Imagination* (1977).
Introduction by Ray L. Hart.

Hartt applies his wit, insight, and critical acumen to questions ranging across metaphysics, truth, authority, history, imagination and more.

VII. What We Make of the World: Memoirs of Julian Hartt (1998-99)

In these memoirs, Julian Hartt practices the "cosmological theology" that he calls for throughout his scholarly work by reflecting on the everyday, ideal, and natural worlds of his own life. These worlds are shaped by significant times, places, and persons. But most important is the unrelenting honesty of Hartt's narrative as it witnesses to the grace that makes truth and truthfulness possible and bearable in our broken world.

Contributors to The Julian Hartt Library

Ray L. Hart is Dean of the School of Theology and Professor of Religion and Theology at Boston University.

Stanley Hauerwas is Gilbert T. Rowe Professor of Theological Ethics at Duke Divinity School.

L. Gregory Jones is Dean and Professor of Theology at Duke Divinity School.

David H. Kelsey is Luther Weigle Professor of Theology Emeritus at Yale Divinity School.

Walter J. Lowe is Professor of Systematic Theology at Candler School of Theology, Emory University.

John D. Sykes, Jr., is Professor of English at Wingate University.

Jonathan R. Wilson is Professor of Theology and Ethics at Acadia Divinity College.